LACAN ON MADNESS

This new collection of essays by distinguished international scholars and clinicians will revolutionize your understanding of madness. Essential for those on both sides of the couch eager to make sense of the plethora of theories about madness available today, *Lacan on Madness: Madness, yes you can't* provides compelling and original perspectives following the work of Jacques Lacan.

Patricia Gherovici and Manya Steinkoler suggest new ways of working with phenomena often considered impermeable to clinical intervention or discarded as meaningless. This book offers a fresh view on a wide variety of manifestations and presentations of madness, featuring clinical case studies, new theoretical developments in psychosis, and critical appraisal of artistic expressions of insanity.

Lacan on Madness uncovers the logics of insanity while opening new possibilities of treatment and cure. Intervening in current debates about normalcy and pathology, causation and prognosis, the authors propose effective modalities of treatment, and challenge popular ideas of what constitutes a cure by offering a reassessment of the positive and creative potential of madness. Gherovici and Steinkoler's book makes Lacanian ideas accessible by showing how they are both clinically and critically useful. It is invaluable reading for psychoanalysts, clinicians, academics, graduate students, and lay persons.

Patricia Gherovici is a psychoanalyst and analytic supervisor. Her books include *The Puerto Rican Syndrome* (Other Press, 2003) winner of the Gradiva Award and the Boyer Prize, and *Please Select Your Gender: From the Invention of Hysteria to the Democratizing of Transgenderism* (Routledge, 2010).

Manya Steinkoler is a psychoanalyst in formation at Après-Coup in New York and a professor in the Department of English at Borough of Manhattan Community College.

LACAN ON MADNESS

Madness, yes you can't

Edited by Patricia Gherovici and Manya Steinkoler

Routledge
Taylor & Francis Group

LONDON AND NEW YORK

First published 2015
by Routledge
27 Church Road, Hove, East Sussex, BN3 2FA

and by Routledge
711 Third Avenue, New York, NY 10017

Routledge is an imprint of the Taylor & Francis Group, an informa business

British Library Cataloguing in Publication Data
A catalogue record for this book is available from the British Library

Library of Congress Cataloging-in-Publication Data
Lacan on madness: madness, yes you can't / edited by Patricia Gherovici
& Manya Steinkoler.
pages cm
1. Lacan, Jacques, 1901–1981. 2. Mental illness. 3. Psychoses.
I. Gherovici, Patricia. II. Steinkoler, Manya.
BF109.L28L3176 2015
362.2—dc23
2014025556

ISBN: 978-0-415-73615-2 (hbk)
ISBN: 978-0-415-73616-9 (pbk)
ISBN: 978-1-315-74275-5 (ebk)

Typeset in Times New Roman
by Florence Production Ltd, Stoodleigh, Devon, UK

CONTENTS

Notes on contributors   vii
Acknowledgements   xii

Introduction   1
Patricia Gherovici and Manya Steinkoler

PART 1
Madness manifest: encountering madness   17

  1 **The case of the baby diaper man**   19
     ROLF FLOR

  2 **Ilse or the law of the mother**   33
     GENEVIÈVE MOREL

  3 **From psychotic illness to psychotic existence: on re-inventing
     the institution**   47
     GUY DANA

  4 **On the suicide bomber: anatomy of a political fantasy**   56
     RICHARD BOOTHBY

  5 **Today's madness does not make sense**   68
     PAUL VERHAEGHE

PART II
The method in madness: thinking psychosis   83

  6 **"You cannot choose to go crazy"**   85
     NESTOR BRAUNSTEIN

  7 **Treatment of the psychoses and contemporary psychoanalysis**   99
     JEAN-CLAUDE MALEVAL

8   Psychotic transference   112
    JEAN ALLOUCH

9   The specificity of manic-depressive psychosis   127
    DARIAN LEADER

10 Melancholia and the unabandoned object   139
    RUSSELL GRIGG

11 Madness, subjectivity, and the mirror stage: Lacan and
    Merleau-Ponty   159
    JASPER FEYAERTS AND STIJN VANHEULE

12 Narcissistic neurosis and non-sexual trauma   173
    HECTOR YANKELEVICH

13 She's raving mad: the hysteric, the woman, and the
    psychoanalyst   187
    CLAUDE-NÖELE PICKMANN

PART III
Madness and creation: environs of the hole   203

14 The *open* ego: Woolf, Joyce and the "mad" subject   205
    JULIET FLOWER MACCANNELL

15 Normality and segregation in Primo Levi's *Sleeping Beauty
    in the Fridge*   219
    PAOLA MIELI

16 Spell it wrong to read it right: Crashaw, psychosis, and
    Baroque poetics   234
    STEPHEN W. WHITWORTH

17 Madness or mimesis: narrative impasse in the novels of
    Samuel Beckett   245
    OLGA COX CAMERON

18 Reading mayhem: schizophrenic writing and the engine
    of madness   254
    MANYA STEINKOLER

Index   268

NOTES ON
CONTRIBUTORS

Jean Allouch is one of the founders and directors of the review *Littoral* and the École lacanienne de psychanalyse (Paris). His study of Lacan's patient, *Marguerite, ou L'Aimée de Lacan* (1990/1994) is known as a masterpiece of scholarly research. Allouch has introduced significant feminist, gay, lesbian, and queer theory works to a French audience. Author of over twenty books, including *Lettre pour lettre* (1984), *Érotique du deuil au temps de la mort sèche* (1995/1997), *Le sexe du maître* (2001), *L'amour Lacan,* (2009), his most recent work is the trilogy *L'Ingérence divine: Prisonniers du grand Autre* (2012), *Schreber théologien* (2013), and *Une femme sans au-delà* (2014).

Richard Boothby is Professor in the Philosophy Department at Loyola University Maryland. His research has focused on the intersection of psychoanalytic theory and contemporary continental philosophy. He is author of *Death and Desire: Psychoanalytic Theory in Lacan's Return to Freud* (1991), *Freud as Philosopher: Metapsychology after Lacan* (2001) and *Sex on the Couch: What Freud Still Has to Teach Us about Sex and Gender* (2005).

Nestor Braunstein is a psychiatrist and psychoanalyst whose work has been paramount in the reception of Lacanian psychoanalysis in Mexico and Latin America. Recent books include *Por el camino de Freud* (2001), *Ficcionario de Psicoanálisis* (2001), *Depuis Freud, Après Lacan. Déconstruction dans la psychanalyse* (2008), *Memoria y espanto o el recuerdo de infancia* (2008), *La memoria, la inventora* (2008), *Memory and Dread: or the Memory of Childhood* (2010), *El inconsciente, la técnica y el discurso capitalista* (2012). His best-known work, *Goce* (*Jouissance: A Lacanian Concept,* 1990, 2006) has been translated into many languages. Other books include *Clasificar en psiquiatría*, published simultaneously in México, Madrid, and Buenos Aires, and a volume co-edited with Betty Fuks and Carina Basualdo published in French, Spanish and Portuguese: *A cien años de Tótem y Tabú 1913–2013* (2013) and *Le malaise dans la technique. L'inconscient, la technique et le discours capitaliste* (2014).

Olga Cox Cameron has been a practicing psychoanalyst in Dublin for the past twenty-five years. She lectures in psychoanalytic theory and in psychoanalysis and literature at St. Vincent's University Hospital and has published numerous articles on these topics in national and international journals. She is on the editorial board of *Lacunae, The Irish Journal of Psychoanalysis* and she is the founder of the Irish Psychoanalytic Film Festival.

Guy Dana is a psychiatrist and psychoanalyst in Paris and clinical director of the psychiatric hospital and treatment facilities at Longjumeau, part of the Bartélémy Durand Administration (France). Past president of the *Cercle Freudien*, he has authored numerous articles, participated in radio and television programs about his innovative psychoanalytic treatment of psychotic patients. In *Quelle politique pour la folie? Le suspense de Freud* (2010) he describes the theoretical and practical aspects of the treatment he has put into place. *Le hasard, les mots et la psychanalyse* will appear in 2015. Involved in conflict resolution in the Middle East, he organized a meeting for psychoanalysts, including Israeli and Palestinian colleagues, at the French Senate (2003).

Jasper Feyaerts (Msc Psychology) is a PhD student in the Department of Psychoanalysis at Ghent University. He specializes in the philosophical cross-reading and critical reappraisal of psychoanalytic and phenomenological perspectives on subjectivity and modern science, with attention to the work of Husserl, Merleau-Ponty and Lacan.

Rolf Flor is a psychoanalyst in private practice in Boston. He is co-curator of the Boston Lacan Study Group and the clinical director of the Eliot Community Human Services in Lynn, Massachusetts. He is a faculty member of the Massachussetts Institute for Psychoanalysis.

Patricia Gherovici is a psychoanalyst, analytic supervisor, co-founder and curator of Philadelphia Lacan Group (Philadelphia) and member of Après-Coup (New York). Her books include *The Puerto Rican Syndrome* (2003), winner of the Gradiva Award and the Boyer Prize, and *Please Select Your Gender: From the Invention of Hysteria to the Democratizing of Transgenderism* (2010). Recent contributions include *The Literary Lacan: From Literature to 'Lituraterre' and Beyond* (2013) and *A Concise Companion to Psychoanalysis, Literature and Culture* (2014). *Psychoanalysis Needs a Sex Change: Lacanian Approaches to Sexual and Social Difference* is forthcoming.

Russell Grigg practices psychoanalysis in Melbourne and teaches philosophy at Deakin University. He has been a major influence in introducing Lacanian psychoanalysis in Australia. A member of the *École de la cause freudienne* (Paris) and the Lacan Circle of Melbourne (Melbourne), he has been closely involved in the translation of Lacan into English, having translated Lacan's *Seminar III The Psychoses* and *Seminar XVII: The Other Side of Psychoanalysis* and collaborated with Bruce Fink on the translation of *Écrits*. His books include *Female Sexuality* (1999), *Lacan, Language and Philosophy* (2009), and with Justin Clemens, *Jacques Lacan and the Other Side of Psychoanalysis:*

Reading Seminar XVII (2006). He has published on questions of logic, language, and ethics, as well as on clinical issues concerning psychosis and neurosis.

Darian Leader is a psychoanalyst practicing in London. Founding member of the Centre for Freudian Analysis and Research, he is President of The College of Psychoanalysts-UK and Visiting Professor at the School of Human and Life Sciences, Roehampton University. He is the author of many essays on art and a frequent contributor to *The Guardian*. His books include *Why Do Women Write More Letters than They Post?* (1986), *Promises Lovers Make When It Gets Late* (1997), *Freud's Footnotes* (2000), *Stealing the Mona Lisa: What Art Stops Us from Seeing* (2002), *Why Do people Get Ill?* (with David Corfield, 2007), *The New Black: Mourning, Melancholia and Depression* (2008), *What Is Madness?* (2011), and *Strictly Bipolar* (2013).

Juliet Flower MacCannell is Professor Emerita of Comparative Literature and English at UC Irvine. She is currently co-chair of the California Psychoanalytic Circle and co-editor of *(a): the journal of culture and the unconscious*. An Honorary Fellow of the Institute for Advanced Study, University of London, she is the author of several books on psychoanalysis and philosophy in a social and political frame, including *Figuring Lacan: Criticism & the Cultural Unconscious* (1986; reissued by Routledge, 2014), *The Regime of the Brother: After the Patriarchy* (1991), *The Hysteric's Guide to the Future Female Subject* (2000), and over ninety articles. Her work has been translated into Spanish, German, Slovenian and French. She is also an artist.

Jean-Claude Maleval is a psychiatrist, psychoanalyst, and professor of clinical psychology at Rennes University, France. He is a Member of École de la cause freudienne and World Association of Psychoanalysis. His voluminous scholarly publications on schizophrenia, paranoid psychosis, and autism are considered to be at the cutting edge of research and theory in the field. His books have become standard for studying psychosis in a psychoanalytic framework. They include *Folies hystériques et psychoses dissociatives* (1981, 1985, 1991, 2007), *Logique du délire* (1997, 2011), *La forclusion du Nom-du-Père* (2000), *L'autiste et sa voix* (2009), *Etonnantes mystifications de la psychothérapie autoritaire* (2012).

Paola Mieli is a psychoanalyst in New York City. Instrumental in bringing a Lacanian clinical presence to the US, Dr Mieli is the founder and president of Après-Coup Psychoanalytic Association and member of Le Cercle Freudien (Paris), Insistance (Paris), and The European Federation of Psychoanalysis (Strasbourg). She has published numerous articles on psychoanalysis and culture in Europe and America. A correspondent editor of the psychoanalytic journal *Che Vuoi* (Paris) and a contributing editor of the journal *Insistance. Art, psychanalyse et politique* (Paris), she teaches in the Department of Photography and Related Media of The School of Visual Arts in New York City. Her books include *Sobre as manipulações irreversíveis do corpo* (2002), and *Being Human: The Technological Extensions of the Body* (co-editor, 1999).

Geneviève Morel is a psychoanalyst in Paris and Lille whose numerous works have been translated into many languages. She is the president of Savoirs et Clinique, Association pour la Formation Permanente en Psychanalyse (Paris), director of their journal, a member of CFAR and president of the Collège de Psychanalystes d'A.l.e.p.h (Association pour l'étude de la psychanalyse et de son histoire). She has written extensively on art, culture, film and psycho-analysis. Her books include *Sexual Ambiguity* (2011), *Clinique du suicide* (2002; 2010), *L'œuvre de Freud. L'invention de la psychanalyse* (2006), *La loi de la mère. Essai sur le sinthome sexuel* (2008), *Pantallas y sueños. Ensayos psicoanalíticos sobre la imagen en movimiento* (2011).

Claude-Noële Pickmann is a psychoanalyst in Paris and a member of Espace Analytique, and The Fondation Européenne pour la Psychanalyse. She is the founder of the research group Asphère, dedicated to the question of psycho-analysis and the feminine. Her work focuses on hysteria and the feminine question in clinic and theory. She has published widely in psychoanalytic journals.

Manya Steinkoler is a psychoanalyst in New York. She is a member of Après Coup (New York) and Espace Analytique (Paris). She is film editor of The Candidate Journal and has published articles on psychoanalysis and film, literature, opera and financial fraud. She is assistant professor and teaches literature and film at Borough of Manhattan Community College. She is co-editor, with Patricia Gherovici, of *Lacan, Psychoanalysis and Comedy* (forthcoming).

Stijn Vanheule is a clinical psychologist, chair of the Department of Psycho-analysis and Clinical Consulting at Ghent University (Belgium), and a psychoanalyst in private practice (member of the New Lacanian School for Psychoanalysis). He is the author of *The Subject of Psychosis: A Lacanian Perspective* (2011) and *Diagnosis and the DSM: A Critical Review* (2014), as well as of multiple papers on Lacanian and Freudian psychoanalysis, psycho-analytic research into psychopathology, and clinical psycho-diagnostics.

Paul Verhaeghe is senior professor at Ghent University and has been chair of the Department for Psychoanalysis and Counseling Psychology. He is a member of the European School for Psychoanalysis and the World Association of Psychoanalysis. His books include *On Being Normal and Other Disorders* (2004), *Does the Woman Exist?* (1999), *Love in a Time of Loneliness* (2012), *Beyond Gender: From Subject to Drive* (2001), *New Studies of Old Villains: A Radical Reconsideration of the Oedipus Complex* (2009) and more than two hundred papers. Recent books such as *What About Me? The Struggle for Identity in a Market-Based Society* (2014) critique contemporary psycho-therapeutic practices and reveal links between contemporary society and the new disorders.

Stephen Whitworth is an associate professor of Renaissance Studies in the Department of English at Bloomsburg University of Pennsylvania, and has published numerous articles on Renaissance poetry and Lacanian psychoanalysis. He is a member of the Washington D.C. Forum of the École de Psychanalyse des Forums du Champ Lacanien, and is currently working on a book on male sexuality and seventeenth-century poetry entitled *Ravage and the Baroque: Masculine Sexuality and the Seventeenth-Century Devotional Lyric*.

Hector Yankelevich is a psychoanalyst who has been instrumental in introducing Lacan's work to Argentina. He taught at the University of Buenos Aires and Rosario. Trained in Paris, he worked in France for more than three decades, writing for several psychoanalytic reviews. He has lectured in Europe, Israel and the US. He is an AME, Analyst Member of the Escuela Freudiana de Buenos Aires. He teaches in the Masters in Psychoanalysis Program at the Universidad Nacional de Rosario, Argentina. He is the author of *Ensayos sobre autismo y psicosis* (1997, 2010), *Del Padre a la letra* (1998), *Lógicas del Goce* (2000) and *Du père à la lettre* (2003). Forthcoming is *The Logical Assumption of Sex*.

ACKNOWLEDGEMENTS

This book would not be in your hands if it were not for the help of many remarkable people. Our heartfelt thanks to the following:

Jennifer (Rivky) Mondal for her promptness, reliability, and discerning attention to detail in the editing of the manuscript.

Jean Michel Rabaté for his kind support and invaluable assistance with style and translation.

Guy le Gaufey for his painstakingly careful proofreading of our translation, his attentive reading of several chapters in this volume, and his helpful editorial suggestions.

Dan Collins and Todd Dean who helped organize conferences on madness and psychosis that inspired our book project.

Vanessa Sinclair and Michael Garfinkle for their support and friendship.

Sofía Rabaté for her good cheer.

Luis Calderón Alvarado for his fantastically good sense of humor and support of the "Locaniana Picapiedra project."

The members of the Smedley Writers Group: Justine Gudenas, Randall Couch, Mona Doyle, Larry MacKenzie Carolyn Kipnis Raskin, Ave Maria Merritt, and Bernard Stehle for their support, adroit criticism, and love of words.

Kate Hawes and Kirsten Buchanan at Routledge for their trust in our endeavor, which made this book possible.

We are very grateful to all the people whose combined support has given us the very power of the "yes" that buoyed up the "can't" so that something new could be born.

INTRODUCTION

Patricia Gherovici and Manya Steinkoler

The aim of this book is to change our perception of madness. Is madness a disease? Does it have a cure? We interrogate the meanings of these words and the assumptions they involve. The essays in this book show how fear can be replaced by thought, how impasse can be resolved by informed clinical intervention, and how a threatening emptiness can be lessened by the invention of a shared word. We will learn that there is a way to work with senselessness, with those patients on the brink of a precipice, or those trapped in a gaping void. We will be able to better intervene with subjects who suffer seemingly inexplicable aggressive explosions as well as with those whose normalcy and extreme rationality may conceal a dormant psychosis. The essays in this collection uncover the hidden logics of insanity to take a first step towards new possibilities of treatment and cure.

Why madness? The term itself, like the vicissitudes of the clinic devoted to it, has protean qualities. It is a shape-shifting oracular monster that only answers to those capable of discerning its wiles. Medical historian Roy Porter called it "the mystery of mysteries" (Porter 2002: 1). When does the question of madness begin? Apparently with humanity itself. As far back as 10,000 years ago, we find archaeological evidence of skulls with holes drilled into them. Medical historians hypothesize that the trepanations were early treatments for those who today we would call mentally ill. Later medieval iconography suggests that the holes in the head were made in the attempt to remove "the stone of madness." Evidently, from the beginning of the history of madness, there has been a hole, and the hole persists.

Literature and myth have wrestled with madness: from a raving Heracles's foaming mouth, rolling eyes, contorted body, to Medea's vengeful frenzy, taking the life of her own children, to Ajax's unrighteous wrath, to Dido's suicidal despair, to Orestes's feverish hounding by the untamable furies, to Lear's stubborn demise, howling on the heath, to Hamlet's real or feigned delusions, to Ophelia's florid musings while losing her mind; all these cultural icons illustrate a continued questioning of the pathos of madness, a plight that exceeds our comprehension and elicits our pity, our fear, and our awe. Yet while the pathos of madness has inspired classics of the Western canon, the mystery of insanity resists explanation.

Nowadays, despite the innovations in pharmacology, diagnosis, and brain research and imaging, madness continues to haunt the layman as well as the specialist. Researchers, scientists, psychologists and therapists in charge of its treatment and management, as well as the discovery of its causes, are repeatedly confronted with the inability to fully account for its opaque and troubling reality while endlessly churning out new diagnostic labels. Since the Enlightenment, the machine model of the human being has continued to enjoy considerable popularity: contemporary psychiatry tries to reduce any form of bizarre or disruptive behavior to a defectively wired brain. When today we talk about "wiring of the brain," or "genetic," rather than familial inheritance, we should not forget that these are metaphors. The "wiring" and "chemical" models have become a new craze of the mental health and pharmaceutical industries that purport to circumvent metaphor and treat the body as if madness itself could be reduced to an affair of the flesh, and the entire human being to a malfunctioning apparatus.

After endless rewritings of the many editions of the bible of psychiatric diagnosis, the *Diagnostic and Statistical Manual of the American Psychiatric Association*, the boundary between madness and sanity remains undefined, permeable, and constantly contested, as several essays in this book argue. Nestor Braunstein, Jean-Claude Maleval, Darian Leader, Paul Verhaeghe, and Russell Grigg rethink the classic taxonomy. They challenge the limitations of the DSM and offer alternative approaches to bring back to the clinic a precision that was lost with the new-fangled psychiatric terminology. Grigg's meditation on clinical impasses and Richard Boothby's analysis of suicide bombing also invite us to rethink classical psychoanalytic notions used in diagnosis such as the Freudian conception of melancholia. Darian Leader's precise exploration of manic depression also provides a welcome clarification of a tricky and seemingly ubiquitous manifestation, restoring its clinical specificity. His contribution has a poignant urgency given the current cultural trend of rebranding classical diagnoses as lifestyle choices applying to almost everyone.

We are aware of the political, social, medical and religious valences of the word madness. It has been used as a coercive instrument of oppression to police people for centuries. Our use of madness in the title is an attempt to de-stigmatize and revitalize the word. Madness may very well be a social creation, as Emile Durkheim maintains in *On Suicide* (2006). A strong critique of the social stigma attached to those deemed insane and a denunciation of the abuse they have been subjected to, has been raised by the eloquent voices of the anti-psychiatry movement. Thomas Szasz (1974) has persuaded us that madness should not be considered within the parameters of "myths" such as that of "mental illness." While promoting the creation of alternative approaches to non-normative behavior, anti-psychiatry has revealed that notions of mental illness are misleading, erroneous, and ultimately aimed at persecuting, restraining, and imprisoning the alleged mad person—Szasz famously compared psychiatric care to a witch-hunt. R. D. Laing (1960) has shown that insanity is a derogatory label to scapegoat and segregate those who deviate from social norms. Whether madness is a social construct, a myth or a label, clinicians still have an ethical responsibility to treat those who are suffering and ask for help. Lacan's idea that the subject's unconscious is both "the discourse of the Other" and "structured like a language" blurs the distinction between the individual and the social, offering us a way out of the binary that has informed this controversy.

Freud was already questioning the distinction between sanity and insanity when he claimed that everyone was insane in their dreams (Breuer & Freud 1893: 13) and developed a theory of dream interpretation based on the analogy between dreams and insanity (Freud 1900). Freud here indicated that he was echoing Kant's assertion of 1764 that "[t]he madman is a waking dreamer" and Schopenhauer's quip "that dreams are a brief madness and madness a long dream" (Freud 1900: 90). While objectors may see the dream as a "useless and disturbing process" or "the expression of a reduced activity of the mind" (Freud 1900: 91), the creator of psychoanalysis claimed that "we shall be working towards an explanation of the psychoses while we are endeavoring to throw some light on the mystery of dreams."

What light does madness shed on dreaming? Elsewhere, in "An Auto-biographical Study," Freud observed "that so many things that in the neuroses have to be laboriously fetched up from the depths are found in the psychoses on the surface, visible to every eye" (Freud 1925: 60). Since repression does not operate in psychosis, we are not talking about a divided subject as we would in neurosis; there is no "un"-conscious as such. Actually, the psychotic is spoken by the Other, as manifested in the delusions, usually experienced as thoughts coming from the exterior, imposing themselves from without. The psychotic is subjected to the Other without mediation through intruding ideas, hallucinations, voices, imposed thoughts and commands. Lacan says that the psychotic is the "martyr of the unconscious," giving to "martyr" its meaning of "witness" (Lacan 1993: 132). If dreams are the *via regia* to a knowledge of the unconscious (Freud 1900: 33), in madness we have already arrived.

The delusion opens a direct access to the unconscious as the discourse of the Other, and it is a spontaneous attempt at a cure. Lacan considers the delusion a metaphor, highlighting its palliative function and its creative aspect. It is ironic that our wish to cure the delusions of the mad is in fact an attempt to cure their own cure. As torturing as it may be, a delusional system of thought can compensate for an experience of collapse, as it did for President Schreber. His elaborate delusion of rays, transformation into a woman, and final marriage with God to start a new race granted him not only freedom (he wrote a memoir about this and was released from confinement) but offered a system of ideas to compensate for his inner collapse. In Manya Steinkoler's essay in this volume, we also see the invention of a delusion as the attempt on the part of a schizophrenic at self-cure. We note that what we call "symptoms" can be a mode of action, a form of reparation and a way of making sense of senselessness, even if it looks like senselessness to us. It is often said that hallucinations are unreal. Given the unmediated relation of the psychotic to the Other, hallucinations are actually the most real. As much as hallucinations are the reality for the delusional person, the scene of the dream becomes the reality for the dreamer but only while she is asleep. Deprived of a structuring prohibition, the psychotic is condemned to an unbearable, untethered freedom, as Nestor Braunstein develops in his essay in this collection, caught in the nightmare of living in a constant dream. Neurotics wake up from their dreams while psychotics do not. Since one third of our life is spent sleeping, it is a logical conclusion that we spend one third of our lives mad. Should the skeptical reader think we exaggerate, we will remind her that we are in good company. Let us recall Cervantes' Don Quixote who warns us "[t]oo much sanity may be madness," and Emily Dickinson's "Poem 620," "Madness is Divinest Sense and Sense the Starkest Madness."

Madness is no longer a technical word in the current psychiatric jargon, although it was once widely used as such by medical practitioners. We nevertheless insist on the use of a commonsensical word in order to open a discussion of a non-specialized, non-nosological term, taking into account Michel Foucault's critique of psychoanalysis. Foucault (1988) conducted a history of madness leading to an analysis of the institutions that secluded and imprisoned otherness. Our choice of the word "madness" pays homage to Foucault's seminal contribution to the awareness of how social, political, and legal structures discipline and punish; they construct discourses that confine the insane, the morally degenerate, and the non-compliant. Let us reclaim madness not just by absorbing Foucault's critique of psychoanalysis, but by thinking beyond it.

We live in a time when many uncertainties are covered up by salesperson-like assurance, a hallmark of today's master discourses. Anyone curious enough to take a look at pharmaceutical companies' explanatory inserts of their anti-psychotic drugs will quickly note that the efficacy of the psychiatric medication is always rendered in the hypothetical conditional tense. This is not the case only for side effects, but also for the mechanism of action of the specific "disorder" or "condition" the medication is prescribed to treat. Peter Breggin, in *Your Drug May be Your Problem* (1999), *Talking Back to Prozac* (1994), *Toxic Psychiatry* (1991), and *Medication Madness: A Psychiatrist Exposes the Dangers of Mood-Altering Medications* (2008), has denounced the risks of what he sees as the over-prescription of psychiatric drugs. He argues that psychiatric drugs have replaced religion. Marx's opium of the masses is back with a twist—nowadays, psycho-pharmaceutical drugs are the opium of the masses, sustaining a colossal, extremely lucrative industry. As of March 2014, the antipsychotic drug aripiprazole or Abilify was the top selling prescription drug in dollar volume in the United States with sales reaching nearly $6.9 billion a year. How many psychotics are there in America? How could a drug initially approved for schizophrenia achieve block-buster sales? Besides launching a very aggressive publicity campaign urging everyone to "Ask Your Doctor If It May Be Right For You—Abilify" and pushing illegal remuneration to physicians and other health care providers to entice sales (in 2007 Bristol-Myers Squibb was forced to pay more than $515 million to settle federal and state investigations into their drug marketing and pricing practices),

Abilify was marketed as an *atypical* antipsychotic; it could be prescribed for all kinds of symptoms from bipolar disorder, to depression, to autism. Today, antipsychotic drugs like Abilify, which are acutely sedating and have dangerous and potentially irreversible side effects, are widely and casually prescribed off-label for people without diagnoses of psychosis and who suffer only moderate symptoms such as anxiety (Friedman: 2012).

Chris Lane (2008) in *Shyness: How Normal Behavior Became a Sickness* has widely documented the alarming consequences of the influence exercised by drug companies on psychiatric practice. Ordinary afflictions get transformed into mental disorders, everyday shyness gets turned into "social anxiety." The astonishing rise of mental illness is simple to explain. Every time a new "disease" appears in the DSM, Big Pharma just happens to be marketing the profitable drug for its treatment. As Lane concludes, "before you sell a drug, you need to sell the disease." Here, we use the word "madness" so that the "conditional condition" can remain an open question and not a commodity, refusing the obfuscation of the jargon of the psychopharmacological salesperson. Influential clinicians such as Darian Leader (2011) have already extolled the benefits of the use of this term in an attempt to make the divide that separates "normal" from "mad" flexible and open to discussion. This is an ethically important consideration that challenges the temptation to demonize, judge, and overmedicate the insane, opening up the possibility of listening properly.

The subtitle *Madness, yes you can't* is a way to express the paradoxes of both neurosis and psychosis. This perplexing formulation refers back to the idea of the double-bind, a contradictory injunction that plays with rationality and twists it around, so widely discussed in the 1960s and considered the cause of psychosis at that time. *Madness, yes you can't* also reminds us that in madness the law operates in a derailed manner. We hope to generate reflection and deliberation with our subtitle. It will send the reader to the heart of the issues addressed in this book. The phrase also evokes negation, both in terms of psychosis as the failure of a "no" at the origin of the law, and of neurotic repression, which is threatened in the dramatic crises we may find in non-psychotic madness.

Indeed, if the term madness elicits inquiry and even controversy, we hope it will inspire the re-emergence of thought in the clinical setting. It is a reminder that in clinical practice it is efficacious to remain curious, open-minded, critical, ready to listen, not too rushed to "capture the disease" or tighten uncertainty with the lasso of a diagnostic label. While most of the time it is possible to make a clear distinction between neurosis, psychosis, and perversion, it is often clinically efficacious to make use of the diagnosis as a "working hypothesis" that is constantly tested and rethought. Occasionally, it may only be confirmed at the conclusion of a treatment. As Dany Nobus and Malcolm Quinn (2005) suggest, "knowing nothing" can be extremely productive. For Lacan, the role of the analyst is marked by *docta ignorantia*, "wise ignorance," as systematized by the Renaissance philosopher Nicolas Cusanus (Lacan 1988: 278). The analyst operates from a place of ignorance, of not-knowing; if there is any knowledge, the analysand's unconscious produces it. Jean Allouch further elaborates this idea in his chapter in this collection, noting that the relation to knowledge, on which transference is predicated, is reversed in psychotic patients: the analyst has to be willing to become a "secretary to the insane" (Lacan 1993: 206), reversing the place of the "subject-supposed-to-know." Not-knowing is not a posture. It is the beginning of a learning and of a possibility of an effective clinical intervention. Ignorance, if it can inspire curiosity, may be the mother of thought.

Indeed, the clinic of madness can serve to remind us once again of the Freudian discovery: the emergence of the unconscious is always surprising—for both the analysand *and* the analyst. We advocate keeping an openness to surprise and contingency, as grounds of fertile possibility not just in the individual cure of a patient, but to impact the general malaise affecting psychoanalysis itself, a malaise in which a will to tame the drives on the part of the analyst, however well-meaning it might seem, gives up on the work of the unconscious. It can concern a passion for interpretation or a theoretical certitude that amounts to the same. At times, psychoanalytic theory becomes not just a defense against thinking but a resistance to listening.

Our subtitle *Madness, yes you can't* alerts us to a structural constraint: nobody goes mad by wanting to. One goes mad because of a disposition, or rather an indisposition: there is structural limitation to the triggering of psychosis. Someone becomes truly crazy only if it is structurally possible. We see this elaborated in Braunstein's contribution to this volume, "You cannot choose to go crazy." We follow a practice of "differential diagnosis." A "mad" symptom does not necessarily mean a psychosis. This distinction concerns cases of neurosis even when they present excessive and outlandish behavior, as shown in Claude-Noële Pickmann's contribution to this volume, "She's raving mad: the hysteric, the woman, and the psychoanalyst" and Verhaeghe's "Today's madness does not make sense." This does not mean that we believe in a continuum between psychic structures, as Melanie Klein proposed with her idea of a progression from a schizo-paranoid position to a depressive position, nor does it mean that we consider madness a latent stage to which one can regress transitorily. Mental structural organization has to be dislodged from symptoms.

Madness, yes you can't is also a formula for neurosis. A yes is premised on an interdiction of jouissance: "You can't," an interdiction that Lacan calls the Name-of-the-Father. The paternal metaphor separates the mother from the child and sets the child on an impossible quest to find the object of the mother's desire, which henceforth is at the level of metaphor, forever exiled from the Thing itself: the divided subject is born. The resulting frustrations of this quest are unsatisfying and even enraging—indeed, they can be maddening. A further reading of this phrase in the context of neurosis and society points to the way the superego commands enjoyment while making it impossible at the same time. Here the cultural and ideological "dream" is posited as the good, and even at times as a moral injunction "to enjoy" (the American dream, the dream of thinness, of riches, of happiness), with its underside, you can't, being the figure par excellence of political and social impotence and contemporary malaise. Our subtitle lets a recent and well known presidential campaign slogan ring slightly off key, allowing us to hear the limitations of willful and even well-meaning optimism.

In the tilting of our subtitle towards the side of neurosis, the word madness relates to anger, as a consequence of something that is not allowed. The subject is frustrated. So while you cannot choose to go crazy, the particular ways in which you cannot choose vary, and can become infuriating. The demands and strictures of civilization are stultifying, driving us mad, if only for a brief period. *Ira brevis furor est*—anger is a brief madness. Anyone can go crazy for a moment. This is made explicit in the semantic proximity in English of "mad" and "angry." Rage can lead to a momentary insanity. Doesn't the standard equivalence of "angry" with "mad" already imply that anger can make us lose our heads? We recognize the difference between being angry and acting out murderous fury, but what matters here in the linguistic and psychological affinity between "mad" and "angry" is the stress on time: a "brief" madness—duration is key. Why do people sometimes go crazy, if just for a while? Moderate anger, in Aristotle's perspective, arises from a situation of injustice that needs to be corrected and has a policing function (Aristotle 1980: 96). This naturally leads to a conception of anger as a handmaiden of justice. Yet, in Aristotle's view, this rage for justice is within measure—never excessive; we are never really *that* mad.

As we continue to helplessly witness senseless explosions of violence in our schools, parking lots, movie theaters, and shopping malls, we find ourselves more bewildered by the terrifying reality before us. And we are even more confounded by a rage for retaliation that is anything but temperate or rational. Wanting to protect our children, we look to science, especially to genetics, only to find ourselves at the mercy of a frightening essentialism increasingly jeopardizing the very rights and freedoms we are aiming to protect. Not all angers are created equal: the notion of foreclosure allows us to make a structural distinction between delusional rage and justified anger. The visibility of madness today makes us denounce the mental health system's failures, the horror of the act, and the suffering of the victims. We wish to move away from the spectacular side of madness and turn our attention to its causes and treatment, to madness before it becomes visible.

Lacan never retreated in the face of madness. While Freud allowed us to hear the logic of neurosis behind its symptoms, uncovering their sense and learning to read the unconscious, he did not feel that psychoanalysis could treat insanity. Indeed, many psychoanalysts after Freud have considered that psychoanalysis has no contribution to make to its treatment. The specificity of structure has been lost for many clinicians who become intimidated by the often dramatic and inexplicable phenomena. More disquieting, some psychoses remain unrecognized by the practitioner, often due to overly normal behavior, extreme rationality, superior intelligence, and at times, apparent social success. Even when it may remain dormant, untriggered, with no visible signs, psychosis is nevertheless the correct diagnosis. Our collection of essays will alert us to the recognition of both forms—visible madness and the more subtle form that Darian Leader (2011) calls "quiet psychosis."

If Lacan did not hesitate before madness, it was because his encounter with psychosis made him a psychoanalyst. Not only was his doctoral thesis on paranoia the beginning of a lifelong development and refinement of his original understanding of madness, as Allouch's essay in this volume shows, but Lacan turned to Freud to make sense of his encounter with Marguerite Anzieu, whom he called Aimée. She presented the full gamut of paranoid symptoms (erotomania, megalomania, prejudice, persecutory ideation, passionate jealousy) while her superior cognitive abilities remained intact. Aimée was committed to Saint-Anne Hospital after having spent one month incarcerated. An intelligent, well read, articulate young mother, she had tried her hand at fiction and poetry as a means of recognition, and ended up institutionalized after attempting to murder a famous actress, a gesture that Lacan would name "paranoiac self-punishment." Studying Aimée and her writings, Lacan came to understand the origins of paranoiac crime, later unveiling the logic of the psychotic structure. The essays in this book continue to advance his theories regarding the various clinical realities he encountered. The texts by Verhaeghe, Pickman, and Yankelevich allow us to revisit what are often considered non-analyzable cases, inviting us to examine our assumptions and the conceptual challenges posed by patients whose clinical presentations do not fit into the classical clinical categories. Lacan's clinical experience taught that psychosis needed psychoanalysis, and Freud's that hysterical madness founded psychoanalysis. Together they show that madness indeed needs psychoanalysis.

One of Lacan's major contributions was the theorization of the mirror stage, which Feyaerts, Vanheule, Yankelevich, and Steinkoler revisit and elaborate on in this collection. This elaboration was directly influenced by his encounter with paranoid psychosis in the 1930s. His later thesis of the Name-of-the-Father and the primacy of the signifier, which he developed in the 1950s, can also be traced back to his reading of another case of paranoia, Schreber's memoirs. For Lacan, foreclosure is a defining term. It concerns the fact that in psychosis the Name-of-the-Father failed, the mother's desire was never metaphorized, that is, it was never replaced by a signifier. What is not inscribed in the Symbolic returns from the Real. With this thinking Lacan is able to make sense of the logic of Schreber's madness. At this point, the primacy of the Imaginary, or mirror stage, which had dominated Lacan's early thinking about psychosis, would be replaced by the deficit in the Symbolic. In the 1970s, in his reading of James Joyce, Lacan invented yet a new theory of madness. The writings of Joyce led him to the invention of the "sinthome," a symptom that does not need to be cured but one that makes life livable and can spare someone a fate of madness. In this instance, using the topological model of the Borromean knot of Real, Imaginary, and Symbolic, Lacan effectively went beyond the classical diagnostic taxonomy. He replaced the Name-of-the-Father with the sinthome, a creation with the potential to make up for errors in the knotting of the three registers. The father becomes just a symptom like many others, and Oedipus, Freud's symptom.

Our contributors invite us to tread the fine line where mad is not necessarily pathological but potentially creative. Madness does not only manifest in suffering or a maladjusted or aberrant response. The sinthome is another way for madness to be transformed into an individual and creative solution, an invention, which becomes another form of cure. In the third section, "Madness and creation: environs of the hole," several essays reflect on the work of great writers to show how creation can avoid madness or make good use of it. Mieli with Primo Levi, MacCannell with Joyce and Woolf, Whitworth with Crashaw, Cox Cameron with Beckett and O'Brien, and finally, Steinkoler with the writings of a schizophrenic patient show that madness has the potential to give access to a profound form of knowing, and that creation is a savoir faire with that knowledge.

This book is a timely collection of state-of-the-art essays by leading international scholars and clinicians responding to an urgency experienced in society today with regard to madness. It addresses a gap in Lacanian psychoanalytic literature in English. Offering new perspectives on a wide variety of manifestations and presentations of madness, this book condenses seminal and innovative work by international specialists spanning several continents. All contributions reflect the state of the art of Lacanian theory today.

This book is divided into three sections. The first: "Madness manifest: encountering madness" provides a combination of clinical case studies, institutional modalities of treatment, and social symptoms of madness such as suicide bombing that we hope will open discussion and debate. The second section: "The method in madness: thinking psychosis" is devoted to a rich variety of elaborations that help us rethink madness outside traditional categories and definitions while maintaining theoretical rigor. The common thread among these chapters is the idea that madness has a logic. The third: "Madness and creation: environs of the hole," demonstrates how madness can be a solution rather than a problem to be "fixed." It illustrates the creative, affirmative aspects of madness.

The section "Madness manifest: encountering madness" opens with Rolf Flor's "The case of the baby diaper man," which disproves the assumption that psychoanalysis cannot treat psychosis. The open-minded intervention of a clinician who is willing to listen to the logic and traumatic personal history behind seemingly senseless and disturbing symptoms, and who is not confined to ideals of "health" or "normalcy," can assist a psychotic subject in leading a less precarious life where he can form meaningful attachments to others. Not concerned with moral correction, the ideology of norms or the indication of deviancy, but respecting the patient's structure and giving dignity to symptom formation, such clinical work allows for change where before there had been only the invisible solitude of a lost social outcast.

In "Ilse or the Law of the Mother," Geneviève Morel relates a detailed clinical case that challenges the usual psychoanalytic paradigms of cure and of sexual difference, showing innovative ways in which the clinic can be re-invented.

9

Lacanian psychoanalysis has been accused of being obsessed with the phallus, the father and, even more misleadingly, with "language games." In Morel's compelling clinical account, Lacanian psychoanalytic treatment is creative, deeply ethical, and concerned with subjective reality; it is a dynamic work where dramatic transformative effects become possible. Morel shows how, by having a child with her female life partner, Ilse was able to position herself in the family history to become a parent, and ultimately to avoid the destiny of madness. The outcome of the treatment places the subject in the family genealogy facing sexual difference without fully relying on the phallus. What is at stake in this case is the dignity of life and the invention of a future.

In Chapter 3, "From psychotic illness to psychotic existence: on re-inventing the institution," Guy Dana, creator of a pioneering clinic for the treatment of psychosis, explains how the Lacanian understanding of psychosis led to his creation of a new institutional treatment structure. Foucault had documented how society tries to control the abnormal, punishing by way of exclusion and seclusion. Dana shows that the seclusion of the psychotic subject is already present at the psychic level. He demonstrates how the clinical setting built on a multi-disciplinary treatment team and a multitude of treatment venues fosters a change in material space, allowing for the formation of a newfound social link. In Dana's invention, influenced by Winnicott as well as Lacan, the institution itself is structurally modified in order to better treat and manage the psychic reality of psychosis. Stressing the move to "psychotic existence" from "psychotic illness," Dana aims to make "madness" something livable and inventive for the patient, as well as for us.

In the following chapter, "On the suicide bomber: anatomy of a political fantasy," Richard Boothby discusses the phenomenon of the "madness" of the suicide bomber, testing Freud's theory of melancholia in the analysis of a socio-political "case." Boothby's examination uncovers the metapsychology of the political mechanism at work in the ideology of the suicide bomber and the fantasy that motivates the suicide. He unpacks the dynamics of terror in terms not just of the act itself, but of the fantasies at play for the perpetrator and for the society in which these events occur. He reveals an intimate connection between the terrorist act and the society and culture it is perpetrated on. Without diminishing their outrageousness, he reveals the logic implied by the seemingly inexplicable and senseless acts of terror and the frenzy they elicit.

Exploring the clinical challenges we face today, Paul Verhaeghe, in Chapter 5, "Today's madness does not make sense," writes about the "difficult" patients we encounter today. These are patients who do not associate freely or seem to have transference to the analyst. They do not give any meaning or relevance to their past experiences in terms of their current suffering, nor do they express any curiosity about their symptoms, tending to act out by engaging in dangerous activities such as drug use, cutting, eating disorders, and putting their bodies at risk. These patients' presentations question the armchair comforts of what Verhaeghe proves are antiquated ways of thinking about them and what they tell us. Challenging the contested notion of "borderline," Verhaeghe proposes to bring back the quasi-forgotten Freudian notion of "actual-neurosis," which can help us discern what looks like psychosis all the while remaining in the field of neurosis. Opening the dialogue with other psychoanalytic perspectives, such as attachment theory, he underlines the crucial role of a positive therapeutic relation while inviting the reader to address creatively the clinical challenges of seemingly senseless madness.

In the opening chapter to the second section, "The method in madness: thinking psychosis," Nestor Braunstein both warns and reassures us: "You cannot choose to go crazy." Braunstein shows that madness is not a matter of will or choice. Indeed, psychosis is the structure where choice is impossible. Lacan nevertheless asserted that the mad person is the only truly free human being. Braunstein explores this seeming contradiction, underlining the paradoxical "price" of that freedom in all its clinical resonance. He shows how the psychotic subject experiences jouissance as a devastating, limitless and painful invasion, not subjected to meaning or social norms. Without the barrier of fantasy, the very being of the psychotic is at stake. Braunstein returns to the question about diagnosis to tell us that since "there are no full time psychotics," both "psychosis" and "psychotic" can become "schematic labels that steer the clinician and the reader off track, instead of orienting them."

Chapter 7, Jean-Claude Maleval's "Psychosis and contemporary psycho-analysis," provides a historical survey of the theorization of psychosis, situating Lacan's development therein as a way of problematizing the contemporary DSM and the pharmacologically-influenced psychiatric clinic. Highlighting the originality of the Lacanian approach, he foregrounds the notion of the foreclosure of the Name-of-the-Father as playing a defining role in the origins of psychotic structure. Explaining the concept of *suppléance*, Maleval shows how invention plays an important part in the cure. Maleval reminds us that modern psychiatry has abandoned its own rich history and theoretical rigor and that it was Lacan's gift to transmit this fruitful heritage via his teaching.

Chapter 8, Jean Allouch's "Transference in psychosis," historically situates the notion of transference in terms of Lacan's encounter with Aimée. Recalling that Freud thought that without transference a psychoanalytic cure was impossible, Allouch explains why the existence of transference has been questioned in psychosis. If in neurosis, transference is an attribution of knowledge, in psychosis, it is not the analyst who is in the position of the so-called subject-supposed-to-know, but the psychotic subject himself. Allouch illustrates this reversal of positions by revisiting Lacan's seminal case of Aimée. This chapter gives us the key to working successfully with psychotic patients who are considered by some clinicians to be unanalyzable precisely because they are incapable of developing transference in the traditional psychoanalytic sense. Alluding to Lacan's own transformative encounter with psychosis, Allouch recommends that the clinician occupy the place of "secretary of the alienated," a perplexing yet clinically astute maneuver. Allouch's work situates the discussion of transference and of psychotic transference as a central aspect of the history of psychoanalysis. This chapter is taken from Allouch's *Marguerite ou L'Aimée de Lacan* (1994), considered a classic in psychoanalytic scholarship, a detailed examination of Lacan's seminal case study. We are proud to make this remarkable contribution finally available to an Anglophone audience.

In Chapter 9, "The specificity of manic-depressive psychosis," Darian Leader also critically reconsiders the use of clinical categories. Offering a thorough historical survey of the concept of manic depression, he draws a distinction between manic-depressive psychosis, mania and depression. Leader emphasizes that Lacanian studies of psychosis have tended to focus on three diagnostic categories: paranoia, schizophrenia and melancholia. Historically, however, the category of manic-depressive psychosis has been the subject of a vast amount of attention in mainstream psychiatry, and is often seen, with schizophrenia, as encompassing the whole field of psychosis. While Lacan's references to manic-depressive psychosis are few and far between, in this chapter, Leader examines them to see what light they can shed on the phenomenon of manic-depressive states, posing the question of the legitimacy of the diagnostic category itself. Are mania and depressive states phenomena found in all forms of psychosis or is manic depression a distinct diagnostic entity unto itself? If it is, what are its links to other forms of psychosis and, in particular, to schizophrenia? He explores these questions using clinical vignettes, memoirs, and textual studies from psychoanalysis and psychiatry.

In the tenth chapter in this collection, "Melancholia and the unabandoned object," Russell Grigg explores another complex clinical phenomenon that raises treatment questions: the patient who enters analysis in good faith, works diligently during her analytic sessions, and yet continues to suffer and gets worse, as if the analysis itself were the cause of the deterioration. Grigg shows that this clinical stagnation or regression can be understood within the parameters of melancholia, as the consequence of an invasive presence of an object. Arguing that Freud's comparison of mourning and melancholia is misleading, Grigg points out that, following Freud, the attack on the ego in melancholia is too devastating for it to be fully understood as internalized aggression against the object. Another explanation of the origins of melancholia needs to be found.

Looking more closely at the origins of madness, in Chapter 11, "Madness, subjectivity, and the mirror stage: Lacan and Merleau-Ponty," Jasper Feyaerts and Stijn Vanheule discuss the model of Lacan's mirror stage to illuminate how madness touches on the essential structure of human subjectivity, effectively erasing the divide between normal and pathological. Feyaerts and Vanheule show how Lacan's mirror stage, the formative developmental milestone in the creation of the ego, can be importantly distinguished from the mirror as theorized by Merleau-Ponty. Further, they develop and elucidate the Lacanian understanding of hallucination in terms of the mirror stage's relation to the Symbolic order, lending theoretical sense to the very heart of madness's opacity.

In Chapter 12, "Narcissistic neurosis and non-sexual trauma," Hector Yankelevich interrogates madness in terms of a discussion of narcissistic neurosis, providing further consideration of the mirror stage's role in the development of subjectivity. Let us recall that, observing the retraction of the libido from the external world in psychosis, "narcissistic neurosis" was one of the names originally suggested for psychosis by Freud, following Abraham. Yankelevich delves into the construction of reality as an early work of the psyche. Developing the clinical consequences of Lacan's theory of the mirror stage, he elaborates a Lacanian theory of narcissistic neurosis by considering Rilke as an example of a successful solution to the limitation of this form of narcissistic madness.

In "She's raving mad: the hysteric, the woman, and the psychoanalyst," Claude-Noële Pickmann takes a close look at mad episodes in the treatment of women that often follow a crisis in their amorous lives. She develops Lacan's concept of "ravage" or *ravissement*, a term taken from the writer Marguerite Duras, to show its use in understanding the differential clinic of hysteria and psychosis. By way of this concept, Pickmann proposes another way to think about madness in women, i.e. as a being stranded or as concerning a theft of the ego. She explains that such madness is not psychotic and can exist in neurotics, when they experience a significant loss of love or are deprived of their support systems. Probing Freud's speculations regarding femininity while proposing a feminist Lacanian theory of women's sexuality, Pickmann's understanding of feminine madness is crucial in the treatment of women who are systematically misdiagnosed as borderline or psychotic, and, as a result, often suffer social stigma and clinical mistreatment. Once again, the puzzling quality of madness is lifted, inspiring new ways of considering clinical challenges.

In Chapter 14, which opens the section "Madness and creation: environs of the hole," Juliet Flower MacCannell's "The *open* ego: Woolf, Joyce and the "mad" subject" shows how the writing egos of two of the most celebrated twentieth century modernist writers, James Joyce and Virginia Woolf, allowed them to overcome the social, familial and gendered conditions they struggled with. MacCannell compares Woolf to Joyce in terms of their "writing egos" to highlight Joyce's unique know-how and Woolf's tragic entrapment in the ideal of a unified ego she protested, but from which she could not finally free herself. She calls Joyce's know-how an "open ego," one that liberates the Imaginary from the confines of a body and situates it in a new and liberating relation to language— protecting him from the madness Woolf endured.

In the next essay, chapter 15, "Normality and segregation in Primo Levi's *Sleeping Beauty in the Fridge*," Paola Mieli analyses one of the most eloquent writers of the holocaust experience, Primo Levi. In one of his less commented on works, the dystopian science-fiction short story, *Sleeping Beauty in the Fridge*, Levi tells the story of a woman who is kept in the refrigerator over hundreds of years and taken out only for important occasions, showing the strangeness and yet perfect comfort of madness in everyday life. In Mieli's analysis of the story, she shows how the intrusion of the past into the present is a source of both life and death, of a sense-making and sense-destroying intrusion of a traumatic reality. She shows how Levi's story illustrates how the uncanny can lose its status as uncanny and become simply banal. This paper not only offers a contribution to Holocaust-survivor literature by touching on the understanding of the madness of technology and the commodification of femininity (and, thus, of otherness), but allows us to consider our current reality in which the madness of consumerism has become commonplace.

In the following chapter, "Spell it wrong to read it right: Crashaw, psychosis, and Baroque poetics," Stephen Whitworth examines the absence of the Name-of-the-Father in the poetry of the seventeenth century English Catholic mystic, Richard Crashaw. Crashaw's solution to the failure of paternal metaphor is to "sing the Name which None can say," suggesting that the Baroque poet had found a creative solution—a substitute for this lacking crucial function. While his art assists him in his work on and with the jouissance that traverses and exceeds him, in Whitworth's reading, Crashaw is never completely sheltered from psychotic returns of the Real.

Olga Cox Cameron's essay "Madness or mimesis: narrative impasse in the novels of Samuel Beckett" discusses Lacan's claim that our relationship to language is one of parasitic dependency. She shows how Beckett unmasks this relation of interdependency in all its alienating dimensions. The maddening effects of language pertain to all speaking beings, not only to the insane. Beckett's tragicomic reduction of the "I" illuminates the darkness we like to deny by way of chatter that occludes a more permanent and abiding silence. By way of Beckett, Cox Cameron shows the Lacanian notion that we are all mad; madness is no longer designating illness but rather refers to what it means to be a being who speaks.

The book closes with Manya Steinkoler's "Reading mayhem: schizophrenic writing and the engine of madness," a reading of a screenplay synopsis written by a psychotic patient. *Le Jeu-Mémoire du Dieu Serpent Mehen* offers a paradigmatic example of schizophrenic writing. Writing, in this case, while opaque and oppressive for a reader, since there is no access to metaphor, acquires sense when seen as an attempt to explain and find a logic to an existence that seems completely random, without fantasy and without the metaphor of the Name-of-the-Father to anchor meaning. In the text, Ixidor finds himself being played in a game the rules of which he doesn't understand and he advances and regresses without understanding why or how. Steinkoler's reading locates the function of the mirror stage in psychosis as illustrated in the story by the progression of the game. Despite the fact of being crazy, *Le Jeu-Mémoire du Dieu Serpent Mehen* is not mad insofar as it makes something legible and grants Ixidor a reader, if not exactly an addressee. This is a good example of the ingenious aspects of psychotic creation that find a creative way to reveal an absolute structural impasse, and can be called a work of art.

Lacan on Madness: Madness, yes you can't intervenes in current debates about normalcy and pathology, causation, effective modalities of treatment, prognosis, and currently popular ideas of what constitutes cure, while offering a reassessment of the positive and creative aspects and potential of madness. This book tries to show that those who dream of lassoing Proteus err, drunk with phallic hubris that the tragedies sought to purge us of. But that does not mean that we are ineffective with the gods. Sometimes, by showing our humility in just being mortals who lack the strength to subdue them, we can be far more effective. These essays show us that we can know a great deal about why Proteus takes the shapes he does and how his shapes, and tempests, and rages can be changed as he stages them for us. And in the event we are not recognized, where we are called to witness a terrible and frightening tempest, silent or deafening, staged for no one at all, the essays in this book show us the modest power to be had in simply witnessing the storm. Sometimes just knowing that the storm matters, that he has affected the mortal realm, that he was seen, is enough for Proteus to leave the seas in peace.

Bibliography

Aristotle (1980). *Nicomachean Ethics*, trans. D. Ross. New York: Oxford University Press.

Breggin, P. R. (1991). *Toxic Psychiatry: Why Therapy, Empathy and Love Must Replace the Drugs, Electroshock, and Biochemical Theories of the "New Psychiatry."* New York: St. Martin's Press.

—— (2008). *Medication Madness: A Psychiatrist Exposes the Dangers of Mood-Altering Medications*. New York: St. Martin's Press.

Breggin, P. R. and Cohen, D. (1999). *Your Drug May Be Your Problem: How and Why to Stop Taking Psychiatric Medications*. Cambridge, MA: Perseus Books.

Breggin, P. R. and Breggin, G. R. (1994). *Talking Back to Prozac: What Doctors Aren't Telling You about Today's Most Controversial Drug*. New York: St. Martin's Press.

Breuer, J. & Freud, S. (1893). "On the Psychical Mechanism of Hysterical Phenomena," in *The Standard Edition of the Complete Psychological Works of Sigmund Freud, Volume II (1893–1895): Studies on Hysteria*. London: Hogarth Press.

Durkheim, E. (2006). *On Suicide*, trans. Robin Buss. London: Penguin.

Foucault, M. (1988). *Madness and Civilization: A History of Insanity in the Age of Reason*. New York: Vintage Books.

Freud, S. (1900). "The Interpretation of Dreams (First Part)," in *The Standard Edition of the Complete Psychological Works of Sigmund Freud, Volume IV*. London: Hogarth Press.

—— (1925). "An Autobiographical Study," in *The Standard Edition of the Complete Psychological Works of Sigmund Freud, Volume XX (1925–1926): An Autobiographical Study, Inhibitions, Symptoms and Anxiety, The Question of Lay Analysis and Other Works*. London: Hogarth Press.

Friedman, R. (2012). "A Call for Caution on Antipsychotic Drugs." *The New York Times*, September 25, 2012, p. D6 of the New York edition.

Lacan, J. (1988). *Le Séminaire, Livre V, Les formations de l'inconscient*, ed. J. A. Miller. Paris: Editions du Seuil.

—— (1993). *The Seminar of Jacques Lacan: Book III The Psychoses 1955–1956*, ed. J. A. Miller, trans. R. Grigg. New York: W. W. Norton.

—— (2006). *Écrits*, trans. B. Fink. New York: W. W. Norton.

Laing, R. D. (1960). *The Divided Self: An Existential Study in Sanity and Madness*. New York: Penguin Books.

Lane, C. (2008). *Shyness: How Normal Behavior Became a Sickness*. New Haven, CT: Yale University Press.

Leader, D. (2011). *What Is Madness?* New York: Hamish Hamilton and Penguin.

Nobus, D. & Quinn, M. (2005). *Knowing Nothing, Staying Stupid: Elements for a Psychoanalytic Epistemology*. New York: Routledge.

Porter, R. (2002). *Madmen: A Brief History*. New York: Oxford University Press.

Szasz, T. (1961; 3rd edn 1974). *The Myth of Mental Illness: Foundations of a Theory of Personal Conduct*. New York: Harper & Row.

Part 1

MADNESS MANIFEST
Encountering madness

1

THE CASE OF THE BABY DIAPER MAN[1]

Rolf Flor

Jay achieved only modest toilet training. At first, this was framed by his parents as a training issue. Thereafter it was framed as a health problem. Doctors were consulted; medications were tried; behavioral methods were laid out. However, the problem remained unsolved and unexplained. Extensive medical efforts to help Jay with enuresis continued into adulthood. Eventually Jay only feigned participation. He lost interest in solving what was no longer a problem. One might say, to the contrary, the problem had become its own solution.

In a particular crisis, his diaper began to feel good to him. Over time he added ways to comfort himself. Jay collected pacifiers and discarded children's clothing. By the time he reached late adolescence, Jay began to photograph himself wearing a diaper, clutching the paraphernalia of infancy. He could admire these pictures and eventually shared them with others in online communities. With these images and objects, he found himself able to develop a quasi-symbolic matrix that made it possible to negotiate the challenges of connecting to others.

Now an adult, Jay sees himself as an "adult baby" and a "diaper lover." His "solution" is not a flawless way of negotiating his connections; some people who know him closely, especially family members, object to his diapers. Despite their complaints, the only thing he wishes to change about himself is certain angry outbursts that punctuate his social experience. "I lose it and when I do I hurt people that I love very much." Rage troubles him and for this he seeks help.

The setting and beginning of treatment

I am a psychoanalyst in private practice. I am also the clinical director for a community behavioral health agency. The agency provides what is called "human services," a description that I personally value more than the notion of "behavioral health," because it emphasizes that we provide our services one person at a time, rather than for the benefit of maintaining a norm. The case I will discuss is from the clinic.

A clinician with many years' experience entered my office.

She said, "We have to figure something else out. This one is not for me. Somebody else should see him."

I responded, "Who is he?"

"A guy sent over by the shelter specialist. At first he said he has urinary incontinence and needs to wear a diaper. Later in the interview he admitted he is registered as a level 3 sex-offender and he really wears diapers all the time because he likes them. Half way through the intake he started sucking on a binky!"[2]

I asked, "Why is he here?"

"He said he comes 'from an angry family' and that it was 'rough at the shelter' and that he is anxious about staying there because it is 'making him mad.' God only knows what he really wants . . ."

She interrupted herself with an apologetic tone and softened her demeanor.

"Look, I am sorry, but I am the wrong therapist for him. He needs someone that can work with his kind." After a pause, she continued, "I bet he is here just for medications anyway . . . or maybe because of some parole officer."

"Did he ask for medications?"

"No, not yet."

"Did he say he was mandated to treatment?"

"No."

"What did he say?"

The volume of her voice rose steadily as she said: "He said he pleaded guilty to sexually assaulting a six-year-old girl when he was eighteen and that was why he was labeled as a sex-offender." Pausing, she added, "He admitted that he offered to lick the girl's vagina."

She continued with an ironic tone, "But then of course he also said he is 'not a pedophile' and he was 'misled to a guilty plea.' I tell you, this guy is a creep."

I asked, "What did you say to him about next steps?"

"I told him that I was just doing an intake assessment and that I will not be his therapist. He is waiting outside. Should we tell him that someone will contact him when someone becomes available?"

"What is his name?"

"Jay."

Meeting Jay

Waiting outside my door was a slender young man with strawberry blond hair. He appeared younger than his twenty-eight years. Jay wore loose clothing: overalls and an oversized baseball cap. Since I was already aware of it, I could not fail to notice the evident padding from a diaper. He seemed to be carrying his worldly belongings in a large diaper bag.

I gestured for him to come in and I introduced myself. He smiled wanly as he looked at my outstretched hand. "I understand you are asking for treatment and I am available. When is it possible for you to come back?" I shook his hand again after we agreed to a time the next day.

I saw Jay in the clinic, twice a week, for less than year. I would describe our work as psychoanalytic psychotherapy. For my work in the clinic I need to modify the range of options for variable-length sessions and must develop treatment-planning language that can withstand the scrutiny of third-party payers. Nevertheless, the work that I asked of Jay began very much like the work I ask of any patient (say everything that comes to mind, complete unfinished sentences, associate to dreams, reflect on parapraxes, etc.).

In the course of treatment, we established that he was not mandated to see me, and I never had any contact with authorities on his behalf. I found him to be engaged in the process and reliable in attendance. He had complaints about the world and how he was treated. There was also at least one specific thing he wished would change: although the events had been infrequent, he had occasionally found himself in a blind rage during which "I lost control of my body." Though he did not develop this point at the beginning of treatment, he described "rage coursing through [his] body."

Family history

Jay was born and raised in a large city in the southwest of the United States. He is the second of three children. He has a brother who is two years older and a sister who is three years younger.

Jay's father, now disabled, was a long-distance truck driver. Early in the treatment, Jay told me that his father had recently been diagnosed with terminal cancer and that his siblings were encouraging Jay to go down and "make peace with him." Jay refused because he thought he would not be able to control his rage in the presence of his father. He described his father as having been a "crazy asshole who beat the shit out of us." He can "rot in hell for all I care."

Jay's mother held numerous unskilled jobs. He first described her as "pushy" and "controlling," but in later sessions it becomes increasingly clear that he thinks he was at one point her favorite and he expressed nostalgia for better times with her. Sometimes he blames the change on the birth of his sister; at other times he blames the abusive father for having "ruined" things. In the arc of their relationship, his mother went from "loving to pissy." His use of that phrase is interesting in the context of his life long struggle with enuresis. We can hear a unique significance in the phrase for Jay about the switch in valence in his relation to the (m)Other— from positive to negative—and about the emergence of a localized body symptom in a place of contestation between Jay as a subject and the Other.

Growing up in relative poverty, the family lifestyle and income were greatly impacted by both parents' abuse of drugs and alcohol. Their habits dominated Jay's childhood. Jay and his brother were taken away by family services and placed into care with his paternal grandparents when he was two. After the parents finished a course of substance abuse rehabilitation treatment, Jay and his brother continued to live briefly with those grandparents while his parents struggled to find employment and housing. In contrast to Jay's father, Jay said that he really respected his grandfather, emphasizing in particular that he was a "church-going man," even while also acknowledging that his grandfather was tyrannical with his faith and quick to use corporal punishment. Jay's grandfather functioned in a more symbolic father role, perhaps setting a limit to jouissance. But it seemed that his mother disapproved of this role. This left Jay eventually in the clutches of his real father, a father who did not recognize such limits and who probably could not facilitate for Jay a metaphorization of the desire of Jay's (m)Other.

Jay's mother became pregnant while Jay was in the care of his grandparents. After the birth of a sister, Jay and his brother returned to live with his parents. The parents stayed close to the grandparents at first, his father making a show of remaining sober and attending church. Jay's mother did not "buy into" his grandfather's piety and expressed frustration with what she perceived as self-righteousness. When Jay's father returned to work they moved again, and his father also gravitated back to a life filled with deadly pleasures. Jay's father frightened everyone in their house with alcohol-fueled rages, magnified sometimes by cocaine abuse. His parents' fights were quite violent, according to Jay's report.

After several courses of rehabilitation, Jay's mother began to avoid street drugs and alcohol and described herself as "in sobriety." She managed her version of sobriety by complaining of pain and obtaining prescription pain relievers. At the same time she began to rely more on Jay. She asked Jay to help care for his sister even when he was quite young, which he says he was happy to do because she really was a "good little baby." But his mother's moods ran, in his words, "hot and cold." This greatly confused him, because his very earliest memories are of a loving mother. When his sister was asleep and his father was away she favored him by waking him up and taking him to bed with her.

After a certain age he changed his own diapers. In sessions, Jay related several charged moments, long after infancy, when she changed his diapers. When his mother helped, it was often because she wanted to hurry him along; but he also suggested that helping to change his diaper was her "wanting to make up with me," a phrase that suggests the patching up of a romantic relationship.

When Jay was six, it was decided that his younger sister should live with the grandparents. He does not understand exactly why that happened. Perhaps the mother did not have the time to take care of a pre-school child anymore. Perhaps the father's doubt about Jay's sister's paternity reached some sort of head. Perhaps the father's rages forced his mother to find a refuge for the girl. Jay raises all of these as options but seems unsure that any of them explains what happened, especially since his mother did not like the grandfather. But Jay is nevertheless certain that the decision to send his sister away came from his mother. It seemed odd to him that she could just "flush her away like that."

Clearly the un-metaphorized desire of the mother remains enigmatic, but not one that leads to formulate this as a question; instead, it is only "odd" that she can "flush" Jay's sister away. His diaper may be a way to hold her back from doing the same to him.

Enuresis and the "baby thing"

Jay had only ever achieved a modest toilet training. Nighttime enuresis forced him to remain in diapers when he went to bed. Daytime accidents led to many embarrassing moments. Until he turned five, the enuresis was framed as a training issue, and thereafter it was framed increasingly as a medical problem. His mother was most troubled that accidents also happened during the day.

After the family reunified, and without the presence of grandparents, Jay's father first ridiculed Jay and then grew ever more frustrated over time. Jay was a target for his father's anger because of the constant washing of sheets and the expense of unsuccessful treatment. The fact that his accidents were more frequent when Jay was upset did not change his father's responses. Jay's accidents became a lightning rod for family problems as his mother protected him by her own acts of violence towards his father.

A few weeks into treatment Jay told me the following story. His father frequently complained about the smell of urine. Jay lived in fear of the days when he was at home alone with the father (Jay's brother would find ways to not be home). Shortly before his eighth birthday, home alone with his father, after his sister had been sent to live with the grandparents, Jay's father sat in the kitchen drinking and smoking. When his father went to the bathroom Jay heard him bellow in anger as he passed Jay's bedroom. "What the fuck is wrong with you? You stupid fucking thing, this room smells like piss!" Associating to these words, Jay remarked that his father often called him a "fucking baby" and he did not fail to notice that his father was equating a "baby" with a "thing."[3] As his father sat on the toilet, he kept yelling out to Jay about the smell of the urine in the house. Jay feared where this was going. He slipped out of his own room and moved anxiously from corner to corner of the house, unsure where to find refuge, desperate to not let his father see him. His anxiety mounted as Jay thought about "how he was going to beat me." Finally Jay slipped through his parents' bedroom and to the small room beyond, a room originally intended for his sister. As his father intermittently bellowed from the toilet, Jay hid himself behind boxes and luggage, wondering how long it would be before his father got up from the toilet and found him.

"I rocked myself to stay calm—I thought my heart was going to jump out of my chest when I realized I had just had another accident—piss got onto the rug —I took off my clothes to try to soak it up—to rub it dry—I could still smell it— I don't know why I but—I was cold?—anyway I reached into a box—then I was putting on my sister's clothes—I don't know why—I crawled into a ball and hid in the corner—rocking—then I—felt—good—and . . . and . . ."

He stopped at this point in his story. After a pause, I asked, "And . . .?" He said the calmness he "discovered" while sitting rocking and wearing his baby sister's clothes faded when he suddenly worried that his mother might find him. I was surprised that his worry was about her. At that moment in his story an enraged father was stewing on the toilet or perhaps even already looking for Jay to beat him. When I repeated his words, "mother might find me," he said, with irritation in his voice, "Yes, well, she didn't."

From that day on, Jay had something he could use to "baby" himself literally. His very own diaper felt good to him. He could also wear things in addition to a diaper that helped him feel okay. Over time he collected discarded children's clothing and other comforting clothes. He hid pacifiers in several places and he would suck on these when he was alone. He preferred to wear nothing but the diaper when he did this. He took pictures of himself, which he would look at later.[4]

The next years involved continued medical efforts to help Jay with his enuresis. He wore special clothing and took precautions at night. His father continued to belittle him. Publicly, his mother defended Jay against the father, deflecting the father's abusiveness. When they were alone, however, she reproached Jay, saying that he should "try harder." Jay says he lost interest in solving what was "not anybody's problem."

Jay's parents separated when he was ten. When the father moved out, the sister returned to live with them. Jay changed school several times, since they moved often, but he appreciated the ability to start over and learn new ways to hide his practices from kids at school. He said nighttime enuresis abated during this time but he still wore a diaper day and night to control "accidents."

A "sissy" in "AB world"

Early in his treatment, as he was relating his family history, Jay casually asked if I had "heard about the adult baby world?" I asked him to tell me about it. He picked up my pen and wrote the address of a website on my notepad. "Check it out. You'll see." His eyes brightened as he excitedly told me what I could expect there. Jay described how an internet search in his early teens unexpectedly brought him to the realization that "there are millions of us." "There are adult babies everywhere. Places you would never even suspect. There are cops who are adult babies and diaper lovers—I have met some online—I even know an FBI agent who is a diaper lover." He explained to me how the community of adult babies and the diaper lovers who admire them "are a family" and how they "stay connected and protect each other." Pointing at his phone he said, "I have at least three numbers that I can call there and get help to almost anyone anywhere."

Social media websites are frequently part of his dreams and were brought up in sessions. Jay had many profiles on social media websites. He belonged to several online communities that he believed were closely monitored to minimize exploitation and harassment. Additionally, he described himself as helping to police the sites, "reporting users who seemed to be a danger to others." After he first mentioned his internet experience in a session, Jay would refer to ABs and DLs, sometimes saying "AB/DL" (much the way one hears people now use the abbreviation "LGBT" as a standard term for the lesbian, gay, bisexual and transgender community). Usually Jay would refer to this as the "AB world."

The ecstasy of his discovery of the adult baby world when he was around thirteen years old was mitigated by another experience near the same time. An older cousin found Jay in bed dressed in an outfit that made him look like a "sissy." This was the word used by the cousin, who took Jay's diaper as an excuse to force Jay to perform fellatio on him. By Jay's report he did not enjoy performing fellatio, but there was something complex about this moment of traumatism. The word "sissy" struck a chord with him and performing fellatio made him feel "gross," but he genuinely liked this cousin and felt close to him. While Jay was discovering the world of "adult babies" and "diaper lovers" on fetishistic websites, he found that the term "sissy" had a generally understood meaning in this context. In the AB world, a "sissy" is a male who identifies as an adult baby but wants to dress and be experienced by others specifically as a baby girl. Jay's cousin privately called him "sissy" in a way that suggested attraction or affection of some kind. So the sexual assault left Jay both anxious and ashamed but also stimulated in other ways. Jay became overwhelmed by the abuse heaped on him by that same cousin in front of others. Jay's cousin had been using the word "sissy" and "faggot" interchangeably in public, "so I tried for a while not to wear diapers and got rid of things" (pacifiers, pictures, baby clothes).

Soon after the sexual assault, feeling stripped of the ability to enjoy or comfort himself, Jay swallowed a bottle of the tri-cyclic antidepressants prescribed for his enuresis. "When I woke up [in the hospital after the suicide attempt], my father was speaking to me. I began screaming for him to go away, and I told them that I only wanted to talk to my grandfather." In the way Jay tells this story, he relished the rejection he was able to express by asking for his grandfather. With the others present, his father was not able to react with his customary rage. The father needed to swallow that rage. "I know that pissed him off," Jay explained; it was a necessary punishment of his father. The use of the expression "pissed off" evokes a theoretical network of connections between urination, anger, and paternity. One might wonder whether the diaper was not a kind of proxy device for containing his subjective dissolution, preventing his getting pissed away in the presence of this all-too-Real father.

The rest of his middle and high school years, from age thirteen to eighteen, "had ups and downs." The "ups" were largely in the form of increasing associations in the AB/DL world. He developed social media skills, profiles, and associations. On the "down" side, there was increasing isolation from his family. His suicide attempt first garnered him sympathy and then later ridicule in his family. During his teen years, his immediate family also made discoveries about his online life.

Finding a "thick black line"

After the sexual assault and the suicide attempt, after years of tolerating the shame quietly, Jay found himself increasingly unable to contain himself when "pissed off." Jay became aware of what he called a "growing problem": his temper. He found himself fighting more regularly, first with his brother, then with ever more people. These arguments were not "just fights," they were "black-outs of rage . . . hissy-fits where I lose control and hurt anyone who got in the way." He was arrested several times as a teenager for fighting.

The phrase "growing problem" seemingly referred to a problem that had been small but was becoming unmanageable. It could also however refer to the experience of becoming physically bigger and the frustration of seeing himself as no longer quite physically baby-ish. Jay recognized that an adult baby has something awkward about it. With the onset of puberty, he seemed to have to reinforce some sort of fundamental balance of what he knows and what he denies, and this did not come without discomfort for him.

These "explosions" became increasingly intrusive events for Jay just as he was starting to have real world contact with self-identified AB/DLs. Some of the people he met online would want to meet for sexual encounters; from Jay's perspective they were predators who were "looking at the AB/DL world in the wrong way." Asked what he meant, Jay explained that he saw a fundamental difference between ABs and DLs. Adult babies may or may not be sexually active, but the AB world is not "really a part of sex." More often than not, AB events are enjoyed "for themselves." Jay said, "Adult babies and their adult baby mommies [were] coming together just to be together," emphasizing the word "be" in order to express the non-sexualness of coming together.[5] In session Jay emphasized that even while sexual relations do happen in the AB world, for him there is a "thick black line" between the things he does in the AB world and ordinary sexual relations between himself and his partners. His sexual partners, usually female, are part of his adult baby world because he does not want to "always hide that," but these partners also know that there is this "thick black line."

Diaper lovers, on the other hand, have to be considered more cautiously according to Jay. Some really are just adult baby mommies and occasionally adult baby daddies. But diaper lovers also include some, usually males, who are "unable or unwilling" to maintain that thick black line. "Things get ugly when they [the diaper lovers] get confused." Jay has many doubts about the role and prevalence of real adult baby daddies in the AB world.

Crossing the "thick black line"

When Jay finished high school at eighteen, he had limited notions of what to do next. He played with the idea of raising money in various ways, including prostituting himself. The internet gave plenty of opportunities for "that kind of hook-up." He said he found the idea distasteful and yet it was implied that he did make some money by allowing himself to meet with DLs. Jay insists he never enjoyed these as sexual activities. Jay preferred to ignore the financial aspects of these encounters. He said he saw this as people helping each other in the AB world (not as prostitution). Far more troubling to Jay was the fact that online fetishistic culture seemed to think everyone was interested in every other fetishistic culture. He was completely perplexed that internet search engines suggested any connection between adult babies and, say, bondage. And yet, a search on adult baby leads quickly from the AB world to shoe fetishes, bondage, bestiality, etc.

Unable to keep any other employment due to his temper, throughout his adolescence Jay primarily made extra money by babysitting, an activity even the very name of which he enjoyed. There was "something funny" in telling people that he was babysitting, because that had very idiosyncratic associations for him. He also got to handle baby clothes and baby toys. He thinks he was "very good" to the children.

When Jay was eighteen he happened to be babysitting a neighbor's six-year-old girl and her two-year-old brother. The six year old, whom he had babysat before, had an accident in which she wet herself. Away from home, in wet clothes, she was ashamed of going home and having to face her parents. Jay described her as becoming inconsolable. Her crying became screams. Her baby brother woke and also began crying, and Jay reports that he became "anxious and angry." He took her to a public bathroom to help her clean up. The filthy bathroom had nothing that could help: a broken sink, an out-of-reach hand drier, and an empty toilet paper dispenser. He said, "I did the only thing I could think of—I offered to, eh, lick it clean." He says, "I never really did it—but I did offer—I don't know why, but it doesn't matter, I might as well have done it—it was wrong."

Jay related a version of this story to the clinician who first saw him. He again related the story to me in a very early session. Certainly this description of his crime pushed my clinician, and would push many people, past the limits of empathy. But what was the description? A well-practiced lie? A self-deluding reconstruction? A deliberate effort to get a rise out of me? Immediately after telling me the story, he said, "I think that hurt her. I would never hurt someone like that again. I would kill myself if I even thought of it." He then related a complex story in which, having uncovered situations online where an adult male was apparently trying to have sexual relations with an underage person, he successfully thwarted them, reported them, had others come to their rescue, etc. He relished descriptions of how his intercessions led to punishments for these "moldy perverts." His family name has a certain similarity to the word "moldy." He had previously used the phrase "moldy-old" to describe other people pejoratively when he wished to suggest they were too old for something. I raised a question by simply stating the word he elided: "Old?" His association was that his mother had often tried to encourage him around his enuresis by saying to him, "You're too old to be wearing a diaper, you can lick this problem Jay, I know you can."[6]

Months later the young girl told a parent what Jay had done (what Jay says he only offered to do). The enraged parent confronted Jay and eventually pressed charges. Many of his practices and photos were brought to family and police attention, leaving Jay "feeling trapped." Unable to deny or explain the experience, Jay's lawyer recommended he plead guilty. Jay went to a prison for five years.[7]

When he left prison he was ranked at the highest level for sex-offenders. That rank is reserved for offenders who pose the greatest risk to the community, those deemed by the sexual offender registry boards as most likely to re-offend if provided the opportunity. Most have prior sex crime convictions as well as other criminal convictions. Their lifestyles and choices may also be what place them in this classification. Some, but not all, have predatory characteristics (i.e. they may seek out and groom their victims). They may also simply have refused to participate in or complete approved treatment programs. In fact, Jay felt the conditions of his treatment were intolerable and onerous. He was offered counseling in which he was "forced into talking about things [he] did not want to talk about." "All they ever wanted to talk about was what happened. They don't care about me at all." Jay felt threatened by forensic clinicians because they would introduce intrusive elements to test his sexual inclinations (penile devices, polygraph tests) and so he refused treatment. Jay sees his "perversion" as the opposite of sexual. This rejection of "treatment" and his legal history of assault charges added weight to the case against him.

Beyond the "thick black line"

After his release, while trying to steer through the many social and legal challenges of being labeled a sex-offender, Jay intensified the practice of meeting adult babies and adult baby mommies through online "AB world" chat rooms. He met his future wife, an AB woman living in New England, in a chat room. They began speaking regularly on the phone. He didn't need to tell her about the diapers, because that is not only accepted but is a core element of the AB world. He did tell her about the enuresis, a bodily issue that stayed with him and had in fact worsened while in prison. Although she herself was a self-described AB who preferred to be treated as a baby, his incontinence "makes me feel," she said, "like I should be the one taking care of you."

Jay reports that they met for a strictly platonic AB encounter. Quickly after their one and only offline meeting, he decided to move up from the southwest to the northeast because she had again offered to "mommy" him. Jay began the process of having his parole moved out of his home state. After months of planning and saving, they had this encounter:

"I got off the bus and walked into the station looking around for Kayla—at first I couldn't find her—I went from nervous to angry—I started calling her cell phone and then I saw her! She was sitting on the floor wearing the cutest dress— her legs spread out—her dress spread out like a blanket—with a little teddy in her lap—and that was it!"

Even though this was technically not their first encounter, Jay described their reunion in this way: "We just clicked . . . it was love at first sight!" The original agreement, that she would be his mommy, changed when they began having sex. That image of her sitting on the floor, with her dress spread and a teddy bear between her legs, had aroused him sexually. My interventions prompted him to talk about the shift. This is when he first spoke of the "thick black line." Some of the time they would be like a couple, having sexual relations, and other times they were in an AB relationship. His wife apparently also understood there to be a "thick black line" separating sex from the AB world. By his report, they never AB role-play while having sex.

Living with Kayla and her family was "tense but okay" at first. Things changed quickly when Kayla's family found out about Jay's status as a registered sex-offender. Further research by her mother led to an angry confrontation between Kayla and the rest of her family. "I heard the whole thing so I started packing my bag—Kayla came in and saw what I was doing, so she pulled out a bag and started packing to come with me." They spent that night sleeping behind a church dumpster. The next day "I forced her to go back home. I knew she should not be on the streets. I couldn't let her do that. So I moved into a shelter."

Eventually Kayla also moved out and they lived together with friends from the AB/DL world. Jay says it was then that they secretly got married. "But we never told anyone—her family doesn't even know—they know we still get together but they have no clue that we are married."[8] Because Jay failed to register at this address, he went back to prison (now in Massachusetts) for a year. During that time he maintained contact with his wife, his mother and some AB friends. Later Jay admitted that the immediate cause of his being sent back to jail was actually instances of domestic violence between him and his wife.[9] He begins to tear up when he talks about how she stuck it out with him; one time he said tearfully, "my baby is my mommy and I will do anything for her and she will do anything for me." On release from this second spell in prison, Jay moved into the shelter near my clinic.

Clinical questions

Jay seems to have lacked a signifier for his mother's desire. What controlled the faucet that made her run hot then cold? Why did she "flush away" his sister? Arguably, even without such a signifier, Jay may have experienced moments in his life when an interdiction was placed on the direct experience of jouissance from/with his mother. But was a prohibition actually imposed by his father? His father had a presence that makes this theoretically possible. But Jay's mother also undermined his particular paternal function in countless ways, even with regard to the paternal grandfather. So with his mother, as he said, things went "pissy." And with "pissy" we can mark some kind of encounter for Jay with the Other of language, yet as a signifier, "pissy" has a strangely fixed connection to the problems of his body.

I tread lightly with these assertions because I cannot be certain whether or not there were moment(s) of alienation and/or separation from an object *a* that could bring Jay to his personal version of the endless hunt for satisfaction faced by a speaking subject. How could I? Given the early stage of his treatment, the only thing I would like to postulate is that, remarkably, Jay has already laid bare for us a kind of inversion of the primal scene. Jay seems to discover (maybe I should say rediscover) the object *a* with which he will identify, the talismanic diaper with which he first sops up his own urine and then incorporates into his AB world. I now find it easier to think of the diaper as a way of tightening Symbolic, Real, and Imaginary aspects of his experience.

From the moment in the closet when he was able to calm himself with children's clothing, it seems to me, he knows where he stands. But this could certainly be read in other ways; perhaps with his own penis sheathed, the image of his entire body may represent the wholeness of a maternal phallus. As a baby, he himself may belie her castration. His role as a "sissy," a female adult baby who happens to be male, underscores that relationship to the mother. This is obviously not a primal scene of parental coitus on which neurotic fantasies are built, but rather one where Jay secures the imaginary role the diaper will come to play for him.

But what happens now in treatment? What can he do?

Playing with the "thick black line"

Jay is an adult baby and he has no wish to change that mode of jouissance. And yet there are problems that seem to threaten the "thick black line" with which he tries to organize his romantic life. From adolescence on, there is the increasingly intrusive question of the diaper lover. With "diaper lover" we should hear not only that there may be love for the one who wears the diaper, but that the one who wears the diaper may be a lover. Jay is an AB, an adult baby, a miraculous identification that constricts dimensions of experience that threaten to be pissed away or pissed off. But "AB" is now also short for "AB/DL." And like "LGBT," it no longer seems enough to reference the "LG" without saying the whole acronym. So Jay is also AB/DL: adult baby and diaper lover. What, we could ask, happens when one subtracts AB from DL?

That very question came up in a session when Jay was rehashing the calculus of letters with which he spells out this story. He related the following dream:

"I was at the shelter being teased for my diaper. Everybody was staring at me and pointing and saying mean things. I was getting mad, really mad, and yet somehow I didn't care. I took the rest of my clothes off just to show them. I don't care. Suddenly everybody was just looking. There I was with a boner sticking out of the top of my diaper. When I woke up I did have a boner and I was really scared that . . . somebody would see me." Because he paused in a notable way before he said "somebody," I repeated for him "Somebody?" He responded, "Well, you too were staying at the shelter in my dream." My presence in his dream at least suggests a transferential investment. How would this investment bring returns?

A number of considerations of how he sees me must be taken up given my appearance in his dream. A part of his own body that seems to have been overrun by jouissance has been bound by his diaper, perhaps preventing the need for more violent management. Yes, he has found a "thick black line" to ward off the "black-outs." On one side of the line we find the unruly jouissance, on the other, the ordinary sexual satisfaction with his wife. Now something threatens to peek out from that containment.

Should one speak of transference here? Perhaps it was possible for him to see me as some kind of subject-supposed-to-know in part because of the way in which his intake-worker made clear that he, Jay, presented some kind of problem for her. She came to see me in an obvious state of anxiety about him. Her demeanor and actions may have actually facilitated his being able to see me in a different light. He sensed her judgment and found my neutrality more inviting. Perhaps because he thinks of himself as being fundamentally innocent, my neutrality showed that I knew something.

When Jay came into treatment I asked him to tell me about his history. I also asked in as many ways as I could what questions he faced. One way of asking that is to ask what he wanted from treatment. Over time, the list, if we draw it from his own expressed complaints, included many things: sleep better, be less anxious, have more real-life encounters, be less depressed, have children of his own. But two things in particular stand out: firstly, he has never expressed any interest in changing with regard to diapers and the AB world. He does not complain even about the urinary incontinence that he says still happens at night. But he has most definitely complained about the need to control his temper. He describes what he calls "black-outs," a phrase that is frequently heard in the context of alcohol abuse. During these "black-outs" he has "assaulted" others, "including people I very much love."

Many of his early sessions contained long sections of material in which he described his policing the virtual AB world and his acquaintances therein. He would insist that the web was a sort of "wild west" that had not yet been civilized; is Jay now propping up the Law that was needed to keep it safe for other ABs? Sometimes he would tell me that he knew I couldn't talk about it to others because of confidentiality, but it would be "ok if [I] did." This makes it a "win-win," because he gets to talk about things and I get to help others stay safe as well.

Every now and then he would turn to me for help. He showed that he thought I was being helpful in that regard, because even if I did not offer advice, he thought it was "clear from the way [I] was listening that if [I] felt he was doing something inadequately [I] would surely speak up." On another occasion, having learned that I had some authority with regard to the local emergency services, he called me between sessions and asked me to help hospitalize his wife when she had called him expressing suicidality. When I gave him the number for the Emergency Service System in her part of the state he said he "was 100% sure that [I] would know how to direct [him] to the right place."

His dream about being in the shelter gives us pause. How can we theorize the "boner" he dreams of and the "boner" he wakes up with? Have I been deputized to keep some kind of Law in place? And what will he do with his "boner" if the point of a diaper is to "prevent black-outs" by keeping things all tied together?

Notes

1 An earlier version of this paper was read at the APW conference "On Madness" in St. Louis in October of 2012. I want to thank Manya Steinkoler and Patricia Gherovici for their reflections on the text. They have essentially challenged me to rethink the case. The presence of some degree of transference and the absence of any clear indicators in the discourse of the patient made it difficult for me to see the case as a classical psychosis. Since then I have found some tools in Jacques Alain-Miller's *Ordinary Psychosis*.

2 Jay carries around a pacifier for when he feels anxious. He never placed it in his mouth during our sessions.

3 Perhaps in this equation, Jay will find his object not in a fantasized dynamic relationship with his subjectivity but directly in the "pocket" of his diaper (Brousse 2003: 3).

4 Jay did not associate this behavior with explicit sexual satisfaction. For example, I have no reason to believe that he ever masturbated while looking at the pictures. He reported having images on his phone that were his favorites. He never shared the photographs with me. And when talking about the online communities he participated in, Jay made clear that the photographs were not shared with people who seemed to see them as sexual images.

5 "Be" as in "B" from the acronym "AB." So one could hear this as "coming together just to baby together"—though the phrase "coming together" could just as well suggest the opposite, being together in a very sexual way. And finally, to "be together" suggests babies and mommies simply being joined, as in being physically connected.

6 One reader of this paper offered the following apt reflection: "Would this be a moment when what is foreclosed returns from the Real, without the metaphor, as if the message was, 'When you pee on yourself, you lick the problem?'"

7 Jay refused to speak about his years in prison.

8 Jay's marriage to Kayla still remains a secret.

9 Jay was arrested for domestic violence, at which point it was established that he was a level 3 sex-offender who had failed to register with the local authorities.

Bibliography

Brousse, M.-H. (2003) "Editorial." Mental: International Journal of Mental Health and Applied Psychoanalysis. Online. Available at: 2013lacaniancompass.files.wordpress.com/2011/05/mentalonline121.pdf_201 (accessed 30 October 2013).

Wulfring, N. (2008) *Psychoanalytic Notebooks of the London Society of the New Lacanian School: Vol. 19 "Ordinary Psychosis."* London: Printek Ltd.

2

ILSE OR THE LAW
OF THE MOTHER[1]

Geneviève Morel

There is no universal signifier for sexual difference in the unconscious. The phallus, which might have played this role, works for both sexes in the dialectic of the castration complex as the signifier for sexual ambiguity, at least in neurosis. Indeed, the phallus authorizes the dialectic of "having" and "being" insofar as they are related to anatomy. The boy *has* the penis and thus resents the failure of his phallic power even more. The girl *does not have* this organ, but this does not stop her from *being* the phallus for her mother, and later on for a man, or even to *have it* in the form of a child. Thanks to this phallic dialectic of having and being, the neurotic subject positions him- or herself on one side or another, slipping towards the other side at times without too much trouble: the pre-adolescent girl has her "tomboy" period, and the boys playing at cross-dressing do not create any lasting confusion. Admittedly, this denotes the neurotic's polarization around the phallic question, contributing to symptom formation.

When a psychotic subject does not enter the phallic language games that constitute what Lacan calls "the sexual discourse," she is confronted with the enigma of sexual difference without having a phallic signifier ready-made by the maternal discourse at her disposal. She therefore has to invent something else in order not to become perplexed. Some cases show that adolescents can suffer from a double difficulty in separating from their parents, in situating themselves in sexuation. This difficulty makes them experience all sexuality as "incestuous" and their own position as "homosexual"—terms that connote in a simple way a confusion between the sexes and the generations. The subject wants certain worlds to remain distinct from one another.

But this is not enough: another sort of difficulty arises once the subject has succeeded in "separating these worlds," worlds that need to be separate, but in which the subject does not manage to find a place. One solution consists in putting a sinthome in place to create a new relation to sexual classification and filiation. The case of Ilse shows that one way of inventing such a sinthome is to make use of the new forms of parenthood taking shape in our societies today.

33

I: Unraveled connections

Ilse, a thirty-year-old woman, came to see me because she wanted to change analysts. She had lost confidence in her analyst, a man, C., because of his silence. Since incestuous memories of her father had come up in the session, she was distressed, anxious, and experienced somatic symptoms. The silence of the analyst, which she associated with her father's silence, became unbearable for her.

She felt that C. would hinder a new relationship she had recently begun after a difficult break-up with her previous girlfriend. Ilse had begun her analysis with C. because she had had difficulties with love in the relations with her partners, who were always women, and because of her troubled family background. Her father, married for thirty years to her mother, had changed jobs and had had several affairs, which led to a divorce. Her mother, panicking at the prospect of this separation, tended to depend on her only daughter for help rather than her three sons. It was difficult for Ilse to find a response to this maternal demand and she felt overwhelmed by her mother's anxiety. What is more, she had become her father's confidante: he would recount his adventures in detail and, feeling like an accomplice, she felt guilty in relation to her mother.

Our sessions, which focused on the fear of incest and rape, began with much anxiety. The "incest" at issue was, however, exceedingly allusive and remained as such—or, more precisely, it was quickly no longer spoken about. It involved a scene with three people: her father supposedly put his hand on Ilse's knees, and her mother supposedly protested, provoking a row between her parents. Also associated with this was the theme of violence and the evocation of a scene in which her father had beaten one of her brothers, Eric. She had heard screaming behind the closed door without seeing anything. Two years older, Eric was, she said, her "incestuous brother," because she had had experiences of sexual fondling with him between the ages of eight and fourteen, also the time of her first homosexual relationship. He was now a father but she interpreted some of his behavior towards her as equivocal and dreaded that he might carry out incestuous acts should he have a daughter.

When Ilse came to sessions, she spoke of how she "felt her sexual organ was hollow," attributing this painful sensation, as well as sensations of being "crushed in her back" and "hit on her back," to what remained from the rape and the incestuous acts of violence. These were forgotten but registered in her body— revealed in this way through a process of remembering. Her preoccupation with the deportation of homosexuals and their massacre by the Nazis ("you could not escape with your life") was associated in the session with other "things" that she herself had been unable to escape from: her menstrual periods, and her father's "massacre" of Eric, which he accepted "passively."

In light of her emotional state, I feared the development of a delusion, all the more so given that she told me she was feeling "paranoid" at work and with those around her. I therefore made two interventions. I remarked that on the one hand these *supposed* "memories" of incest (I insisted on this qualifier to loosen her conviction) had occurred after a face-to-face encounter with a man, C., the analyst that she had now left. On the other hand, referring to her recent comments in the session, I revived her historical interest in the massacres of homosexuals and highlighted the link of these to her more personal fears (I was thinking of her menstrual periods, of the idea of "massacre" and "rape" by the father).

These interventions offered her relief by separating her from what was confirmation of a catastrophic paternal transference and refocused her on her history. Indeed, for a few sessions she continued to feel "penetrable," to have the idea that she had "foreign bodies in her vagina," and to feel threatened by men, while evoking a desire tinged with fear, particularly in her dreams. Her position in these dreams was one of silent paralysis when confronted with men. She experienced a sexual excitement that seemed obscene to her and that made her feel shame when there were demonstrations against Le Pen and when reading news items about incest. These fantasies soon disappeared to be replaced by a somewhat laconic reconstruction of the stages in her history.

II: Two compartmentalized worlds

Until the day when, at the age of six, her mother had had Ilse's long hair cut, Ilse had no particular memories. That day, when she returned home and her brother Eric didn't recognize her, she broke down. On that day, she felt she had lost her femininity. But what was this femininity before the age of six? She said nothing about it other than to mention her long hair.

The closed world of men

After this event, she entered definitively into a world of boys: she had three older brothers, was "her father's daughter" and "a tomboy." Between eight and fourteen years of age, there was some sexual fondling, initiated by her brother Eric, which she would describe as incestuous a long time afterwards, and which she stopped engaging in when she had her first same-sex relationship at the age of fourteen.

At around nine or ten years of age, after a clash with her schoolteacher, she strongly felt the support and silent sympathy of her father. She had planned to run away, but she gave up on this because her brother had discovered what she was up to. The death of her paternal grandmother when she was twelve left her in despair.

At thirteen, in an essay she wrote, she expressed her wish to change her sex. At fourteen, after her first relationship with a girlfriend, she knew that she was homosexual, but she did not tell her parents until she was twenty.

We note very few events in a past apparently without much neurotic disturbance. In six years of analysis, however, numerous dreams enabled her to reconstitute what had been played out behind the smooth façade of a problem-free childhood. Two worlds confronted each other.

The world of men was characterized by cruelty. The father, "a mad, monstrous king," incarnated absolute power in the home. In a dream, he is sitting in front of

Ilse on a throne, exhibiting an enormous, "disproportionate" sexual organ, which she finds ridiculous. She evoked times when he would hit her brothers; she could hear these "massacres" even though she was not present. On one occasion, her mother got a black eye. She remembered her grandfather who used to cruelly kill rabbits on their farm. However, her father also had a protective role, as the episode with the schoolteacher indicated. He transmitted a certain professional ambition that was however damaged by the contradiction between the esteem he demonstrated towards his daughter and the scorn he showed for her mother. It was a silent, speechless transmission. Ilse chose the same profession as her father.

The closed world of women

Opposed to this, the world of women was essentially represented by her mother and her paternal grandmother. As a young girl, her mother had been "abandoned" by her fiancé "because of her refusal of sex." So, she threw herself onto Ilse's father and, in order not to lose him, became pregnant. The paternal grandmother was opposed to this marriage and looked down on her daughter-in-law, an attitude that she shared with her son. The father would systematically interrupt his wife and would never let her express her ideas. Ilse's mother confided in her that she did not feel respected and constantly spoke badly to her of her father and of men. From this Ilse got the idea that the feminine sexual organ was "mutilated."

If she experienced compassion for her mother, her mother's submission to her husband revolted her. She remembered one occasion when the family was leaving to go on holiday and her mother had insisted that Ilse not disturb her father who was preparing the trailer: her mother's meekness troubled her deeply. As a consequence, she refused the feminine model that her mother incarnated, the model of a woman who "only" had children, who had remained dependent on her own mother for a long time, who could do nothing on her own, and who found herself, despite all her sacrifices, once again rejected by the divorce.

The paternal grandmother was "a strong woman" who could have presented the little girl with another dimension of femininity, but she died too early. Her death, when Ilse was twelve, felt like "a catastrophe." In short, Ilse rejected the model of the "mutilated" sexual organ and attempted to side with the boys. But there was an obstacle: the masculine sexual organ as an emblem of violence.

Imaginary feminine and virile identifications

Ilse succeeded all the same in siding with the world of boys by using an imaginary identification with her brothers when, at six years of age and with short hair, she was admitted into their world and recognized as one of them. She continued all the same to look for a place for femininity. Around the age of ten, she recounted having felt inexplicably good when the daughter of friends of her parents had joined her, without saying a word, in the bathroom. It was as if she then had a place, but only momentarily. We can deduce that she had to constantly rely on imaginary identification to find an evidently fragile identity. Suddenly, we understand why the relationship with Eric did not seem sexual to her: her "incestuous brother" was used mostly as a virile support for her. In an analogous way, from the age of fourteen, she tried to constitute a feminine identity for herself, though unsuccessfully, with same-sex, often platonic, relationships. She had a name for these relationships of support, calling them "imitation-couple" relationships, contrasting them with relationships as couples, which were more difficult to sustain, as we shall see.

Rape and the mutilated sexual organ

We can see what begins to emerge as a possible relation of complementarity between the two closed and separate worlds of men and women; on one side, the mutilated sexual organ, and on the other, masculine power—rape. Something bordering on delusion suddenly appeared, in the manner of the return in the Real of a long foreclosed idea. This was what had precipitated her leaving her male analyst C., whose silence evoked her father. Ilse, as we have seen, felt in her body that "her sexual organ was hollow" and "mutilated," she experienced her body as "dismembered," and she "remembered" being raped by her father. This worrying emergence was contemporaneous with her parents' separation, when each of them had solicited her attention more than usual. Her father was looking for her approval, and her mother for her pity and company. She then had some dreams in which she found herself with a married couple. In one dream, the woman asked her to make love, but the man arrived and she felt paralyzed. She interpreted it as an Oedipal dream, which evoked a childhood memory, a scene in which her father had rejected her mother and Ilse had remained mute. Indeed, she was scared of remaining voiceless and paralyzed when confronted with violent men like her father, as she had been during "the massacre of her brother." In an analogous way, she dreamt that one of her girlfriends was raped but that she herself remained mute and paralyzed. Afterwards, the girlfriend reproached her for not having intervened.

Her mother had transmitted the fear of men and the idea that "one" could not defend oneself against them: all these dreams were therefore attributed to the mother—negatively, obviously. Ilse longed to free herself from this maternal suffering and, due to this, her place in the feminine world was unsustainable. She recalled holidays during which she was the only little girl among nine boys playing a stripping game (*le pouilleux déshabilleur*). When she lost, she had to do a striptease in front of the boys and couldn't get out of it. Fortunately, the unexpected appearance of her mother—still without any words—saved her from the shame of being exhibited. This confirms that femininity for Ilse was reduced to a mutilated sexual organ, to be exhibited to boys without being able to say no.

Feminine relationships

As soon as she had sexual partners, Ilse's position was compromised, given the rigid framework of these two separate worlds. The imaginary identification with her brothers was no longer sufficient to ensure a relationship with a woman.

At the beginning of her analysis, Ilse had a tendency to put herself in the place of her father. She had already confronted her mother who had reproached her, when she was an adolescent, for being as nasty as he was. Stricken with nausea, she then felt invaded, inhabited by him: "I am my father," she used to state with anxiety. She dreamt several times: *that her father was making love with his wife, and that she was taking his place. The woman now in front of her was her "dismembered" mother, whom she wanted to satisfy, and to whom she wanted to give what her father had deprived her of.* Transposed into reality, this produced relationships that were intolerable and given to fusion.

In another dream, *she could neither stay with her partner, nor leave her side at all, because something terrifying threatened them.* This terror was associated with her mother, whom she described at the time as a manipulator. She remembered having pretended to be asleep one morning as a child so that her mother would come and give her a cuddle. Her mother, who had not been fooled, left her alone and spoke to her in "a sardonic tone." This demand for love from her mother was— without any possible dialectic—associated with the fear of being dropped and with archaic anxieties about dismemberment. When she had to leave her companion each day to go to work, it was "a tearing away from herself," "a loss of identity" and "a roaming," all of which were unbearable.

Her transference dreams were of the same basic structure: *either she drove me in the car, she made me scared, and I felt bad, "directed" by her this way, or I was given blows to the back at the moment when she spoke to me in the dream about her mother, at the precise place where she felt pain.* "So I was in the humiliated place that women are assigned to in this rigid sexual bipartition of the world."

There was therefore barely any alternative between these two worlds that were mirrors of each other. Confronted with men, Ilse was plunged, speechless, into the world of raped women. And, confronted with the women, and against her will, she could easily inhabit the world of rapists.

After her troubled start in analysis and my two interventions, which had distanced her from the "remembering" of paternal incest, her somatic symptoms and preoccupations with diverse massacres gradually stopped. The cure reoriented her towards the preceding construction. That is to say, she set up these two worlds, as well as the impasse where she found herself without a place. She got the measure of this impossibility and was able to break off the difficult relationship she found herself in with her partner, before finding her new girlfriend, Marie, with whom relations were different. Ilse let herself be talked into it and, appeased, did not expect anything in particular. The relationship took a more sexual turn, in a reciprocal mode, which displaced the confrontation between these two worlds that were mirrors of each other. Marie liked Ilse's body, and she accepted reciprocal penetration with a finger, which Ilse's former partner refused—as, moreover, did most lesbians, Ilse told me.

In a dream, *she was bathing with an amorous young man and her mother's voice told her to be wary.* She interpreted the dream as a sexual inhibition issuing from her mother, to which she was no longer obliged to conform. "I can feel an opening," she said, still very close to language of the organ. In any case, she seemed to have found a place, which some new transference dreams confirmed. In one of them, *her family consulted me, each one for themselves, separately, in turns: like her, each of them had found their place in the analysis.* She took up the previous material again retrospectively in the analysis and re-elaborated it, returning again to "the two separate worlds" and their signification. Ilse thought she had gotten out of it.

III: The inseminating father

Marie, however, wanted a child. After some thought, consultation with various lesbian groups, and an in-depth study of the question, Ilse and Marie opted for artificial insemination for Marie in a European country that authorized AID (Artificial Insemination by Donor) for lesbians in a relationship (which is not the case in France). Ilse did not at all envisage becoming the biological mother of a child herself, but the plan and then the decision, taken together, of the insemination of Marie suited her. "I want to make a choice that connects me definitively," she said, without clarifying any further the coordinates of this connection. However, even if she consented to it, this decision destabilized her a great deal, as was shown in two dreams about "conception" that she raised just before their trip for their first consultation at the specialist at the fertility clinic.

The first dream was a variant of a recurrent dream. *Her father was having a sexual relationship with an unknown woman and Ilse took over from him, with the same woman.* "It could have been my mother, but it was another woman" (in fact, in a previous dream, it had been with her mother).

We could have deduced from this that Ilse's father was taking the place of the anonymous inseminator, of the real father of the child to come. But Ilse's associations did not go in this direction. She found this dream pacifying, as it effaced the "memory" of the raping father and introduced a new, more idealized image of him: she "constructed herself as a homosexual" by now taking the place of the father "who loves women."

In the second dream, *Ilse found herself with a naked man whose sexual organ she could see, and over which she vomited after they made love: I had to explain to him that I loved women.* It probably concerned a dream linked to the announce-ment to her father of her decision to become a homosexual parent. This incestuous dream also shows that she, too, receives a child from the father (which she gives birth to by vomiting), at the moment of Marie's insemination, which she was required to attend.

If we read these two dreams together, it emerges from the first that the father gives Marie a child on Ilse's behalf (since she substitutes herself for the father with the woman), and from the second, that he also gives a child to his own daughter. He therefore takes the place of the real father (the anonymous donor) and he impregnates the two women simultaneously with just one and the same child. The father therefore intervenes in this affair as a third party, like a hyphen between the two women, a *Deus ex machina*, an agent of liaison, to give the same child to both of them.

We remember how the encounter of Ilse with analyst C. had caused the sudden appearance of ideas of paternal incest, which could evoke the triggering of a psychosis.[2] Now, curiously, the father was summoned, as a third party, to a symbolic place,[3] in order to give in an imaginary way a real child to a female couple, without bringing with it the least delusion. On the contrary, the present situation was accompanied by a certain stabilization for Ilse because it was the sign of the end of an anguishing sexual bipartition of the world from which she had been excluded.

Questions of structure: hysterical disgust or phallic foreclosure?

We could deduce from this that foreclosure, in the case of Ilse, is concerned more with the phallus (and the link between the masculine sexual organ and the phallus) than the Name-of-the-Father as a symbolic instance.

Foreclosure of the phallus and body phenomena . . .

The rejected signifier is indeed the phallus, as an imaginary emblem of rape and massacre. It is the phallus in its capacity as signifier of an evil power that Ilse's feminist culture links firmly to the masculine sexual organ. However, this idea, borrowed from the current cultural climate, is not tempered by a neurotic dialectic. Henceforth there was for her, on the one side, "women plus children," and on the other side, "fathers plus the phallus." Just before the "insemination dreams," a previous dream had indeed represented this kind of separation exactly: *Some men were sitting down around a giant phallus. It was the world of her childhood, while in another room, a widow, a colleague of her father's, she was alone with her children.*

This dream seems to go in the direction of rejection of the phallus. I never noticed in our sessions any elementary phenomena at the level of language, and therefore no decomposition in the Symbolic register. Only bodily phenomena, "events of the body," denoted a problem at the level of the body's imaginary. These disturbances are undeniable; they have been repeated with much clarity and cannot be confused with conversion symptoms, which always rest on unconscious repressed metaphors. Only analytic deciphering can bring to light and undo them (like the *vermögend* in the case of Dora). Far from the complexity of the condensation and displacement that characterizes Freudian repression, it concerns bodily synesthetic sensations that Ilse immediately translates into the idea of receiving blows. In turn, these blows take on the signification of an idea, already there, of a rape, or are interpreted as maternal persecutions. In fact, Ilse confided to me on more than one occasion that she had "received blows" when coming to the session: "*Someone* was leaning on her back and *Someone* was making her sit down in the road."

This "Someone," supposedly the agent of the bad treatments she was subjected to, was the sign of the existence of a mental automatism. This "Someone" is mute, as the father and mother are when they are the agent of torment. If this "Someone" begins to speak, the mental automatism worsens to become a verbal hallucination, which, fortunately, has never happened, but is not to be excluded as a possibility.

Ilse had associated the ill treatment with a traumatic anesthesia she had undergone at the age of five at the dentist, and for which her mother, who hadn't warned her about it beforehand, appeared to be the person really responsible. I also received blows in one of Ilse's dreams, just because she had spoken to me of her mother. This denotes a transitivist mechanism of projection and an imaginary identification in the transference. These elementary phenomena confirm Ilse's psychotic structure.

. . . or hysterical conversion?

I had hesitated from the beginning of the cure. Was it a question, triggered by her entry into analysis with C., which had unfortunately evoked the phallus and the paternal silence—a revival of an incestuous fantasy incarnated in hysterical conversion symptoms? We could indeed have interpreted these corporal phenomena as a hysterical disgust for the masculine sexual organ. The connection of paternal incest with the veiled scene of the blows delivered by the father to the "incestuous brother" could, in this interpretation, evoke the Freudian fantasy "A child is being beaten." The blows "received" in the street would then be the expression of a fantasy of being beaten (but why this curious way of presenting it as the initiative of the Other?). The analysis with C. would have provoked this strong return of the repressed. This is what I was inclined to believe at first. But, if this was the case, how to explain that in six years of analysis the castration complex never emerged? Why has no construction of the fantasy of flagellation ever been elaborated?

Is it not rather a question, in this difficult analytic beginning, of the outline of a delusion provoked by the appeal to the Name-of-the-Father in the transference towards C.? It is not easy to be categorical in a case in which there are no disturbances of language and the subject has a perfectly "normal" life. All the same, I opted for a psychotic structure,[4] on account of the character of mental automatism of the somatic phenomena that repeated themselves ("someone" acted on her body, "someone" made her carry out an action) and because of a total absence of a phallic dialectic, which would be difficult to conceive in a neurotic context. Indeed, we do not find in Ilse any problematic around *Penisneid* as we do in the cases of neurotic homosexuality. Moreover, I have never glimpsed the least phallic demand in her. Nor do we find any possible passage between the separate worlds of men and women, marked by fixed and rigid traits, in which the subject only manages to integrate herself with the men, and only in an imaginary and fragile way.

Two divided fathers: the lover of women and the rapist

The foreclosure of the phallus as the signifier of generation emerges in the dream of "conception," when Ilse vomits on the man's sexual organ, even after her fertilization. The father as agent of generation is idealized as "the one who loves women," at the moment when he is summoned to unconsciously "explain" the conception of the child. The father is then completely dissociated from all the allusions to castration that we would inevitably find in a case of neurosis: here, as soon as it concerns the father or a man, the foreclosed symbolic castration returns in the Real in the form of the idea of rape.

There are therefore two paternal images that remain disjointed and independent of each other: the rapist and the lover of women, as if we could turn the page between these two paternal figures without any remainder, as if a cut materializes what is not of the order of repression but of foreclosure.

On the side of the women, castration is realized and non-symbolized, and is confused (in a manner similar to the confusion in the idea of rape) with the horrifying idea of a mutilated sexual organ and a massacre of women. The mother is the center of gravity of this sinister field, into which she is likely to continually drag her daughter with her.

In a certain way, the relation to the child of the other woman seems more "simple" for Ilse than for a neurotic woman. Owing to this disjunction between the father of love and the gift and the father as the agent of the foreclosed castration (i.e. the rape), this solution avoids conflicts and gives Ilse greater social liberty.

In a later dream, Ilse sees "a sun father." She associated on "the paternal shining light" in her present life, all the while saying that she had had to leave her father in order to find him.

IV: Being "the parent"

What place is Ilse going to occupy, then, in relation to her partner, the future biological and legal mother? After the successful insemination of Marie, now pregnant, some dreams presented Ilse and her mother in the same scene, and Ilse had to reconsider her bipartition of the world. How was she going to situate herself? She announced to me that she was going to be "the parent" of Marie's child. The parent, she explained to me, was neither the mother (this was Marie) nor the father, who was an anonymous donor. She considered this term "parent" as a sort of neologism, a new concept that would perfectly name, in its neutrality, her role with the child about to be born, a place that "linked her definitively" to Marie and the child. She didn't want to be "a second mother"—a designation that often prevails in analogous situations. Nor did she want to take the place of a "father."

The couple would therefore not be based on the man-woman bipartition that up until then had governed the world order, but would be that of "a parent" and "a mother." The parent would have moral authority, which corresponded well with her character and qualities, she thought. She would have no legal bond with the child, to her great regret, because an adoption turned out to be impossible. But she envisaged all the same, with Marie's agreement, initiating steps in order to secure legal guardianship of the child.

Ilse's parents took the news calmly, all the while pointing out to her that her legal bond with the child would be fragile; they would have hoped for a little girl from her. On this occasion, when the theme of the law emerged, particularly in the discussion with her parents, it did not awaken anything terrible in Ilse: no specter of a commander arose, and there were no serious upheavals. Ilse was serene. Fundamentally, the neurotic and guilt-inducing debate concerning rights and duties simply did not take place. Ilse had found a solution to make do without the permission and blessing of the moral majority, all the while remaining within the limits of legality. She was not outside-the-law; she respected the law, but she exploited the loopholes in the system. The fact that there wasn't the least psychotic emergence at that particular point again confirms the sinthomatic value of the solution Ilse found to the problems of generation and sexual difference.

Marie's labor, which they spent much time preparing for together, returned Ilse to the circumstances of her own birth, which she spoke about in the session. Her mother had tried to abort her, she had confided to Ilse when she was twenty, because she did not want a fourth child. After Ilse's birth, her mother, exhausted by the labor, supposedly did not have the strength to breastfeed her baby, nor to receive her adequately. Listening to this sad account, Ilse had felt guilty for what she had inflicted on her mother by being born and she knew that it was through the willingness of Marie "to agree to have herself inseminated that she herself avoided the terror of labor." Labor, like her periods, was associated with "massacre" and "the mutilated sexual organ," and even with "a murderous maternal wish" towards the fetus that she compared to Nazism. The labor, at least in terms of the possibility of her own family, therefore also referred to a foreclosed castration. Moreover, Ilse was worried about Marie's labor, which she "was supposed to attend." I pointed out to her that it was not an obligation, which gave her some relief. But she insisted on being there and participating in (almost) everything. She lived "all the physical details" of this pregnancy; the child "slept by her side" and she spent a lot of time touching it on the mother's stomach; this concerned a sort of "communication" and "recognition." Maternity was unacceptable *via* her mother and she had to "appropriate it for herself" in another way through the intermediary of Marie, breaking away, at the same time, from her "murderous" mother. Before the labor, Marie had to take to her bed and Ilse spent some difficult moments looking after her. She dreamt *that she had to seduce a young woman and at the moment of sleeping with her they found themselves in two separate beds, with the young woman dressed in a wedding gown.*

If the mother was offering herself, the woman remained forbidden. Ilse was tempted by infidelity while Marie and she did not have sexual relations and slept apart, but she resisted. One summer morning, during the holidays, she called me at last to tell me that a child, a boy, had been born and that all had gone well. I congratulated her soberly.

V: The invention of a sinthome

In her analysis, Ilse put in place a sinthome, "the parent," an invention of a new relation to woman and to filiation. At the outset, the sexes were distributed between two worlds, which were rigidly separated. Ilse had no place among them: the imaginary identification with her brothers was not sufficient to sustain her in the confrontation with women, except to form an "imitation-couple," and it was out of the question for her to join the clan of feminine victims, of which her mother was a terrifying emblem. Following an intense elaboration in the analysis, and a minor delusional transferential episode accompanied by "events of the body," the encounter with a new partner who wanted a baby transformed the initial given situation by allowing Ilse to construct a "couple." Now, confronted with the "mothers with children," it was not a question of placing herself on the side of "the men with the phallus"; such was the new sexual dichotomy that her uncon-scious was offering her. And this was all the more the case since the phallus turned out to be a foreclosed symbol for her, as it always had been. By leaning on the discourse of homosexual parenthood that the gay and lesbian movements offered her and to which she referred, Ilse invented—confronted with the future mother— "the parent." This term has a neologistic value: it is full of what it avoids while alluding to it—the father and the mother.

The rapist father became "the paternal shining light" as a result of an unconscious process that symbolically installed him as a third party between the two women. The process also effaced his initial value of phallic rapist to make of him both the real father—in the place of the anonymous sperm donor—and the imaginary father of the same child given conjointly to the two women.

The mother, victim of the man but a potential murderer of the child, was effaced thanks to the advent of this new being. Furthermore, "being a parent" abolished Ilse's sad arrival into the world by "repairing" the poor welcome her mother gave her when she was born.

The new given situation is as follows: a "parent" faced with "a mother plus child," with whom a definitive bond has been made; the disappearance of the "men plus phallus"; and, in one corner, "the paternal light" who guides the subject as her guardian angel. Such is the way the sinthome "being a parent" is written and it is thanks to this sinthome that Ilse is able to invent a new mode of filiation without the phallus, but not without a support taken from the father. We can observe the "quadripartite structure" (Lacan 2006a: 653; Lacan 2006b: 460–1) in which the sinthome is included, holding together the mother (the Real), the child (the Imaginary), and the father (the Symbolic) by confirming the exclusion of the phallus. Furthermore, the sinthome inscribes a possible sexual relation with a woman by using the social symptoms of the era. In this case too, as in Joyce's case, we note that the father is an essential element for the sinthome, without however there having been any paternal metaphor. This confirms the interest of Lacan's late teaching.

The case of Ilse, if my diagnosis of structure is correct, demonstrates something further: there are cases in which the phallus is foreclosed. This provokes disturbances in the Imaginary register, producing body events. Yet the father as a signifier of creation and generation, as Name-of-the-Father, still functions. Speaking in the terms of "The preliminary question" (Lacan 2006b: 571), there are cases where we note the foreclosure of the phallus (Φ zero) without a foreclosure of the Name-of-the-Father (P zero).[5]

The sinthome "being a parent" focuses Ilse's sexual ambiguity and stabilizes her. Ilse is no longer neither on one side nor the other, she no longer needs to define herself in the "old" categories of man and woman that have tormented her to such an extent. She has taken on a new identity, sexual but not sexuated, and she has given it a name. From this point of view, "the parent" plays an analogous role to the phallus in neurosis—it is valid for both sexes. Its difference from the phallus is that "the parent" does not belong to the universal dialectic of Oedipus; it is Ilse's singular invention using a minority discourse.

But who knows what the future holds? Nothing can guarantee that the signifier of the phallus as emblem of sexual discourse will not be taken over by a multitude of individual sinthomatic solutions. There are signs of precursors. In order to console those with a nostalgic bent, we will say that the phallus has been a universal signifier for a very long period of history.

Translated by Lindsay Watson

Notes

1   An earlier version of a section of this chapter was published in Morel, G. (2006). "The Sexual Sinthome." *The Incurable Umbr(a): A Journal of the Unconscious.*

2   Indeed, following Lacan, a triggering of this kind can be caused by the appeal to the Name-of-the-Father on the basis of an imaginary confrontation, here between Ilse and C., the man-analyst (as we have seen, Ilse was until then sustained by an imaginary identification via her elder brother) (Lacan 2006b: 577).

3   "Car, si l'exige le contexte symbolique . . . ne saura jamais rien" (Lacan 2006b: 556).

4   I speak here of structure in the psychoanalytic sense; psychotic structure does not necessarily imply madness.

5   Lacan envisaged the possibility of a disjunction between these two "chasms" of foreclosure, but not that one could exist without the other; Ilse's case would therefore be an example of this second figure (Lacan 2006b: 571). See Morel, G. (1999) "Research on the Beginning of Psychosis," in *Ordinary Psychosis*, Paris: Le Paon. As

concerns feminine homosexuality, Lacan emphasizes in 1958 (Lacan 2006b), as we have seen, the difference between the affirmation of being a man in the female homosexual (the naturalness with which such women call on their qualities as men) and the transsexualist delusion. In 1971 he takes up this parallel by trying to be specific about the difference between the modes of rejection of the phallus in the two cases: this could throw light on the diagnostic discussion above, by showing that the rejection of the phallus in feminine homosexuality can be structurally close to psychosis. Perhaps it would be necessary then to make of it a fully-fledged structure. In the case of Ilse, however, the affirmation of being a man does not exist consciously, but we may wonder, as I have done, whether her phallic rejection is psychotic or not.

Bibliography

Lacan, J. (2006a) "Kant with Sade," in *Écrits: The First Complete Edition in English*, trans. B. Fink, New York: W.W. Norton, pp. 645–68.

—— (2006b) "D'une question préliminaire . . ." [On a Question Prior to Any Possible Treatment of Psychosis] in *Écrits: The First Complete Edition in English*, trans. B. Fink, New York: W.W. Norton, pp. 445–88.

3

FROM PSYCHOTIC ILLNESS TO PSYCHOTIC EXISTENCE

On re-inventing the institution

Guy Dana

Let us begin with a simple question: Is psychosis curable? We have learned that delusions and other disturbing psychotic phenomena are almost always curable. In psychosis, we are concerned with what remains recalcitrant, resistant to treatment. These include psychic fortification, taciturn reclusiveness or what we call psychotic solitude, a solitude where social isolation is substantially marked. Interestingly, it is precisely the radical solitude of psychosis and the difficulty of constructing social ties that will provide the key; by understanding it, we will be able to discern the trajectory of a cure that would allow for a solitude more open to chance events and alterity, and distinguishable from agonizing solitude. Of course, we can generalize and say that all analytic encounters entail encounters with solitude. However, the particular solitude of psychosis is one that can never be shared. Here, the issue of the social link to others remains of primary concern.

Even in "successful" cases where social ties have been established, one may still ask the question whether the patient has actually been cured. Looking for meaning or signification to resolve problems of a psychotic individual is not as efficacious as it often is with neurotic patients. In psychosis one must introduce other therapeutic parameters. That is why I have found the idea of perspective, as developed in the visual arts, useful within the structure of the clinical encounter. The notion of perspective insofar as it concerns the creation of space pertains to clinical work under transference, as the fundamental therapeutic position of "being with." I shall return to this point and it will be part of the key to transforming psychotic solitude.

The notion of solitude permits us to make distinctions in psychoses. One type of psychosis is that of the well-known case of Antonin Artaud, for whom the presence of someone, of anyone—not necessarily that of an analyst—was helpful. This proximate other helped Artaud's ability to think and to tolerate the void.

In Artaud's statement in a letter addressed to George Soulié de Morant, this idea is made palpable; he writes: "My thought grabs what is alive and reacts to the ideas that someone emits alone" (Artaud 1996: 201). Here we see him intimately reacting to the other. When he is alone, however, it is quite a different matter. "I am mortally bored. I am nowhere. The nothingness and the void: that is what represents me." When Artaud says "grabs on to what is alive" (Artaud 1996: 201), in his words we can hear the resonance of Gaetano Benedetti's statement, "To be with: that is our answer to negative existence" (Faugueras 2011).

Unlike the first modality of psychosis Artaud presented, one in which the other is necessary, in a second modality of psychosis, we see the exact contrary. In this form of psychosis, any other person is an unwelcome excess. Here, the experience of what Benedetti calls "negative existence" is so powerful that therapeutic attempts are almost always futile. The subject is alone, and comfortable with this aloneness. He may manifest social withdrawal by his own volition, looking for and at times even finding the way to spontaneously cure himself. This is possible when the patient's search is not interrupted by pressure from the analyst that would cut short the time necessary for understanding, or by an authoritative decision coming from another person that would preclude the patient's own search for a cure.

Finally, the third modality of psychosis is one in which transference is possible—with all its tumultuous, unexpected rebounds and ruptures that require years of engagement by both parties. In this instance, something, but mostly someone, wants to wrest the patient from solitude. Even though transference may occur, solitude remains an issue. Many authors have discussed the notion of "opaque compactness" (*compacité*) with regard to the psychoses, a term that pertains to this solitude. Here we witness a surprising adhesiveness to words, a lack of psychic space, and a quasi-impossibility of reflexive thought. In addition, we note the impossibility of considering what is said and detaching from it. This is illustrated in the words of a patient as they were reported to his analyst, Franco De Masi: "Unfortunately, the unconscious can only listen without seeing, just as the eyes can only see without hearing, and since the unconscious doesn't have eyes to look within, it hallucinates internal images by way of its eyes that it lacks within" (De Masi 2011: 85). In other words, this patient can hallucinate or hear voices outside of himself. One may say then that from the moment he can hear himself speak and therefore consider himself engaged in social ties, it is probable that the relation to his hallucinations (hearing voices) will change.

One comment on the handling of the psychotic transference: we cannot take for granted that we can occupy the position of analyst or therapist for psychotic patients. Transference in psychosis requires attention, presence, and composure. What is at stake is the presence of someone rather than the specific person of a given analyst. At times, we are called on to establish a limit, changing positions from a place of submission, and this intervention is often tumultuous and dramatic. The stakes for the analyst are to know at what moment one should wait for an elaboration, be it minimal, and at what moment one should interrupt the patient and cut into the jouissance. This delicate work is therefore like a dance step; one must know how to adjust in an encounter that is far from being assured. What the patient makes of what we think of him is important to consider, and yet risks becoming the slippery slope of an erotomanic transference where the analytic relation could intensify or end. Neurosis does not allow the same approach, or the same direction of treatment.

The psychotic's *stabitat*

Starting with Lacan's notion of the "stabitat," a neologism condensing stability and habitat[1] in my therapeutic approach to the cure of psychosis, psychic space and language form parallel roads. This "stabitat" is something the analyst can offer, but so can the institutional space as well. Gisela Pankow proposed this notion when she spoke of "backups." Jean Oury added that "to see someone, even daily, if there are no back-up supports for living the rest of the time, for example, public transportation: on the metro, the bus, or in the street, amounts ultimately, to dishonesty" (Oury 2008: 138). The institution as a "back-up" is key in this regard.

Conscious of this necessity, I am in agreement with the implementation of an unconditional welcome. This first step assures the preconditions of psychic security. The next step concerns a choice in the modalities of the work. An example of this can be found in Winnicott's remark regarding this choice to Herbert Rosenfeld in 1953: "If an analyst or a psychiatric service is capable of curing a schizophrenic patient, a mother should certainly be capable of doing the same even though the child is only at the beginning of life, and the logical conclusion is that the mother prevents schizophrenia in driving things along well and in an utterly ordinary way" (Winnicott 1953: 98). In this remark, Winnicott makes us hear the disposition that I follow in my own practice. I find a good deal of clinical know-how in the alternation between the analytic setting and the psychiatric service. It is not for naught that Winnicott remarks, and not without some humor, that this strategy is like that of a mother!

Given the considerable challenges in the treatment work with psychotics, we are concerned with putting psychoanalytic tools into play in a variety of ways. These are often not decided in advance but are invented, and they constitute what I will call analytic invention or analytic know-how, or in this case we could call it "analytic engineering" put into practice. This engineering has its own internal intelligence, with modalities of operation respecting analytic methodology while adapting it. I define this engineering as a secular, material know-how, one that includes constructing bridges, tunnels, links, and walkways. This is why I make use of multiple treatment venues, where different therapeutic facilities are housed. They constitute the "tangibles," what Foucault called "heterotopias." They become the stage where at least one alternative to psychotic solitude is played out.

I make use of the multi-venue treatment layout, and I place my bets on this multiplicity's ability to bring forth a grammar that will allow perspective to come into play. The multi-venue treatment facilities welcome a language proper to subjectivity, however extravagant it may be. Finally, the various venues will allow the subject to be represented by a narrative account or a story, or even a multiplicity of stories.

The narrative will at once be the environment and the condition for the constitution of a new imaginary. Many psychotic patients lack an early childhood narrative; this seems increasingly the case today. There is often a lack of a discourse regarding what the "*infans*"[2] felt or did. In short, this lack of stories told about the child results in a lack of psychic continuity between the child and his immediate environment. In such cases we have the conditions for the worst kinds of traumas since they cannot even be remembered. Here the subject molds himself precisely around this lack of narrative history.

At times a traumatic past can be filtered through a transferential space and can therefore be worked with, allowing the re-establishment of a signifying chain. But, alas, this happens rarely. Small archaic traumas that could not be verbalized or transmitted, and therefore repressed, must be taken into consideration. In such circumstances, the ego folds back onto itself, building more or less indestructible walls. Winnicott's contributions are relevant here, since his thesis is not incompatible with the Lacanian notion of the failure of the paternal metaphor. These failures may have occurred during times of psychic suffering, to have taken place completely unnoticed. They could be qualified as "soul murders," as Schreber called them, the never-constituted psychic massacres unavailable to memory. Unable to remember them, the psychotic's isolation deepens and may produce a more radical solitude.

This solitude is only exacerbated by the regrettable changes taking place today in psychiatric hospitals, which give priority to action rather than to relationships. In socially marginalized areas, looks trump words, rendering the therapeutic effect of language ineffectual. Yet language plays a fundamental role in the treatment of psychosis. In my approach, the Lacanian concepts of the Other, the body, and jouissance guide the therapeutic work, both in the psychoanalytic and in the institutional dimension.

"Syntonia" is a term I take from the clinic of psychosis to introduce the connection between the Other and the body. We note this connection in the following clinical vignette of a neurotic patient and mark the distinction from what we will see in psychosis. The neurotic patient tells a story of an armchair (*fauteuil*) that he carried around in his car for several weeks without being able to find a place for it. The armchair (*fauteuil*) was a sort of blind spot (*faut à l'oeil*).[3] This signifying equivocation illustrates the over-determination one sees in neurosis of the interplay between the Other and the body. We see that the fact that he keeps carrying the armchair around, not knowing why, betrays that jouissance is implicated and put into words possessed by the Other. Stemming from a bodily source of jouissance, it allows us to realize not just that the Other is the body (Lacan 1967), but that we are spoken unbeknownst to ourselves, always a source of surprise.

For neurotics, the end of analysis allows the emergence of a novel relationship with jouissance and an increase in knowledge made possible due to a relation of speech with meaning. It is precisely this change that psychotic patients will never experience. In psychosis, when this jouissance is displaced, or when it falls, we can speak of a fall of "syntonia," which implies a missing appeasing relation, a lack of stability between the Other and the body. We find this in psychosis where "syntonia" is notably absent. Let us posit a few hypotheses about this absence. Does this disharmony stem from a lack of ballast or anchoring point, seen in the difficulty in handling semblance[4] and sexual drifting? Since in psychosis the paternal metaphor has failed, and there is a rapport, there is a sexual relation between the Other and the body. But this connection is fusional and does not work as a representational counting system, what in mathematics is called a base or radix. This disharmony stems from a "non-place" that makes counting impossible. The psychotic can approach this disharmony by way of irony, which is common and expresses the "out of sync" and "out of play" of the psychotic subject. From this de-regulation of jouissance, a spontaneous solution, what we may call *suppléance*, may emerge.

Let's consider two clinical situations involving psychosis where such disharmony exists. Julien constantly fiddles with his Adam's apple. He couldn't tell you why he is obsessed with it, but this obsessive touching follows a recent state of depersonalization during which he mutilated his leg, wanting to cut it off completely. We can hypothesize that what is at stake is an impossible negativation, which is then followed by a failed symbolization. Cutting the leg is an unimaginable act in which reality is called forth. But this reality is a visible material reality, a "live" castration the subject cannot do without because it cannot be symbolized. While I am stunned, faced with the scope of this disaster, I tell Julien that maybe he is afraid of losing his voice, as he seems to be invaded by the influence of the voices.

The words of the analyst are never forgotten as the patient hears them. As they often do, the effects of words resonate elsewhere. While not inhibiting his curious tic, my remark at least calmed his anxiety because a subject was re-introduced into the game. This effect is only possible on the condition that the patient is able to re-appropriate in some manner what is suggested to him. The Other and the body are thus conditionally reconciled, allowing for some narrative. For Julien, the Adam's apple is stranded without a signifying anchoring. With the psychoses we are without the resource of signification; we are forced to invent something else where signification works for neurotics.

Let's look at another case. Jerome repeats a soccer corner kick maneuver all day long. Does he actually enjoy playing ball? No one knows, yet he repeats the word "corner," a signifier which insists, haunting him. Is he calling to others to come and play with him? If he was, he would surely have found them a long time ago. Perhaps it might be a call to another player who would strike the ball with his head and conclude the maneuver of the corner which usually requires one other person. Is Jerome's "sick head" part of this repetition? Or is it a movement of admiration or even envy towards another head that does not leave him alone? Who knows? What is clear is that this "corner" for the time being, works as a signifier in the Real, as an ultimate signifier that paradoxically could open the road towards a form of supplementation (*suppléance*). All these conjectures can only be confirmed by the subjective response of the patient. Progress is when disharmony or "a-synthonia" resolves by a supplementation that affects the patient's signifying chain. In other words, it allows the unconscious, even through secondary pathways, to reduce jouissance and liberate emotions and effects that have been fixated, in some cases, for years. In a psychotic situation one must reduce the Other's alienating presence that is persecutory and insistent since, in psychosis, we find either a body not related to the Other, or a body suffering from too much Other.

We can further observe "a-syntonia" in Antonin Artaud's letter to Georges Soulié de Morant. Artaud speaks of his suffering as "troubles" occurring in his thoughts. Artaud writes that he is "at the mercy of a kind of terrifying crushing and tearing of consciousness, truly *baffled* with respect to my most elementary perceptions, unable to connect anything, to assemble anything in my mind or still less to express anything, since nothing could be retained. . . . It seems to me that I have forgotten *how to think*" (Artaud 1988: 289–90). Like Jerome, Artaud indicates that what we consider the potential for association, which allows for the fundamental rule of psychoanalysis to work, in his case does not function. Artaud suffers "a lack of continuity, a lack of development, a lack of persistence in my thoughts" (Artaud 1988: 294). To attempt to resolve this, he produces an invention. Artaud's solution tries to avoid the Real as the winner.

The psychotic's invention

Freud gives us directions that help us further understand the psychotic's invention. One direction was actually set by Freud the pessimist, the proverbial doubter, who thought that analysis was not suitable for psychotic patients. Freud's remarks to Lou Andréas Salomé in 1915, however, shed light on the issue of symbolization in psychosis. He wrote: "What interests me is the separation (*Scheidung*) and the breaking up into its component parts (*Gliederung*) of what otherwise would revert to an inchoate mass" (Freud and Salomé 1966: 32). Freud suggests that any act of symbolization supposes separating and creating distinct parts. This fails in psychosis: in psychosis, to organize would be the equivalent of symbolizing since this logical trajectory between separating and organizing does not function; it is blocked by the Real due to the attraction, or the weight, of the original inchoate mass.

There is a kinship between the original inchoate mass evoked by Freud and the notion of *lalangue* theorized by Lacan. The baby's playful gurgling denotes an enjoyment of the word, of its musicality, of its nonsensical sound. This enjoyment is erased so that words can become intelligible, establishing meaning and a social tie. This erasure of jouissance is far more difficult in psychosis. At the same time, the direction towards meaning is important since it gives us a signpost as to how to direct the cure. We must invent a detour for that enjoyment, for that jouissance, in order to distract it and even repress it. That is the space where the therapeutic work between the individual and the collective meet. While Freud makes distinctions, Lacan's *lalangue* introduces excess, *lalangue* says more than shared common language can—it is there that its Real value lies.

To summarize, to convert jouissance into knowledge requires a shared language. This means creating a shared language out of solitary mad distortions, out of internal limitations, from which we can invent a place of awakening, a third place, namely, a place of transference. Jouissance thus serves as a compass in our practice, regulating it. For this conversion to occur we must tolerate the discontinuity or the void will reveal itself as soon as the analyst introduces regulation. This essential question inspired me to construct a multi-faceted institutional treatment plan in order to help with symbolization, to measure, organize, and tolerate the void.

Practically speaking, the jouissance triggered by psychotic transference puts into play one or several separations or cuts: considering that jouissance is a substance made of words and body, the trajectory of the analytic cure must allow for this jouissance to be worked on, reducing it and molding it in such a way that the interdictions of thought are lifted. The analyst intervenes to welcome, reorient, enlarge, and solicit an awakening that stems from the work of separation. This is key to the treatment of psychosis. If the jouissance is too strong, as is seen in logorrhea or mutism, a separation is called on between the Other (words) and the body. We are reminded of Freud, the pessimist, the very one who in 1904 affirmed, "Psychoses, states of confusion, and deeply-rooted (I might say toxic) depression are therefore not suitable for psycho-analysis; at least not for the method as it has been practiced up to the present. I do not regard it as by any means impossible that by suitable changes in the method we may succeed in overcoming this contra indication—and so be able to initiate a psychotherapy of the psychoses" (Freud 1905: 253).

I am not dissuaded by Freud's pessimism and interpret it rather as a challenge to adjust our method. The psychoanalysis of psychosis may be considered a conquest of jouissance, a conquering of the substructure of language, all the while ensuring language's value, and even its pleasure. For the psychotic, language says much more than the word can connote, inviting a private and particular jouissance. Creation grants the aptitude for tolerating the erratic and discontinuous. It allows for a means to extricate oneself from the quicksand of the original inchoate mass. How can the analyst best act to solicit creation, and enable the regulation of jouissance?

With the taming of disruptive jouissance in mind, I have constructed a series of institutional treatment venues that are all very distinct from one another, and I have tried using the analytic method to confront the deregulation of jouissance as we experience it with psychotic patients. Between the treatment venues, a notion of space-time is introduced, attempting the connection between signifiers, thus very literally creating psychic space. This connection attempts to introduce a third term to exit the binary of outside/inside as well as the repetition of the couple hospital/home. The grammar of place, a grammar that is built up in terms of material space through hospitality, allows for ways of working with psychosis by breaking up jouissance. The experience of places and transfers, of space and time, allows for a new conjugation. This traversal affects the void, which can slowly become introjected and supported. A new grammar is thereby created. This grammar seeks, by way of differentiating between venues, to treat the linguistic difficulties associated with psychosis.

One of the problems of psychosis is the inability to inscribe history diachronically. The therapeutic aim here would be to support a discontinuity that "stops not being written," as Lacan would say. This could explain why certain patients find writing a way to structure their relation to the world, sometimes to the point of "graphorrhea." In reality, the Symbolic, but also the Imaginary are deficient in psychosis, and finding a way into a story is an important element of a coming to grips with the Real, and being able to sustain social ties.

I propose a change of paradigm; I compare it to the invention of perspective in the Renaissance. My aim is to offer a more tolerable experience of discontinuity of space and time as enacted and emerging between the treatment venues. This allows an encounter with other treatment teams, and the formation of multi-dimensional transference. The subject's history is created or re-created. What a particular staff member had not been able to hear, another will be able to welcome. Over time, a sort of supplement is thus constructed, making up for the lack of narration that insists in psychosis.

Finally, this narrative construction is a buffer against excitation; it appeases the subject. One can see a modification of the Imaginary that goes from the specular to a more constructive Imaginary; continuity occurs between past and future. The venues, the frames, the gaps, the vacation breaks, help make up the experience of grammar of presence and absence. The experience of continuity and the gaps in between all make up this "analytic engineering." All serve to regulate jouissance and take hold of the Real.

Within this context, Kurt Lewin enlightens us with a verifiable formula: "Fixity of procedure, liberty of content." This relates to institutional work where continuity is a way of working with the patients' radical discontinuity. It is another way of looking at madness, albeit one less defined by medical aspects and where the social tie is able to act as a compass providing an additional gauge for our work.

Translated by Manya Steinkoler and Patricia Gherovici

Notes

1 In Lacan's *L'Étourdit* (1972) we read: "Mais de quoi s'agit-il ? Du rapport de l'homme et de la femme en tant justement qu'ils seraient propres, de ce qu'ils habitent le langage, à faire énoncé de ce rapport. Est-ce l'absence de ce rapport qui les exile en stabitat ? Est-ce d'labiter que ce rapport ne peut être qu'inter-dit? Ce n'est pas la question : bien

plutôt la réponse, et la réponse qui la supporte—d'être ce qui la stimule à se répéter— c'est le réel [But what is at stake? The relationship of the man and of the woman in as much as they would be suitable, from the fact that they inhabit language, to make a statement about this relationship. Is it the absence of this relationship that exiles them in this stable habitat (stabitat)? Is it by inhabiting it in a labile way (*d'labiter*) that this relationship can only be inter-dicted (*inter-dit*)? This is not the question: much more rather the response, and the response that supports it by being what stimulates it to repeat itself is the real]." *L'Étourdit, The Letter* 41 (2009): 31–80, p. 46–7 and in Lacan (2001) *Autres Écrits*, Paris: Seuil, p. 455.

2   *Infans* in Latin means without speech, not able to speak.

3   Translator's note: The semantic equivocation can find an equivalent in English if the hypothetical case of a patient not find place for a love-seat; the polyvalence of the word brings into play body (seat) and love.

4   Lacan's notion of semblant is crucial for understanding the notion of object *a*, the place of the analyst in the cure, the positioning of woman in the sexual encounter, the Phallus, and jouissance. It has to do with the ability to make-believe, that is, the capacity granted by language to represent the Real by way of fiction in a manner that appears illusory. This possibility is often deficient in psychosis where representation loses its metaphorical qualities.

Bibliography

Artaud, A. (1932; 2nd edn 1988) *Selected Writings*, ed. Susan Sontag, Berkeley: University of California Press.

—— (1996) *Oeuvres Complètes*, Paris: Gallimard.

De Masi, F. (2011) *Vulnérabilité de la Psychose*, Paris: Ithaque.

Faugeras, P. (2011) *Rencontre avec Gaetano Benedetti: L'expérience de la Psychose*, Paris: ERES.

Freud, S. (1905 [1904]) *The Standard Edition of the Complete Psychological Works of Sigmund Freud, Volume VII (1901–1905): A Case of Hysteria, Three Essays on Sexuality and Other Works*, London: Hogarth.

Freud, S. and Salomé, L.A. (1966) *Letters*, ed. E. Peiffer, trans. W. Robson and E. Robson, New York and London: W.W. Norton & Company.

Lacan, J. (1967) "La Logique du Fantasme," Seminar delivered 15 May 1967.

—— (2006) *Écrits*, trans. B. Fink, New York: W.W. Norton & Company.

Oury, J. (2008) *L'Homme Qui Marche*, in *Autour de Gaetano Benedetti*, Paris: Campagne Premier.

Winnicott, D. (1953) *Lettres Vives*, Paris: Gallimard.

4

ON THE SUICIDE BOMBER

Anatomy of a political fantasy

Richard Boothby

It is a virtual axiom about madness, the sort of truism that offers a reliable fulcrum for jokes, that the madman never regards himself as mad. Madness appears to be fundamentally incapable of perceiving itself accurately, so much so that the lacking of the capacity for an objective perception of oneself can serve as a shorthand definition of the condition. Madness is always and essentially someone else's problem, which means, among other things, that we can reasonably expect interesting political effects to cluster around assertions of madness. The post-9/11 world is routinely charged with low-grade, "code orange" paranoia about security issues, a paranoia not infrequently re-inflamed by the apparent madness of suicide attackers. It would seem particularly important to reflect not only on the psychical states that drive people to such extreme acts of violence but also the ways we perceive such actors. This paper is devoted to a brief exploration of the place suicide bombers occupy in our collective imagination.

The title's reference to fantasy is in no way intended to deny the brutal reality of suicide bombing, a prime signature of political violence in our time. My intention is rather to pursue an inquiry into the psychic means by which we protect ourselves from the traumatic effects of such attacks and the collective uses to which those means are put. In the larger scheme of things, the number of casualties caused by most suicide attacks is relatively low. The attacks' wider psychological and political impact, however, is immensely greater, often powerfully influencing public opinion and driving far-reaching national security measures and policy decisions. Such disparity between actual body counts and larger political effects is itself a central feature and generally an explicit aim of terrorist activity. All the more important, therefore, is the task of better understanding our own reactions to terror, reactions that are rightly called fantasmatic to the extent that they not only play on but also positively produce exceptionally powerful fears and prejudices. How, then, to grasp the structure and function of that fantasmatic dimension?

As a first approach to the topic, it is worth noting the ways in which a suicide attack appears to violate some of the basic patterns of human struggle. There is, for example, the way that the suicide bomber, most often striking out across a lopsided asymmetry of power, short-circuits the standoff described by Hegel between master and slave (Hegel 1977: 111–19). Suddenly and unexpectedly, the suicide attacker proves spectacularly willing to pay the price of death, defined by Hegel as the escape from serfdom and oppression.

Suicide bombing upends other conceptions of violent conflict as well. Think, for instance, of Hannah Arendt's perspicacious definition of violence as requiring implements (Arendt 1970: 4). The point is that the reliable wielding of violence in direct combat over another human being necessitates augmenting one's own bodily powers with supplementary tools, preferably specially made for the purpose, and the bigger the better. The suicide bomber comes close to inverting this logic of the implement, returning in the most grisly way to the materiality of the body. He or she dons an explosive vest, which will function less as a violent implement than as a mere propellant, so that the body itself assumes the role of the weapon. When the explosive vest is detonated in a crowded café, pieces of the attacker's very body—limbs, bone, teeth—become lethal projectiles. In the most brutally literal way, suicide bombers kill by throwing their own bodies at their victims.

How can such an atavistic recourse to the pure corporeality of the body fail to be experienced as anything but a primitive insult to a culture that prides itself on technological advance, and that has invested itself so elaborately in implements of violence, particularly those that succeed in killing at a distance? It is as if the suicide bomber is breaking the rules of a game that we have long struggled to establish. What utter contrast there is, for example, between the grisly immediacy of suicide bombing and the near-perfect virtuality of assassination by drone attack.

Maybe it is not accidental that the bludgeon-like violence of suicide bombings and the abstract unreality and "surgical" character of our now-preferred means of pre-empting terrorist attack form such a striking asymmetry. The two tactics comprise a kind of binary couple, as if based on the necessity of a structural opposition. Aside from the technological abyss that separates the relative crudity of the suicide vest from the computerized aerial drone and its remotely guided missiles, the binary opposition at stake is also one of psychic impact. In the public eye, the one is as traumatically spectacular and mesmerizing as the other is deceptively invisible.

Suicide attack also turns on their heads other aspects of conventionally established power relations. One thinks of the underlying logic of sovereignty identified by Giorgio Agamben with the figure of homo sacer, the human being reduced to "bare life," whose abject body furnishes the medium of exception that defines the sovereign authority (Agamben 1998). According to its origin in Roman law, Agamben reminds us, homo sacer is the condemned man who can be killed but not sacrificed. The suicide bomber appears to be the perfect opposite, a human being who is sacrificed, indeed sacrifices him- or herself, but who cannot be killed.[1]

To this neat opposition between homo sacer and the suicide bomber, it is crucial to append a further note about their deeper linkage, if not identity. Agamben's intention in highlighting the concept of bare life in the figure of homo sacer—a figure most directly embodied in the contemporary world by the concentration camp prisoner—is to suggest that a greater and greater proportion of the world's population finds itself approaching this very position. The virtual prisoners of refugee camps, for example, cannot be eliminated outright (such was the method employed by the Nazis and our laws raise a few more obstacles to such indiscriminate murderousness) but they also cannot be sacrificed (which we can take to mean that such persons are deemed to fall outside the bounds of established community and as such are deeply compromised in their ability to call on our protection or even our recognition). From this point of view, suicide bombing can readily appear as a last-ditch revolt of homo sacer, utilizing bare life itself as if it were the only resource still available to him (or her) in order to insist on being taken into account. The suicide bomber says, in effect, "I'll make you pay attention to me, even at the cost of detonating my own body."

To cite a last and very significant moment of inversion: the terrorist suicide bomber overturns, at least on an individual scale, the implicit logic of avoidance of suicide that formed the indispensable underlying premise of the classic doctrine of nuclear deterrence as MAD, or "mutually assured destruction." In the Cold War confrontation between nuclear powers, a tense peace seemed guaranteed so long as each adversary could assume that the other would avoid the virtually self-destructive option of a first strike. Triggering the inevitable retaliation would be tantamount to suicide. Yet recent experience has presented a new kind of deadly proliferation, that in which the certainty that no one would willingly embrace self-destruction proves to be alarmingly false.

In this way, the menace of the suicidal terrorist is internally connected to the most fearsome prospect of future terror: the willingness of attackers to use a nuclear bomb, without regard to consequences for themselves. With the suicide bomber, the Cold War specter of annihilation overspills any promise of containment in nuclear monopoly and threatens to break out anywhere, anytime. Nor does such renewed nuclear anxiety seem limited to non-state actors. Was not an assumption of this sort of suicidal willingness part of the implicit logic that informed the American attack on Saddam Hussein? To fear that Iraq possessed weapons of mass destruction and was prepared to use them was to assume that Saddam might become a suicide bomber on a national scale. It should be clear that the current debate about Iranian nuclear ambitions relies implicitly on a parallel assumption.

Already in these ways, the act of the suicide bomber is rightly said to constitute a special source of political anxiety, yet we have not exhausted the traumatic potential posed by suicide bombing. In a recent book, titled *On Suicide Bombing*, Talal Asad puzzles over the meaning of the particular horror provoked by the suicide attacker, a horror that presents a striking contrast, for example, to our often blithe acceptance of massively greater civilian slaughter by aerial bombardment. How is it possible that a suicide bomber can, and often does, produce a more atrocious-sounding headline than a B-52? The question is a provocative one, of course, because the casualties in the latter case are routinely many times greater.

Among the first hypotheses Asad considers is that put forward by the psychoanalyst Jacqueline Rose, who focuses on the way in which suicide bombing uncannily closes the gap between perpetrator and victim. In the familiar scenario in which a bomber mingles in the thick of the crowd at a wedding, a funeral, or a marketplace, victims are drawn for a horrendous instant into a peculiar intimacy with their destroyer. The tender proximity of Eros has unbeknownst been joined by utter lethality. Suicide attack in Rose's apt formulation is a "deadly embrace." "Suicide bombing," she says, "is an act of passionate identification—you take your enemy with you" (Rose 2004: 21).

A further reference to assassination by aerial drones seems irresistible at this point. By contrast to the horrifying erotic proximity of the suicide bomber, the drone attack, directed by remote control from bases a hemisphere away and quite literally striking out of thin air, appears as an embodiment of pure lethality from which every trace of messy erotic connection has been meticulously eliminated. In the aerial drone, the abstract essence of death, like a pure tincture of the Freudian *Todestrieb*, appears to have been perfectly distilled from all admixture with Eros.

Asad embroiders Rose's approach, illuminating the paradoxes of suicide attack, particularly around the way that it effects a coincidence of the act of murder and its own punishment. The suicide bomber achieves both in the same instant. Yet Asad is ultimately unsatisfied with Rose's analysis and proposes an alternative that highlights the way the suicide bomber achieves a kind of primitive ontological rupture. By its very nature the most successful suicide attack occurs wholly unexpectedly in the midst of the most mundane social intercourse, the frame of which is blasted into unrecognizability. The suicide bomb effects an instantaneous destruction of the reassuring existential horizon of the mundane life-space that Heidegger called "everydayness." It is not just that one or more people are killed but rather that some local stage of existence is torn utterly asunder. In this way, Asad suggests, suicide bombing embodies Stanley Cavell's definition of horror as "the perception of the precariousness of human identity . . . the perception that it may be lost or invaded, that we may be, or may become, something other than we are, or take ourselves for: that our origins as human beings need accounting for, and are unaccountable" (Asad 2007: 68).

And yet, we are prompted to ask a pesky question: wouldn't any sudden outbreak of catastrophic violence produce such a "perception of precariousness"? What is so horrible about suicide attack in particular?

Asad anticipates the question and answers it by supplying a crucial additional dimension to his argument. He notes first how suicide attack, as a strategy of killing others by means of voluntarily sacrificing oneself, resonates uncannily with religious traditions. Asad rightly notes that all three monotheisms found themselves on the willingness to sacrifice. Christianity is particularly striking in this respect, as it so clearly elevates virtually suicidal sacrifice to the status of divinity. Even more crucial, however, is the way in which the act of the suicide bomber intensifies the central contradiction that underlies the moral and political foundations of secular liberal society. The social contract that undergirds liberalism must continually resolve the tension between the maintenance of order in the community and the exercise of individual freedom. What the suicide bomber ultimately detonates is precisely that unstable tension. Asad thus concludes that "what horrifies is not just dying and killing (or killing and dying) but the violent appearance of something that is normally disregarded in secular modernity: the limitless pursuit of freedom" (Asad 2007: 91). By an act of spectacularly unrestrained and violent freedom, the suicide bomber explodes the balance between freedom and its disciplinary regulation for the good of the community that forms the very basis of liberal culture.

Though a good deal more could be said here to elucidate Asad's point, which is a complex and interesting one, it is difficult not to feel that his account misses an enormously important dimension of the problem he has set for himself. It is a dimension forcefully indicated by a psychoanalytic perspective. Approaching the matter in psychoanalytic terms, we are led to wonder whether the most important psychical function of the horror aroused by suicide bombing resides less in the way that it triggers a recognition (about the precariousness of the human life, about our fragile stability, etc.) than in the way that it effects in us a failure of recognition. To put the question in other terms, what if the primary effect of the suicide attack is less to introduce a traumatizing new knowledge than to violently establish an especially impenetrable zone of not-knowing? On this view, the really salient thing about the horror of suicide attack consists in the way that it stuns cognition somewhat in the way we may be blinded by a brilliant flash.

At stake, then, is the production of a selective unknowing that might also and more appropriately be compared to the psychoanalytic conception of the phobic object. Freud's teaching insists that the object of phobic horror is not itself the issue. In fact, the particularly intense terror that is stimulated by the confrontation with the dreaded object, or better, the mere anticipation of that confrontation, effectively furnishes a screen behind which certain other things can remain hidden. In being terrified by spiders or insects, there's something else at stake that remains concealed behind the fear of little bugs. The business of psychoanalysis is then to find and name that something else. Following a parallel approach in the present case, we need to ask whether, in the grip of the visceral horror aroused by suicide bombing, we are not likewise blinded to important aspects of its larger meaning? And doesn't the production of that blindness have to be recognized as part of the very function of the horror that grips us in the face of suicide bombing?

Asad is right to focus on the special horror evoked by the suicide bomber. What he cannot clarify, however, is how that horror, produced by the spectacle of a violent exercise of freedom, also provides the means by which we may succeed in obscuring from ourselves the meaning of that very exercise. The resources of psychoanalytic theory are useful here because such a contradiction is exactly what Freud meant by the bi-fold structure of the symptom. The symptom is a paradoxical, double-sided process: it successfully denies the very thing that it compulsively reproduces. The symptom repeats the traumatic impact, indeed insistently forces it upon us, precisely as it represses its potential effect on us. The classic instance is that of sexual repression, which obsesses itself with the very substance of sex that it otherwise cannot tolerate. Is this not a similar mechanism operating in the present case? If we accept Asad's claim that what horrifies about suicide bombing is a traumatizing excess of freedom, then should we not add that it is precisely this freedom that our horror most decisively covers and renders invisible?

To grasp this interpretation requires squarely facing its paradoxical implication. The detonation of a suicide bomb understandably elicits an immediate reaction of profound horror, even in people not directly present at the site of detonation. Moreover, the incitement of that force of horror is presumably a key part of the attacker's intention. What I am suggesting, however, is that that very reaction of horror submits almost immediately to a kind of psychical reprocessing, virtually automatically and without conscious effort, that redeploys it as the means by which the potential meaning of the horrific act can be more easily contained and dismissed. In this way, the sense of horror is enlisted in a process that prevents further reaction to or reflection on its cause. The real effect of the horror response is to produce a powerful blind spot in the consciousness of those horrified by it.

If this view of the matter is valid, it means that suicide bombing tends, by its very nature, to miss its real target. The aim of most suicide bombers is to bring attention to some desperate cause, to call attention to the plight of aggrieved people by engaging in the most desperate form of violence. The suicide attacker is most often a martyr in a struggle for recognition. Yet the psychic dynamics that are set in motion by suicide attacks tend to obscure the stakes of that very struggle for recognition. One might even find in this paradox of self-produced failure a limited cause for optimism. Perhaps the recent vogue of suicide attack will quickly fade, deflated by the realization that its desired effect, that of bringing desperately needed recognition to desperate causes, is finally self-defeating.

But let us go on to specify more precisely the most common means by which this failure of recognition is accomplished. The suicidal gesture is taken to be either, first, completely irrational or, second, mindlessly robotic. In the first option, the suicide bomber is thoughtlessly dismissed as simply insane. The calculated willingness to die strikes most people as almost unimaginable. Suicidal attack appears cavalierly to reject the self-preservative impulse that underlies everything we do. This apparent rejection seems immediately unthinkable, yet more measured reflection after the fact confronts us with an insurmountable opacity. All suicide compels us to confront an ultimately unanswerable question. Absent the testimony of the one who has taken their own life, or sometimes even in the presence of such testimony, it is impossible to settle once and for all the question as to why they did it. In both of these senses—for its apparently crazy rejection of self-regard and for its intrinsic opacity of motive—the act of the suicide bomber, amplified atrociously by its spectacular consequences, readily announces itself as an irrational and gratuitous outburst.

The second option construes the bomber's intention not as a product of individual irrationality but of collective brainwashing. Here, the assumption is that only psychological manipulation by maniacal "handlers" could induce someone to blow themselves up. For the purpose of erasing awareness of the bomber's own free will, however, this second course of interpretation is no doubt just as effective as the first, though by reliance on even more dangerous means, as it invites even more sweeping judgments about whole cultures, presumed to be mired in irrationality, that do not or cannot value life. In the wake of 9/11 attacks, Islam itself was referred to as a "culture of death."

In either case—dismissed as irrational acting out or as robotic automatism— the real freedom of the suicide attacker, that is to say, his or her subjective intentionality, is obscured. It remains a closed question. And we can immediately understand the reason for this closure. The immensely convenient thing about ascribing complete irrationality to the suicidal gesture is that it allows us to side-step consideration of any more comprehensible motive. Gone is any cognizance of the point made by Robert Pape and others that the majority of suicide attacks around the world are undertaken by members of communities suffering under foreign occupation or oppression (Pape 2006). The apparent craziness and essential opacity of suicide thus combines with our own need for political obtuseness to produce a self-serving blind spot. It is a blind spot that was already perfectly displayed by the response of Secretary of State George Shultz, fully twenty years before 9/11, when asked by the Yugoslav foreign minister about the causes of Palestinian terrorism. Reddening in the face, Shultz pounded the table and bellowed, "There is no connection with any cause. Period" (Ahmad 2003: 49).

We have so far taken our clue from the Freudian perspective but are now in a position to benefit from the contributions of Freud's most innovative follower, Jacques Lacan. The question of unknowable intention at stake here touches directly on the central concern of Lacan's entire outlook on the unconscious: the enigma of the desire of the Other. According to Lacan, it is in relation to that enigma that the most inaccessible kernel of subjectivity is constructed and around it that the play of fantasy is spun. It is a point of immediate relevance to our discussion because it is the unanswerable question of the Other's desire that energizes the obsessive search for traces of the Other's enjoyment, a search that is inevitably driven to merely suppose what it cannot certify. It is in this light that we ought to interpret the apocalyptic dream of the seventy virgins attributed to the 9/11 attackers. This supposed dream of the martyrs' heaven, conspicuously more sexualized than the Islamic tradition behind it actually warrants, says much more about the victims of the attacks than it does about the attackers themselves. The conclusion to be drawn is that this image of an anticipated sexual enjoyment is inserted at precisely the point at which the question of other motives for violent acts has been eliminated from consideration.

Of course, the entirety of my analysis here takes as its object the immediate and relatively thoughtless reaction of ordinary people, and as such it is an exercise in reconstructing the background of unexamined assumptions and opinions that inform everyday perceptions and judgments. The point is to excavate some of the reasons why the drift of public doxa after 9/11 was decisively turned away from serious questions about the real motives of the attackers. The huge quantity of scholarly writing over the decade following 9/11 devoted to fathoming the motives of suicide bombers—a veritable flood of books and articles—poses less a counter-argument to this point than additional proof, as that volume of university discourse seems posed as a corrective to the sense of the majority of people on the street that suicide bombing is essentially something opaque and unimaginable.

That opacity and unimaginability, in fact the entire complex of denial that I have been pointing to, was massively and elementally summed up and sealed by George Bush's description of the 9/11 attackers as consummate "evil-doers." Repeated like a drumbeat, the rhetoric of evil served ever more completely to communicate the pointlessness of any inquiry into comprehensible motives. Indeed, is not "evil" a prime figure, perhaps the prime figure, of the incomprehensible? One of the stranger things about evil is that, aside from understanding that it is something very, very bad, we know almost nothing about it, a circumstance, one might recall, that gave St Augustine plenty to think about.

A final series of questions might be considered, all clustered around the use of the term "fantasy" to describe the psychical residue of the horrified apprehension of suicide attack, a usage that may sound strange when compared to the more ordinary meaning of fantasy. I've argued that the most important thing about the idea of the suicide bomber, the real meaning of our horror in the face of that idea, is a fundamental opacity or even emptiness. The central feature of this "fantasy" seems to be a vacant and indeterminate lack. At this point, the resources of Lacanian theory are again indispensable, insofar as Lacan defines the luring power of fantasy in relation to an obscure core that remains completely unspecified. This core of lack he calls, famously if enigmatically, "*objet petit a*," the "little object *a*."[2] It is possible to glimpse its operation in even the most pedestrian motions of fantasy. Take the dream of winning the lottery. The fact that we are typically unable to supply any answer to the question of what exactly we might do with the jackpot were we to win, that the actual consequences of winning remain almost completely unknown to us, far from damping the driving force of the fantasy, is precisely the source of its greatest power. The deepest potency of fantasy is rooted in what it does not and cannot picture to itself. It is in this way that Lacan returns to the teaching of Plato's *Symposium*, asking us to recognize the mostly hidden but absolutely decisive role of lack in the production of desire (Lacan 1991).

We can usefully expand for a moment on this theme of lack specifically in connection with the dream of winning the lottery. At the core of this dream is the attraction of money, about which Lacan had a number of interesting things to say, prime among which was the peculiar status of money as a signifier. Money is simultaneously a signifier of perfect plentitude, virtually the material definition of pure potency, while at the same time being completely lacking in determinate meaning. Money is a strangely open, empty signifier. As Lacan puts it at one point, money is the signifier that destroys all signification. Money destroys signification precisely because the only thing greater than the power of money to signify (or buy) anything, in fact, the very source of this power, is its utter emptiness of signification. Linking this point to the fantasmatic lure of the lottery enables us to see very precisely in what that lure consists. When a giant pool of money is generated by an artificial process of accumulation for the express purpose of one person's winning the pool by a throw of chance, the intrinsic power of money to capture and stimulate fantasy, the power to put into play the open lack of signification in a particularly potent way, is expanded geometrically. The lottery is the magical power of money squared. No wonder so many people find the temptation to play the lotto irresistible. A moment's rational reflection would reveal their chances at winning to be less than those of being struck by lightning twice, even three or four times. But such reflection is impotent to counter the attraction of the fantasy.

To return to the theme of terrorist bombings, the point I am making is that the specter of suicide bombing injects the function of lack into the very concept of terrorism in a particularly powerful way. The first result is to intensify the idea of terrorism itself by virtue of locating within it a nucleus of something unfathomable, all the more disturbing for the fact that this unfathomability concerns the inner motives of the terrorists. In this way it is easy to imagine how the enigmatic and especially unnerving figure of the suicide bomber tacitly animates a phrase such as that used by the Bush administration to justify detention at Guantanamo, namely, that it housed not just enemies of the state, not just terrorists, but "the worst of the worst." What is the suicide bomber if not "the worst of the worst"?

We've considered the way in which the assumption of this unthinkable nucleus at the heart of terrorism can function to blind us to a more accurate appraisal of the enemy's motives. It can also, and perhaps even more ominously, blind us to our own. It may, for example, blunt reaction to, or even help mobilize support for, wide-ranging and dangerous political and policy choices. One thinks immediately of the paucity of public outcry to many disturbing revelations during the post 9/11 War on Terror: the momentarily shocking photos of torture at Abu Ghraib that quickly faded from view, the news of CIA secret prisons and black sites that have functioned in foreign nations as staging areas for rendition and torture, the widespread abuses of official powers of surveillance, at home as well as abroad, the summary assassination of terror suspects, even American citizens, by drone attack, etc. By inflating the public's sense of horror at terrorist attacks, the specter of suicide bombings needs to be seen as an especially powerful part of the incentive to accept any means, however morally or legally questionable, that serve the ends of security.

Let us venture a couple of final remarks about the fantasmatic dimension of the suicide bomber, posed in a somewhat larger frame of reference. Attending to the deep grammar of public opinion, it is particularly interesting to ask how the threatening figure of the "terrorist," and that of the suicide bomber in particular, relates to an older and more familiar figure, that of the Cold War "communist." What we have is a sort of update of a foreign bogeyman that serves similar functions as political excuse, whipping boy, scapegoat, self-justification, etc.

Indeed, it seems immediately tempting to assign to the old-style communist and the new Islamic suicide terrorist virtually identical roles in altered historical circumstances. During the Cold War years, fears of totalitarian communists or of shadowy Marxist infiltrators were played on to justify both reactionary policies at home and aggressive adventurism abroad. The Cold War boasted plenty of "regime change" of its own. In the contemporary context, the figure of the Islamic suicide bomber appears to be a powerful justification for similar actions and objectives, though now more decisively centered on the increasingly pressing challenge of access to resources, particularly petroleum.

In fact, even a brief backward glance at the recent history of political rhetoric makes it clear that the communist and the terrorist have been for some time serving a common role as embodying mortal threats to the free market system. We do well to remember that the first "War on Terror" was declared by an American president—Ronald Reagan—two decades before 9/11. The enemy was not Islamic suicide bombers but El Salvadoran rebels and the Sandinista revolutionaries in Nicaragua on whom the Salvadoran FLMN was said to model itself. However, there is arguably an important distinction between old-style red-baiting and today's hysteria over terrorism. The difference consists in the fact that the ideological battle against communism in the twentieth century, a battle that now seems to have been almost completely successful, the words "communist" and even "socialist" having become terms of almost universal disapprobation in American political discourse, was a battle that had to be fought against hundreds of thousands, if not millions of Americans for whom "socialism" was not yet a dirty word. That broad range of citizens, from trade unionists, journalists, and teachers to grassroots populists and New Deal politicians, was deeply sympathetic to the essential goals of a socialist alternative. A massive ideological campaign was required to dissuade them from those views.

How, then, do things stand with today's battle against terrorists? Now that the anti-communist battle is essentially over, for the moment anyway, and the vocabulary of socialism has been rendered politically radioactive, there is no apparent alternative to capitalism. Within the existing horizon of viable political ideas in America, there is no credible counterweight to free-marketism. There is, however, still a danger that new throngs of disenfranchised people, used up and spat out by the free market, even if they no longer have a clear alternative system to look toward, may increasingly recognize something deeply wrong with the present regime. Indeed, it is astonishing that such a mass renewal of discontent with capitalism was not produced by the great crash of 2008 and the subsequent period of economic unraveling and suffering that followed. True, the Occupy Wall Street movement appeared for a brief moment to be the beginning of such a recognition, but that flicker of light appears to have faded almost as quickly as it sprang up.

In this context, the figure of the suicide bomber has played a useful role in buttressing a whole-hearted American commitment to capitalism. Just when the rapaciousness and callous profiteering of the financial system seemed to be most starkly laid bare, just when the "mad dance of capital"[3] threatened to appear most nakedly in all of its obscene social destructiveness, we had another, even more spectacular madness to point to: that of the mad bombers who blow themselves up in utterly crazed acts of vengeance and protest. In the face of such an electrifying spectacle, who could conceive—as we should, after all—that the total losses for average American families from the great recession of 2008 far exceeded the damage done by the attacks of 9/11, punishing though they were to the larger economy. The fact that the 9/11 hijackers were foreign in every sense of the word— nationally, ethnically, religiously, and above all behaviorally, willing, as their suicidal gesture proved, to commit an act that most Americans found unthinkable— made it possible for the majority of those Americans not only to dismiss any meaningful reflection about the real motives of the attackers, to try to understand their perspective, but also made it possible for the attack to bounce off the main body of the "American way," leaving completely intact the basic assumptions and self-definition of American society. It is deeply significant that, in the immediate aftermath of the September 11 attacks, Americans were told by the president that the best thing they could do for their country was to go shopping. Yet what is perhaps most significant about that amazing remark is that so few people found it a strange thing to say.

As our period is analyzed by historians of the future, they may well judge the horror of the 9/11 suicide attacks and the percolation of similar, less monumental suicide bombings around the world in the following decade as having served for a brief but crucial time as an important conservative influence on the American political climate. In the face of such apparently mad attacks, the underlying premises of our own system of life are bound to appear less mad. Indeed, the fantasy-inflated figure of the suicide bomber has arguably served as a reinforcing supplement to that other great fantasmatic distortion of our times, the most fundamental of our current political consciousness, that by which we forestall any recognition of the inhumanity, irrationality, and ultimate destructiveness of unrestrained capital behind the assertion of its precise contrary: a celebration of the free market as a panacea. We conceal from ourselves what Sheldon Wolin and others have called the "inverted totalitarianism" (Wolin 2008) of corporate-directed society behind the image of free market capitalism as a redemptive, even divinely sanctioned, dispenser of the unlimited good. The companion, equally deluded assumption is that all government intervention to regulate markets—for some, even government taxation—is tantamount to fascism.

Viewed along these lines we have pursued, the current international rash of suicide bombing, far from being an unmitigated evil, might be regarded as one of the best things that ever happened to business as usual, so handy a tool of the status quo, in fact, as to recall Voltaire's quip about God: if the Muslim suicide bomber didn't exist, it would have been necessary to invent him.

Notes

1   This point is made by May Jayyusi: "If 'homo sacer' is he who can be killed and not sacrificed then the martyr here inverses this relation to sovereignty, transforming himself into he who can be sacrificed but not killed." Jayyusi's remark is from an unpublished paper, "Subjectivity and Public Witness: An Analysis of Islamic Militance in Palestine" (Asad 2007: 48).
2   See especially Jacques Lacan (2004) *Le Séminaire de Jacques Lacan, Livre X: L'Angoisse*, ed. Jacques Alain-Miller. Paris: Editions de Seuil.
3   A favorite phrase of Slavoj Žižek's; see especially his brief but useful 2008 book *Violence: Six Sideways Reflections*. New York: Picador.

Bibliography

Agamben, G. (1998) *Homo Sacer: Sovereign Power and Bare Life*, trans. D. Heller-Roazen. Stanford: Stanford University Press.

Ahmad, E. (2003) "Terrorism: Theirs and Ours," in R. Howard and R. Sawyer (eds.), *Terrorism and Counter-Terrorism: Understanding the New Security Environment*. Guilford: McGraw Hill.

Arendt, H. (1970) *On Violence*. Orlando: Harcourt.

Asad, T. (2007) *On Suicide Bombing*. New York: Columbia University Press.

Hegel, G. W. F. (1977) *The Phenomenology of Spirit*, trans. A. V. Miller. Oxford: Oxford University Press.

Lacan, J. (1991) *Le Séminaire de Jacques Lacan, Livre VIII: Le Transfert*, ed. Jacques-Alain Miller. Paris: Editions de Seuil.

—— (2004) *Le Séminaire de Jacques Lacan, Livre X: L'Angoisse*, ed. Jacques-Alain Miller. Paris: Editions de Seuil.

Pape, R. (2006) *Dying to Win: The Strategic Logic of Suicide Terrorism*. New York: Random House.

Rose, J. (2004) "Deadly Embrace," *The London Review of Books 26*, 21.

Wolin, S. (2008) *Democracy Incorporated: Managed Democracy and the Specter of Inverted Totalitarianism*. Princeton: Princeton University Press.

Žižek, S. (2008) *Violence: Six Sideways Reflections*. New York: Picador.

5

TODAY'S MADNESS DOES NOT MAKE SENSE

Paul Verhaeghe

The extraordinary diversity of the psychical constellations concerned, the plasticity of all mental processes and the wealth of determining factors oppose any mechanization of the technique; and they bring it about that a course of action that is a rule justified may at times prove ineffective, whilst one that is usually mistaken may once in a while lead to the desired end.

Freud 1913

Past and present

Thirty years ago I received my first patient. It took only one session to recognize a full blown hysterical structure: conversion symptoms framed within a *belle indifférence*, extreme ambivalence towards sexuality, and a positive transference from the start. The further the treatment advanced, the more convinced I was of the efficiency of all that I had learned. Much material surfaced by means of free association, leading to interpretations almost self-evidently, although not without some resistance, etcetera.

This very first clinical experience met my implicit expectations based on my classical training. Looking back I can define those expectations as follows: In former days, analysts expected a patient with symptoms in our meaning of the word, i.e. conversion symptoms, phobic constructions, obsessive-compulsive symptoms, and so on. Furthermore, analysts assumed that the analysand had a notion that his or her symptoms meant something, and that they had a connection with his or her history. On top of that, we expected a more or less positive transference in which we obtained a position described by Lacan as that of a *sujet-supposé-savoir*, a subject-supposed-to-know. This is more or less the summary of the criteria presented by Freud as the requirements for psychoanalytical treatment (Freud 1905a). In short, this is the field of psychoneurosis, with a clear accent on the prefix "psycho."

A hundred years later, we are confronted with completely different problems. Instead of phobic anxiety, we encounter panic disorders; instead of conversion symptoms we find somatization and eating disorders; and instead of acting out we are confronted with aggressive and sexual enactments, mostly in combination with self-mutilation and drug abuse. Moreover, patients have little or no notion of the potential implications of their symptoms and they are hardly aware of a historical context. Last but not least, we have been ousted from our armchair's comfort. A positive transference does not come easily. In the best cases today, therapy starts with a rather indifferent attitude. Often enough, we are even confronted with distrust and a distinctly negative transference.

This is the type of patient Freud undoubtedly would have refused. With a slight exaggeration I can state that the well-behaved psychoneurotic of yore, who, due to an unresolved Oedipal problem fantasizes about forbidden sexual acts and who out of sheer feelings of guilt develops phobic or obsessive symptoms within a largely imaginary mental world, is threatened by extinction. Today we are dealing with a promiscuous, aggressive and/or self-mutilating borderline patient with a complex traumatic history, who nourishes an addiction in addition to eating disorders. This is the new madness. In practice, this means that we meet in our consulting room, for example, an obese male patient, reeking of stale beer, arriving twenty minutes late who, clearly but non-verbally, gives us to understand that we should not expect him to co-operate easily. If we, slightly alarmed, review his file and learn that he has a history of violent outbursts, chances are that we, as therapists, will respond with our own negative bias. We may thereby repeat precisely the patient's etiology and reinforce his problem.

Differences

The supposedly new character of contemporary madness is highly relative, as it has undoubtedly always been present. The only new thing is that it presents itself more often, or receives more attention than before. As early as 1975, Green mentioned a malaise in psychoanalysis because of a change in the post-Freudian patient (Green 1996). Green applies a generic interpretation of the borderline state and psychosomatics. Some twenty-five years later, Hartocollis (2002) argued that in the second half of the twentieth century psychoanalysts from different backgrounds studied patients with predominant actual-neurotic problems and pinpointed poor or even absent psychical representation in domains of functioning where analysts would classically expect conflict and defense.

This leads us to the question of the distinction between classic symptoms and new symptoms, and we can note at least four remarkable differences between them. Firstly, these new symptoms mainly have to do with the body. Secondly, their nature is often performative. Thirdly, they lack the layers of meaning that are typical of classic symptoms. Lastly, the patient does not link these symptoms to his history. These four features fit within a bigger picture, one in which the therapeutic relationship itself can be quite difficult.

Concerning the physical aspect, the body takes a central position in a direct, real, and non-mediated way. In contrast, classic symptoms deal with the body in an imaginary, phantasmagorical way. As a reality, it stays out of range. To be sure, some classic symptoms do affect the body. Conversion symptoms are a distinct example, but it is not so hard to spot the difference with the new ones. Conversion symptoms leave the body intact, while disrupting a function such as movement or affecting the senses. The new symptoms do not leave the body intact. On the contrary, self-mutilation, addiction, eating disorders, and somatization violate the body.

Concerning the performative element, with the exception of obsessional acts, classic symptoms are limited mostly to an imaginary field (i.e. phobic symptoms, hallucinations, compulsive thoughts or delusions), and do not act. When an act does happen, our terminology, "acting out," defines its exceptional nature. Moreover, the psychoneurotic "acting out" is meaningful, like the other psycho-neurotic symptoms, and can be analyzed through analytical interpretation. It is precisely this lack of meaningful symptoms in combination with a focus on "acting out" that explains why our "new" patients are notoriously difficult to treat.

Difficulties concerning treatment

Contemporary empirical research confirms something Freud already knew. Therapeutic efficacy has everything to do with the transferential relationship and the way it is handled. Applied to the contemporary patient, the failure of classic treatment must be linked to a failure in the therapeutic relationship. The treatment of addiction, self-mutilation, eating disorders and so on is not successful because the patient does not co-operate. In caricatured terms: instead of a well-behaved neurotic, begging to be heard and willing to please, we are confronted with a reluctant, aggressive drug-addict, a borderline patient, or a lying and cheating anorexic patient. Often enough, a negative counter-transferential reaction follows. This can go quite far: such patients have been designated *therapy resistant* (Lydiard and Brawman-Mintzer 1997; Rosenbaum 1997), and an empirical study describes the therapist's predominant reaction as contempt (Rasting, Brosig and Beutel 2005). In terms of the dialectics of the therapeutic relation, this amounts to blaming the patient. It is the patient who is the reason for the therapeutic failure; he is *resistant*, and does not have a genuine demand for help.

Ethically and clinically, it is far more correct to say that these patients do not present us with the demand for help that we expect, nor do they allow us to occupy our position as subject-supposed-to-know. In the unlikely case that they assign us this position and present us more or less with a classic demand for help, we are confronted with yet another complication. Psychoanalytic technique is always a deconstruction: using free association and interpretation we analyze psycho-neurotic symptoms by deconstructing them to reach more original, nearly always conflicting, layers of meaning. The two conditions necessary to this technique are that the symptoms carry a multilayered meaning and be deployed within a positive transference relation. The new symptoms lack both of these; hence, classic psychoanalytical treatment does not work.

Lacan states that the principal resistance during analysis arises from the analyst. Countertransference has to do with our prejudices and biases. Our bias is that we expect a certain type of patient. If the patient does not fit that expectation, we react in a negative way, to the detriment of the patient. If we want to work with the new madness, we have to leave our comfortable armchair. In the first instance, it is necessary to understand, in terms of psychoanalytical theory, the distinctions from classic psychoneurosis. Subsequently, we can develop, based on that understanding, a different and more efficacious therapeutic approach.

About twenty-five years ago I could no longer escape this conclusion. In my search for understanding, I re-interpreted a classic Freudian diagnostic differentiation, namely the distinction between actual-neurosis and psychoneurosis.[1] Combining this distinction with Lacan's theory on subject formation and attachment theory, I was able to improve my understanding of the development and history of this distinction. In retrospect, this is a plea for a clinically useful diagnostic reasoning, in contrast with a diagnostic labeling as steered by a sterile DSM. The usefulness resides in its attention to the etiology, i.e. the developmental history of the subject and his symptoms in relation to the primary others. This permits us to understand how this relation and these symptoms are likely to repeat themselves in relation to others, including the therapist. As I will argue, in the case of the new madness, it is precisely this basic relation to the Other that needs to be changed by therapy.

A forgotten Freudian category: actual-neurosis

From 1894 onward, Freud introduced a differential diagnostic distinction, which he retained throughout the course of his oeuvre. On the one hand, as he distinguishes in the *Neuropsychoses of Defense* (Freud 1894, 1896b), these are disorders whose cause can be found at the level of psychic elaboration, representational and defensive, of infantile sexuality. The accompanying symptoms are signifying, and the typifying characteristic for this group is a defense against an inner conflict concerning sexual desire. On the other hand, he describes the category of the *actual-neuroses*. Their cause is similarly located at the level of the drive, but specifically relates to the patient's present life, not the past. Symptoms are limited to bodily phenomena, unprocessed anxiety and somatic anxiety equivalents, and have no defensive significance (Freud 1895, 1896a, 1950a). Notice that at that time, *neurosis* and *psychoneurosis* are general terms, indicating both neurosis and psychosis as we understand them today. In the following part of this essay, unless otherwise indicated, I will concentrate on the neurotic part within the larger Freudian category of actual-pathology.

At this point it is necessary to consider the concept of the drive, because at that time it was not yet fully developed (Freud 1905b), although the idea is easily recognizable. A major problem that bothers Freud from the start is the inner rise in tension, i.e. the energetic flux that arises from within the body and therefore cannot be avoided. Later on, this becomes a central characteristic of the drive, namely the pressure (*Drang*) or excitation (*Erregung*) (Freud 1915). A central idea that is already present in the *Studies on Hysteria* is that this pressure has to be abreacted. Its binding via representations (i.e. words) is the necessary condition. In case of psychoneuroses, this psychological processing has taken place, but the representations have been distorted because of the defense mechanisms. The final result is the psychoneurotic symptom. In case of actual-neurosis, the step towards representation has not been successful and the innervation remains on the level of the body.

The categories of psychoneurosis and actual-neurosis, however, are not to be regarded as mutually exclusive. In stating that psychoneurotic symptoms can hardly ever appear without actual ones, although the latter can appear without the former (Freud 1910), Freud legitimizes the fact that actual-neurotic pathology is a study on its own. Besides that, he considers the actual-neuroses as the nucleus and first stage of the psychoneuroses, particularly within the relationships neurasthenia-conversion hysteria; anxiety neurosis-anxiety hysteria; and hypochondria-paranoia. The latter indicates again that Freud's original actual *neurosis* can also be applied to our contemporary category of psychosis.

Freud's remark about the dynamic relationship between these two categories is important from a therapeutic point of view. Actual-neurosis and psychoneurosis must be considered as two extremes on a continuum, with the possibility of moving from one to the other. The movement backwards is well known; we call it regression. The movement upwards will be a psychotherapeutic goal.

In the course of his career, Freud focuses on psychoneuroses, leaving the actual-pathology relatively unexamined, despite the fact that he continues to confirm its existence. The reason for this is pragmatic: he considers it to be unresponsive to his psychoanalytic treatment. As the symptomatic superstructure and associated phantasmagorical development are completely lacking, there simply is nothing to analyze. Despite this, Freud does describe this group thoroughly. At first he distinguishes two types of actual-neuroses: anxiety neurosis and neurasthenia (Freud 1895; Freud 1896a). Later, he adds hypochondria to this list (Freud 1912; Freud 1914). And lastly, he completes the list with addictions. In each case the focus is on the drive arousal and on the damming of libido, along with the impossibility of psychic elaboration. All actual-neuroses are consequently to be considered as different manifestations of a similar underlying process. This brings me to the etiological question.

Freud describes this underlying process as an interplay between a somatic-sexual factor that serves as an endogenous source of excitation and the subject's failure to psychically master this excitation and thus discharge it associatively via words. As a result of this failure, the excitation exerts a *toxic* effect on the body (Freud 1895). Freud's reflections on causation converge in the idea that, in the case of actual-neurosis, the drive is handled in a non-representational way. Quanta of somatic-sexual excitation are not coupled to psychical representations, and the excitation remains present in a free-floating state. Whereas in psychoneuroses endogenous excitation obtains a representational coating (Freud 1912) and finds its symbolic expression via classic analyzable symptoms, the representational process is short-circuited in cases of actual-neurosis. As a result, excitation reaches excessive proportions and is expressed in bodily phenomena.

For Freud (1925), the direct etiologies lie in the patient's *abusive* sexual practices, i.e. the way the patient practically handles somatic-sexual excitation. In the case of anxiety neurosis, he points to the role of an inhibited sexual life: abstinence or imperfect or interrupted coition (Freud 1895; Freud 1950a); in the case of neurasthenia, to masturbation or spontaneous emissions (Freud 1896b; Freud 1912).

After Freud, this part of his theory was nearly forgotten by post-Freudians. To my knowledge, Mitrani (1995) and Hartocollis (2002) were the only ones who returned to the idea of actual-neurosis. This also undoubtedly has to do with the specific direct etiologies that Freud attributes to actual-neuroses. Nowadays, sexual abstinence and masturbation do not have the same significance as they had in the early 1900s. In my reconsideration of this diagnostic category, I will focus on the lack of psychic processing of the drive through the form of representations.

Actual-pathology and new madness

At the start of this essay I discussed the core features of the contemporary madness, namely a central position of the body, dealt with in a direct and non-mediated way; performative symptoms, instead of psychological ones; the lack of meaningful layers; and a complex, often negative, therapeutic relationship.

It is not difficult to connect these features to Freud's description. The connection becomes even more obvious if we take into account the categories he files under actual-neurosis. Neurasthenia may have disappeared from our diagnostic vocabulary, but its description resembles the contemporary somatization closely; Freud's anxiety neurosis coincides completely with contemporary panic disorder (Verhaeghe et al. 2007). Addiction fits in as well (Loose 2002). Obviously, the body and the lack of meaning are at the heart of these disorders.

What does not fit is what Freud describes as the direct etiology, namely sexual inhibition. On the contrary, the new madness deals with sexual release rather than inhibition or abstinence. This explains the accent on performativity and enactment. The fact that Freud does not mention the difficult therapeutic relationship is not that odd, since he chose not to treat these patients.

The principal feature of Freud's actual-neurosis is the lack of psychological, representational processing of the inner excitation. Indeed, this is likewise the nucleus of the new madness. As I will explain, we must consider the complicated relation with the Other as well, not only during treatment but also in terms of its dynamic at the root of the actual-neurosis.

Identity development and drive regulation

From the start, Freud wrestles with a central issue related to his etiological considerations. Both actual-neurosis and psychoneurosis originate from the same problem, namely, the experience of an internal tension that has not been, or is unable to be, psychically elaborated (Freud 1985, Draft G). In the case of actual-neurosis, the arousal continues to be active on the somatic level, causing panic attacks and somatization. In the case of psychoneurosis, the transition towards psychical processing has taken place, hence the construction of hysterical and obsessional symptoms and the possibility of interpreting them. The question is how this transition towards psychical elaboration comes about. Once we understand this transition, we can address the question of its failure in actual-neurosis. Here, we must turn to Freud's unsurpassed *Project for a Scientific Psychology* (Freud 1950a).

At the time of the *Project*, Freud was developing a theory on the origin of psychical functioning. The point of departure of human development was found in an original experience of unpleasure (*Schmerz*, or "pain"), caused by an internal need and whose prototype was hunger and thirst. Freud considers this pain a quantitative accumulation of tension, whose stimuli break through the so-called *protective shields*, just as with physical pain (Freud 1895). Later, he will compare this to the trauma caused by the drive (Freud 1950a; Freud 1915: 146–7). In other words, pain, drive excitation and trauma are brought into a single line: the subject originally experiences them as an arousal coming from the outside, and this arousal is such that the subject cannot cope with it (Verhaeghe 2001).

Because it originates in the somatically immature, infantile body, the usual flight reaction is impossible. The infant's reaction to this unpleasant experience is prototypical and will prepare a basic form for all later relationships. The baby turns to the Other with a cry.[2] The caretaker is to provide a specific reaction to neutralize the inner arousal (Freud 1950a: 317–321; Freud 1926: 169–172). This intervention from the Other will always consist of a number of acts and words, indicating that the child's appeal has been understood and dealt with. Notice that, because of this prototypical basic form, originally physical pain and excitation becomes inextricably bound up with the Other. In other words, from the very beginning, the somatic arousal acquires an inter-subjective dimension, marking the point at which the transition from the somatic to the psychical takes place.

Today, we know that this transition can scarcely be overestimated. It prepares the foundation for our identity along with the ability to regulate the drive arousal. Firstly, the child literally internalizes images and words received from the Other; this idea returns in Lacan's mirror stage theory, and later, in attachment theory. These representations are the basis for the identity of the child. Freud describes such a process of internalization in terms of incorporation and identification, which are the foundational mechanisms of the ego. Secondly, the regulation of the drive is in keeping with this. The images absorbed from the Other not only give subjects access to their own arousal, but moreover teach subjects how to

74

handle this arousal via the Other, that is to say, in a symbolic way. This process culminates in a special kind of identification during the Oedipal period, namely the *Über-Ich*.

The acquisition of identity and the regulation of inner tension have repercussions in the way anxiety is experienced. The original experiences of unpleasure and anxiety are chiefly of a somatic nature. Freud calls this automatic or traumatic anxiety (1926: 136, 148). This is closely connected to what is nowadays called a panic attack. Such an anxiety is meaningless and has clear somatic qualities, such as palpitations, respiratory problems, or tremor (Freud 1916–1917: 395). In addition to anxiety as such, Freud also describes the somatic equivalents of anxiety, what nowadays is called *somatization* (Freud 1895). The connection with the Other ensures that the original anxiety (helplessness with respect to the arousal) shifts towards separation anxiety (because the Other is supposed to provide an answer) and later to signal anxiety (signaling either the potential return of the original anxiety and/or the potential absence of the Other). The physical displeasure becomes psychic distress the moment the Other fails to turn up. This kind of separation anxiety will be powerfully present at the beginning of development. It diminishes as identity and acquisition of object permanence are securely established. As the Other is internalized, her actual presence is no longer needed.

What I especially want to emphasize in my reading of Freud's theory is the close relation between identity development and drive regulation, and the fact that both are based on representations taken from the Other. This has two important implications that I have not yet addressed. Firstly, disorders in the field of drive regulation are inevitably identity disorders, because drive regulation and identity acquisition are based on the same processes. Secondly, these two processes are only possible if the relationship with the Other is positive. Freud discusses a love relationship, one attachment theory calls "safe."

The importance of the Other

Lacan extends the Freudian theory significantly. The gain is the central position of the Other. From 1948 onwards, Lacan develops his theory of identity acquisition wherein the Other plays a central role. In short, his starting point is the assumption that, at birth, the child has no given identity. Identity is acquired through identification with the mirror image offered by the Other. This mirroring results in an initial awareness of bodily identity, through which the subject-to-be gains access to the psychical experience and processing of the component drives. The subsequent development, called subject formation, comes down to identifications with and separation from the signifiers presented by the Other. Because he starts from Freud's idea of a non-bridgeable gap between the Real of the drive and the symbolic-imaginary elaboration, for Lacan, identity acquisition is a never-ending process (Lacan 2006; Verhaeghe 1998).

Attachment theory has recently been taken up again from a psychoanalytic perspective and, as result, an impressive corpus of empirical research has been produced. The main conclusions clearly confirm that the original relationship between mother and infant determines later relationships. Furthermore, they show that identity is developed via the caretaker's mirroring of the child's internal experiences with regard to arousal (Fonagy et al. 2002). It is through this mirroring that the possibility of affect regulation emerges. The correlation with Lacan's mirror stage is obvious, even though these authors do not make this connection.

It is not so difficult to see that these three theories (Freud, Lacan, and attachment theory) put forward an identical point of departure: an internal rise in tension leads to an appeal to the Other, and it is the Other that presents the foundations for a first identity, via his/her mirroring reaction. Representations from the Other result in a *theory of the mind* that provides the subject with both access to and a means of regulating its own drive.

Joining Freud's theory of the development of the ego with his distinction between actual-neurosis and psychoneurosis, we can outline the impact of the Other and delineate this distinction much more clearly. In the case of a psycho-neurotic development, the pressure resulting from the drive is processed via the mirroring reaction of the Other. On these grounds, the subject acquires a representational identity, whose further Oedipal elaboration may lead to the construction of meaningful symptoms based on unconscious fantasies. This transforms the original automatic anxiety into a defensive signal anxiety. The nature of the symptoms will be determined by the specific mechanisms of defense.

In case of an actual-neurosis, however, this elaboration does not occur. Because of a failure in the relationship with the Other, the subject remains stuck in this transition. The effect with regards to the clinical picture of actual-neurosis is an absence of meaningful symptoms and the preponderance of anxiety-related somatic phenomena, these being expressions of the automatic anxiety. The typical characteristic of actual-neurosis is the continuing, unregulated and real nature of the arousal in combination with a very ambivalent relation to others.

The possible causes of the failed relationship with the Other are diverse: a depressive parent, not capable of suitable mirroring; a preoccupied parent being too close and therefore a threatening mirroring; or an abusive parent. In any case, the basic relationship with the Other is anything but safe. The effects of this failed relationship will become clear on three levels: drive regulation, identity, and relations with others.

In the field of drive regulation, the step towards a representational processing is barely executed. The processing is situated close to the point of departure, namely the body. Therefore, the focus is on the performative: hence, aggressive and sexual *enactments*, self-mutilation, and eating disorders. The reflective position and the ability to talk about their problems are often extremely limited. At the same time, we also meet with patients who chatter nonstop, but do not say anything. This manner of speaking must be understood as an act with a clear abreaction function, a type of action-speaking (Mitrani 1995). The focus on a performative processing fits a disturbed development in early youth. Meaning is absent because the initial mirroring, leading to representations, is hampered due to the unsafe basic relationship with the Other. The symptoms are non-mediated attempts to cope with the jouissance, focused on the Real of the body.

A second, predictable, consequence is to be found in the field of identity development. If this crucial development is marked with a lack of or with unsuitable mirroring, the result is not only a lack in the field of psychic processing of arousal; the lack will be found in the field of identity as well. The experience of identity is rather empty or chaotic, and above all dependent on the look of the Other. There is hardly object permanence, and therefore hardly ego permanence. The literal presence of the Other and his or her gaze is necessary, because otherwise these patients will not know who or what they are.

This leads us to the third and most important consequence, namely the typical nature of the interpersonal relation. In a best case scenario, the patient will not expect much from the Other because the initial important others did not have much to offer either. In a worst case scenario the patient will only expect a negative response and is armed with a negative and hostile attitude towards anyone. Instead of basic trust, we are confronted with basic distrust.

The line of expectation is that the actual-pathological patient will always take an ambiguous stand. On the one hand she makes an appeal to the Other in order to receive an answer, and primarily asks for recognition. On the other hand, the patient will reject the Other. Here we find an ambiguous combination of separation anxiety and intrusion anxiety. The fear of an intrusive other continuously thwarts the need for an immediate presence of the other. Metaphorically speaking, this is like going full speed and slamming the brakes on, all at the same time. Obviously this is not healthy, either for the car or, in this case, the body.

This applies mainly to more complex types of actual-pathology, today often described as borderline patients (Verhaeghe and Vanheule 2005). Attachment studies on borderline personality disorder clearly link the development of these disorders to a failure in the original process of mirroring as either inadequate or lacking (Fonagy et al. 2002). Borderline is without any doubt a negative term, and calling them attachment disorders is a better option. Still, I think this denomination is too vague, because psychoneurosis is also an attachment disorder. Actual-pathology pinpoints the specific combination of a negative interpersonal basic relationship and an inability to process the drive on a psychic level. This description is both diagnostically and therapeutically clear and functional.

Therapeutic implications

This leads us to the crucial question: what about treatment? Freud already concluded that classic analysis does not work because, simply put, there are no symptoms present to be analyzed. A first, naive, therapeutic response is often the following: These patients are cognitively not able to phrase affections and arousal, as is the case with alexithymia. Therefore, we must teach them. This seems a logical approach; it is nevertheless doomed because the underlying cause, i.e., why these patients are not capable of phrasing affections, is dismissed. It is essential that the typical inter-subjective relation be taken into account. It is this relation that blocks the transfer of representations coming from the Other. Often enough, this impossibility is understood by the therapist as resistance, with a total neglect of the interpersonal structure and its history.

The first therapeutic objective is therefore the development of a positive therapeutic relationship, and this remains crucial during the entire treatment. Only a trustful therapeutic relationship will make possible the transfer of representations coming from the therapist. During the initial phase the patient is more interested in the style and pitch of our interventions than in the content. The patient has a constant interest in all forms of non-verbal communication, because he verifies again and again if the other will reject him. Separation anxiety is quite powerful. Everything that can be understood as a rejection is immediately experienced as such, and contributes to the unwilling attitude the patient takes. It is important that the therapist set up a solid and predictable framework and repeat the same message over and over again: I am here for you and I am willing to listen.

Due to the developmental history it is clear that the classical approach is out of the question. The use of the setting of a couch, a talkative patient and a tight-lipped therapist out of eyesight does not work. The patient experiences such a setting as another rejection, or at least considers the therapist to be unwilling to provide answers, which is an iteration of the initial etiology. On top of that, when this patient cannot see the eyes of the other, he will lose himself because his identity can only be constructed by using the gaze of the other.

Consequently, the therapist must be more active. We need to identify issues and elucidate context. We need to take an ethical stance as well. We will have to intervene actively in order to symbolize and historicize the patient's impulsive and affective experiences, whereupon these experiences become accessible for a new and fruitful type of processing. We thereby risk provoking a second basic anxiety, namely intrusion anxiety. Hence, we walk a thin line during the entire treatment between separation anxiety and intrusion anxiety.

The primary goal of the therapy is not the transfer of certain contents, but the creation of a relation that facilitates that transfer. Only when the therapeutic relation is relatively stable can the therapist help to develop a psychological processing of the drive. To be sure, this is not the development of an isolated competence, because drive regulation goes hand in hand with identity development. Elsewhere I have called this "subject amplification" (Verhaeghe 2004).

This is only possible when an effective therapeutic relation has been successfully installed. It is clear that the therapist has to engage himself. As Lacan states in his seminar on ethics, "[the analyst] pays with his person" (Lacan 1992: 291). Mitrani gives this a concrete meaning when she tells us that we must incorporate and experience the patient's non-representational experiences: "[We have to keep] these experiences in [our] mind for a sufficient period of time to be able to suffer and to think them and to give them logical, verbal meaning, to be conveyed to the patient, all in good time" (Mitrani 1995).

Conclusion

As a young therapist, I had the experience that a number of my classic patients got worse. As a result, I seriously doubted my therapeutic skills. Apparently, my unease became clearly visible during a certain period because some of them tried to comfort me: "But sir, you do not have to be too concerned. It is only here, with you, that I feel bad. When I step out of this room, things are much and much better." In other words, the neurosis had become a full-scale transference neurosis, and was gradually limited to the consulting room. A transfer from the outside to the inside had taken place.

With actual-pathology, we get the opposite message. If the treatment starts to be successful we hear: "This is the only hour of the week, and the one place where I feel more or less at ease, but outside this room there is only misery." As such, this message undoubtedly indicates progress, but it is clear that this is no final objective. We need a reversed transfer, the development of a basic trust, built within the therapy and transferred to the outside world. This is the challenge we face when dealing with this group of patients.

Notes

1   The very first publication goes back to Verhaeghe (1989) "Le diagnostic psych-analytique: le symptôme entre névrose actuelle et psychonévrose." It took a book to elaborate this approach: Verhaeghe (2004) *On Being Normal and Other Disorders*, New York: Other Press; original publication in Dutch in 2002.
2   We use the Lacanian concept of the Other, with a capital O, indicating both the Other and the Symbolic Order. Its starting-point is the (m)Other, presenting the child with the necessary words and symbols for its inner arousal, and eventually, for its identity.

Bibliography

Fonagy, P., Gergely, G., Jurist, E. and Target, M. (2002) *Affect Regulation, Mentalization and the Development of Self*, New York: Other Press.
Freud, S. (1894) "The Neuro-Psychoses of Defense," *Standard Edition*, 3: 41–61, London: Hogarth.
—— (1894; 2nd edn 1895) "On the Grounds for Detaching a Particular Syndrome from Neurasthenia under the Description 'Anxiety Neurosis,'" *Standard Edition*, 3: 87–115, London: Hogarth.
—— (1896a) "Heredity and the Aetiology of the Neuroses," *Standard Edition*, 3: 141–56, London: Hogarth.
—— (1896b) "Further Remarks on the Neuro-Psychoses of Defense," *Standard Edition*, 3: 157–85, London: Hogarth.
—— (1898) "Sexuality in the Aetiology of the Neuroses," *Standard Edition*, 3: 261–85, London: Hogarth.

—— (1904; 2nd edn 1905a) "On Psychotherapy," *Standard Edition*, 7: 255–68, London: Hogarth.

—— (1905b) "Three Essays on the Theory of Sexuality," *Standard Edition*, 7: 123–245, London: Hogarth.

—— (1910) "The Psycho-analytic View of Psychogenic Disturbance of Vision," *Standard Edition*, 11: 209–18, London: Hogarth.

—— (1912) "Contributions to a Discussion on Masturbation," *Standard Edition*, 12: 239–54, London: Hogarth.

—— (1913) "On Beginning the Treatment (Further Recommendations on the Technique of Psycho-Analysis, I)," *Standard Edition*, 12: 121–44, London: Hogarth.

—— (1914) "On Narcissism," *Standard Edition*, 14: 67–102, London: Hogarth.

—— (1915) "Instincts and Their Vicissitudes," *Standard Edition*, 14: 109–40, London: Hogarth.

—— (1915–17; 2nd edn 1916–17) "Introductory Lectures on Psycho-Analysis, Part III: General Theory of the Neuroses," *Standard Edition*, 16: 243–463, London: Hogarth.

—— (1924; 2nd edn 1925) "An Autobiographical Study," *Standard Edition*, 20: 1–74, London: Hogarth.

—— (1925; 2nd edn 1926) "Inhibitions, Symptoms and Anxiety," *Standard Edition*, 20: 75–175, London: Hogarth.

—— (1887–1902; 2nd edn 1950a) "Extracts from the Fliess Papers," *Standard Edition*, 1: 173–280, London: Hogarth.

—— (1887–1902; 2nd edn 1950b) "Project for a Scientific Psychology," *Standard Edition*, 1: 283–397, London: Hogarth.

—— (1985) *The Complete Letters of Sigmund Freud to Wilhelm Fliess*, trans. and ed. J. M. Masson, Cambridge, MA: Belknap Press of Harvard University Press.

Green, A. (1975; 2nd edn 1996) "The Analyst, Symbolization, and Absence in the Analytic Setting," in *On Private Madness*, London: Rebus.

Hartocollis, P. (2002) "'Actualneurosis' and Psychosomatic Medicine: The Vicissitudes of an Enigmatic Concept," *International Journal of Psychoanalysis*, 83: 1361–73.

Lacan, J. (1964; 2nd edn 1973) *Le Séminaire, Livre XI, Les quatre concepts fondamentaux de la psychanalyse*, Paris: Seuil.

—— (1973) "The Mirror Stage as Formative of the I function as Revealed in Psychoanalytic Experience," in Bruce Fink (trans.) (2006) *Écrits*, New York: W. W. Norton & Company, Inc.

Lydiard, R. B. & Brawman-Mintzer, O. (1997). "Panic Disorder across the Life Span: A Differential Diagnostic Approach to Treatment Resistance," *Bulletin of the Menninger Clinic, 61* (suppl A): 66–94.

Loose, R. (2002) *The Subject of Addiction: Psychoanalysis and the Administration of Enjoyment*, London: Karnac Books.

Mitrani, J. (1995) "Toward an Understanding of Unmentalized Experience," *Psychoanalytic Quarterly*, 64: 68–112.

Rasting, M., Brosig, B. and Beutel, M. E. (2005) "Alexithymic Characteristics and Patient-Therapist Interaction: A Video Analysis of Facial Affect Display," *Psychopathology*, 38: 105–11.

Rosenbaum, J. F. (1997) "Treatment-Resistant Panic Disorder," *Journal of Clinical Psychiatry*, 58, 2: 61–4.

Verhaeghe P. (1989) "Le diagnostic psychanalytique: le symptôme entre névrose actuelle et psychonévrose," *Quarto*, 37–8: 15–19.

—— (1998) "Causation and Destitution of a Pre-ontological Non-entity: On the Lacanian Subject," in D. Nobus (ed.) *Key Concepts of Lacanian Psychoanalysis*, London: Rebus Press.

—— (1998; 2nd edn 2001) "Trauma and Psychopathology in Freud and Lacan: Structural versus Accidental Trauma," in *Beyond Gender: From Subject to Drive*, New York: Other Press.

—— (2004) *On Being Normal and Other Disorders: A Manual for Clinical Psychodiagnostics*, trans. S. Jottkandt, New York: Other Press.

Verhaeghe, P. and Vanheule, S. (2005) "Actualneurosis and PTSD: The Impact of the Other," *Psychoanalytic Psychology*, *22*, 4: 493–507.

Verhaeghe, P., Vanheule, S. and De Rick, A. (2007) "Actual Neurosis as the Underlying Psychic Structure of Panic Disorder, Somatization, and Somatoform Disorder: An Integration of Freudian and Attachment Perspectives," *The Psychoanalytic Quarterly*, *76*, 4: 1317–50.

Part II

THE METHOD IN MADNESS
Thinking psychosis

6

"YOU CANNOT CHOOSE TO GO CRAZY"

Nestor Braunstein

For patients who are "crazy" ("psychotic, if you will") (Lacan 1967), there is a structural obstacle that makes the tying together of knowledge and love difficult, in other words, an impediment to forming transference. In such cases, interpretation becomes futile, if not persecutory or dangerous. This has been the case since the time of Freud. The issue of the existence of transference in psychosis became the title of a well-known article by Lacan: it was the question prior to "any possible treatment of psychosis." "Not just anyone can go mad" (Lacan 2006a: 144). Freud asserted, and with reason, the existence of *Neurosenwahl,* the choice of neurosis. But he never spoke of a choice of psychosis. The lesson of psychosis, I propose, is that there is no choice; psychosis is not a choice.

Lacan said, "The mad person is the only free human being" (Lacan 1967). Soon after, Lacan formulated his theory of the four discourses and the condensed syntagm: the social link (*lien social*). *Lien,* link, connection, tie. The madman is free from participating in the dialectic of meaning in his own speech, outside of discursive ties. To enter into discourse is to engage in a link and, therefore, a loss of freedom. Madness creates an exception placing itself outside the exchange of speech, of discourses. This idea is already present for Lacan in the beginning of his teaching, when he discusses the "negative freedom of a kind of speech that has given up trying to gain recognition" (Lacan 2006b: 280).

At this time, Lacan reiterated what he had already said twenty years earlier in "Presentations on Psychic Causality":

> [R]ather than resulting from a contingent fact—the frailties of his [the psychotic's] organism—madness is the permanent virtuality of a gap opened up in his essence. And far from being an "insult" to freedom, madness is freedom's most faithful companion, following its every move like a shadow. Not only can man's being not be understood without madness, but it would not be man's being if it did not bear madness within itself as the limit of his freedom.
>
> (Lacan 2006a: 144)

Lacan's position is clear: freedom has a frontier, and the name of this borderline is madness. Once crossed, unconditional freedom is lost and generalized servitude ensues. Lacan added: "The psychotic presents essentially as the sign, the sign of an impasse, of what legitimizes the reference to freedom" (2001b: 363). This absolute impasse separates freedom from its absence. We either have madness, where freedom runs amok, or sanity, where programmed obedience is mandated by culture.

Let us note that in Lacan's four discourses, there is no room for another discourse, that of the psychotic. Here speech would not be a semblance, but would be placed precisely at the point of union of truth and the Real, what Julia Kristeva termed the "*vreél*" or "true-real" (Kristeva 1985). All discourse is a semblance because it presents itself as true without being so. Semblance pertains to all discourse because it speaks of entities that exist only in the discourse that produces them as fictions, giving them a linguistic status. Finally, semblance pertains to all discourse because semblance is its agent, displacing truth and at the same time placing it at a cautious distance, be it in the form of the discourse of the master, the university, the psychoanalyst or the hysteric. The psychotic is not and cannot make semblance. He lives outside it, even when he is able to cross its frontier and make himself understood (Braunstein 2007). To sum up: all discourse is semblance; this is why there is no psychotic discourse. If paranoia speaks—and above all, it writes—then it speaks as truth, a true-real, outside the semblance that is all discourse.

This does not mean that the madman is free to make choices in the sense of making decisions. In fact, insofar as his condition is psychotic, others choose for him. The madman is free from having to choose. One cannot choose without losing, without renouncing a measure of jouissance. The psychotic cannot say "no" to the imposed renunciation of jouissance inherent to discourse as a link; he does not need to protect himself with the barriers to jouissance that pleasure, desire, and fantasy provide.

Psychosis "spares" the subject symbolic castration, saving him from obligatorily dislodging jouissance from the body and participating in a discourse where the object is lost. He is "saved" from the barriers that lodge subjectivity in phallic signification, making the sexual rapport impossible. In immediate contact with the object, not subjected to the task of making metaphors and metonymies about their relation with the object in the chaining of signifiers, the mad are not constrained by "sense-making."

Thus, madness shows us the image of a freedom from which the *normals*[1] (Lacan 1985: 304) are alienated. Neurotic or perverse subjects, who so scarcely defend themselves from the Real by way of the Symbolic, clutch to their narcissistic image and install themselves in a supposed "reality" made of links between signifiers and arbitrary signifieds. Such "reality" (*Wirklichkeit*), in which we all live, away from the Real, is not much more than a fantasy shared by many; it allows us to (mis)understand each other and support the illusion that we are not mad. We live in the kingdom of sense; we are not bonkers, whether we like it or not.

The madman, in particular the so called schizophrenic, does not know that he denounces the presumption of self-confirming reason. He excludes himself from the socio-cultural exchanges and ends up subjected to the psychiatric medical order, locked up, his body controlled by pharmaceuticals. Psychoanalysis thus confronts this dilemma: to idealize madness as a paradigm of freedom (on the side of antipsychiatry) or to objectify it with the notion of "illness" (on the side of psychiatry), thereby justifying manipulation and reclusion. We denounce the error of such a dilemma, and open a different path congruous with the still pertinent determinism of Freud and Lacan: madness does not occur by chance.

The risk is double: to reduce the madman to a condition of animality, treating him with a veterinary schema, or to extol the madman's freedom as an imaginary poultice for our lack of it. Because the Other takes possession, the mad do not own their bodies and suffer. This situation bears resemblance to that of the addict and the suicidal person, who abandon their bodies and leave them in the hands of the Other. The "freedom" of the madman is lived within the walls of the asylum or in miserable little rooms in shabby hotels where nowadays they are isolated after being doped up with chemicals.

Let us ask then, how does someone become psychotic? Lacan claims in "Science and Truth" that one "is always responsible" for one's subjective position (Lacan 2006d: 729). Neurosis, addictions, suicide, and perversions are choices. Choice is not about deciding which object to enjoy; in taking this point of departure, one would end up in the most rudimentary psychologization of the autonomous conscience.[2] Choosing means accepting loss, and renouncing jouissance. The paradigm of choice, of a forced choice, is offered by Lacan in his well-known alternative: "Your money or your life" (Lacan 1973: 193). The choice imposed on the subject excludes the possibility of the conjunction of both. The psychotic is precisely someone who, not being a someone yet, cannot respond and choose; he is unable to forsake, to accept a loss of jouissance. Placed on the side of "being," he loses on the side of "meaning." Whoever chooses accepts the loss of the object and therefore makes a dent (*écornement*) in jouissance, choosing to relate to the object insofar as it is a lost object. This is what is at stake in the Freudian *Neurosenwahl*. This does not take place when the confrontation with the Other results in a psychosis.

Let us carefully follow Lacan's development of this issue. Lacan first spoke of psychosis as an "unfathomable decision of being" (Lacan 2006a: 145).[3] This expression appeared in an article devoted to psychic causality, written at the request of Henry Ey in 1946. There, Lacan confronted the veterinarian pretentions of psychiatry, even those disguised as organodynamism. The "unfathomable" or "unsoundable decision" is pervaded by a Sartrean spirit dominant at the time. This position is openly contradicted by the Lacanian concepts presented a decade later in the period of elaboration that extends from Seminar III (1955–6) on psychosis to "On a Question Prior to Any Possible Treatment of Psychosis," already mentioned. Here the question of psychosis is centered on the concept of foreclosure (Lacan 1985: 361), which opposes the idea of an "unsoundable decision." This new thesis puts forward a non-intervention (linked to the juridical notion of "preclusion") of the paternal metaphor; this is to say, of the signifier of the Name-of-the-Father substituting for the desire of the mother. Through the intervention of the Name-of-the-Father, the budding subject will see himself separated from the primal object of jouissance; this results in an originary privation (*Versagung*), a dissatisfaction, a painful displeasure, and an unrelenting search for the lost object. We call this nostalgic search "desire." When the father's law, with language as its vehicle, intervenes in the rapport with the mother, the subject is removed from the maternal sphere, prior to which the mother was fantasized as a part of the child's own body. The emerging subject is forced to localize jouissance in the exchanges of language. Speech orients and reroutes the satisfaction of the drives' ambitions. But speech cannot produce satisfaction because it is condemned to wait for and depend on the response of the other.

The determinism proper to psychosis should be looked for in the subject's relation to language. The signifier that would be the axis of all articulation (the Name-of-the-Father) has not taken its place in the chain and all the other signifiers are wandering unmoored and aimlessly: the highway is blocked and the subject is condemned to roam, taking minor roads where the sign speaks on its own (Lacan 1985: 293). "[I]n this buzzing that people who are hallucinating so often depict to you on this occasion, in this continuous murmur of these sentences, of these commentaries, which are nothing but the infinity of these minor paths, the signifiers begin to talk, to sing on their own" (Lacan 1985: 294). What is produced here is an unchaining in the rapport of the discursive link (of one signifier with the subsequent one), in the rapport of the Borromean chain (of Real, Symbolic, and Imaginary), and in the generational chain (the structures of kinship that generate identifications). This noise of broken chains renders the psychotic deaf.

Let us oppose the "election" of a psychosis to the "fall" into psychosis. In both there is something that is "unfathomable" or "unsoundable"; in one, a philosophical presumption, in the other, a clinical fact. Whose unsoundable decision? "Of being," the early Lacanian formula makes explicit (1946). How could being, anterior to the entry into language, anterior to the self, the subject, the ego, actually "decide" what to be? The being in that proposition is already subjectified, like a "jouissance of being," a jouissance of life itself, if the desire of the Other does not intervene (an Other we may call "maternal") in taking care of the newborn's basic needs. This being, of flesh before body, cannot decide anything in the confrontation with the Real of the Thing. Instead, the Other decides in a manner that is unfathomable, enigmatic, and ignored, due to the stubborn intervention of the unconscious. This Other, personalized in the mother or her substitute, is inhabited by the Name-of-the-Father that exercised its influence on her. It is an Other that desires and enjoys, linked to the world of exchanges, inhabited by speech, full of the best and the worst expectations for this new life. This Other is the one who has to formulate a call to the ex-sistence of the child. The Other may not do so, delivering it in the equivocal manner that phenomenologists call the double bind: "I want and do not want you to exist; I want and do not want you to reach autonomy (the spectral autonomy of subjectivity); I want and do not want you to integrate your body with your image with a name that I impose on you; I want and do not want that you know Real, Symbolic, and Imaginary and that you insert yourself into a genealogical chain, in a network of kinship, in the equivocal qualities of language and of lalangue." This message is the "unsoundable"; it is not the being, but rather the Other that will decide what will become and what will happen to that being. The subject is the result of this invitation-intimation of the Other to ex-sist on its "own" account.

The future psychotic is structured by the Other: ambiguously called (or not called), excluded, exiled, deprived, expelled, unnamed, curtailed, rejected[4]—all the ways of saying foreclosed—of language and of dialectics (also quite frequently, full of an overwhelming food that comes too early, before it is demanded). This is the Other's desire, here, "unsoundable." For the being to become "structured"— whether in psychosis, perversion, or neurosis—we must always take into account the Other. This Other could be absolved of any responsibility if we consider that it is an unsoundable "decision of being," which would be equivalent to a destiny (*até*) written by the gods. There is a "decision" and an "election," but they are made by the Other, who is waiting and receiving this new being. The psychoanalysts who work with children (Maud Manonni and Melanie Klein are paradigmatic examples) have demonstrated the vicissitudes and determinations of infantile psychosis in the clinical treatment of autism.

When the signifier of the Name-of-the-Father is missing, the clinic teaches that what remains is not a subject of indetermination or absolute freedom, but a subject sunken in an ineffable state of jouissance, subjected to the caprices of the mother's desire. Since the paternal metaphor is an effect of the operation of the mother's absence, it is also an indicator for the child that the mother desires something other than him. There is something that the child cannot fulfill, something mysterious and ineffable, whose place the Name-of-the-Father comes to occupy. The paternal function consists in creating an obstacle to the mutual enjoyment in the relation between mother and child. "All human formation," says Lacan, "has, by essence and not by accident, to limit jouissance" (Lacan 2001b: 364).

For this failed operation to occur, for the foreclosure to ensue, a chain of three generations is necessary. Returning to Françoise Dolto's famous thesis, Lacan in 1968 says, "[it takes] two generations of neurotic grandparents and parents to make a psychotic child" (Dolto 1971: 242).[5] This thesis of the three generations, which is openly deterministic, is clearly opposed to the mysticism of the "unsoundable decision" posed twenty-five years earlier, and can be added to the understanding of psychosis as an uncompensated defect in the knotting of the Borromean chain (R, I, S) developed by Lacan from 1974 to 1977.

The father will curtail the worst. There is no doubt that he is an impostor and that the consequence of his imposture is the subject's subjection to the ties of discourse. Thanks to the metaphoric interference of the signifier of the Name-of-the-Father, the subject is evicted from jouissance, from the burning bush of the Thing. The desire of the mother, on the other hand, is not imposture; it is the one that takes the place of meaning in the paternal metaphor; it is very real. The effects of the failure of the paternal imposture are well-known: the subject does not enter into the discursive formations of the unconscious that are nothing but semblance. What follows is the worst, and this is what any treatment of psychosis should avoid in order to not "toil at the oars when one's ship is stuck in the sand" (Lacan 2006c: 485).

To avoid both the Master's solution that locks up and devalues the madman and the idealist's appeal to an unsoundable and phantasmatic freedom, psychoanalysts must find a third approach. Freud's determinism and Lacan's genealogic (three generations) and structural (Borromean) causality indicate the path to follow, a path of not turning back in the face of madness.

There is no escape for the psychotic. For the one who never chooses anything, there is no possibility of a manageable, operative entry and exit for language transactions, whose model would be the alternation of sleep and wakefulness. The estrangement from the signifying chain is a consequence of a flaw in the subjective structure. The psychotic places himself, and is placed, outside the ring of discourse.

One difficulty appears when one writes in a general manner about psychosis: the tendency is to use a global model that would apply to all psychotic patients, despite the fact that this general model is rarely confirmed in particular cases. There are no full time psychotics. This is how "psychosis" and "psychotic" become schematic labels that steer the clinician and the reader off track, instead of orienting them in the process. At the end of his life, Freud was quite aware of this. In *An Outline of Psychoanalysis* (1940 [1938]) Freud wrote:

> The problem of psychoses would be simple and intelligible if the withdrawal of the ego from reality could be carried through completely. But that seems rarely if ever to happen. . . . We may probably take it as being generally true that what occurs in all such cases is a *split* in the mind. Two mental attitudes have been formed instead of a single one— one, the normal one, which takes account of reality, and another which under the influence of the instincts detaches the ego from reality.
>
> (Freud 1940: 76)

This *Spaltung* between two simultaneous subjective positions has to be taken into account.

The Lacanian definition of discourse as a social link among bodies inhabited by language is the essential conduit to the psychoanalytic concept of subjective position. A subjective position is always one of a kind, in particular when speaking of the psychoses. The definition "a signifier is that which represents as subject for another signifier" (Lacan 1981: 207), found in the Master's discourse, is incomplete without the surplus of the object *a*, a fugitive Real that escapes the discursive articulation of S1 and S2.

The subject ($) is in the position of truth. The general formula of the discourses is

$$\frac{\text{agent}}{\text{truth}} \rightarrow \frac{\text{other}}{\text{production}} \text{ which is read in the discourse of the Master as: } \frac{S\,1}{\$} \rightarrow \frac{S\,2}{a}$$

In between truth and production, as the necessary missed encounter between the two elements, $ // *a*, the cut marks a disjunction. The subject is separated from the object, which is a surplus jouissance and the cause of his desire. This condition is proper to the neurotic, the so called "normal." Once the places in the four terms in the formula of the discourse of the Master are occupied, the cut or disjunction between the subject and the object *a* becomes evident, and we read the formula of fantasy; the cut becomes the lozenge or diamond: $ ◇ *a*.

How can we apply this formula to the understanding of psychosis? Already in Seminar XI (1964), years before producing the mathemes of the four discourses, Lacan stated that the key was found in the link (*liaison*) between two signifiers, in the interval that separates them, "for (*pour*) another signifier" in the well-known definition of the subject. The S1 does not represent the subject before the S2, either because there is no differentiation between both signifiers, or because the syntactic articulation that would link them is broken. This is the effect of foreclosure.

Discourse produces a fugitive remainder of jouissance—the object *a*, which is inaccessible to the subject. The function of speech and discourse are radically perturbed in psychosis because the agglutination into one signifier (holophrase) or the disarticulation of two signifiers produces a structural flaw in the constitution of the fantasy. This disturbs the relation between the subject $ and the object cause of his desire *a*. Psychosis is a process affecting the signifying interval between S1 and S2. It affects the interval in the matheme of the fantasy, where the lozenge ◇ makes fantasy possible. The lozenge stands for the conjunction and disjunction of subject and object. Lacan spoke about this in three different ways: as a cut, as the unconscious, and as desire. These three modalities fail in psychosis. One could say that the lozenge is broken or absent, and that is the reason there is no fantasy or that the term "fantasy" would have to be redefined if we were to sustain the uncertain syntagm of "psychotic fantasy." The paths of desire and fantasy are defenses against jouissance, closed off for the psychotic. The third defense, pleasure, is experienced as a jouissance without limits, an inescapable, invasive, deleterious jouissance.

The function of fantasy is to sustain a healthy distance between the subject and the object cause of desire. This space produces an excess to phallic jouissance (a surplus), or jouissance as object. Thanks to fantasy, the subject is protected in his rapport with the Other's jouissance; the subject is kept outside it. The lozenge in the formula is equivalent to an image of the glass of a window in a shop (or a mirror) that would separate the subject from the desired and forbidden object. Psychosis is a fracture in the crystal, a juncture where the subject is exposed to jouissance and finds himself besieged and torn apart by it.

Let us return to the matheme of the Master's discourse, that of the definition of the signifier discussed above, to illuminate the anomalous situation we find in psychosis:

S1 and S2 are amalgamated in an indistinguishable mass, agglutinated, in what Lacan defined as holophrase.[6] This merging can be observed not only in psychosis, but also in mental retardation and psychosomatic conditions that can be characterized as falling within a "psychotic dimension." There, the couple of signifiers is petrified, the S1 is repeated without producing meaning, and S1 and S2 are unarticulated, lacking syntax, inevitably and definitively separated from each other. In both cases, discourse as a social link cannot exist. Taking the matrix of the Master's discourse, we can pose the relation of the psychotic to speech as:

$$\frac{S1}{\$} \quad \diamond \quad \frac{S2}{a}$$

In the above, the lozenge has been displaced to the relation between S1 and S2. The cut between subject and object, the barrier that kept them apart and encouraged the imaginary of a search for an ulterior rediscovery, is gone.[7] There is a double break in psychosis: of one signifier with another, and of fantasy as a barrier against jouissance. There is also a double clinical effect: the interruption of the intersubjective dialectic and an uncontrolled invasion of the Other's jouissance, which is not subjected to phallic regulation or to the Law that orders desire. In psychosis, the hallucination substitutes desire and fantasy.

The metaphor of the Name-of-the-Father allows for the linking of the signifiers (S1 → S2) and produces an effect of signification linking signifier and signified. Its failure makes the S1 lack meaning in the phrase that could receive it, retroactively, from the S2. In such a situation, the signifier loses its symbolic dimension and, as Freud intelligently anticipated, the word-representation is real and cannot be distinguished from the thing-representation. The Real appears without the buffering of speech; the hallucination is its clinical manifestation. This is madness. The delusion is an attempt at a metaphor to make sense of the chaos of dissociated signifiers. Without it, we only have the harassment heard incessantly, the litany, the verbal stereotypes, the syllabic perseverance, and the allocutions without interval—in other words, the holophrase.

We are left with an either/or: either jouissance, which is proper to madness, or discourse, which is proper to the subject. Lacan spoke of a "subject of jouissance" only twice. The "subject of jouissance" is a strange syntagm, because "[i]f the subject is not divided, he is mad," as Lacan said with glaring clarity in 1958 (1998: 433). He used this syntagm first in 1963 (Lacan 2004: 203), when he proposed a mythical beginning that culminated in subjective division (a formula of subjective division and causation), and second in 1966, when he presented the publication of the French translation of the memoirs of Schreber (Lacan 2001a: 215). He referred then to the polarity between the "subject of jouissance" and the divided subject, who is represented by a signifier for another signifier.

Foreclosure operates on the relation of the signifier of the Name-of-the-Father with the rest of the chain. Unmoored, the speaking being aimlessly roams the discourses, dependent on the Other's response, trying to signify himself in his own speech, in existence. This is why for the psychotic, insofar as psychotic (and neither "full time" or completely), the word is not a symbol: it is not an invitation for exchange; it does not work as a diaphragm to filter and regulate jouissance.

The signifier represents the subject who is not psychotic. The subject is in the place of meaning; he is what is meant; he is what is signified for (*pour*) another signifier, by/next to another (*auprès d'un autre*). Of course, this is never completely accomplished, because there is always a remainder: the object *a*. In psychosis, the articulation with the second signifier is missing. A signifier replaces the subject completely; it does not represent him. This signifier does not need to conjugate with another; there is a coalescence of signifier and subject (meaning). There is not an inassimilable remainder, a residue of the operation. The psychotic is invaded by a jouissance from which the common, "sane" person is excluded. Words are things for the psychotic. In psychosis, there is an S1 that represents the subject in an absolute manner, without remedy, remission or any symbolization of lack. This is why, let me insist, we speak of psychotic jouissance and not of psychotic desire. There is no lack that would put discourse into motion.

The psychotic cannot maintain his distance from jouissance; he identifies with his jouissance. He is jouissance. In this regard, the hallucination is not an individual's perception. There is no distinction between *perceptum* and *percipiens*. Since the lozenge that distances the subject of jouissance from the object *a* is missing, there is a condensation between the two terms of the fantasy: the subject and object are conglomerated. We should think of a word analogous to "holophrase" to designate this coalescence between $ and *a*, of which the most conspicuous example is the hallucination. In the subject's perception, there is an object that can be subjected to the Freudian "reality testing." In the hallucination, however, the subject is confused and fused with his object. They are not two but rather one; they do not maintain a relation of reciprocal exteriority.

In psychosis, jouissance is not localized in a bodily region. Not contained or limited by the phallic signifier (φ), the representative of what is lacking of the desired image in the body, it invades the body entirely. Transformed into a screen, where the most horrifying metamorphoses are projected, the subject is astonished and reduced to being the passive stage of transformations that obey the obscure will of an omniscient Other, who regulates the organic happenings. Influence, hypochondria, command hallucinations, persecution, magnetism, irradiations, transsexualism, *pousse à la femme*, negation, putrefaction, and cadaverization of a body where no will but the Other's reigns are all like the will governing the flesh of President Schreber for centuries to come.

Before, after, and in lieu of: these are the three temporal and spatial vectors along which jouissance[8] deploys itself facing speech in its rapport with the Other. We situate the jouissance of the psychotic before speech, as we have seen, but not beyond language. There is indeed a mythical jouissance of being posited at the beginning, anterior to the entrance into the world of exchanges inherent to life itself. This mythical jouissance is unable to sustain its life without appealing to the Other as capable of satisfying needs and demands. This jouissance of being, screaming and senseless, precedes the existence of the subject and of the ego. This is the jouissance of the flesh thrown (*geworfen*) into the world.[9] It precedes the imaginary and symbolic representation of the body.

But also after speech: in the speaking being (*parlêtre*), jouissance must go through customs, passing through the flexible diaphragm of the speech that doses it out, subjecting it to phallic signification. Through the palliative force of speech, the subject can traverse the barriers of narcissism and the pleasure principle so that the drive historicizes and inscribes the subject, marking her passage into the world. Speech allows the subject to leave an imprint on the Other, who is ready to receive her baggage.

In lieu of speech, instead of speech: as the underside of speech, jouissance appears in the neurotic symptom in its perverse staging, under the banner of the supposedly strong ego. There jouissance flaunts itself as a curse, while not quite in speech; it is pure being, prior to the fall of man that resulted from his using speech. This incommunicable jouissance independent of the Other escapes symbolization and lodges in the body. This is the material used by the psychotic to express himself or herself without an addressee. For psychotics, speech does not function as a regulating diaphragm; they are inundated and displaced by a jouissance resistant to exchange. This jouissance proliferates so invasively that it does not allow for speech or for the other, thus preventing the Other or the semblant from containing and limiting it.

The imaginary Phallus Φ (capitalized, impossible to negativize) is the signifier of the jouissance interdicted from the speaking being. Not yet symbolized, the body has not yet been emptied of jouissance. Since lack in being has not been installed, the subject is not yet desiring. This is why psychoanalysts should never speak of psychotic desire. Without the space for this fertile lack, without the realization of the imaginary function of castration $(-\varphi)$, there is nothing to look for, or to expect as a response, in the field of the Other.

The Phallus does not fulfill its function of signifier per se, except through another signifier, the Name-of-the-Father. It allows for the establishment of a foundational pivot: the S1 to which the S2 of unconscious knowledge can be linked. The Phallus cancels out the Thing, allowing for the emergence of the subject as represented by the Name-of-the-Father.[10] If the stem of the Name-of-the-Father is missing, the branches break loose; there is no tree or root system to hold them. This quick approximation of the notion of "foreclosure"[11] is key to understanding psychosis. There is no limit to jouissance, no spigot able to bear the pouring speech that spills every which way without a container. The localized and temporal absence of a signifier of the Law leaves the subject at a loss, deprived of the identifying references that would allow him to navigate the world.

Another effect of the non-regulation of jouissance is that, lacking the paternal orientation of the superego and the inheritance of the Oedipus complex, the psychotic cannot be guided towards a woman, as promised and possible. Unstoppable and incoercible, the obscene and ferocious order of the maternal, Kleinian, and archaic superego commands an impossible "Enjoy!"—the unlimited jouissance of the Thing before castration.

His defective integration into the Symbolic order makes distance from the Real impossible. This produces a complete disorganization of the Imaginary of the body. Over this background of fragmentation, over this radical disturbance of existence, the restitutive function of the delusion tries to link the subject to the signifying chain and account for his lived experience. The whole of the psychotic adventure results from this dispersion of signifiers that are left unrelated to the social link. The delusional metaphor attempts to remedy the failure in the paternal metaphor, bestowing meaning on the lack in the Other. It tries to return the subject to the network of social relations, restoring the link between the *Bindung* of jouissance and speech.

What I have summarized in these pages corresponds to the later revision of Lacan's thoughts on the relations between jouissance and speech. Such revision raises many questions. It is not a coincidence that Lacan presented the theory of the paternal metaphor and the "foreclosure" of the Name-of-the-Father as the essence of psychosis in January 1958, some time after finishing his Seminar III on "The Psychoses," and introducing the theme of jouissance in March of that year. The development of the concept of "jouissance" forced him to rethink the issue of madness, reworking the theses centered on disturbances in the organization of signification. The "desire of the Mother" that had to be substituted for the "Name-of-the-Father" to save the subject from psychosis had to account in theory and practice for the enigmatic "jouissance of the Other," that real substance that subsists, resisting dissolution into the relations between signifier and signifier. The quotient that is impossible to settle in language exchanges will be transformed into the object *a*.

Finally, with the later introduction of jouissance, the strict distinction between neurosis and diverse forms of madness was impugned every time surplus jouissance appeared outside speech in every motion of the drive. The frontiers of madness became blurred, forcing a "nosological revision" (Lacan 1965). Lacan wonders whether Joyce can be called mad or not. He adds that "to be mad is not a privilege." He also says that "for most people the Symbolic, the Imaginary, and the Real are entangled to the point that they bleed into each other for want of an operation that would distinguish them as in the Borromean knot" (Lacan 2005: 87). Besides highlighting the evident (that Schreber had managed to become a distinguished jurist while suffering a dormant psychosis that was triggered when he was well into his forties; that Joyce was able to navigate all his life making of writing a "supplement of the Name-of-the-Father," not because that signifier was foreclosed in the symbolic but because it was de facto foreclosed), Lacan states that madness remains within the horizon of all speaking beings. Madness lurks in the constitutive amalgam of jouissance and the signifier.

To conclude more simply and radically, we can say that madness is a transitory disruption of the relationship of the subject and the other. Madness is a separation, an interruption of the social link. It is in this sense that even if one cannot choose madness, a madman is the "last free man," who has been freed from the restrictions imposed by shared conventions. Yet such separation is never complete or definitive; mad subjects never lose all their bonds to reality, at least to the Other's reality. The responsibility of psychiatrists or psychoanalysts is then to place themselves on the psychotics' side, to try and see things from their perspective and not from the perspective of cultural, familial, and political demands and social expectations. Such demands and expectations include the manual of psychiatric diagnostic standards, and concerns all the "norms" corresponding to the abstract construction of this fiction called the "common" or "normal" person. If madness asserts the impossibility or the rejection of life in the world of others, it is also a call to be heard, an appeal to be understood in a singular position.

Notes

1 This is one of the few times in which Lacan employs the term "normal" without irony—but not without reservations: "the minimal number of fundamental points of insertion between the signifier and the signified necessary for a human being *to be called normal*, and which, when they are not established, or when they give way, make a psychotic" (Lacan 1985: 304) (italics mine).

2 The aporias of the ideology of free choice are addressed by R. Salecl in *Choice* (2010).

3 Editors' note: In Bruce Fink's translation, *unsondable* (unfathomable) is rendered as "unsoundable."

4 Or with the access denied by the guardian of the door, as in Franz Kafka's emblematic story "Before the Law."

5 Dolto's thesis differs from that of Maud Manonni, who linked infantile psychosis uniquely with the parent's fantasy.

6 The concept of holophrase appears quite early in Lacan's work; it is already mentioned in his first seminar in 1954. In linguistics, holophrase refers to the use of one word to express a whole phrase. In Lacan's last reference to this concept (1964: 215), he talks about the absence of connection between one signifier and another, that is, a dissolution of the signifying chain that prevents the subject form being present in discourse. He is thus placed outside discourse in a situation we call *a-diction*, which we can observe in psychosis, mental retardation, and in psychosomatic phenomena. See the remarkable work of Stevens (1987) on this subject.

7 Such was the fantasy ($ ◇ a) as a response to desire in the graph of "Subversion of the Subject and Dialectic of Desire."

8 To give a succinct definition, we will say that jouissance is the sum of the incidences in the body resulting from the effect of the encounter with language. As Lacan says in *Seminar XX Encore* (1998: 55): "there is not an other apparatus than language. That is how jouissance is fitted out [*appareillée*] in speaking beings . . . language is . . . the

apparatus of jouissance." One could also say that the subject is a battlefield whe
enjoying (living) body confronts the world in which the Other of language reig
9 The reader versed in German may have already thought of the relationship be
    the condition of throwness into the world, *geworfen*, Heidegger's use of the noun
    Geworfenheit, and the concept of *Verwerfung* (rejection, repudiation), a term highlighted
    by Lacan in Freud that we will translate, accepting that it is a psychoanalytic neologism,
    as "foreclosure."
10 See Braunstein (1990/2006; 2005: 78–93).
11 On the essential notion of foreclosure see Maleval (2000), Rabinovitch (1998) and Porge
    (1997).

Bibliography

Braunstein, N.A. (1990; 2nd edn 2006) *El goce. Un concepto lacaniano*, Mexico: Siglo
    XXI, (2006) Buenos Aires: Siglo XXI [Available in French as *La jouissance. Un concept
    Lacanien*. Ramonville: Erès].

——— (2007) "Le concept de semblant chez Lacan," in *Depuis Freud, Après Lacan*,
    Ramonville: Erès.

Dolto, F. (1971) *Le cas Dominique*, Paris: Seuil.

Freud, S. (1940). "An Outline of Psychoanalysis," *International Journal of Psycho-Analysis*,
    21: 27–84.

Kristeva, J. (1979) "Le vréel," in *Folle vérité: Vérité et vraisemblance du texte psychotique*,
    Paris: Editions du Seuil.

——— (1985) *Loca verdad. Verdad y verosimilitud del texto psicótico*, trans. M. Caparros
    Madrid: Fundamentos.

Lacan, J. (1946) "Propos sur la causalité psychique." Reprinted in *Écrits*, trans. B. Fink
    (2006a), Paris: Seuil.

——— (1953) "Fonction et champ de la parole et du langage en psychanalyse." Reprinted
    in *Écrits*, trans. B. Fink (2006b), Paris: Seuil.

——— (1956; 3rd edn 1985) *Le Séminaire. Livre III. Les psychoses*, Paris: Seuil.

——— (1958; 2nd edn 1998) *Le Séminaire. Livre V. Les formations del l'inconscient*, Paris:
    Seuil.

——— (1959) "D'une question préliminaire à tout traitement possible de la psychose."
    Reprinted in *Écrits*, trans. B. Fink (2006c), Paris: Seuil.

——— (1963; 2nd edn 2004) *Le Séminaire. Livre X. L'angoisse*, Paris: Seuil.

——— (1964; 2nd edn 1973) *Le Séminaire. Livre XI. Les quatre concepts fondamentaux
    de la psychanalyse*, Paris: Seuil.

——— (1965) "La science et la vérité." Reprinted in *Écrits*, trans. B. Fink (2006d), Paris:
    Seuil.

——— (1965) *Le Séminaire. Livre XII. Problèmes cruciaux de la psychanalyse* (Unpub-
    lished).

——— (1966) "Présentation de la traduction de P. Duquenne des Mémoires d'un névropathe
    de D. P. Schreber." Reprinted in *Autres écrits* (2001a), Paris: Seuil.

——— (1967) "Petit discours aux psychiatres," speech delivered at the Cercle d'Études
    directed by Henry Ey, 10 November 1967. Online. Available http://www.ecole-lacanienne.
    net/pastoutlacan60.php (accessed 28 August 2013).

——— (1981) "Seminar XI," in *The Four Fundamental Concepts of Psychoanalysis*, trans.
    A. Sheridan, New York: W.W. Norton & Company.

—— (2001) "Allocution sure les psychoses de l'enfance," in *Autres écrits*, Paris: Seuil.

—— (2005) *Le Séminaire. Livre XXIII. Le sinthome 1975–1976*, Paris: Seuil.

Maleval, J.-C. (2000) *La forclusion du nom-du père. Le concept et sa clinique*, Paris: Seuil.

Porge, E. (1997) *Les noms-du-père chez Jacques Lacan*, Ramonville: Erès.

Rabinovitch, S. (1998) *La forclusion. Enfermés dehors*, Ramonville: Erès.

Salecl, R. (2010) *Choice*, London: Profile Books.

Stevens, A. (1987) "L'holophrase entre psychose et psychosomatique," *Ornicar?* 42: 44–71.

7

TREATMENT OF THE PSYCHOSES AND CONTEMPORARY PSYCHOANALYSIS

Jean-Claude Maleval

Today, psychiatric practice finds itself split between two modalities of clinical procedure. The first is blinded by psychopharmacology as a cure-all and the second is crumbling to pieces as a result of the latest DSM. The hoped-for moment when the coming together of each of these two clinical paths would finally take place, when each syndrome would find its "partner molecule," has continued to evade us.

Psychopharmacological clinical work functions by trial and error, attending to the effects of each prescription on the patient. From the discovery of neuroleptics, anti-depressants, and anxiolytics, one can presumably "deduce" the existence of psychotic, depressive, or anxious patients. Such a clinical approach doesn't have much use for the semiological knowledge garnered by classical psychiatry since it is only the authority of the drug that matters for this sort of work. It can, at most, pick and choose little tidbits of older clinical knowledge all the while remaining totally indifferent to the formal envelope of the symptom.[1] For instance, if the anti-depressants aid the disappearance of patients' complaints, it is because, according to this "logic," the subject was "depressed without knowing it." Ergo, we invent "masked depression," often called "cheerful" or "smiling" depression, while the Freudian notion of conversion is relegated to the clinical garbage can.

The last DSM did not completely ignore the gains made by classical psychiatry, since it initially used them to invent its principle syndromes. However, by trying to objectivize them, to render the knowledge of them statistically relevant and reliable, it ignored the data about the dynamics of the "disorder." The rich observations made at the end of the nineteenth century, for example, on the stages of the evolution of chronic delirium, would be lost (Maleval 2011). Aiming to reduce the clinical criteria to a few simple traits to obtain a "true evaluative diagnosis," we arrive at a veritable decomposition of the psychiatric clinic by way of an exponential increase in syndromes, difficulties, and disorders. We note 106 such disorders in DSM-I; 182 in DSM-II; with DSM III there are already 265;

we find 292 in the DSM-III-R; and in the DSM-IV we see a jump to 392. The DSM-IV-R operates on a significant new advance: being able to distinguish 542 disorders.[2] The logic of this approach aims for a standardized precision that the singularity of the subject continues to resist. This accounts for the persistent multiplication of the syndromes, ad infinitum. In amplifying the DSM, we will only end up with more and more diversified descriptions of the modalities of the human subject's jouissance. This quest for formulaic diagnostic rigor results in failure, since as we continue to enlarge the field of mental disorders, we blur the distinction between normal and pathological, ultimately dissolving any real or useful concept of mental illness.

Long before the publication of the DSM in the 1950s, the eminent psychiatrist Eugene Minkowski clearly discerned the consequences of a clinical practice centered on isolating symptoms:

> There is hallucination and hallucination, just like there is anxiety and anxiety. Separated from its lived context, the isolated and generalized symptom [is already] excessively, an "abstraction." In this sense, it is placed automatically in terms of a neurological perspective, while in reality, it draws its signification in the mental depths it stems from [. . .]. It's obvious [. . .] that maniacal euphoria, paralytic euphoria, and the beatific euphoria of the idiot are not the same [despite all having the name euphoria]. It is the mental depths, [what Minkowski calls the "mental fundament"], that is the most important. It is the same for anxiety and depression, and in reality, for all symptoms [. . .]. Psychopathology arises from the symptom, but the various mental fundament, is characterized by structure. It is thus closer to the syndrome than to the symptom. However, the syndrome is not necessarily the appropriate term to speak of the mental fundament and its dynamism.
>
> (Minkowski 1997: 150)

The clinical approaches of modern psychiatry based on the DSM, as well as that of medication concerned with the objectivization of disorders, impose an epistemic reduction that is quite costly for the patient. This cost concerns what Minkowski named the "mental fundament and its dynamics"—in other words, the subjective dimension, the subject's desire and his demands.

Psychoanalysis advocates a different clinical approach, which stems from the classical psychiatric clinic. Contemporary psychoanalysis has become the heir apparent to the treasure trove of clinical knowledge gathered between 1860 and 1930. This seminal work began with the brilliance of Jean-Pierre Falret (1794–1870), who passed the flame to Gaétan de Clérambault (1872–1934), whose work was then codified by Emil Kraepelin (1856–1926). Psychoanalysis has kept this heritage alive, enriching it with new observations and adding a dynamic dimension by introducing the notion of transference. As a result, since 1950, many psycho-analysts have ceased to doubt the ability of psychotic patients to enter into a transference relationship, but they continue to debate how to best manage it. A decisive step was taken in the 1980s with the hypothesis of the foreclosure of the Name-of-the-Father, affecting the direction of the cure. Since then, many psychoanalytic treatments have demonstrated the possibility of relying on the psychotic subject's capacity for invention as a way of treating his suffering. Two major points at the turn of the twentieth century were responsible for the future of psychoanalytic work with psychotic patients. The first of these was the continuing compilation of symptoms and modes of functioning. Second, we have learned, and the subsequent analyses of psychotic patients have shown, that it is more beneficial to wager on the psychotic subject's capacity for invention than to think of him as someone suffering from a deficit.

Freud essentially adopted Kraepelin's nosology. "It is certain," noted Jacques-Alain Miller in 1979, "that we have to use the language that the psychiatric clinic has handed down to us, to the extent that Lacan could say: in fact, it is the only clinic that we have" (Miller 1979: 244). However, the power of this clinical knowledge has diminished, having lost its dynamism in the 1930s. "In the last 30 years," Lacan told his audience in 1967, "there hasn't been any discovery in psychiatry concerning its rapport with the madman, not the slightest clinical modification, no contribution whatsoever. We are left with the beautiful tradition of the nineteenth century; all we have since are a few touch-ups by Clérambault" (Lacan 1967). Obviously, we could note a few minor discoveries after de Clérambault: Kanner's autism (1943), Asperger's syndrome (1944), transsexualism (1949), Munchausen's syndrome (1951), typus melancholicus (1961), Ferjol's syndrome (1967), and Munchausen by proxy (1977). Notwithstanding appearances, this list seems to confirm that classical psychiatry approaches its own internal limit when we observe that only two of the discoveries just listed are due to the work of a psychiatrist (Kanner, Tellenbach); all the others are credited to non-psychiatrists and endocrinologists (H. Benjamin), a hematologist (J. Bernard), an internist (R. Asher) and two pediatricians (H. Asperger, R. Meadow).[3] Since the 1980s, the classical clinic has been fragmented in a mini-syndrome format with nothing solid to sustain it.

Psychoanalysis proposes a new clinical practice: treatment under transference. It can only succeed by introducing the presence of the analyst as a surrogate for the Other. The psychoanalytic clinic is able to note three structures: neurotic, perverse, and psychotic. These structures introduce the dynamic of desire into these fixed nosologies. "There are of course phenomena that resist transference," Miller notes:

> But it allows a scientific or para-scientific knowledge that is much more refined than what is obtained by pharmacological substance use. This use erodes phenomena; they disappear without ever having been understood, confusing very different symptoms—for example, under the name of "depression." The differentiation that allows for psychoanalysis is incomparably more powerful. I am sure that in the United States, an

impressive number of hysterical women are treated as schizophrenics. The first thing that American feminism ought to do is to carry the militant movement towards re-establishing the diagnosis of hysterical neurosis.

(Etchegoyen and Miller 1996: 24)

In short, Miller continues today, "Psychiatry says to molecular biology: 'I love you!' and it answers back, 'Die!' We psychoanalysts are the true friends of psychiatry. If psychiatry would cut itself from its roots and cease to pay meticulous attention to what Lacan calls, 'the formal envelope of the symptom,' it would be lost" (Etchegoyen and Miller 1996: 19).

Today's psychiatric clinic, championing the argument that all the manifestations of the madman are classifiable, has become incompatible with the experience of psychoanalysts. If Freud makes of the *Memoirs of President Schreber* a Freudian text, it is because he introduces the notion of the subject. This means that he does not evaluate the madman in terms of a deficit or a dissociation of functions; a simple reading of Freud's text shows that nothing of the sort is relevant in this case (Lacan 1966: 70). Contrary to the opinion of many clinicians and of most Freudian analysts, the psychoses are not a failure of thought. The philosopher Jean-Jacques Rousseau, the physicist and founder of thermodynamics Julius von Mayer, the mathematician and founder of non-Euclidian geometry János Bolyai, the founder of sociology Auguste Comte and many others would attest to the fact that delirium is compatible with very high functioning intellectual faculties. Those who advocate an approach to psychosis that concerns "deficiency" usually object to the theoretical concept of foreclosure of the Name-of-the-Father and risk stigmatizing the psychotic by emphasizing what is missing. What a proper approach really concerns is a dynamic concept that places the emphasis on the psychotic's creative resources, and opens new possibilities for the treatment while freeing the subjective capacity to supplement (*suppléances*).[4] The flaw in the Symbolic that the psychotic bears no more interferes with thought than does the neurotic's repression or the pervert's disavowal. The flaw in the Symbolic no more precludes the psychotic subject's position from being modified and elaborated in analytic treatment than it would with a neurotic subject.

For some time, the notion of the foreclosure of the Name-of-the-Father more set up barriers to the treatment of psychotics than opened new perspectives. Let's recall that although he told us not to recoil before psychosis, Lacan also advocated an attitude of prudence in its treatment. His rare technical indications pertain largely to what the clinician should avoid doing: one should not authenticate the Imaginary, not interpret homosexuality, not make meaning resonate, and not demand that the subject lie down on the couch. He could see in the "Preliminary Question" that a specific maneuvering of transference would have to be invented to guide the cure of psychotics, but he himself was not able to design it in advance. For the next thirty years, from the 1950s to the 1970s, Lacanian works were rarely concerned with the treatment of psychotic adults. It is logical, then, that the main principle in the research produced on this theme in the Freudian school of Paris was dedicated to institutional psychotherapy (Jean Oury, Ginette Michaux) and not to individual cures. In the Freudian Field Collection directed by Lacan (1964–81), no one was able to surpass Lacan's formulations in "A Question Preliminary to Any Possible Treatment of Psychosis": no work was dedicated to it. We also note that the only published work in this field, *Psychiatry and Anti-Psychiatry*, came from someone who was not a member of the Freudian school of Paris, David Cooper. This research gives no credit to the analytic cure, but it demonstrates the benefits of an institutional approach without medication of subjects said to be schizophrenics (Cooper 1970). Lacan only once alluded to work from outside his school in his collection (*Champ Lacanian*), in reference to the treatment of psychotic patients. This has left a hole in his teaching, revealing a heuristic lack in his conceptualization of the 1950s.

Insofar as the hypothesis of the foreclosure of the Name-of-the-Father (Maleval 2000) prevented the opening of a new orientation to treat psychotics, those who followed Lacan were tempted to dress up antiquated practices in a new vocabulary. In the 1970s, some of them affirmed that one must analyze the "foreclosed desire" of psychotic children; these include, for instance, Françoise Dolto (1971: 249). Others considered that one must trust the possible hystericization of psychosis —for instance, Maud Mannoni (1979: 133). These analysts conceived foreclosure as a modality of repression, certainly more profound, but analyzable in the classical manner. In 1956, Lacan already warned against a "fundamental Imaginary" that is too widespread. He said that "there is something that must communicate between neurosis and psychosis, between the pre-conscious and the unconscious in a way that would 'push, nibble,' and be able to 'break through the fortification'" (Lacan 1981: 187).

The concept of the foreclosure of the Name-of-the-Father nevertheless allowed for certain diminished functions observed in psychotics in treatment to become more precise. It was not through new therapeutic perspectives that this arose; Lacan was betting on his new work in 1967. He thought a new approach would emerge due to his research and he named this "an other centering" (Lacan 1967). Lacan progressively put in place the possibility of "an other centering" through scattered notations, all of them post-1964, no longer stemming from the logic of the signifier but founded on the axiom of jouissance. He situates the psychotic as a subject who is out of discourse, who is invaded by a deregulated jouissance the major utterances (*enoncés*) of which are "holophrased,"[5] and who is therefore at risk of developing an erotomanic transference. In 1958, he had already affirmed that when the subject is no longer divided, "he is mad."[6] He resumes this line of thought in his final research, highlighting the fact that it is not only in the field of the signifier that the schism of the subject has failed. Now, he will place the accent on the invasion of a deregulated jouissance. The psychotic has the object in his pocket, he adds in 1967; that is why the voice tends to sonorize in verbal hallucinations and the gaze tends to present in the feeling of being watched. Moreover, the psychotic subject presents a paradoxical normality in the sense that his major difficulty demonstrates the primacy of the discourse of Other, which is manifested in a mental automatism that exposes the neurotic illusion that we speak for ourselves when, in fact, we are spoken. "Mental automatism is normal" says Lacan in 1977 (1979: 22). Automatism is a rejection of the unconscious, conceived of as something that lends itself to interpretation. We must add a difficulty inherent to the transference. Here the mortifying erotomania hardly hides the presence of the Other's jouissance, an Other who is always inclined to make the psychotic his thing. This is where we locate the risk in the transferential relation to the analyst (reported by Lacan in "On a Question Preliminary to Any Possible Treatment of Psychosis"), which can precipitate an outbreak of the psychosis (Lacan 2006: 582), constituting the clinician as the persecutor.

His varied teachings pertaining to the psychotic's modality of jouissance nevertheless maintained a great coherence. Each of them proved the result of the same process: the non-extraction of the object places the subject outside of discourse; this lack of a barrier to jouissance predisposes the psychotic to be subjected to the Other's jouissance.

The new approach to psychosis through jouissance does not seem to open therapeutic perspectives further. On the contrary, they seem to augment the obstacles already encountered; they underline the difficulties inherent in the transferential relation, block the interpretation of the delusion, and situate the subject outside of discourse. However, they no longer place the accent on the unchaining of the signifier but on the invasion of jouissance, the very one that Schreber attested to with extraordinary precision. He writes, "An excess of voluptuousness will render man unfit to fulfill his other obligations: [. . .] God demands *constant enjoyment*" (Schreber 2000: 249–50). God demanded to see Schreber as both man and woman, as a unique person, in order to have intercourse with himself. God demanded a constant state of jouissance.

In exposing the implications of the deregulation of jouissance, in 1967, Lacan was able to elaborate the concept of "the other centering" that he hoped would overcome the challenges stated in the essay "On a Question Preliminary to Any Possible Treatment of Psychosis." However, he did not realize the implications of this for the direction of the cure. If one accepts the thesis that ultimately it is the invasion of jouissance that the psychotic subject suffers from, does it not make sense that the analysis should oppose it? Michel Silvestre was the first to draw this conclusion during the years following Lacan's death. "If in his initial request," he writes in 1984, "the psychotic expects signifiers from the analyst able to organize the upheavals of his world, in his second request, the transferential one, the psychotic offers his jouissance to the analyst so that the analyst will regulate it" (Silvestre 1984: 55).

In the 1980s, following the establishment of these fundamental orientations, many psychoanalytic treatments of psychotics, conducted by analysts of the Ecole de la Cause Freudienne, confirmed this to be effective. When the psychotic subject addresses himself to the psychoanalyst, he first asks for help to bring order to his world and supposes that the physician knows better than he does how to go about it. At the same time, the psychotic affirms that he possesses certain knowledge, transmitted to him by the elementary phenomena at the onset of the triggering that he was witness to without his consent. "What the psychotic wants to affirm," claims Briole, "is on the order of an affirmation that does not leave room for any doubt, nor does it allow for dialectic—at least not at first. The psychoanalyst can only be the witness to the psychotic's experience of victimization, wherein he is unable to act. The analyst can't do anything about it either. And in the end, the psychotic doesn't ask him to do anything about it—and even, if one really listens well, the psychotic will warn the analyst not to get mixed up in it" (Briole 2006: 7). Indeed, to answer the request to structure the psychotic's invasive jouissance with a pre-fabricated knowledge tends to mobilize the mortifying erotomania rather than hinder it. It is in acting against the delocalized jouissance that the psychotic transference will actually be appeased. The resulting feelings of persecution are effectively counter-balanced by transference love; the treatment can continue, even until the dissolution of the transferential bond. In the case of neurosis, the analysand addresses the analyst insofar as he is supposed to know. In the case of psychosis, the analysand presents a certitude with which he tries to interest the analyst.

Since the 1950s, all psychoanalysts have agreed that psychotic subjects are able to develop massive fusional and ambivalent transferential relations. Federn (1952) and Rosenfeld (1967) proposed naming this "transference psychosis." At the end of the day, it is nothing but an extension of the transference neurosis in the field of psychosis bringing about a concept of psychosis on the model of acute neurosis and the postulate of the existence of a psychotic core in neurosis itself. The decisive division between neurosis and psychosis, the foreclosure of the Name-of-the-Father, challenges the concept of transference psychosis with a new concept that we can designate by a more precise term: "erotomaniacal transference."

In 1967, the concept of erotomaniacal transference was introduced. This term indicates a certain inversion of the protagonists in comparison to what we observe in the transference of neurotics. Such erotomania shows the feeling that the psychotic subject experiences as the object of the clinician's love, but it is a cumbersome love and cannot be compared to the transference love of the neurotic. This phenomenon, Freud affirms, is not actually an avatar of love; it cannot be mistaken with the erotomaniacal test imposed on the psychotic during which he sees himself as the object incurring the abuse of the malicious Other. The erotomania shows that psychotic transference tends to articulate itself within the web of the delusion. Erotomania, according to the classics, is characterized by an assumption: the absolute knowledge of being loved, often by an eminent person, one who took the initiative. We know that this delusion goes through several phases: from hope to rancor. Erotomaniacal transference does not take place in every treatment of a psychotic; as a paranoicizing relation, it can often remain quite temperate. We nevertheless note a downward slope of the subject's relation to the Other that must be countered, in both the cure and in its direction. Failing to construct a fundamental fantasy, the psychotic subject finds himself in a rapport of intimate proximity with the Other of jouissance. What marks the psychotic structure within the analytic treatment under transference is the propensity of the subject to answer with a sacrifice of himself that he supposes is expected by the Other. Auto-mutilation and suicide, as well as many failures including alcoholism, substance abuse, and other existential problems, can be resorted to in this regard. Moreover, the specular relation to the semblant excites the subject to carry out this sacrifice through others with whom he identifies.

To establish the dynamic of the cure, many psychotics want to keep the analyst in the position of witness, so as to protect themselves from desire, yet this remains insufficient. The analyst must try to direct the jouissance, at times limiting it by blocking the de-regulated jouissance, and at other times in a positive manner by sustaining certain of the subject's ideals. Therefore, it is not appropriate for the analyst to use "the rule of free association" with the psychotic. It is best to initiate a directed conversation with him, inspired from the "free flowing exchanges" Lacan used in his sessions with Aimée (Lacan 1975: 213), conversations directed by the idea of preserving the subject from the menacing jouissance of the Other.

The end of the analytical work with a psychotic varies greatly with regards to the modes of stabilization. Usually these involve the shoring up on a partner, and the construction of a *suppléance* through the intermediary of an object (Laurent 1987) by the work of the letter, with the will to make a name for oneself (Laurent 1992). This regulates the distance to the Other and encapsulates the delusion (Maleval 1997). The same subject may develop several of these succinctly: some of them remain entirely dependent on the presence of the analyst, some less so, and some not at all. Consequently, it is not inevitable that the psychoanalytic treatment of the psychotic be interminable.

Let us note that during the last decades, several analysts, after many years of working with psychotics, related stabilizations built on the construction of a delusional order: Dominique Laurent (1993), Collete Chouraqui-Sepel (1993), Colette Soler (1987), Yves Kaufmant (1987), Didier Cremniter (1987), and Augustin Ménard (1987). Let us note in this case that the Lacanian approach radically breaks with what had previously been presented under the name of the psychoanalysis of psychoses. It is important to take seriously Freud's discovery that the delusion is already an attempt at a cure. The delusion constitutes a metaphor that functions as a *suppléance* to the foreclosed paternal metaphor so that in its most elaborate forms (paranoid and paraphrenic) it succeeds in framing the subject's jouissance. Wedded to idealized signifiers, it can stabilize reality. At times it happens that a favorable end of a psychotic cure can in fact be the structuration of a delusion. Because of the popularity of psychoanalysis in today's world, some subjects are able to formulate original requests in this regard that should be taken seriously. We know of one recently addressed to L. Solano: "What I expect from my analytic sessions with you, is to be able to exit this destiny that has driven me to a psychiatric hospital three times. Perhaps you could help me produce a delusion that would make sense [. . .] a delusion that would match the collective one. It doesn't bother me to have a different perception. What bothers me are the police, the hospital security and the highly stressful situations I find myself in" (Solano 1937: 108–11). Indeed, as early as 1984, Broca related a treatment in which the patient was constructing a pacifying delusion. As a starting point, Broca saw his role as one of consent. The staff perceived the patient to have experienced a certain horror in response to her delusion, "always marked by a pejorative note justifying repeated psychiatric interventions" of the kind that essentially, Broca says, the psychotic can find in the person of the analyst, someone who consents to incarnate or become the place of address. "It is not sufficient to be an analyst to incarnate this in a good way. For proof, I note what had happened with the past four psychiatrist-psychoanalysts she had met with. She says of this failure: 'They butchered my transference'" (Broca 1984: 50). According to an elegant formula used by a group of Argentinean psychoanalysts, in such analyses, in order to avoid similar failures, it is necessary to "be able to tolerate the certitude without being complicit with the delusion" (Casenave 1992: 178).

The direction of the cure oriented on the tempering of jouissance cannot be planned. What sort of *suppléance* might the subject find to elaborate in the work? In this respect, the gap between psychiatry and psychoanalysis only widens; the clinician armed with the DSM sees the delusion with horror. He takes this invention as a cancer of the psyche, and not for the black flower it is. He does not allow for the positive perspective that would permit the delusional subject to find a place of address in the analyst.

The developments in psychoanalytic theory within the past two decades have opened new perspectives on the direction of the cure for psychotic patients, including knowledge about their termination. Still obscure, knowledge about termination is only now being tapped. This touches on the current proliferation of psychoanalytic theory concerning analytic work with psychotic patients.

There are other incidents in which psychoanalytic theory has affected clinical practice. Certain merit mention: a renewal of the clinical case presentations, the triggering of certain clinical phenomena (the push-towards-Woman, the gap in phallic signification), and, finally, the development of the notion of ordinary psychosis where the signs are discrete, since they are not medicated and remain untriggered.

These last two points of the psychoanalytic clinic would of necessity have consequences not only for the direction of certain cures but for their practice and expertise. We note that these are diminished before subjects who are otherwise "normal" in every way but who have committed serious acts. The DSM does not permit us to discern a psychotic structure in subjects who do not manifest signs of psychosis. Analytic listening allows us a more refined ear, in discerning the first signs of the push-towards-Woman, by noting initial misuses of the signifier, or alerting us to fugitive de-localizations of jouissance. Such elements can have a predictive value in alerting us to a danger for the subject. When the experts— psychiatrists and psychologists—orient themselves on behavior, they consider all subjects perverse if their delusion concerns sex. This mistake considers phallic jouissance (that of the neurotic or the pervert) to be the same as the jouissance of the Other (that of the psychotic). It is also a mistake insofar as the diagnosis of perversity stigmatizes the subject, without discerning that the disorder of their world is far more radical.

Sergeant Bertrand was considered a "monomaniacal erotomaniac" by psychiatric experts who examined him in 1849.[7] They understood him to be a madman, someone who today would be classed in the catch-all term of "sadism with necrophiliac features," a common current diagnosis for serial killers. The diagnostic mistake was not to notice that his jouissance was of a very particular sort. One only has to listen to what the subjects themselves insist on. Unfortunately, the DSM categories get in the way of listening. What was Sergeant Bertrand telling us? "Jouissance with a live woman," he said, "was nothing compared to jouissance with a dead woman" (Dansel 1991: 149). He strongly underlined this point, and there are good reasons to believe him; by checking with other references, his extreme jouissance was obtained not through coitus with the cadaver, but by actually cutting it up. This is why, to counter Dr. Michéa's diagnosis of "monomaniacal erotomania," Bertrand insisted that his jouissance would be better characterized as "destructive monomania." "Yes!" he averred,

> the destructive monomania was always stronger than a monomaniacal erotic one. This is incontestable. And I believe that I would have never raped a cadaver had I not been able to destroy it afterwards. Thus the destruction wins over the erotic dimension, and whatever one says, no one is able to prove the contrary; I know better what is going on in me than anyone else. The mutilation of bodies had only as a goal, as some people had wanted to say, to hide my passion, and the excesses to which I delivered myself: the desire to mutilate was more imperious in me than the one to rape.
>
> (Dansel 1991: 173)

Bertrand's most destructive jouissance did not concern sex: it exceeded the limits of phallic jouissance, opening up onto the Other jouissance. When phallic mediation does not operate, an Other jouissance emerges that gives direct access to the body. Or, we could say that in order to get off on the body of the other, Bertrand had to have total power over it by cutting it to pieces. Such phenomena disengage the death drive from the sexual drive and only happen when the jouissance of the subject is crushed by the constraints imposed by the signifying chain. More recently, Schaeffer, a serial killer, condemned in the United States, expressed similar views. He writes in his *Journal of a Killer*: "When one looks up close, particularly in terms of these murders, there is nothing particularly sexy in this thing. The popular authors give the impression that the murder is something erotic, as if it were the height of sexual excitation, but in reality, it is quite something else. It's dirty" (Dansel 1991: 64). He reports that one of his victims "thought she was in the hands of a sexual beast"; his perception of himself is decidedly different: "this was not at all the case," he clarifies. "She was actually in the hands of a murderous maniac" (Dansel 1991: 98). His description of his victims as stinking and disgusting, his fascination for bodily decomposition confirms that Schaefer, in the manner of most killers, finds his jouissance in a de-sexualized object: none other than a drive object, and in his case, an anal object. When the phallic function fails and an other, unsublimated jouissance emerges, one that finds direct access to the body of the Other, the sexual drive withdraws and the object cause unveils its affinity with necrophilia. What is left is a purification of the drive, reduced to its fundament, i.e. the death drive. The most evident manifestations are discernible in diverse behaviors: from lust killing to auto-erotic suicide to necrophilia. Certain forms of alcoholism and drug addictions can find a place in this series when they extend beyond phallic jouissance towards a total degeneration of being, sometimes even aiming at a quick death. All of this is quite different than the staging of the pervert where the rapport with the object is mediated by the *semblant*. A form of "lack of seriousness," Lacan notes, "is all there is to define perversion" (Lacan 2006b: 74). There is no doubt that the psychoanalytic approach is helpful in distinguishing, diagnosing and treating psychosis today.

We should also note that the "clinical case presentation" as practiced by Lacan had few commonalities with classical psychiatric practice. Lacan already had reservations about this practice in his youth. He writes in his doctoral thesis (1932): "Interviewing has few advantages being nearly always disadvantageous" (Lacan 1975: 212). In 1955, his critique becomes more radical: "Three quarters of the time that we show the subjects how to proceed, we note nothing else but what we ask of them—what we suggest they respond to us. We introduce distinctions and categories in what they experience that are of concern only to us. [. . .] Proceed according to order, and the chapters are already written" (Lacan 1981: 126, 137). Contrary to this practice oriented towards classification, Lacan emphasizes that the first approach to good interviewing and to a "good investigation concerning psychosis" involves "letting the patient talk as long as he or she wants to." It concerns a presentation where one "listens" (Lacan 1972: unpublished conference), founded on the supposition that the subject can teach us and not on trying to insert him into a grid. By way of this alone we come to see a subject as dynamic in his own treatment, and this will reverberate on the attitude of the treatment team where such listening will be practiced. It makes for a rupture with the DSM modality of treatment, allowing a humanization in psychiatry.

We conclude on this point concerning the ethics of the psychoanalytic approach to the psychiatric patient that breaks with the idea of approaching the patient scientifically. According to Lacan, such scientism denotes an ideology of the suppression of the subject of the unconscious. Science is animated by one goal—knowledge—such that neither desire nor guilt would hinder the development of its logic. No one today takes notice of this, and this is why we need to have so many ethical committees. This lack of awareness can have, Lacan says in 1973, "stifling consequences for what we call humanity." Psychoanalysis finds itself in the place of exception in terms of the discourse of science. With regard to this place of exception, as well as to the effects that are sometimes "stifling," Lacan assigns the function of an "artificial lung thanks to which one tries to find jouissance in speech so that history will continue" (Lacan 1974: 46–7). The psychoanalytic practice of one by one is a counter-balance to the scientific treatment of the subject by universalization. The task of the psychoanalyst in the modern world, Lacan affirms, must be "compensatory."

Translated by Manya Steinkoler

Notes

1   See Lacan (1953) "Function and Field of Speech and Language." Reprinted in *Écrits*, trans. B. Fink (2006a), Paris: Seuil; and Miller, J.-A. (1991) "Reflections on the Formal Envelope of the Symptom," *Lacanian Ink* 4: 13–21.
2   Editors' note: The numbers increase continually; the fifth edition of the manual, the DSM V, published in 2013, added 15 new mental disorders.
3   We cannot consider the concept of borderline as used in the 1940s by American psychologists as a consistent contribution (Maleval J.-C. (1985) "Les variations du champ de l'hystérie en psychanalyse," in *Hystérie et Obsession*, Navarin: Paris.)
4   Editors' note: The Lacanian concept of *suppléance* is occasionally translated as supplement. It concerns a subjective invention, a new way to supplement a structural deficiency due to foreclosure.
5   Editors' note: Lacan borrows the term "holophrase" from linguistics to refer to an earlier stage in a child's language acquisition: a one-word utterance is used to express a complex meaning that would normally require a phrase. It can be found in psychosomatic disorders as well as in psychosis. The holophrase is a soldering of S1 and S2.
6   "The human subject," Lacan indicates during the seminar *The Formations of the Unconscious*, (June 4, 1958), "is a divided subject. If he is no longer divided, he is mad."
7   Francois Bertrand, aka Sergeant Bertrand aka the Vampire of Montparnasse was found guilty of exhuming women's bodies from various Parisian cemeteries and having sex with and mutilating them.

Bibliography

Briole, G. (2006) "Why Talk with Patients?" in *Clinique Bonsecour*.

Broca, R. (1984) "Sur l'érotomanie de transfert" (On the Erotomania of Transference), in *Actes de l'Ecole de la Cause Freudienne*, Paris: Ecole de la Cause Freudienne.

Casenave, L. (1992) "L'humour comme stratégie dans la stabilisation d'une psychose" (Humor as a Strategy of Stabilization in Psychosis), in *Les Stratégies de Transfert en Psychanalyse*, Association de la Fondation du Champ Freudien, Paris: Navarin.

Chourauqi-Sepel, C. (1993) "Le Comptable, Dieu et le Diable," in *Actes de l'Ecole de la Cause Freudienne*, Paris: Ecole de la Cause Freudienne.

Cooper, D. (1970) *Psychiatrie et Anti-Psychiatrie*, Paris: Seuil; also *Psychiatry and Anti-Psychiatry: Studies in Existential Analysis and Phenomenology* (1967), London: Tavistock.

Cremniter, D. (1987) "Artifices de la Cure," in *Actes de la Cause Freudienne*, Paris: Ecole de la Cause Freudienne.

Dansel, M. (1991) *Le Sergent Bertrand, Portrait d'un nécrophile heureux*, Paris: Albin Michel.

Dolto, F. (1971) *Le cas Dominique*, Paris: Seuil.

Etchegoyen, R.H. and Miller J.-A. (1996) *Silence Brisé*, Paris: Agalma.

Federn P. (1952) *Ego Psychology and the Psychoses*, New York: Basic Books.

Kaufmant, Y. (1987) "Le Psychotique et l'analyste : demande ou commande?" in *Actes de l'Ecole de la Cause Freudienne*, Paris: Ecole de la Cause Freudienne.

Lacan, J. (1932; 2nd edn 1975) *De la psychose paranoïaque dans ses rapports avec la personnalité*, Paris: Seuil.

—— (1953) "Function and Field of Speech and Language." Reprinted in *Écrits*, trans. B. Fink (2006a), Paris: Seuil.

—— (1956; 2nd edn 1981) *Le Séminaire. Livre III. Les psychoses*, Paris: Seuil; and also (1981) *The Psychoses, Seminar III*, Paris: Seuil; (1993) *The Psychoses, The Seminar of Jacques Lacan: Book III 1955–1956*, ed. J.-A. Miller, trans. Russell Grigg, London: Routledge.

—— (1966) "Présentation des 'Mémoires d'un névropathe,'" in *Cahiers pour l'analyse*, Paris: Seuil.

—— (1966) "On a Question Preliminary to Any Possible Treatment of Psychosis." Reprinted in *Écrits*, trans. B. Fink (2006a), Paris: Seuil.

—— (1967a) "Petit Discours aux Psychiatres," speech delivered at the Cercle d'Études directed by Henry Ey, 10 November 1967.

—— (1967b) Conférence inédite à l'hôpital Sainte-Anne-Paris (November 1967).

—— (1972) Conference in St Anne, 6 January 1972, unpublished.

—— (1974) "Déclaration à France Culture," *Le Coq-Héron*.

—— (1975) *Of the Paranoiac Psychoses and Their Rapport with Personality*, Paris: Seuil.

—— (1977) "L'insu qui sait que l'une bévue s'aile à mourre," *Ornicar?* 17/18 (1979).

—— (2006b) "D'un Discours qui n'est pas du semblant," *Seminar XVIII*, Paris: Seuil.

Laurent, D. (1991) "L'Homme aux noms," in *Revue de l'Ecole de la Cause Freudienne*.

—— (1993) "Une femme intelligente," in *Revue de l'Ecole de la Cause Freudienne*.

Laurent, E. (1987) "Pour la vérité," *Actes de l'Ecole de la Cause Freudien* 23: 169–73.

Maleval, J.-C. (1985) "Les variations du champ de l'hystérie en psychanalyse," in *Hystérie et Obsession*, Navarin: Paris.

—— (1997) *La logique du délire (The Logic of Delusion)*, Paris: Masson.

—— (2000) *La Forclusion du Nom du Père*, Paris: Seuil.

—— (2011) *La logique du délire*, Rennes: Presses Université de Rennes.

Mannoni, M. (1979) *La Théorie comme fiction*, Paris: Seuil.

Ménard, A. (1987) "La rencontre d'un psychotique," in *Actes de l'Ecole de la Cause Freudienne*.

Miller, J.-A. (1979) "Complément aux journées des cartels sur la psychose," in *Lettres de l'Ecole Freudienne de Paris*, Paris: École Freudienne de Paris.

Minkowski, E. (1957) "Voie d'accès aux analyses phénoménologiques et existentielles," *Annales Médico-Psychologiques*, II, 115; reprinted in (1997) *Au-delà de rationalisme morbide*, Paris: L'Harmattan.

Rosenfeld, H.A. (1965) *Psychotic States*, London: Hogarth Press.

Schreber, D.P. (1903) *Memoirs of My Nervous Illness*, trans. Ida Macalpine and Richard Hunter (2000), New York: New York Review of Books.

Silvestre, M. (1984) "Transfert et interprétation dans les psychoses : une question de technique," *Actes de l'Ecole de la Cause Freudien*, in Angers VI.

Solano, L. (1937) "Charon, passeur-dames," in *Actes de l'Ecole de la Cause Freudienne*.

Soler, C. (1987) "Quelle place pour l'analyste," in *Actes de l'Ecole de la Cause Freudienne*.

8

PSYCHOTIC TRANSFERENCE

Jean Allouch

A madman saw himself as a morsel of grain. Having come to understand that this was a delusion, his psychiatrist was able to discharge him. But as soon as the man stepped out of the hospital, he sprinted right back to his psychiatrist's office. "Goodness! What's happened?" Panting, out of breath, the man stated, "My God! I've just met a hen!" "But you know by now that you're not a morsel of grain!"—"Oh, yes, doctor, I know very well! But does that hen?!"

Lacan's encounter with Marguerite Anzieu produced two new ways of tying love and knowledge together. First, he gave Marguerite the name Aimée, or "beloved." Second, she became for him what he later designated as the "subject supposed to know." What can we make of this new knotting of love and knowledge, a phenomenon that Lacan defined as transference? It is all the more striking to assume that someone else actually knows, since Lacan never stopped saying that there is not the least desire on the part of the speaking being to know anything at all. He adds that this phenomenon of assuming knowledge of the other does not concern desire, but love. Moreover, he will specify that this "subject supposed to know" is not exactly concerned with a love of knowledge. What is transference really about, then?

Transference: the one and the many

The fortuitous discovery we call transference is one of the fruits of the deployment of the psychoanalytic method, all the more noteworthy since it appeared unexpectedly. Freud discovered it around 1912, and used the term *Übertragung* not in the plural, but in the singular. If we posit a transference specific to psychosis, are we not forcing a plurality and imposing a distortion that Freud subtracted at the moment of his discovery? In doing so, would we not distort an essential concept of psychoanalysis as we do when we qualify transference as maternal or paternal? The discovery of transference, whose importance cannot be downplayed, has crystallized a particular relationship of psychoanalysis to paranoid psychosis. This is indicated by the affirmation that there is no transference in psychosis.

There is no transference in psychosis? In fact, nothing could be further from the truth! It was not after discovering the concept of transference that Freud concluded that psychotic transference does not exist, but during his elaboration of the Oedipus complex. In 1906, Freud insisted that paranoiacs did not have the kind of free-floating libido that neurotics did (Freud 1911). This deficit was attributed to a regression to autoeroticism. The paranoiac's inability to transfer free-floating libido onto the figure of the psychoanalyst would render him incurable. The hackneyed aphorism that there is no transference in psychosis amounts to a prejudice against the specificity of psychotic transference. In 1924, Freud wrote:

> The neuroses were the first subject of analysis, and for a long time they were the only one. No analyst could doubt that medical practice was wrong in separating those disorders from the psychoses. . . . It would seem, however, that the analytic study of the *psychoses* is impracticable owing to its lack of therapeutic results. Mental patients are as a rule without the capacity for forming a positive transference, so that the principal instrument of analytic technique is inapplicable to them. There are nevertheless a number of methods of approach to be found. Transference is often not so completely absent but can be used to a certain extent . . . the chief consideration in this connection is that so many things that in the neuroses have to be laboriously fetched up from the depths are found in the psychoses on the surface, visible to every eye. For that reason the best subjects for the demonstration of many of the assertions of analysis are provided by the psychiatric clinic. It was thus bound to happen before long that analysis would find its way to the objects of psychiatric observation.
>
> (Freud 1925: 59)

Would Freud have made the psychoanalytic study of the neuroses the condition *sine qua non* for approaching the psychoses? It seems that he did. When Freud speaks of psychosis starting from neurosis, does he end up erecting an almost insurmountable wall between psychoanalysis and psychosis? He writes that working with the concept of narcissism allowed "a glimpse beyond the wall" (Freud 1925: 60).

From the very beginning the psychoanalytic approach to psychosis was primarily hypothetical. There is something that resembles a false start regarding psychotic transference in Freud's thought. Lacan does not adhere to certain givens that stem from neuroses in his approach to psychosis. His trajectory does not follow

Freud's but rather crosses it. This divergence was not heresy since he was not following Freud's steps in the first place.

To understand the Lacanian divergence, we need to explore certain canonical psychoanalytic aphorisms; for example, human beings are supposed to follow a predestined path from autoeroticism to a felicitous relation with the object. This is one of the doctrinal bases supporting the idea that there is no transference in psychosis. Is such a dogma the holy grail of psychoanalysis? Is psychoanalysis condemned to disappear if it stops affirming the historical and structural primacy of the "auto" over the "hetero"? Even after substituting primary narcissism for primal autoeroticism we still cannot rectify this false start. Lacan would begin elsewhere. One of the major factors that allow for his theoretical progression was his refusal to take autoeroticism as primary. For Lacan, autoeroticism is defined differently: it concerns a disorder of object a that occurs in the absence of a self. There is thus nothing "auto" involved here, except to designate what is present when the "auto" is absent.

The case of the delusion is the same. Far from being solipsistic and showing the latent presence of some sort of primary narcissism, the delusion will show how a subject "enter[s] at full tilt upon the domain of inter-subjectivity" (Lacan 1956: 193). Thus we can see the exemplarity of delusional phenomena that in Freud are reduced to megalomania, whereas in Lacan they are situated within the persecutory delusion.[1]

The notion of loss of reality correlated to depersonalization can be found in both Lacan and psychoanalytic orthodoxy. Lacan argues in "The Family Complexes" (1938) that the access to reality, and in parallel the constitution of personality, are subtended by a process: psychosis comes about not from a deficiency, but as a stasis in a process that is cut short. There is not a loss, but a non-constitution of reality; not a de-personalization, but a "non-personification." We see this manifest in the fortuitous clinical revelation of the hyper-normality of people who, confronted with a certain situation, became insane.

Now we are faced with a puzzling reversal of values. The psychotic transference, posited by Freud as non-existent, becomes exemplary of all transference for Lacan. Could we say, then, that psychotic transference is nothing but another name, even the true name, of transference itself? We return to the question of "the one and the many" of transference, present in the concept since its discovery. This time, however, the "one" would be obtained on the basis of the very thing that had originally been excluded, namely, psychotic transference.

Clinical experience, however, does not call for such a reduction to "the one." Transference in neurosis and psychosis seem to be of so different a respective valence that the problem is rather to explain both the singularity of the concept and the disparity of its modes of realization. Lacan's writing the matheme of transference in 1967 satisfies the demands of both the one and the many.

The signifier of transference

Let's take a closer look at the matheme of transference:

$$\frac{s - - - - - - - - s^q}{s(S1, S2, \ldots Sn)}$$

In order to grasp the elements at stake in the matheme, we will review some texts concerned with this problem. Lacan proposes the matheme of transference, revisiting what had put Freud on the right track at the beginning. Freud recounts that a patient threw her arms around him just as the maid entered the room, surprising them. Humble and inveterately skeptical, Freud does not believe the patient's amorous gesture is due to his personal charm, and discerns something discordant at work. Discussing an article on transference by Thomas Szasz, Lacan glosses the argument as follows: "According to the author, the analyst is supposed to point out to the patient the effects of more or less manifest discordancies that occur with regard to the reality of the analytic situation, namely that two real subjects are present in it" (Lacan 1964: 136).

How did we fail to notice from the beginning that "discordancy with regard to reality" is an issue that is not posed but imposed in psychosis, especially where the delusion or hallucination is concerned?

Let's take another look at this problem of transference from the perspective of discordancy, revisiting a discussion first inspired by psychosis. Just as we invite the madman to come to the conclusion that he is not a morsel of grain, as in the joke that is the epigraph to this chapter, in the so called "interpretation of transference" we would supposedly push the analysand to accept that her psychoanalyst does not actually have a head of luxuriant blond locks, as he had done in her dream,[2] and that she was actually "distorting reality."

Lacan's thought stems from a questioning of psychosis that led to his conceiving of transference in terms that differed from those just mentioned. Lacan notes that we forget that in analysis somebody is actually talking to somebody else, addressing an other "supposed to know." He first presented the subject supposed to know in 1964.[3] Lacan himself notes that he speaks almost phenomenologically. If one addresses, or supposes a knowledge on the part of, someone else, should we not conclude that the regulating figure of the transference be more properly named (cf. Russell's definite descriptions) not a subject, but an other supposed to know? This is precisely what Lacan does not do, despite the fact that aspects of this thought could have led him to his initial definition of the unconscious as the discourse of the Other.[4] Choosing "subject" over "other" suggests Lacan's acute attentiveness to psychosis. Let's follow this operation step by step. He would elaborate this, discussing both a supposed knowledge and also the one who will become the subject supposed to know: "It is clear that this relation is established on a plane that is not reciprocal, not symmetrical. This much Szasz observes, only, quite wrongly, to deplore it—in this relationship of the one with the other, there

115

is established a search for truth in which the one is supposed to know, or at least to know more than the other" (Lacan 1981: 137). It is obvious that knowledge is attributed to "the one" and not to "the other." This passage continues:

> the one is supposed to know, or at least to know more than the other. From the latter, the thought immediately arises that not only must he not make a mistake (*se trompe*), but also that he can be misled (*on peut le tromper*). The making a mistake (*se tromper*) is, by the same token, thrown back upon the subject. It is not simply that the subject is, in a static way, lacking, or in error. It is that, in a moving way, in his discourse, he is essentially situated in the dimension of the making a mistake (*se tromper*).
>
> (Lacan 1981: 137)

Lacan does not conclude the sentence that introduces the supposed knowledge. He brings it in with a subordinate clause; then he puts "*et que*" (and that), thus opening another subordinate clause, which introduces something entirely different and unexpected, namely, dupery. What kind of knowledge is supposed of the other if, in this very supposition, one admits that the other could be mistaken? Posing the fact that the other cannot be duped implies that I am not supposing him to know all that much! Or, do we prevent his being duped at any cost, in order to maintain him as the possible support of the supposed knowledge? In the first case, the supposition is not consistent with itself; in the second, the dupery is not really dupery.

Phenomenologically speaking, this question is poorly constructed. The solution proposed still does not solve the problem of the discordance with reality. That same day, Lacan defined transference as "the enactment of the reality of the unconscious" (Lacan 1981: 146). As elegant as it sounds, this formula is nevertheless flawed since it does not take into account the exclusion of the Other supposed to know. In fact, if the unconscious is the discourse of the Other, and the transference is the enactment of the reality of the unconscious, is this reality not *ipso facto* the very one of discourse itself? And, furthermore, if this discourse carries a knowledge, as Lacan continues to hammer into us, isn't the enactment of this reality that of the "knowledge of the Other"? The matheme of transference excludes this syllogistically inevitable conclusion.

It is not accidental that the question of dupery interrupted the introduction of the supposed knowledge. The essential character of the relation between knowledge and dupery is in fact confirmed a month and a half later in a seminar delivered on June 3, 1964 (Lacan 1981). Here Lacan introduces no longer a "supposed knowledge," but the "subject supposed to know." The terms of "knowledge" (*savoir*) and "dupery," as well as "certitude," refer to Descartes.[5] Lacan reads the *cogito* (I think) as predicated on the annihilation of knowledge[6] and as an error. Descartes's error—in the act of the *cogito*—would later be described by Lacan (1981: 222–7) as a *passage à l'acte* that allowed him to say that he knew something. Explaining Descartes's error, Lacan introduces for the first time the subject supposed to know, while nevertheless refuting Descartes's claim that it could be an Other supposed to knowledge. The experience of the *cogito* is supported by the affirmation that God is not a deceiver; God, for Descartes, is the knowing subject. What is important here is that we see that the "supposed to know" is not attributable to an Other, but to a subject. The designation of the subject supposed to know comes about in a Cartesian space precisely where one gets rid of such a subject. We will find the exact same "paradox" in the Lacanian questioning of the end of analysis in the 1967 text where Lacan writes the matheme of transference.

Lacan reads Descartes as he is questioning psychosis, because in psychosis we encounter the Other supposed to know. This is most evident in the delusion of supposition where the subject believes the Other actually knows. The rule, in the field of the paranoid psychoses, is not that the subject "takes himself for" but that he "is taken for" that morsel of grain, in the place of the Other.[7]

Knowledge is first that of the Other. Thus, to exclude this figure of the Other supposed to know is equal to unhinging an unhinged knowledge. Lacan's coining of the term "subject supposed to know" opens up a question: Where does the subject stand when he addresses the subject supposed to know? (Lacan 1968). Lacan's answer emerges not from transference, but from a fortuitous discovery in the definition of the subject: "A subject supposes nothing; he is supposed, supposed by the signifier that represents him for another signifier" (Lacan 1968: 19). This definition does not permit us to make the subject the agent of a supposition. The subject supposed to know—if we are really talking of a subject—can only be supposed and, moreover, can be supposed only by a signifier—the one who, from then on, will be named "the signifier S of the transference."

To transfer/to position transferentially

Lacan concluded his year-long seminar devoted to the study of Schreber's case by saying: "I wanted to demonstrate that the delusion becomes clarified in all of its phenomena; I could even say in its dynamic, which can be essentially considered, without any doubt, as a disturbance in the relation to the Other, and, as such, therefore, linked to a transferential mechanism."[8]

How does this transferential mechanism disturb the relation to the Other? We will get closer to its particularity by noticing, with Lacan, the Freudian matrix of the variations of the sentence, "I love him." These variations allow us to understand where Schreber ends up—in what Lacan calls "divine erotomania" (Lacan 1993: 126, 311), an erotomania in which, Schreber tells us, the Other speaks and is alive (Lacan 1993). Schreber tells us of the divine nerves that speak the fundamental language (Lacan 1993: 26, 27, 140, 210). For Lacan, Schreber's speech

comes close to the preponderant, crushing, proliferating, aspect of the phenomena of verbal auditivation, the formidable captivation of the subject in the world of speech, which is not only co-present with his existence, which constitutes not only what last time I called a spoken accompaniment of acts, but also a perpetual intimation, solicitation— summation even, to manifest itself on this plane. Not for one instant must the subject cease testifying, at the constant inducement of the speech that accompanies him, that he is there present, capable of responding—or of not responding, because perhaps, he says, one wants to compel him to say something silly. By his response, as by his non-response, he has to testify that he is always awake to this internal dialogue.

(Lacan 1993: 315)

The term "testimony" is mentioned many times throughout Lacan's seminar, showing that we are witnesses not just to a specific case, but to the very structure of paranoia itself. The paranoiac "speaks to you of something that spoke to him. It is the very foundation of the paranoid structure: the subject understood something that he formulates, something I just referred to regarding signification. There is something that has taken the form of speech and speaks to him. . . . The paranoiac renders testimony to you concerning what is at stake in paranoia."[9]

The specificity of transference in psychosis is inferred from the structure that we could call almost-normal. Jakobson's linguistic schema reduces communication to a speaker and a listener. It reminds us of the fact that someone speaks to someone of something from someone else. In psychosis, "the décor is reversed" (Lacan 1993), which shows that the delusion starts the moment the initiative comes from the Other.

What then is the result? It follows that the psychiatrist or psychoanalyst has no choice but to sustain himself in the position of "witness," as secretary of what the madman has received from the Other. Lacan continues with one of his reversals, as he so often does,[10] and this time speaks of the position of the alienist recommending that we should become secretaries to the madman and take what they tell us, verbatim. "Up to now, this was considered precisely the thing to avoid" (Lacan 1993: 206).

Being secretary to the insane concerns not only registering what the psychotic witnesses, but recording what he has received from the Other. This implies that the madman and the alienist find themselves on the same side of the wall: there is no wall of alienation separating them. This gives all the more meaning to an observation Freud made while reading Schreber's memoirs; he had never before seen something so closely resembling his own theory of libido (Lacan 1993: 27). Indeed, just like the psychoanalyst, the psychotic is forced to become the theoretician of his own experience. They are brothers in this necessity[11] since they are related in their common fear of becoming mad.[12] At times the madman proposes rectifications to the theses of psychoanalysis, as Schreber does contesting Kraepelin: "They say that I am a paranoiac and that paranoiacs are people who refer everything to themselves. In this case, they are mistaken, it is not I who refers

118

everything to myself, it's he who relates everything to me, it's God who speaks non-stop inside me, through his various agents and extensions" (Lacan 1993: 135).

The madman's discourse can rival that of the alienist; hence, their discourses must happen on the same level. If a wall exists, we have to know where it is situated, not where people say it is: between the insane and the sane, between the madman and the rational man, between the doctor and the patient. If there is a wall, the alienist and the madman are on the same side. On the other side, there is a being that talks to the subject, and to whom the subject must respond, given the disarray he finds himself in; he addresses an invocation. He has to respond in order to put an end to the persecution. He appeals directly to this being. This ternary structure is homologous to the structure implied by the experience of sainthood.

Situated beside the alienist or the psychoanalyst, the madman is a theoretician of his own experience of madness. One cannot actually say that the psychotic has transference, as one would say of the neurotic. We can propose, however, that the psychotic positions himself transferentially just like the analyst does. Schreber positions a divine erotomania transferentially; in other words, Schreber positions himself as a possible object of transference (i.e. as possible support for the subject supposed to know) in making it known that the Other speaks to him. For Freud it is the same. In terms of the mode of enunciation that we have qualified as "paranoiac," there is no difference between the Schreberian act of publishing his *Memoirs of My Nervous Illness* and the Freudian act of publishing *The Interpretation of Dreams*. In both cases, the authors do not have transference to their readers, but in testifying to their rapport with the Other, they present themselves for their readers as figures of the subject supposed to know. We add that Lacan's "return to Freud" employs the same structure of enunciation; Lacan engages us not by telling us what he thinks, but what Freud said.

Freud gives us a dazzling confirmation of this enunciative homology in telling us that he has succeeded precisely where the paranoiac fails. Indeed, Freud does not speak of succeeding anywhere other than precisely where the paranoiac fails. The question of investing (in the sense of banking) of homosexual libido (that Freud admits to here) remains problematic. It is clear that if Freud succeeded at something, it was in provoking numerous transferences to his person. Freud succeeded in being believed or, more precisely, in establishing that by believing in him, one believed in Freud's thing, or that, in believing in Freud's thing, one believed in Freud. Of course, there is no reason why this cannot be questioned: was this really Freud's intention? Or is it a question of a demand (that the didactic analysis puts an end to when the candidate is convinced of the existence of the unconscious)? When the analytic candidate realizes that the unconscious exists, does that mean that we have tricked him, satisfying his demand? In the crucible that introduces this question, we could also ask whether this concerns the production of an infinite transference or simply producing psychoanalysts. Do we not find ourselves in a case of infinite transference, the very situation that we thought we had surmounted? One sees that this "success" of Freud is not so certain;

the split with Fliess raises questions. In that regard, the problem is much more complex than it seems at first glance. The paranoiac usually has far more difficulty than Freud in finding believers in his thing. Do we not underestimate the incidence of the tertiary structure of madness? At least we see here how the questions that emerge revisit the ones elicited by psychotic transference. Is it not also the case that those who professionally concern themselves with madness do so precisely to "protect themselves from this concern" (Lacan 1967)?

We can now grasp why the psychoanalyst was able to state that the psychotic does not have transference; both the psychoanalyst and the madman position themselves similarly in the transference, lending themselves as support for it. How would the psychoanalyst invite the psychotic to say "whatever comes to mind"? The fundamental rule does not take into account the fact that for the psychotic to say whatever comes to mind is to let the Other speak precisely in order to try to get rid of it. He cannot tell the psychoanalyst what he thinks, not because he is not thinking of anything—far from it—but that is not his problem; it is the Other's problem.

A possible treatment of psychosis is analytically conceivable only once this incompatibility between the psychoanalyst and the psychotic is acknowledged. This is born of the fact that they both become candidates for the position of subject supposed to know. Additionally, the psychotic will not let go of this candidature since he is unable to do so. The only choice left for the psychoanalyst is either to limit himself to treating neurotics or to leave the psychotic the task of "positioning transferentially" so that the psychoanalyst will find himself in the position of the one transferring. This is why Lacan stated that the psychotic transference is, at first, transference to the psychotic.

This is how the function of "secretary to the insane" is realized. The opposition we noted earlier between the one and the many of transference is resolved. There is only one matheme of transference, but two different readings of this matheme, depending on whether we are dealing with neurosis (someone who has transference) or psychosis (someone who positions himself transferentially). In neurosis, the non-subjectified signifier of the transference is of the Other in the sense of the objective-genitive. In psychosis, the signifier of the Other is of the subjective-genitive. We will find an example of the signifier of transference as the signifier of the other, in the sense of the subjective-genitive, in the signifier "Aimée," a signifier that is neither subjectified nor unconscious. Lacan uses this signifier to address Marguerite as the subject supposed to know, and by way of this address, he acquires the function of secretary.

Psychotic transference is a transference to the psychotic. This can be formulated differently, not in regards to the Other but as a function of the object a, as Lacan develops in his seminar on transference. The psychotic is someone who has his object in his pocket (Lacan 1967). In the subjective disparity of our relationship to him, he is the *eromenos* (beloved) and we can only deal with him as an *erastes* (lover).

The relation of the subject to the place of subject supposed to know is direct; it is a place of "you will have to know." These two points concern the psychoanalyst as well as the psychotic. It is not a game of presence-absence that will differentiate them, but rather the style by which one and the other will give support to the function of the subject supposed to know. What the psychoanalyst "will have to know," as soon as he is placed as the subject supposed to know, will only become an effective knowledge if he is able to put his own knowledge "in reserve."[13] The fact of occupying the position of the psychoanalyst does not concern "playing the analyst" too soon. That is where the gap exists, the potential disconnection between transference and the analysis of transference. Unlike the psychoanalyst, who does not take himself for what the neurotic assumes him to be, the psychotic puts too much of himself there. He cannot not play the analyst. The psychotic believes that in imitating and interpreting, he will be able to outwit the Other's action towards him. Or, to put it differently, the psychotic tries to block the Other's jouissance, or, better yet, to definitively destroy it. "I put too much of myself there" seems like the formula of the demand that the psychotic addresses to us. It would be an error to force the psychotic to free associate. The secretary to the saint intervenes for his sanctity, and in the same manner, the psychoanalyst intervenes for the psychotic's testimony, thereby making analysis possible.

Letting knowledge be known

Aimée is the signifier that, by way of his transference to Marguerite, Lacan will address as the subject supposed to know. Aimée is also a sign, which represents something to someone. Aimée is a sign of love, *the* sign of a love. From the preceding analysis we deduce the following: the link between the nomination Aimée (beloved) and the love felt for her is more or less common. What loving experience does not make use of pet names? This was made explicit in 1970 when Lacan revealed to his colleagues: "My patient, the one I have called 'Aimée,' was truly touching" (Lacan 1970). The admission of being touched by her, however, was already noted in Lacan's thesis: "One day she opened up, under the condition that we would avoid looking at her while she spoke. She then revealed her daydreams, which became moving, not only in terms of her childish manner, but for their enthusiastic candor" (Lacan 1932: 166).

Lacan was moved, and consequently no longer remained strictly in the position of observer. This is when she revealed her most intimate daydreams to him. And yet, having noted the banality of such an amorous nomination, there is something particular to it. In most cases, private names are used in intimacy—if a man calls his wife "honey bunny" or "cutie pie," for instance, this term of endearment remains private, used only in the presence of close friends or family. On the contrary, calling Marguerite "Aimée" is a public act for Lacan. Was this already part of Lacan's habit of calling everyone *cher* (dear) as a way of not naming anyone at all? The amorous naming of Aimée remained extimate and not intimate; Aimée became the name of a clinical type (Lacan 1932: 267).

Aimée moved Lacan, but was she moved by Lacan? The simple fact that she confided in him is insufficient evidence to answer this question affirmatively. Perhaps the answer to this question lies in the question itself: Lacan gives a public sign of his love for Marguerite after encountering the tangible signs of a lack of love. Lacan identifies Aimée with the heroine of *Le Détracteur*[14] in her lack of love: "In *Le Détracteur*, an amorous longing is expressed. Its verbal expression is more contrived, even more discordant with life . . . this affective discordancy bodes well with . . . an infantile sensitivity: sudden revelations of brotherly thought, thirst for adventure, pacts, pledges, and eternal bonds" (Lacan 1932: 179–80).

Forty-three years later, Lacan will be even clearer. "We can certainly say that a psychosis is a sort of insolvency in regards to the accomplishment of what is called 'love.' In the realm of love, the patient of whom I was speaking [an erotomaniac] could surely feel much resentment towards destiny" (Lacan 1976: 16).

The naming of Aimée represents Lacan's love for her. The childish character of this love is foreclosed. This love, marked by a fraternal seal, is more *agape* than *eros*.[15] This is in keeping with what we discussed before in terms of the function of secretary.

When Lacan's thesis was published for a second time in 1974, this time for a broader audience, he was more precise in how he was touched by something in Marguerite, i.e. her rapport with knowledge. She *knew*. Lacan went as far as to describe her as a "person who always knew very well what she was doing" (Lacan 1975). Marguerite's rapport with knowledge is a *savoir-faire*, but also a seasoned shrewdness, because Marguerite knows rather than does. Lacan's encounter with Marguerite's invented knowledge led him to question, "What is knowledge?" This question allowed him to theorize the workings of the *passage à l'acte*,[16] which sent him directly to Freud.[17] Two quotes from the 1970s are worth mentioning:

> It is clear that I'm talking to the walls. It took me a long time to figure out that, before hearing what they send back, meaning my own voice preaching in the desert—way before that—I have heard very decisive things, but that is my own business. What I want to say is that the people who are here, namely the ones inside the walls, are capable of making themselves heard, as long as there are good-enough ears. In one word, to honor her for something that does not concern her—this everyone knows—this patient that I have designated by the name Aimée, which was not hers, of course; I was the one who was sucked in by psychoanalysis.[18]
>
> (Lacan 1972).

A few months later, Lacan commented further, "I entered psychoanalysis just like that, a bit late. . . . I made the mistake of having seen what we may call a psychotic. I wrote my thesis on this subject. In the end, it led me to experience psychoanalysis for myself" (Lacan 1978: 42).

Marguerite's rapport with knowledge was such that, far from closing in on the two of them, it opens up, sending Lacan to Freud. The young psychiatrist, a student of de Clérambault, finds in psychoanalysis something like a response to the experience of Marguerite, an experience he feels he is still living through. We know today that he began analysis with Lowenstein while he was still working on the case of Marguerite.

Even if Elizabeth Roudinesco's two hypotheses—that Lacan did his analysis with Aimée[19] and that Aimée was for Lacan what Fliess was for Freud—are more specious than illuminating, they both still speak of Lacan's "transferential rapport" (Roudinesco 1993: 134–6). Roudinesco is nevertheless able to recognize that in the connection between Lacan and Marguerite, the transference is on Lacan's side.

Marguerite's rapport with knowledge would gnaw at Lacan. Her knowledge implied a stasis and this brings the question "What is knowledge?" to the foreground. Lacan had already situated knowledge as such in the Real, which, not being able to be spoken, can only be approached by the Symbolic that "only lies when it speaks." Once again we find here, although differently expressed, knowledge's relation to dupery, so important and decisive for the writing of the matheme of the transference.

Lacan claims that conscience comes from the Imaginary. He writes:

> Conscience is far from being knowledge since it lends itself very precisely, to falsehood. "I know" never really means anything at all, and we could just as easily bet that everything we know is false but sustained by a conscience, whose very characteristic is precisely to sustain this falsehood to maintain its own consistency. . . . It's quite striking—I could also start with secrets that are imposed upon me by my day to day analytic patients—that an "I know" does not only concern knowledge, but a will not to change; it is something—and I tell you this in confidence—that I felt very early on.
>
> (Lacan 1977: unpublished seminar,
> session of February 15, 1977)

Marguerite's rapport with knowledge is anchored in a will resistant to change. Marguerite sustains knowledge as "what she knows, she wants it to be known." In her erotomaniacal appeal, she writes novels addressed to her supposed protector, and to the public at large, whose recognition she seeks. Apart from Marguerite's criminal *passage à l'acte*, it is clear that all of Marguerite's attempts to publicize what happened to her and what came from the Other were failures. Marguerite, for more than ten years, found herself permanently confronted with her impotence in making something known (using the term "impotence" in the Lacanian sense of "a power of not being able to," as a suspension of the act).

Lacan lifts this impotence and exposes where making known was not impotent, i.e., her *passage à l'acte*. He publishes her writings, writes up her case, and makes known the knowledge that she has invented, including her literary creations, to a public that is no longer restricted only to Jeanne, the actress she attacked, as the addressee. As secretary, in this matter, Lacan is eminently active, not without giving some satisfaction to the megalomaniacal ambition of his patient. Lacan's intervention does not concern calming, containing, or inspiring her ambition either. If it has a calming element, it is because it has given a legitimate satisfaction to the mentally ill patient in the sense of "social legitimization." A few intellectuals, notably surrealists, will confirm the merits of this work: the psychiatrists, without exception, badmouthed him while the psychoanalysts would dedicate themselves to reducing Lacan to this impotence once again, i.e., likening it to the same impotence of his patient. In recounting the events that followed, Lacan discussed the "effect of horror" provoked by his thesis. "Finally, it brought me to psychoanalysis myself. This was followed by the war, during which time, I continued with this experience. When the war ended, I thought I could begin speaking about this." The "this" here is equivocal. Are we dealing with Lacan's experience of psychoanalysis as an analysand, or is he speaking of his thesis? What follows seems to confirm the latter. "Absolutely not—I've been told—no one understood anything . . . we know you, we've had our eye on you already for some time" (Lacan 1978: 42).

Realizing Marguerite's wishes to make herself known, Lacan lifted the impotence precisely where her wish for recognition remained at an impasse. Three points are worthy of mention in this regard. First, Lacan does not substitute himself for Marguerite. He does what she is not in a position to do. Would the "notoriety" she obtained from her *passage à l'acte* have allowed her to be published? In his doctoral thesis, Lacan published excerpts from her novels, poems and letters, accompanied, of course, by the write up of the case he named "Aimée." Marguerite did not make her writing known by herself but as a part of this "letting something to be known." In this regard, Lacan will find himself fraternally linked to Freud. He explicitly formulates these two points (and he was encouraged by reading Freud to speak of this) in one of the lectures presented in the United States: "In my thesis, I found myself applying Freudianism unbeknownst to me. . . . I saw insane patients and speaking of them was thus led to Freud who spoke in a style that I found necessary due to my contact with mental illness" (Lacan 1975: 15).

Lacan's point needs correction. If Lacan recognizes that he has applied Freudianism "unbeknownst to himself," he does not admit to explicitly having applied Freudianism at the time of his thesis. Whenever Lacan employs Freud in his dissertation, he misses the mark. Lacan's contact with mental illness forces him to recognize not this or that particular Freudian thesis, but Freud's overall style in his approach to mental illness. When Lacan's *Écrits* were published—and we recall that the word "style" opens the book—Lacan will explain precisely which style is at stake, one that demands "faithfulness to the symptom's formal envelope, which is the true clinical trace for which I acquired a taste" (Lacan 2006: 52).

The third characteristic of this "letting it be known" concerns the name, Aimée. What we have developed in this chapter has allowed us to see that the "Becoming known/*faire savoir*" intimately links the case study and Lacan's transference towards Marguerite. It is the organizing signifier of this transference: Aimée is the sign of Lacan's love for Marguerite, recalling that of John of the Cross for Saint Theresa. Lacan's publication of the case of Aimée took place just at the moment he was about to understand the case in a different way than the one that he had called attention to in the thesis itself. Today, in considering this publication in terms of Lacan's transference to Marguerite, we can render the "symptomatic" writing up of the case more precisely as "sinthomatic." Lacan makes explicit the place that the analyst should occupy in the structure. The case is neither reducible to "The Case of Aimée" nor to "The Case of Marguerite." It is inseparable from the collective character of madness, of a case of psychotic transference in the sense that we have elaborated, and we can further note that, as a published work of Lacan, it is unique. The publication is part of the case, and, like any symptom in psychoanalysis, is caught up in the transference. This is another way of saying that the publication, as such, is not the end of the story.

In view of what we have just said, we hope to give a more precise sense to how Lacan's publication of his thesis, taken as the act of love that it was, will have served the "letting it be known" (*faire savoir*, in the two meanings of "letting it be known": to transmit knowledge (*transmettre le savoir*) and to simultaneously constitute it (*faire le savoir*)).

Translated and abridged by Manya Steinkoler and Patricia Gherovici

Notes

1 Abraham's formula that every persecutory delusion in dementia praecox implicitly contains a delusion of grandeur is ratified by Freud.
2 It seems then that we can only speak of transference in reference to this caricature of a beautiful woman who has only one aim: to sleep with her male psychoanalyst. Freud has contributed to the promotion of this topos, notably in his *Papers on Technique*, 1911–15, his most comic text.
3 Seminar of April 22, 1964.
4 This definition appears for the first time in the Rome Discourse, and this formula is written as "the discourse of the other" with a small a. See "The Function and Field in Speech and Language in Psychoanalysis" in Lacan (2006) *Écrits*, trans. B. Fink, New York: W. W. Norton, pp. 197–268.
5 See Jean-Luc Marion (1981) *Sur l'ontologie grise de Descartes*, 2nd edn, Paris: Vris (available in English as (2013) *Descartes' Grey Ontology: Cartesian Science and Aristotelian Thought in the Regulae*, trans. S. Donohue, South Bend: St Augustine Press) and (1981) *Sur la théologie blanche de Descartes*, Paris: PUF.
6 Descartes's error concerns the "Romanesque" character of Cartesian physics; see Jean Claude Milner (1989) *Introduction à une science du langage*, Paris: Seuil, pp. 138–9, 158–60, 217 (note 28).
7 I have developed this in a discussion of a case of Serieux and Capgras. Cf. (1986) "Vous êtes au courant, il y a un transfert psychotique" ("You are aware, there is a psychotic transference"), *Littoral*, 21 (October): 89–110.
8 This section of the meeting of July 4, 1956 of *The Psychosis Seminar* is not included in the published version.

9   Editors' note: The author uses an unpublished version of the seminar. See Lacan 1993: 41.

10 See the discussion of the *lapsus calami* "schizobrother" (*schizophrère*) in F. Dupré (1984) *La 'solution' du passage à l'acte*, Toulouse: Erès, 250.

12 See Lacan (1993) "Aren't you sometimes afraid of going mad?" p. 123. To assess the fear of going mad it suffices to open any book in which a psychiatrist relates a little bit of his experience.

13 In referring myself to Lacan's notion of four discourses, I have shown elsewhere that this putting knowledge into reserve had a constitutive effect on the analytic discourse that was the determining consequence of Freud's internship under Charcot (Allouch, *Lettre pour lettre*, Toulouse: Erès, 45–70).

14 Editors' note: this is the title of Marguerite Anzieu's unpublished novel.

15 Editors' note: *agape* is the love that gives and expects nothing in return; *eros* is physical, passionate love.

16 Self-punishment bridges the *passage à l'acte* and the calling to Freud via Alexander N. Staub. Cf. J. Lacan (1966), *Écrits*, p. 66. For "On the Problem of Self-Punishment," one can refer to chapter 9 of F. Dupré (1984) *La 'solution' du passage à l'acte*.

17 Didier Anzieu also will address himself to Freud in regard to his experience of his mother's madness but in a different manner than that of Lacan.

18 J. Lacan (1972) *Le Savoir du Psychanalyste*, unpublished seminar of January 6.

Bibliography

Freud, S. (1911) "Psycho-Analytic Notes on an Autobiographical Account of a Case of Paranoia (Dementia Paranoides)," in *The Standard Edition of the Complete Psychological Works of Sigmund Freud, vol. XII*, London: Hogarth.

—— (1925) An Autobiographical Study, in *The Standard Edition of the Complete Psychological Works of Sigmund Freud, vol. XX*, London: Hogarth.

Lacan, J. (1932) *De la psychose paranoïaque dans ses rapports avec la personnalité : thèse de la Faculté de Paris*, Paris: Le François éditeur.

—— (1938; 1984) *Les complexes familiaux dans la formation de l'individu*, Paris: Navarin and (2001) *Autres écrits*, Paris: Seuil, pp. 23–84. Partially translated by Carolyn Asp (1988) as "The Family Complexes," *Critical Texts* 5: 12–29.

—— (1964) *The Four Fundamental Concepts of Psychoanalysis, Seminar XI*, trans. A. Sheridan; also (1977) London: Hogarth.

—— (1967) "Petit discours aux psychiatres," speech delivered at the Cercle d'Études directed by Henry Ey, 10 November 1967.

—— (1968) "Proposition of October 9, 1967 on the Psychoanalyst of the School," *Scilicet 1, Champ Freudien*, Paris: Seuil.

—— (1970) Exposé chez Daumézon, unpublished.

—— (1972) Le savoir du psychanalyste, unpublished seminar of January 6, 1972.

—— (1976) "Conférences et entretiens dans des universités nord-américaines," *Scilicet* 6/7, Paris: Seuil.

—— (1978) *Lacan in Italia*, Milan: La Salamandra.

—— (1956; 1993) *Seminar III: The Psychoses 1955–1955*, trans. R. Grigg, New York: W.W. Norton.

Roudinesco, E. (1993) *Jacques Lacan*: Esquisse d'une vie, histoire d'un système de pensée, Paris: Fayard, translated by B. Bray as Jacques Lacan (1997), New York: Columbia University Press.

9

THE SPECIFICITY
OF MANIC-DEPRESSIVE
PSYCHOSIS

Darian Leader

Clinicians working in a Lacanian framework will be familiar with three main diagnostic categories of psychosis: paranoia, melancholia, and schizophrenia. All predicated on the mechanism of foreclosure, they tend to be differentiated in terms of the relation to the Other, the treatment of morbid excitation and the establishment of meaning. Depressive states outside melancholia are considered on a case-by-case basis, and the same can largely be said for periods of elation and exuberance.

But what of manic-depressive psychosis? One of the central categories of classical psychiatry, Lacan nonetheless had little to say about it as a nosological entity, whether through acknowledgment or critique. There are a few references in the early psychiatric work, and later some comments on mania and depression in his seminars and writings. These are often quoted, yet the actual question of the diagnostic category has received far less attention. Despite the fact that the label of manic-depressive psychosis is used in clinical presentations, there seem to be no real distinguishing features beyond the standard conceptualizations of foreclosure and mania.

And this brings us to our first problem. Even the most cursory reading of Lacan's remarks on these themes gives a clinical picture that is, to say the least, non-specific. The comments on mania, for example, apply just as much to the states of intense agitation and verbal association found in schizophrenia as they do to the so-called "flight of ideas" of manic-depression. The remarks on "manic excitation," on the other hand, could qualify just as well certain forms of hallucination or perturbations within the field of affects. And when Lacan uses the term adjectively to qualify the experience of the end of analysis, he is clearly not suggesting a diagnostic judgment.

A similar difficulty is found in Freud's work. In "Mourning and Melancholia" he includes mania with melancholia, despite the fact that clinically the occurrence of melancholias that never generate manias is far more frequent. Indeed, there are many reasons to question Freud's association, and the cautious tone of his text seems justified. It could be argued that the lows of manic-depression are fundamentally different from those of melancholia, with far less fixity on a single motif, and, equally, that the phenomenology of manic-depression is in fact much closer to schizophrenia than it is to melancholia.

As we start thinking about these questions, a number of clinical and conceptual problems are raised that might help us to consider more critically our use of diagnostic categories and the delimitations we establish between them. Let us look first at some historical issues.

Just as analysts tend to claim a special atemporal pedigree for hysteria, so psychiatrists frequently accord a comparable place to manic-depression. Citations from Aretaeus of Cappadocia inevitably precede excerpts from medieval writers on accidie, and a line is sketched from the classical world to Kraepelin's clinic of late nineteenth century Germany and then on to the bipolar disorders of today. The clinical phenomena of exaltation and dejection are taken to indicate a historical unity, as if all documented descriptions were circumscribing the same form of human distress.

Yet these ubiquitous histories are rather misleading. Note first of all that the endlessly iterated Aretaeus quotations always contain points of ellipsis, which, if filled in, present both a varying clinical picture and confirmation that the Greek writer was not trying to frame a distinct diagnostic category. Medieval notions of accidie are similarly decontextualized and linked far too casually to contemporary theories of depression. Indeed, medieval writers frequently associate accidie with gossiping and diversion rather than the stupor and silence we might hope for. But the key discontinuity here is really to be found in pre-Kraepelinian psychiatry, and especially in the work of Jean-Pierre Falret and Jules Baillarger (Falret 1853–4; Baillarger 1853–4; Ritti 1883).

It was well recognized in mid-nineteenth century psychiatry that states of acute depression and elation could be found in any number of diagnostic structures. From the 1840s onwards, there was an effort to distinguish a specific clinical entity that involved a sequential passage through such states from the many other clinical forms that alienists had documented. Falret's circular madness and Baillarger's double form madness were formulations of this entity, although both authors admitted that they had only ever seen a handful of cases.

In contrast to the mainstream psychiatry of today, they were trying to move beyond the question of mood fluctuations to study the quality of such states, the relation between them and the thought processes underlying them. In agreement with many of their contemporaries, they argued that mania and melancholia were in no way diagnostic of the entity they were describing. A manic episode or a melancholic depression would not point to a diagnosis of circular or double form madness, and the new categories were introduced precisely to make this point.

With Kraepelin, this careful work would be sadly undone. Starting from the sixth edition of his *Psychiatry*, he forged a notion of "manic-depressive insanity" that annexed nearly all manias and melancholias to manic-depression, regardless of rhythm or sequence, as well as all forms of periodic and circular psychosis. Despite hundreds of critiques, many given impetus by the hostility to German scholarship after the First World War, this reductionist view would eventually achieve a certain dominance over American psychiatry. The bipolar diagnoses of today often cite Kraepelin as their historical precedent and certainly share with him an enthusiasm for over-inclusiveness. But we should note that, contrary to the usual claims, Kraepelin had no concept of affective disorders and he makes hardly any reference to problems of mood.

Now, if Kraepelin had at first divided the psychoses into two main groups (manic-depression and dementia praecox), by 1920 he was no longer so sure (Kraepelin 1991). Both his critics and his students had been struck by the difficulty of maintaining the differentiation. What of the manic-depressive who showed the "symptoms" of dementia praecox—the stereotypies, the hallucinations, the negativism, the suggestibility? And what of the praecox patient who was angry and excitable at one moment, yet withdrawn and silent the next? Interestingly, these observations tended to move from manic-depression to dementia praecox rather than the other way round, a fact echoed in the studies of diagnostic practice in the 1940s that found that a very high percentage of those initially diagnosed with manic-depression were later diagnosed with schizophrenia, although the reverse was not the case (Hoch and Rachlin 1941).

The difficulty in differentiating certain cases of excitement as circular or schizophrenic led to several compromise suggestions, such as Bleuler's "schizoid manic reactions." Psychiatrists such as Bleuler, Gaupp and Courbon were interested in the intersection between the two categories, and the new label of "combined psychosis" gained increasing currency (Bleuler 1922; Gaupp 1913; Courbon 1925). There was clearly a problem here. The categories were attractive, yet clinically no hard and fast distinctions could be relied on. Hence the creation of the new hybrids.

In the psychoanalytic literature, opinion was also divided. Ernest Jones was one of the first to publish a psychoanalytic study of a case of hypomania in 1909, yet a few years later he would write to Freud that he doubted manic-depression really existed. In a letter of February 15, 1914, he admits that, "It looks to me as if there were no such disease [as manic-depressive insanity], some cases being psychoneuroses, others paraphrenia (especially paranoia), the prominence of the affective symptoms replacing the other mechanisms of distortion (as they do in dreams sometimes)" (Jones 1993: 263).

Karl Abraham and Melanie Klein of course wrote a great deal on this subject, yet curiously the popularity that their concepts enjoyed was not reflected in any increased attention to the category. Although Abraham had a real interest in differentiation, certainly present in his pre-analytic work on the development of the chick, Klein did little to elaborate category distinctions. On the contrary, mechanisms supposedly specific to manic-depression were described across the diagnostic board. The great irony of Klein's work is that it is essentially a brilliant theory of manic-depression applied to all other clinical structures, yet the international success of the theory did not produce any renewed scrutiny of nosology.

The early American analysts were more focused here, exploring the clinical category and trying to formulate it using Freudian concepts. Ultimately, they would run up against the same problems that had bedeviled the psychiatrists. The research group on manic-depression run by Frieda Fromm-Reichmann from 1944 to 1947 at the Washington School of Psychiatry would conclude that "[o]ur investigation led us to question the justification of Kraepelin's classification of the manic-depressive disorder as a specific clinical entity of its own" (Cohen 1954). Indeed, the same reclassification seen in the psychiatric studies would occur in the analytic ones.

If Jones could cite a 1907 case treated by Otto Gross as the first example of analytic work with a manic-depressive patient, he would later point out that it was in fact a case of dementia praecox. Even Jones's case was not immune. Jung immediately sensed that it was also a dementia praecox, and five years later the psychiatrist John MacCurdy asked the hospital to consult its records, confirming Jung's opinion (MacCurdy 1925: 306).

A similar fate awaited the longest and most detailed study of manic-depression to be published within the ambit of Freud's circle, the monograph *On Flight of Ideas* that Ludwig Binswanger brought out in 1932. Several hundred pages of minute analysis of the speech of a manic patient are followed by a discreet appendix in which we learn that later events showed that he was in fact schizophrenic, with ideas of influence and hallucinations (Binswanger 2000).

By 1951, Bertram Lewin could state in "The Psychoanalysis of Elation" that "many deny that there is a manic-depressive psychosis" and that "What seems to be well-understood now is that the old emphasis on the up-and-down swings of mood was obscuring more important psychological issues" (Lewin 1951: 45). What could these issues be?

Let's start with mania. In his seminar on dread, discussing the relations between *a* and *i(a)*, Lacan points out that "in mania, it is the non-function of *a*, and no longer simply its misrecognition, that is at stake. It's that something in which the subject is no longer ballasted by any *a*, which delivers him, sometimes without any possibility of freedom, to the pure, infinite and ludic metonymy of the signifying chain" (Lacan 1963).

Now, this comment seems to raise more problems than it solves. How would this non-function of *a* differ from the so-called "word salad" that we sometimes find in schizophrenia or any of the other language phenomena in the psychoses where the signifying chain lacks the support of an object? Secondly, the idea that in mania the signifying chain is infinite and ludic seems clinically incorrect.

The most obvious feature of the manias is precisely that they stop. As Patty Duke observed, when asked what's worse for kids, manias or depressions: "neither, of course, is easy but at least with the manias, my children knew there would be an end within a reasonable period of time. They knew that the mania would stop" (Duke and Hochman 1992: 208).

Likewise, as many analytic and psychiatric students of mania have shown, it is highly structured. What seems to be an infinite and ludic play is in fact, when listened to carefully, restricted in its concerns and follows an underlying logic.[1] Clang associations, for example, are actually quite rare. The chain is neither infinite nor inherently ludic, although the penchant for humor, punning and verbal jest may sometimes be pronounced, and requires explanation.

As for the non-function of a, one would then have to explain how it is that manias end and so-called free intervals can occur: does a start to function once again? Can a be integrated into $i(a)$ as it can in mourning? If a is a result of a structural construction of subjectivity, how could it function and then not function? There is the risk here of falling into the trap of seeing mania as what happens to language if you remove the a, as if this simply made the subject the puppet of purely associative links between words, exactly the misconception that students of mania such as Falret, Liepmann and Binswanger had done their best to dispel. We would be moving towards rather than away from Greisinger's famous definition of mania as a state in which "the soul is free, no longer bound by anything."

But let's stay with the idea of non-function. Doesn't it illuminate certain clinical phenomena here? It is striking how often we hear from manic-depressive subjects about their efforts at housecleaning, and there can be hardly any memoir of manic-depression that does not include some mention of this activity. Something has to be extracted, and if the function of a consists, in a sense, in its removal, such activities, which extend from excising dirt to excising part of the brain via ECT, show a certain coherence.

In his memoir of manic-depression, Andy Berhman describes the strange gratification he would feel when vacuuming up dust balls and detritus in his home, and sweeping the dirt into a neat pile, "an act with a purpose and an end result" (Behrman 2002: 217–8). This operation of segregation and then extraction mirrors quite precisely his experience of ECT: "Like the hard concrete that filled my brain has been liquefied and drained from my skull" (Behrman 2002: 226).

The tempering effects of the removal of dirt and "hard concrete" contrast with the extreme vitalization of the body and the senses in manic-depression. For Terri Cheney, "The slightest sensation feels like a volcanic eruption" that "lights up every nerve ending" (Cheney 2008: 212); for Behrman, "Sounds are crystal clear, and life appears in front of [me] on an oversized movie screen"; "my eyelashes fluttering on the pillow sound like thunder" (Behrman 2002: xxi). One could read such descriptions of sensory intensification as indications of the non-function of a: with its extraction, life will seem less vibrant, less alive. The problem here, once again, is differential: why is it that where the manic-depressive can celebrate this porosity of sensory boundaries (at least at the start of mania), for the schizophrenic it can be a source of absolute terror: sounds are too loud, touch goes too deep, tastes are too strong . . .

Lacan's point about non-function, if we take a different perspective here, is simply to make mania appear as the opposite of the process by which *a* does function as the support of the signifying chain, called in Seminar X desire. Mania and desire represent the polarities, depending on the place of the object. Strictly speaking, the reference is to mania rather than to manic-depression. The comments in "Television" nuance the earlier idea, and form part of a series of references in 1973 in the introduction to the German translation of *Écrits* and "L'Étourdit" (Lacan 2001: 526, 556).

Speaking of affect in "Television," Lacan remarks that sadness, which people "qualify" as depression, is

> simply a moral failing, as Dante, and indeed Spinoza, put it: a sin, which means a moral weakness, which is ultimately located only in relation to thought, that is the duty of speaking well (*bien dire*), to situate oneself in relation to the unconscious, to structure. And if ever this weakness, as rejection of the unconscious, ends in psychosis, there's the return in the real of what is rejected, that is, language: it's the manic excitation by which such a return becomes fatal.

(Lacan 2001: 526)

The surprising description of depression as a moral weakness would have raised no eyebrows within the context of Christian ethics. Medieval debates on accidie focused first on whether it was a sin, and if so, what kind, and later on accidie as negligence of a higher good. Gloom becomes sinful only when we recognize that we are called to God and that hope and joy are duties linked to attainment. Sadness becomes a sin when opposed to the duty of rejoicing in God, and can hence be classed along with hatred, envy, pride and anger.

The duty here is not the Christian life, however, but that of *bien dire* and "finding oneself" in the unconscious, and the most extreme forms of rejection of this are equated with psychosis, a categorical not wanting to know about the unconscious. The fact that it is Dante here rather than St Thomas whom Lacan evokes is perhaps due to the former's famous connection in the fifth circle between accidie and the inability to speak: hymns gurgle in the throats of these wretches, for they "cannot speak it in full words."

The reference to mania here is curious. The rejection of locating oneself in relation to the unconscious may offer a definition of psychosis, but why mania? As Colette Soler points out, Lacan does not say mania here but "manic excitation," which could be taken in a much more general sense as indicating any return of libido in the body (Soler 2002). But again, this is non-specific: why would it take the form of manic excitation rather than any of the myriad forms of morbid agitation and intrusion found, for example, in schizophrenia? Or indeed, following the formula that what is rejected from the symbolic returns in the real, why not in the form of hallucination?

As to its "fatal" aspect, it is well known that manic excitation rarely leads to death. On the contrary, suicide is more likely in the depressive phases, and more likely still in times of apparent convalescence. Whatever we make of these details, Lacan's comment still leaves little ambiguity as to his position in the analytic debate on mania: here it is clearly an effect of foreclosure rather than, as Abraham, Rado, Klein and many others believed, a defense against its effects.

But why mania in some cases and not others? We should return here to the work of the early alienists, and separate states of excitation, elation and agitated confusion from mania as such. Loquacity, grandiosity and the apparent absence of "guiding ideas" are hardly hallmarks of mania. Real mania does, however, have certain parameters, which I have explored elsewhere: the initial sense that "The right words are there," that one has a position from which to speak, the necessity of an addressee, the intense feeing of a connection to the world, the conviction that supplies won't run out, the oscillation of a fault, and the rigid separation of binaries, most frequently "good" and "bad" (Leader 2013).

As the arc of mania continues, speech becomes more difficult. Barriers, obstacles and frustrations become magnified. The world "seems to be on a different page." And this brings us to the vital question of how manic episodes end. Lacan had an interest in this problem in his early psychiatric work, and suggested that ideas of persecution played a role here (Lacan 1973). Clinically this is borne out by the fact that the periods that follow mania so often contain repetitive thoughts of someone "bad," and it is difficult not to guess that these have a stabilizing rather than an aggravating function.

If we turn now to the differentiation of the psychoses, we find perhaps more questions than answers. Paranoia, melancholia, and the group of schizophrenias can be separated using the variables of meaning, localization of libido and distance from the Other. For the paranoiac, the world has a sense: he has succeeded—via delusion—in giving a meaning to the desire of the Other. Libido has been localized in the Other, making the paranoiac subject innocent and the Other guilty. Distance to the Other has been regulated, as there is a clear separation between self and Other.

In the schizophrenias, in contrast, meaning has not been fixed. Despite the efforts at delusional construction, the question of meaning remains open, and the subject is often suspended there. Libido is not localized in the Other but returns in the subject's mind and body. Boundaries between self and Other may be indistinct and unreliable, and the schizophrenic is often engaged in the lifelong task of trying to maintain them in any way possible.

As for melancholia, the problem of meaning is generally fixed: the subject is guilty. Libido submerges the ego, as we see in the pervasive self-reproach and devaluation, and the relation of self to Other takes the form of the equation that Freud discovered in "Mourning and Melancholia." When we turn to manic-depression, things become trickier. As Henri Ey pointed out, the subject's productions do not seem as anchored in beliefs as, say, those of the paranoiac (Ey 1954: 55). This, indeed, led some commentators to deny the presence of delusion in manic-depression altogether, or to separate "manias with delusion" from manias "without."

If anything is consistent at the level of sense here, it is less that the Other contains something bad than that the Other is in danger. The altruism of manic episodes and the well-known devotion to charitable and environmental projects are forms of saving the Other, of keeping the Other from harm. Where for the paranoiac the Other harbors a point of toxicity and must be denounced, for the manic-depressive it must, on the contrary, be restored, like the damaged church for St Francis.

Klein recognized this preoccupation in manic-depression, yet linked it too hastily to the subject's own aggressive tendencies: the Other was being protected ultimately from oneself. Yet case after case suggests that what is at stake here is not merely the subject's death wishes but the question of responsibility for a death, situated earlier in the family history. A death or tragedy in a previous generation has never been properly inscribed, and so the weight of responsibility hits the subject in the lows and evaporates in the highs. The Other must be kept from danger, or declared "not guilty." Where the paranoiac and melancholic have resolved this question—"The Other is guilty" and "I am guilty" respectively—in manic-depression the fault oscillates from the subject to the Other and back again.

Doesn't this also help us to explain the curious vacillations around the sense of identity in manic-depression? One of the most frequently voiced questions is whether it is some kind of foreign body or in fact an intrinsic part of the self. "How much of me is me," asks Lizzie Simon, "and how much of me is the illness?" (Simon 2002: 210). Would the person really be themselves after the proposed chemical excision of their mania? Do the highs and lows reveal or obscure who they really are? Should manic-depression be seen as constituting or as compromising the self?

The remarkable ubiquity of these questions perhaps echoes the underlying uncertainty about a responsibility. Not knowing whether the manias and depressions belong to them or not reflects the difficulty of not knowing whether the responsibility is theirs or someone else's. The hyperidentification with the Other means that the fault is both theirs and the Other's, but never entirely their own. Note the way that, as Duke puts it, in mania, "I never really accomplished anything that I could call my own" (Duke and Hochman 1992: 158). And isn't the most common thought after a manic episode precisely to ask, "What have I done?" Any analytic approach has to explore the reference of this "I," charting its movement from subject to Other and back again.

Although suicide in manic-depression can occur for a number of different reasons, it can sometimes aim to settle this agonizingly open question of responsibility. Law codes frequently treat suicide as a crime here, yet it would be more accurate to see it, as early English and Roman law did, less as a crime than as a means to eradicate a crime. When manic-depressive subjects appeal for pharmacological or surgical help, it is often to "wipe the slate clean," as if a single act could absolve them, rather like Behrman's vacuuming away of dust and dirt.

If we turn now to the question of libido, it returns for the manic-depressive, as for the schizophrenic, in the body, but also surely in language—although one could make the same claim for many cases of schizophrenia in which the chain of words is a source of libido, either as an enjoyment or as a mortifying, intrusive vehicle. Cheney makes the brilliant point here that the bodily excitation she experienced was no more and no less than an effect of language: the constant jiggling, movement and physical tension of mania were for her simply forms of the pressure to speak, experienced directly in the body (Cheney 2008: 68).

As for the distance from the Other, this takes on a benign rather than a malignant quality: the subject is joined to the world in a beatific harmony, or at least at the start of the manic arc. There is an acute sense of participation in the Other, understood by many post-Freudians as a stakeholding in the imagined omnipotence of the love object. The fact that it is the Other rather than the other is reflected in the choice of impersonal bodies such as Nature or Civilization or The Universe, which the subject feels deeply a part of, rather like Sister Maria at the beginning of *The Sound of Music*.

These are not the only features that may encourage a separation of manic-depression from other forms of psychosis. The phenomena of thought insertion, thought withdrawal and feelings of influence seem to be absent, suggesting that the topological relation with the Other is in marked contrast with schizophrenia. And yet at the same time, we find plenty of cases where these phenomena are inverted: the person believes during the mania that they are influencing others and transmitting their thoughts to them, just as the sense of identity can undergo strange mutations.

For students of mania such as Greisinger and Ey, there was always an "as if" quality here. The manic-depressive subject somehow never quite believes in the role they are playing out, yet this view may be the result of other factors. The lability of beliefs, which indicates to them the absence of delusional fixity, may simply be a consequence of the need to keep the Other present, alive and out of danger.

For Fromm-Reichman, a schizophrenic subject may be less afraid of attacking this Other because they are less afraid of loneliness. In her terms, the manic-depressive, unlike the schizophrenic, has not accepted the bad mother as his fate (Cohen 1954: 126). He can sell out his ideals to gain love. Note the way that hospitalized manic-depressive subjects so frequently manage to gain small privileges on the ward, thereby making themselves special for the nurse or warden they interact with. Where analysts once saw as a sign of orality the fact that admission of manic-depressive subjects would inevitably be followed by a request for a meal, we can understand it here as another example of a small favor to be granted.

The subject here may dispense with surface ideals that have apparently oriented their projects, but the weight of the Other's ideal will always be present. This could take the form of a parental expectation about the child's future, and the subject tries, often desperately, not to disappoint it. The absolute character of the ideal here has been noticed by analysts. From a Kleinian perspective, since the subject has to keep good and bad apart, objects can become terrifyingly moral and exacting. Where others located here an accentuation of superego function, the pressure to be perfect that proves so ravaging for the manic-depressive subject can be seen as simply a consequence of this separation of predicates.

There are plenty of cases, likewise, in which mania elevates the subject to a divine position, but, in contrast to other examples, it is always within a nexus of participation: a god to know other gods, or to recognize the godlike in their fellow human beings. The fact that these ideas can so easily be contested after the manic arc has run its course or been arrested chemically perhaps confirms the logical priority of the subject's relation to the Other, so often idealized, rather than to their own insignificance.

It is crucial for the manic-depressive subject to guarantee the Other's belief in them, and this sheds light on the remarkable frequency of Truman Show ideas in which the person is part of an experiment. Whereas for others the idea that the world is staged for them usually has a menacing quality—to trick them, deceive them etc.—in manic-depression it is once again benign: it is part of a test to help them move to another level, it is something they are in on. The Other includes them, believes in them, wants them to go forward.

We see this illustrated in the idea, voiced by a manic-depressive patient, that the reality around her was a vast illusion, created to test her: it had all been made up, she said, and she would eventually arrive at the thought that she herself had been made up. Rather than dismissing this as simply a bizarre quirk of psychosis, why not read it as the logical consequence of the structure of manic-depression itself? The Other's belief has to be maintained at all costs, even at the price of according oneself an illusory status.

Mania here can hardly be identified as a direct effect of foreclosure, even if manic excitation can be. Its function must be restorative, a "flight into object relations" as it was once called. The idealizations at play can be quite remarkable, and as Fromm-Reichman observed, whereas for many schizophrenic subjects the Other has feet of clay, for the manic-depressive there will be a continued elevation of at least one person to a position of authority or wisdom.

To conclude, I've done my best to sketch out some possible differences between manic-depressive psychosis and the other forms we are familiar with. It seems important to distinguish real mania from the many varieties of excitement and elation that can be mistaken for it. Once we recognize its particularity, the real question is whether we should annex it to the schizophrenias or accord it a separate status.

For my tuppence worth, I would be tempted to include it, primarily because of the forms of mediation employed in relation to the Other. We see so many of the classic features of schizophrenia in reverse that it is difficult not to infer that the same space of overproximity is in question. The different forms of schizophrenia can then be understood as different ways to manage this space. The ideas of persecution at the beginning and end of manic episodes that Lacan drew attention to in 1932 can be recognized as attempts to reinforce the boundary between self and Other, a boundary that is continually in jeopardy in such a space.

Note

1   See Binswanger's *Sur la fuite des idées* and Liepmann, H. (1904) *Über Ideenflucht*, Halle: Marhold.

Bibliography

Baillarger, Jules (1853–4) "Note sur un genre de folie dont les accès sont caractérisés par deux périodes régulières, l'une de dépression, l'autre d'excitation," *Bulletin de l'Academie nationale de Medecine*, 19: 340–52, Paris: Octave Doin.

Behrman, A. (2002) *Electroboy: A Memoir of Mania*, New York: Random House.

Binswanger, L. (1932; 2nd edn 2000) *Sur la fuite des idées*, Paris: Millon.

Bleuler, E. (1922) "Die Probleme der Schizoidie und der Syntonie," *Zeitschrift für die gesamte Neurologie und Psychiatrie*, 78: 373–99.

Cheney, T. (2008) *Manic: A Memoir*, New York: Harper.

Cohen, M.B. et al. (1954) "An Intensive Study of Twelve Cases of Manic-Depressive Psychosis," *Psychiatry*, 17: 103–37.

Courbon, P. (1913) "Démence précoce et psychose maniaco-dépressive: contribution a l'étude des psychoses associées," *Encéphale*, May: 434–6.

Duke, P. and Hochman, G. (1992) *A Brilliant Madness: Living with Manic-Depressive Illness*, New York: Bantam.

Ey, H. (1954). *Etudes Psychiatriques*, vol. 3, Paris: Décslée de Brouwer.

Falret, J.-P. (1853-4) "Mémoire sur la folie circulaire," *Bulletin de l'Académie nationale de Médecine*, 19: 382–400, Paris: Octave Doin.

Gaupp, R. (1925) "Die Frage der kombinierten Psychosen," *Archiv fur Psychiatrie und Nervenkrankheiten*, 76: 73-80.

Hoch, P. and Rachlin, H. L. (1941) "An Evaluation of Manic-Depressive Psychosis in the Light of Follow-up Studies," *American Journal of Psychiatry*, 97: 831–43.

Jones, E. (1911) "Psychoanalytic Notes on a Case of Hypomania," *American Journal of Insanity*, 2: 203–18; and also in Andrew Paskauskas (ed.) (1993) *The Complete Correspondence of Sigmund Freud and Ernest Jones*, Cambridge, MA: Harvard University Press.

Kraepelin, E. (1920; rpt 1991) "The Manifestations of Insanity." *History of Psychiatry*, 3: 509–29.

Lacan, J. (1932; 3rd edn 2001) *De la psychose paranoïaque dans ses rapports avec la personnalité*, Paris: Seuil.

——— (2001) *Autres Écrits*, Paris: Seuil.

Leader, D. (2013) *Strictly Bipolar*, London: Hamish Hamilton.

Lewin, B. (1951) *The Psychoanalysis of Elation*, London: Hogarth.

Liepmann, H. (1904) *Über Ideenflucht*, Halle: Marhold.

MacCurdy, J. (1925) *The Psychology of Emotion*, London: Kegan Paul.

Ritti, Antoine. (1883) "Traité clinique de la folie à double forme: folie circulaire, délire à formes alternes," *Bulletin de l'Académie nationale de Médecine*, 19, Paris: Octave Doin.

Simon, L. (2002) *Detour: My Bipolar Road Trip in 4-D*, New York: Simon & Schuster.

Soler, C. (1990) "La manie: pèche mortel" in (2002) *L'Inconscient à ciel ouvert de la psychose*, Toulouse: Presses Universitaires du Mirail.

10

MELANCHOLIA
AND THE UNABANDONED
OBJECT

Russell Grigg

There is a form of psychosis that presents some quite special difficulties to psychoanalytic treatment. It is what we can call melancholic psychosis or, more simply, melancholia. In this chapter I discuss the nature of melancholia, understood as a form of psychosis, and articulate a structural account of it. I describe some of its more significant features with the aim of analyzing and describing its underlying structure.

First, a point of clarification: psychiatry tends to distinguish between "psychotic depression" and "melancholia" according to whether hallucinations and delusions are present or not. Lacanian psychoanalysis has clearly demonstrated why it is that a subject may have a psychotic structure even where there are no indications of either delusions or hallucinations. This is a valuable discovery that allows us to look beyond overtly psychotic phenomena for more subtle signs of a psychosis in subjects prior to the onset of psychosis or those in whom the onset has taken a discreet and subtle form.[1] As I hope to show, Lacan's structural understanding of psychosis is particularly valuable in helping us to understand this special kind of psychotic structure irrespective of the presence or absence of classic psychotic symptoms. Moreover, the significance of this understanding is not limited to psychoanalysis, since even within psychiatric approaches, where the question whether melancholia is a psychosis is moot, some have concluded that "psychotic depression" is but a particular sub-type of melancholia.[2]

Many analysts have had the experience of an alarming, sometimes rapid, decline in the condition of an analysand during the early period of an analysis. This may occur as quickly as within the first three months but generally takes longer. I do not think that the following scenario is uncommon: a person comes to see you with a history of "depression." He has been on antidepressants, sometimes for years, perhaps from adolescence, which are often prescribed and managed by his doctor. There may be a history of substance abuse, whether of prescription medication or of a banned substance (i.e. methamphetamine, possibly cannabis), but I have a hunch that the substance is more likely to be a stimulant.[3] He may be reasonably productive, in that he is able to work, study, and enter into relationships. Although he comes with a history of depression, owing to the vagueness and prevalence of this diagnosis it would be unwise to draw any conclusions from it alone. He may have been hospitalized, and this may have occurred during adolescence or perhaps following a suicide attempt. Perhaps during this stay in hospital the person was diagnosed with "depression" or perhaps "borderline personality disorder." It is not uncommon for hospitalization never to have been repeated.

While the background of such patients may vary, the pattern of behavior in analysis is remarkably similar: a persistent adherence to the treatment combined with an alarming deterioration in the patient's condition as the transference develops. In the analysis itself, he is a "good patient." He works hard, is committed to the analysis, and "believes in" analysis, regarding it as his last hope. He is often disenchanted with medication, which he says he dislikes for its side-effects, just as he is unhappy about the stigma of mental illness that accompanies not being able to manage without medication. He has a great desire to be well again, and holds fast to the thought that his analysis will accomplish this for him.

Then, as the analysis unfolds, he becomes increasingly unwell, which is to say that his symptoms intensify. Increasing the frequency of sessions does not seem to make any difference, and, while the analysis may help to avoid the worst excesses of *passage à l'acte*, self-criticism and self-loathing move increasingly into the foreground. Sometimes—though not all that often, fortunately—things can go very badly indeed, to the point where it may be necessary for the patient to be hospitalized.

How are we to understand this reaction to analysis? Although it is thankfully rare, it is not unknown. The timing and evolution of the patient's decline would suggest that this reaction is related to the libidinization of the transference. If we add Freud's observation in "Mourning and Melancholia" ([1915] 1917a) that the melancholic's object-choice is narcissistic, in that it is easily taken up and easily abandoned, then I think we have a lead, which I explore in this chapter. This is the possibility that some, perhaps special, cases displaying such a negative therapeutic reaction are a melancholic form of psychosis. If we maintain that melancholia is a form of psychosis and, with Freud, analyze it structurally as distinct from neurosis and not just as a serious form of major depression, then we may be able to understand some of our own clinical work better, and also just possibly do a service to other forms of treatment, including even those that use medication.

I should say at the outset that the explanation for the negative therapeutic reaction originally developed by Freud does not fit the dramatic and apparently spontaneous reaction to the analysis I have just outlined. As Freud explains, the negative therapeutic reaction originates in an unconscious sense of guilt that may manifest itself in several ways in the treatment, not just as a worsening of the patient's symptoms as the analysis progresses. Freud reasons that symptoms become worse for the patient in the grip of a negative therapeutic reaction because she is counter-suggestive; indications of satisfaction on the part of the analyst with the work of the analysis are met with an aggravation of symptoms. This makes it sound as if the negative therapeutic reaction is a response produced by the transference, and that all that is required is a dispassionate or disinterested attitude from the analyst. But this is a misleading impression; as Freud goes on to say, even when we allow for the attitude of defiance towards the analyst, the greater part of the analysand's negative response remains unexplained. It is this unaccounted-for portion that Freud says contributes to an unconscious sense of guilt and associated need for punishment.

The reason I do not think this account fits the melancholic's response to the transference is related to the fact that, as I argue below, unconscious guilt does not offer an adequate explanation for melancholia. Because melancholia is not a malady of the superego, but a form of psychosis, the transference in melancholia is to be considered different from the negative, guilt-motivated reaction described by Freud. As we know, psychotic transference has a tendency to take on an erotomanic or persecutory dimension,[4] making its handling in the treatment a rather delicate matter. The erotomanic/persecutory dimension results from the subject's conviction that what comes from the Other takes the form "He loves me" or "He hates me." Perhaps we can consider that the more solipsistic form of love we find in the megalomanic, "I love myself," has an equivalent in the conviction of the melancholic, "I hate myself."

There is, however, one potentially confusing point in Freud's analysis of the negative therapeutic reaction. Freud notices a close connection between one form of the negative therapeutic reaction and melancholia: it is a form that arises from a "borrowed" unconscious sense of guilt—that is, when it is the result of an identification with someone to whom the person has been erotically attached; and it is "often the sole remaining trace of the abandoned love-relation and not at all easy to recognize as such" (Freud 1923: 50n). These remarks point to an odd, even bizarre, form of melancholia where the unconscious sense of guilt in the melancholic is the result of a direct identification with the sense of guilt carried by his abandoned love object; that is, the subject's guilt is not a response to his own recriminations against the lost object, as in mourning, but the result of an identification with the lost object's own superego. This is not the typical formation of a melancholic in which the libidinal tie to the object is narcissistic and we must therefore consider it a special and I think rather unusual case; it is one, moreover, with which Freud claims to have had "brilliant" success through uncovering the underlying attachment to the abandoned object.

It is difficult to know what more to say about these cases Freud reports. Their outcome is very much at odds with the cases particularly resistant to analytic treatment, and my inclination is to conclude that "melancholia" is not the right term to describe them. Be that as it may, they bring back the earlier question concerning the downward spiral and subsequent resistance to treatment of the type of analysand indicative, as I say, of a melancholic form of psychosis.

"Melancholia," not "depression"

Why use this term "melancholia"? It is preferable to "depression," which is now recognized to be too diffuse and broad a term to be of clinical use. As has been noted by Michael Alan Taylor and Max Fink,

> In clinical practice, depression describes a normal human emotion, a pathologic state if it is retained too long or too deeply, or a psycho-pathologic syndrome that may be mild or severe. A clinical depressive episode may be defined by its associated adverse life events or it may strike a subject without cause. Accepting "depression" as a medical diagnosis is equivalent to accepting "infection" as a definitive diagnostic term in clinical medicine.
>
> (Taylor and Fink 2006: 2)

"Melancholia" was already an old and familiar term by the time Kraepelin introduced it into modern psychiatry as a distinct clinical category under the name of "involutional melancholia," though it disappeared from his system of classification in the eighth and final edition of his textbook in 1913 (Kraepelin 1913). Contemporary psychiatry has been divided over the usefulness of the term. Some have advocated that it is more precise in meaning than "depression." Taylor and Fink, for example, describe it as a key pathology of mood characterized by a "pervasive and unremitting apprehension and gloom that colors all cognitive processes, resulting in a loss of interest, decreased concentration, poor memory, slowed thinking, feelings of failure and low self-worth, and thoughts of suicide." It is, they say, a recurrent and debilitating condition that "alters mood, motor functions, thinking, cognition, perception and many basic physiologic processes" (Taylor and Fink 2006: 15). Then when psychoanalysis adds an even more precise understanding of melancholia, including as it does the melancholic's reproaches, guilt and self-accusations, the vague term "depression" becomes even more unsatisfactory.

Freud brings a structural analysis to all psychopathology, and his structural analysis of melancholia is particularly important for several reasons. First, melancholia is more than just a severe form of depression. In general, we need to be wary of the current practice of the Diagnostic and Statistical Manual for Mental Disorders (DSM) and other contemporary approaches to mental illness that diagnose according to the severity of symptoms. This wariness is particularly important where melancholia is concerned because classifying forms of depression and depressive-like states into major and minor categories on the basis of their severity and/or their duration is to assume that all have roughly the same psychopathology. This approach obfuscates the interesting questions about melancholia, because it no longer sees it as a distinct condition but rather as a phase of illness that is not structurally distinct from other depressive illnesses; it regards melancholia as lying on the same scale of severity as other depressive illnesses, as merely a depressive illness of the highest severity.

The DSM assumes that mild and severe conditions are expressions of the same underlying condition, and its approach to depressive illnesses is no exception. One of the consequences of this—and maybe even the underlying motivation— is that in practice it often leads to the one standard treatment pattern, typically involving medication. It is recommended that for a diagnosis of depression the criteria for a major depressive disorder set out in the DSM-5 must be met (American Psychiatric Association 2013). However, the increase in categories and "specifiers" in successive editions of the DSM has tended to obscure the more fundamental distinctions, and the latest edition continues this trend. Since so called "minor depressive episodes" are frequently encountered and associated with the same negative effects as major depression, it is not surprising that there has been gradual "boundary creep." Not only are possibly different conditions treated in the same way, but the use of antidepressants recommended only for serious depression has also gradually been extending to minor episodes as well.[5] It also seems that in actual clinical practice there is an informal practice of prescribing higher doses the more severe the symptoms are, just as it is common to find antipsychotic medication prescribed for the more intractable cases of depression. Adopting different forms of treatment altogether for different forms of "depression" seems to be implicitly ruled out. It has not been lost on commentators that seeing what has come to be called "mild depression" as requiring medication is an approach that benefits the pharmaceutical industry, and yet it is well documented that a high percentage of those people who are prescribed antidepressants are not depressed by any of the standard diagnostic criteria and are therefore being prescribed a range of medications for which they are not suited.

Even from the perspective of biological and medication-based approaches to treatment, this flattening-out of distinctions between forms of depression, which assumes that they can all be laid out on a single spectrum from least to most severe, might account for some of their failures. For instance, there is a group of subjects diagnosed as depressed who are resistant to treatment by medication and frequently referred for electroconvulsive therapy (ECT), just as there is also a group of patients resistant to treatment by ECT itself. It would be useful to know whether there are significant differences underlying these cases of "depression."

Freud's "Mourning and Melancholia"

For Freud's structural analysis of mourning we should turn to his "Mourning and Melancholia," which is justly considered one of his master works and a major contribution to the study of affective disorders. It is a persuasively argued text, working with a distinction between mourning, in which the subject is aware what it is that he or she has lost, and melancholia, where the loss has an unconscious source and the true nature of the loss is unknown to the subject. Freud contributes both a careful observation of the phenomenon of melancholia and a structural analysis of its origins, one that changes our views about affective disorders ranging from different forms of "depression," as this term is now used, to whatever since de Clérambault has been known as "passionate psychosis."[6]

As masterful as Freud's little work is, not only does it leave some unanswered questions but there are some serious problems with Freud's analysis as well. One quite crucial problem is that the comparison and contrast he makes between mourning and melancholia is fundamentally misleading. The main difficulty is that Freud's analysis leads to the conclusion that melancholia arises from the loss of an object to which the subject is unconsciously attached. I argue here that the opposite is true: the melancholic response arises because of the proximity of the object through its failure to have become lost. The crisis for the melancholic arises with the proximity of an invasive and what Lacan calls "ravaging" object—to use this term in its old sense of wreaking havoc—causing devastation and destruction, an object from which the subject is unable to distance himself and to which he is constantly prey. There are several advantages to regarding the object as invasive for the melancholic, and I will just mention a particularly significant one here: the object that ravages is similar to, indeed a variant of, the object that persecutes; and this is as it should be, since, as I have already said, we should regard melancholia narrowly construed as a form of psychosis.

Mourning

Looking in closer detail at Freud's text, one is struck by the fact that the discussion of mourning focuses on the psychological features and almost completely ignores the ritualized aspect of mourning. Ritual is integral to the process of mourning, as the poet W. H. Auden emphasizes in his celebrated poem, written as a griever's lament, "Funeral Blues." The poem begins with the practice of mourning, but it soon weaves the personal grief of the griever into the description of the public, ritual nature of mourning:

> Stop all the clocks, cut off the telephone,
> Prevent the dog from barking with a juicy bone,
> Silence the pianos and with muffled drum
> Bring out the coffin, let the mourners come.

> Let aeroplanes circle moaning overhead
> Scribbling on the sky the message He Is Dead,
> Put crêpe bows round the white necks of the public doves,
> Let the traffic policemen wear black cotton gloves.

The ritualized practice of mourning is so prominent that the noun "mourner" does not refer to a person's grief, or at least does so only indirectly. A "mourner" is first and foremost someone performing a ritual. She is someone who attends a funeral or who is said to be "in mourning," frequently in a way that is prescribed either by religious law or popular custom. Mourning can mean wearing black; it can last for two weeks or forty days, where the period of mourning is frequently calculated to the day. In some cultures, it is even possible to employ professional mourners to make a public demonstration of grief to honor the deceased. In any case, the practice of mourning is less an indication of the extent of a person's grief than a ritual that is more or less correctly carried out as a mark of respect for the deceased. Again, even where the practice of mourning is not clearly circumscribed, there are still considerations of propriety that bear on the activities associated with mourning. As Hamlet sarcastically puts it, "Thrift, thrift, Horatio! The funeral baked meats / Did coldly furnish forth the marriage tables."[7]

Why is it so important to observe the rituals of mourning? Part of the answer has to be that love for the mourned object is capable of demanding respect for the person, for his dignity. However, while love for a person can demand respect for him, it is not just a question of love; mourning is not just about one's feelings for and affective relationship to the other but about the respect due to the person *qua* person. It may be true that mourning is also a mask placed over the Other that reflects back on us in inverted form the narcissism of our own survival—this is what Freud says when he writes in "Mourning and Melancholia" that the pleasure of being alive compensates for the loss of the object and thereby contributes to the overcoming of mourning. I would call this Freud's "cynical attitude" that regards mourning as a narcissistic process in which the loss of the object is entirely overcome and leaves not a trace; the person is free to live and love again. However, there is something else going on as well. When we mourn we are not just narcissistically pained by our loss, which is the "narcissistic wound" Freud refers to elsewhere, but we also have a moral attachment—a commitment, if you will—to the memory of the person who has gone; we have a commitment to memorializing the object we have loved. While there are obvious narcissistic components to this process, the symbolic memorialization of what is lost entails leaving a record in the Symbolic of the object's disappearance. This record is both public and private, or material and psychical. Auden's poem subtly weaves together the narcissistic and symbolic elements, as well as the public and private aspects that are present in the mourning process.

In the two quoted stanzas, Auden quite precisely brings out the narcissistic dimension of grief; a grief great enough to make the world stop and take note of the loss. Although this poem can be, and has been, seen as sentimental, to see it as nothing more than this would be to miss its subtlety. Auden himself was no sentimentalist. He is a poet who starts a poem called "Lullaby" with the lines, "Lay your sleeping head, my love, / Human on my faithless arm," that are without illusion about the permanence of love even as he recognizes its beauty and charm. His poetry is troubled, inquisitive, uneasy, both sad and anguished, and here in this poem about mourning—or, more accurately, poem of mourning—the narcissistic aspect of grief invokes the overvaluation of the love object: "The world has lost something precious"; "Stop all the clocks"; "The breaking of so great a thing should make a greater crack"; "Let the world come to a halt."

I return to this topic of narcissism below. To continue with the poem, note that Auden turns away from the public to speak of his own personal grief:

> He was my North, my South, my East and West,
> My working week and Sunday rest,
> My noon, my midnight, my talk, my song;
> I thought that love would last forever: I was wrong.

Then the poem concludes with a precise depiction of the destitution of the griever who has withdrawn all interest from the world:

> The stars are not wanted now: put out every one;
> Pack up the moon and dismantle the sun;
> Pour away the ocean and sweep up the wood;
> For nothing now can ever come to any good.

Note, however, that however grief-stricken the mourner may be, however inconsolable, however painful his loss, his sense of self-worth is undiminished. He does not feel guilty. He blames the world, God, destiny, bad luck—anything—for his suffering, but scarcely holds himself to blame. Now this seems to be at odds with the psychology of mourning, one of the most prominent features of which is sometimes said to be depression; indeed, this is even acknowledged as one of the five stages of the Kübler-Ross model of grief. This is, however, merely another illustration of the shortcomings of the term "depression." The "depression" of a griever is the depression of someone who has withdrawn her interest from the world and libidinal investment in it. This is the characteristic listlessness and introversion of the mourning subject, for whom "the stars are not wanted now" and for whom the moon can be packed away, the sun dismantled and the wood swept up. This depression is to be distinguished from the aggressive attack on the self, the remorseless punishment of the ego, which lies at the heart of the melancholic. Sartre got it wrong, at least for the melancholic: hell is not "other people"; the real hell lies in a place much closer to home, in the depths of one's own heart, a place from which there really is no exit.

Freud claims that in mourning each of the memories and expectations in which libido is bound to the object is brought up and hyper-cathected so that the libido can detach itself from it and, at the end of the process, the ego can be "free and uninhibited again" (Freud 1917a: 245).[8] This is such a manifestly untrue remark that I find it curious Freud should have made it. It is obvious to the most casual observation that mourning always leaves traces behind, in the form of painful memories of a loved one, that are liable to resurface at particular moments such as anniversaries, just as they can also emerge in connection with the most unexpected things: a movie, an item of clothing, a memory of a holiday, or even with a new love. A lost object rarely disappears entirely; an object that was once loved and lost is never abandoned without leaving a trace. And yet, according to

Freud, mourning involves a slow and painful process of withdrawal of one's attachment to the memories related to the lost object and a return to the *status quo ante*. But even in normal mourning the lost object always casts its shadow on the ego. Even if it is true that the normal process of mourning is over when one is free of the object's hold and free to live and love again, the ego never completely loses the mark of the object that has been lost.

Strangely, it took the tragic death from Spanish influenza of Freud's fifth child, Sophie, at the age of twenty-six in 1920 for Freud to recognize that when a once loved object is lost, it is never completely abandoned and remains irreplaceable. Indeed, he recognized that the reason for this continued attachment to the object that keeps the object alive, as it were, is the very love for the object itself. On February 4 of that year he wrote to Ferenczi of his "insurmountable narcissistic insult" (Falzeder, Brabant, and Giampieri-Deutsch 2000: 7), while some years later, on April 11, 1929, in a letter consoling Ludwig Binswanger who had undergone a similar loss, Freud wrote, "We know that the acute sorrow we feel after such a loss will run its course, but also that we will remain inconsolable, and will never find a substitute. No matter what may come to take its place, even should it fill that place completely, it remains something else. And that is how it should be. It is the only way of perpetuating a love that we do not want to abandon" (Fichtner 2003: 196).

"And that is how it should be," writes Freud. The mourning does not and should not bring an end to the object's presence in one's life. Otto Kernberg comments that the process of mourning a lost object can go hand in hand with a persistent memorialization of the lost person and one's relationship to him. As Kernberg puts it, there is not just an identification with the lost object, but also the setting up of an internal relationship with that object in its absence (Kernberg 2010: 607). It is as if out of respect for the person and one's attachment to him, one is bent on maintaining the memory of one's attachment to the object so that it outlives the psychical work of mourning. As Goethe once wrote, "We die twice: first when we die and then when those who knew and loved us die," and it is as living memorials that we carry the mark of lost loved ones on our souls (as cited by Kernberg 2010).

When the mourning is over, the object is still preserved in some way; and this is as it should be. As distressing as the persistent memory of a lost loved one may be, there may be no question for the person who has suffered a loss to want to forget his loss. Moreover, the sadness, the regret, and the pain experienced over a loss can be experienced without having any impact on the person's self-regard. One's life may be impoverished by the loss of a loved one, but without one's sense of one's own worth being diminished.

In thinking about mourning it is, then, important to emphasize the push to memorializing and the respect for the dead demanded of and by the bereaved, those who loved and have, in a sense, been left behind by the death of a friend or loved one.[9] The process of mourning involves a slow and painful repairing of the rent in the Symbolic produced by the subject's loss. The rent can only be patched through the two aspects of mourning: ritual, a symbolic process that mobilizes the entirety of the Symbolic order; and the psychical work of bereavement. It is important that the two processes be interwoven; the psychical work of bereavement is better achieved when accompanied by ritual at the level of the group or the community.

Melancholia

Freud discerns two essential preconditions for melancholia: narcissistic object-choice and regression to the oral phase. The narcissistic nature of the investment explains the strong attachment to the object alongside a readiness to abandon the object when obstacles arise. The narcissistic investment means there is an unconscious withdrawal of libido from the object and its investment in the ego, which is the same process by which Freud explains the collapse of the world, or "world-catastrophe," that occurs in the case of Schreber and other cases of paranoia (Freud 1911: 69ff).

This lends support to my argument that there is an underlying psychosis in melancholia, and that the negative reaction in the treatment arises from the circumstances of the transference. If this is so, then appealing to a negative therapeutic reaction is not decisive when enquiring whether the reaction is psychotic or not, given that this reaction can be present in other conditions, obsessional neurosis in particular. I also doubt whether the melancholic is suffering from a malady of the superego, as Freud believes.

While the narcissistic object-choice, which combines a strong attachment to the object with a paradoxical readiness to relinquish it, is crucial, it does not explain why the ferocity of the criticism addressed to the melancholic ego is as intense as it is—and yet, this is precisely what needs to be explained, since it is what is so specific to and so puzzling about melancholia. It may well be, as Freud holds, that attacks on the ego are really attacks on the lost object, yet we are left with no idea *why* these attacks should be so ferocious. We know that, with one major exception, which I come to below, the aggressive attack on the self and the remorseless punishment of the ego are specific to melancholia and are absent from mourning. For the melancholic, the loss of self-respect is the loss of the narcissistic illusion that he is a meritorious human being. The melancholic believes that it is his misfortune to be alive when being alive is a fate worse than death.

Freud explains this by saying that the self-criticisms are really directed at another person. He reasons that the ego identifies with the abandoned object and is subjected to harsh and cruel punishment by the superego as if it were this object.

The withdrawal of libido from the world and its narcissistic investment in the ego is further indicated by the absence of shame and the insistence with which the melancholic repeatedly reasserts worthlessness. But the self-criticism, which is a sort of collapse of narcissism, is different. Not only is it the most dangerous, even potentially fatal, aspect, but it is also the aspect that is the most paradoxical and difficult to explain. It simply cannot be explained in terms of the ego, which is now the target of the criticisms of the lost object. Criticisms levelled at the lost object are often present in mourning, but in no way do they acquire the horrendous level of the devastating attacks on the ego.

Freud is aware of this, which is why he adds a second dimension to the mechanism of melancholia; as he puts it, the regressive identification with the object is accompanied by a second form of regression, *to sadism under the influence of ambivalence*. This is fine so far as it goes, but it does look like a redescription rather than an explanation; explaining the severity of attacks on the ego by appealing to a regression to sadism is like saying sleeping pills work by virtue of their dormative powers. We are forced to conclude, then, that Freud's explanation is inadequate, since it does not explain the ravages of melancholia as an identification that is then subject to the criticisms to which the object was previously susceptible.

There is another problem as well. The account in terms of regression to sadism allows for no distinction between melancholia and obsessional neurosis, where, for Freud, the depression so typical of obsessional neurosis also arises from the aggression towards the object with which the ego has identified. Therefore, if we are to distinguish between obsessional neurosis and melancholia, there must be some important transformation that takes place when the forsaken object is "internalized."

I earlier described regression to the oral phase as the second of two preconditions for melancholia. Can this explain the devastation of melancholia? The question of regression to the oral stage in melancholia was taken up by Freud as a result of discussions over many years with his disciple and collaborator, Karl Abraham. The significance of the discussion is that it was clearly seen as a way to capture the very different nature of the relation to the lost object displayed by the melancholic subject. It is in this relation that Freud seeks to discover what is specific to the melancholic's response to loss, in the hope that it will clarify why the response is so different from mourning, on the one hand, and, on the other, from what unfolds in obsessional neurosis.

Having described oral eroticism in the first (1905) and second (1910) editions of the *Three Essays on Sexuality*, it is only in the third (1914) edition that Freud speaks of an actual oral or "cannibalistic" *phase* prior to the anal phase. He deepened his understanding of this phase and further elaborated it in his study of the Wolf Man, which was completed but for the appendix by November 1914. Thus, when Freud wrote the first draft of "Mourning and Melancholia" in February 1915 and finished it by May 4 that same year, he already had a detailed under-standing of the oral, cannibalistic stage. Freud writes in "Mourning and Melancholia" that the oral phase is the earliest stage of object-choice and thus the first way in which the ego picks out an object; that it does so by seeking to incorporate the object into itself; and that, in accordance with the oral or cannibalistic phase of libidinal development, this means devouring it. The same view finds expression in "Instincts and Their Vicissitudes," where Freud reiterates the view that incorporation of the object is the "preliminary stage" of love or "a type of love which is consistent with abolishing the object's separate existence" (Freud 1915: 138).[10]

The point of these remarks is that, while subsequent views about the oral stage such as Klein's emphasize that oral incorporation is an aggressive and destructive attack on the object, this is not Freud's view. Freud considered that indifference to the fate of the object would be a more accurate description of the ego's attitude; the intention is not one of aggressive attack and destruction. This is borne out in many places, including a comment in "Instincts and Their Vicissitudes," where Freud says that incorporation is a primitive form of love in which we can speak of unconcern or indifference but not of love and hate in the true sense of these terms (1915: 138–9).[11]

Freud never considered aggressive impulses to be primary. He viewed aggression and associated murderous impulses towards the object as secondary to, and derivative of, the desire to incorporate the object, and he relates sadistic impulses specifically to obsessional neurosis, not to melancholia. When, in *Introductory Lectures on Psycho-Analysis*, he refers to the sadism of the obsessional, it is to point out that it is a disguised form of love for the object. The "obsessional idea 'I should like to kill you,'" he says, "means at bottom nothing other than 'I should like to enjoy you in love'" (Freud 1917b: 344). Time and again Freud emphasizes the erotic dimension to oral incorporation and oral fantasies. On the other hand, when murderous impulses are directed towards the Oedipal rival they are motivated by the desire for exclusive access to the love object. In no circumstance do we ever find expression given to a primary aggressive or sadistic impulse in Freud.

In short, we see Freud pinpointing oral incorporation as a feature that is specific to melancholia but that does not help explain the fundamental issue: the melancholic is ravaged by an object he is unable to separate from. Freud's claim that in melancholia the regression is to an oral, cannibalistic relationship to the internalized object[12] actually goes to the heart of melancholia. Still, the ravaging nature of the relationship remains to be explained.

I will now examine some similarities and differences between melancholia and obsessional neurosis. The obsessional's reaction to loss can resemble the ravages in melancholia, with aggressive attacks on the self and remorseless punishment of the ego that resemble melancholia quite closely. Freud attributed this feature of obsessional neurosis to the ambivalence of the obsessional's relationship to his object. We can now pursue the comparison between melancholia and obsessional neurosis further. [13]

Melancholia and obsessional neurosis

First, melancholia in remission, when the melancholic is neither manic nor depressed, may have strong obsessional characteristics. It is not clear how widely this applies, and it is a matter for further enquiry. Psychiatry has not taken much interest in melancholia in this state, viewing it as simply the absence of mania and depression and in no particular need of attention. This is unfortunate, since melancholia typically has long periods of remission and these periods are also part of being a melancholic. Now, in many cases, we find numerous similarities between melancholia in remission and obsessional neurosis—so many, in fact, that if we only ever saw a melancholic in a state of remission it would be easy to take him for an obsessional. The obsessional character of the melancholic is displayed in a concern for cleanliness and order, where traits of obstinacy and defiance combine with an apparent docility and well-meaning attitude. I refer you to the description above of the melancholics one encounters clinically. One can also find, in sharp contrast with the profligacy of the manic, a frugality with money and attentiveness to personal possessions.

Second, in obsessional neurosis mourning can take on a pathological aspect that is apt to turn into a kind of depression.[14] As Freud writes, "Obsessional states of depression following upon the death of a loved one show us what the conflict due to ambivalence can achieve by itself when there is no regressive drawing-in of libido" (Freud 1917a: 251) such as is found in melancholia. Obsessional mourning is the result of the self-reproaches with which the obsessional blames himself for having wished the death of the object he loves. Freud subsequently points out that while the sense of guilt in the obsessional is particularly garrulous, its accusations are rejected by the ego whose protestations are not to be taken at face value, given that the sense of guilt has unconscious sources. In melancholia, on the other hand, the ego acquiesces in the accusations of guilt and submits to the punishment inflicted by the superego. The difference, Freud says, lies in the fact that in obsessional neurosis the superego's ferocity falls on impulses foreign to the ego while in melancholia the object of its wrath is now part of the ego, which has identified with it (Freud 1917a: 51).

In circumstances in which the self-reproaches and morbid depressive reaction to loss in the obsessional can be indistinguishable from the melancholic condition, knowing in any individual case that there has been an actual loss is diagnostically important. It is possible for melancholia to be triggered by loss, though it is not necessary, and knowing that there has been no actual loss can assist in deciding between a diagnosis of obsessional mourning or melancholia and, consequently, the risks being run in the treatment. Freud was probably correct in his assessment that obsessionals are unlikely to commit suicide, perhaps owing to the depth of ambivalence of the obsessional.

There are clear similarities between melancholia and obsessional neurosis, but when it comes to the differences between the superego's criticisms in obsessional neurosis and melancholia Freud's analysis highlights the *regression* of the libido back into the ego in melancholia and the absence of such a process in obsessional neurosis. This indicates, as Freud says, a more narcissistic investment in the object in melancholia.

The mention of narcissism returns us to the question of melancholia in relation to psychosis, since the withdrawal of narcissistic investment from the object onto ᴜᴇ ego is a crucial step in the psychotic process. As we are now heading into the field of psychosis, let's try to figure out how this works in relation to foreclosure of the Name-of-the-Father. On the assumption that melancholia is a form of psychosis, how does foreclosure operate in melancholia?

Melancholia and foreclosure

Freud never had a strong grasp of psychotic transference. He thought that psychotics were not suitable for analysis because they did not form a transferential bond with the analyst. We know this to be false; psychotics do form a transference, but, as discussed, one that is always liable to become erotomanic or persecutory.

It is possible that it was Freud's inexperience with psychotics that led to his misdiagnosis of the Wolf Man. Freud originally diagnosed Pankejeff as obsessional, which is understandable since it seems that Pankejeff was an undeclared psychotic at the time of his analysis with Freud. But by the time Freud referred Pankejeff to Ruth Mack Brunswick for a second analysis, he was paranoid if not overtly psychotic and, had Freud been more experienced with psychosis at the time of his return for treatment and subsequent analysis, he might well have detected the change in Pankejeff's condition.[15]

Work with psychosis is one of the areas that our clinical experience has extended since Freud. Thanks to Lacan's contribution to the psychoanalysis of psychosis and the work of those trained in the Lacanian approach, we can be confident about taking psychotic patients into analytic treatment. Lacan encouraged us "never to back away from psychosis," not only because it was a duty but also because of what we could thereby learn.

While Freud investigates the obvious similarities between mourning and melancholia, his analysis needs to be examined in light of the structural distinction introduced by Lacan between neurosis and psychosis if we are to understand melancholia. The reaction to the transference on the part of the melancholic indicates, as I have said, that it is the very presence of the object, rather than its loss, that is critical in the melancholic response to the transference. Freud writes that sometimes in melancholia an object has been lost, as in mourning, but that the real difference between the two is that while in melancholia *who* has been lost is known, *what* has been lost is not (Freud 1917a: 245). However, if the typical response to the transference is produced by the proximity of the object, then this suggests that melancholia is not about object *loss*. It follows that mourning, which is produced by the loss of an object, is a misleading model for melancholia; it might even be the case that melancholia does not arise from a loss at all, or at least, not from the kind of loss we find in mourning.

How are we to think about melancholia from a Lacanian perspective? To answer this question, we first need to take a step back and consider what Lacan has to say about mourning. We can begin by briefly considering an interesting comparison he makes between mourning and foreclosure (*Verwerfung*) in his seminar on desire and its interpretation, where he says that the death of a loved one makes "a hole in the real by means of which the subject enters into a relationship that is the inverse of . . . Verwerfung," adding that this hole in the Real "sets in motion . . . the signifier that can only be purchased with your own flesh and your own blood, the signifier that is essentially the veiled phallus" (Lacan 1977: 37–8). The suggestion here, then, is that in mourning the loss of a loved one creates a breach in reality, thereby setting in train, in the reverse direction, the process typically involved in the triggering of a psychosis. Instead of the calamitous collapse, as in psychosis, of signifiers that reveal the absence of the Name-of-the-Father, in mourning, the loss unconsciously activates afresh phallic signifiers that libidinally bind one to objects in the world. Whereas Freud wrote that the work of mourning is a process of relinquishing the features of the object one by one, Lacan sees the process as one of the preservation of the object by constructing a memorial to it in the symbolic; in other words, the work of mourning consists of codifying imaginary features of the object, $i(a)$, into signifiers lodged in the Other. The painful process of mourning stems from the fall of the semblants that love and desire attach us to (Lacan's "phallic significations"); the work of mourning is the transformation of these semblants into signifiers registered in and endorsed by the Other. It is the combination of ritual as a community event ("Stop all the clocks") with the individual's work of mourning that achieves this commemoration. Identification with the lost object, or rather with traits of the lost object, should be seen as part of this process.

But this does not tell the whole story about mourning, which also contains a real dimension, involving the subject's relation to the object a. In mourning, the painful loss of one's semblants exposes the underlying object a, the cause of one's desire and the object that one has put in place to support one's castration.[16] This is the exposure of the real of the object a, or at least a particular aspect of it, that is ordinarily hidden by the object's ideal features.

What makes melancholia so different from mourning is that the melancholic subject turns out to be defenseless against the object. The object cannot be memorialized, as in mourning, and instead remains forever there in the Real. The collapse of the semblants that otherwise veil the object persists, and the "grimace" of the object, like the grimace of a skull behind a beautiful face, is exposed; for the melancholic, the veil of semblants, the $i(a)$, over the object a falls altogether.

How can we understand this as a psychotic process? An account might look something like this. The Symbolic order regulates imaginary jouissance, subtracting it from the subject in the process. This subtraction of jouissance, which we write as $(-\varphi)$, takes place at the level of libido and the drive. Now, because in psychosis the key signifier of the Symbolic order, the Name-of-the-Father, is foreclosed, the possibility opens up of an excess of imaginary jouissance that is both unregulated and invasive. The disarray and confusion that Schreber, for instance, initially finds himself in is accompanied by invasive imaginary jouissance. Then, over the course of his psychosis, he discovers a new way of regulating jouissance, which involves constructing a new relationship to the world, a new "order of the world," to use his phrase, which emerges with his delusional metaphor.

The stability of Schreber's paranoid delusion contrasts with the earlier phase of the disorder when the excess of jouissance simply overwhelms him. In his "On a Question Prior to Any Possible Treatment of Psychosis," Lacan accounts for this crucial, confused period of the psychosis by appealing to the "subject's regression —a topographical, not a genetic regression—to the mirror stage," wherein the relationship to "the specular other is reduced here *to its mortal impact*" (Lacan 2006: 473; emphasis added). Schreber's voices, for instance, speak of him as a "leper corpse leading another leper corpse"; and his body is merely "an aggregate of colonies of foreign 'nerves,' a sort of dump for detached fragments of his persecutors' identities" (Lacan 2006: 473). Lacan's analysis is in terms of the distinction between the Imaginary and the Symbolic, as in Schema I, which is also cast in terms of this same Imaginary-Symbolic distinction (Lacan 2006: 476). The mortification in question is the result of the structural regression to the Imaginary relationship. The object in the Real plays no part.

It does not seem unreasonable to speculate that if Lacan had written this text after 1964 instead of in 1958, he would have invoked the role object *a* has to play. He would have referred the mortiferous role to the object, not to a regression to the Imaginary. And he would have distinguished between the collapse of phallic signification, "Φ_0," in Schema I, and the unmediated presence of object *a* with respect to the relationship to the object. In a 1967 address by Lacan to a meeting of psychiatrists at the Sainte Anne Hospital, as part of a series of lectures under the auspices of his friend Henri Ey, we find this comment: "It is the free men, the truly free men, who are mad. There is no demand for the *petit a*, he holds it, it is what he calls his voices, for instance. . . . He does not cling to the locus of the Other, the big Other, through the object *a*, he has it at his disposal. . . . Let's say that he has his cause in his pocket, and that is why he is mad" (Lacan 1967).[17] What we should note is that the proximity of the object *a* in psychosis means that the subject has not separated himself from it as the object cause of desire. This separation, which for the neurotic subject is produced by the Other as locus of speech and language, both regulates and limits his jouissance. In the absence of this separation a plenitude of jouissance is apparent in such typical psychotic formations as erotomania, hypochondriasis, and the persecutions characteristic of paranoia. One should also mention the feminization of the psychotic subject, or what Lacan calls the "*pousse-à-la-femme*" we find in many transsexuals, with their unbridgeable certainty and sometimes persistent pursuit of surgical interventions to more closely resemble their particular ideal of femininity.

In melancholia we encounter the same failure of separation from the object. The depressive function is explained by the fact that the unseparated-off object, in being a "piece of the Real" ("*un bout de réel*," as Lacan says) leaves the subject exposed and defenseless to its ravages. A comparison with paranoia might help: the paranoiac is prey to the evil Other who wishes him ill; the melancholic is likewise defenseless against the Real of a horrific object, unmediated by the Symbolic.

154

Let me illustrate the function of object *a* in melancholia with some observations concerning the case of the French author and playwright, Jean Genet.[18] Genet tried to take his own life on at least one occasion and also went through some serious periods vaguely described as "depressive." But one does not have to look very closely to detect an intimate relationship to the abject. Guéguen states that one of the paradoxes of Genet's life was the recognition given him, "a subject who presented himself as effaced and marginal," by "highly visible anti-authoritarian writers such as Cocteau, Sartre, Simone de Beauvoir and others" (Guéguen 2009: 101). In his biography of Genet, Sartre rightly came to attribute an existential role to "abjection" in his life, and Sartre described this abjection "as a methodical conversion, like Cartesian doubt and Husserlian epoche: it establishes the world as a closed system which consciousness regards from without, in the manner of divine understanding" (Sartre 2012: 141).

Guéguen persuasively argues that whereas in his writing Genet tries to elevate waste to the level of an agalma, his homosexuality would constantly place him in a position of detritus, of reject—homosexuality described in Edmund White's biography as "a curse, or worse as a sentence that could not be lifted." This identification with waste, this object *a* as a piece of shit, returns constantly in an aesthetic that, one might say, reveals the turd behind every object of beauty. As the title of one of his writings eloquently puts it, "What Remains of a Rembrandt Torn into Little Pieces and Flushed down the Crapper." Or, more existentially, he wrote of himself that "something that seemed rotten to me was turning my entire previous view of the world gangrenous" (Genet 1968: 21, my translation).

My suggestion is not that Genet was melancholic, necessarily; rather, his life and literature can be seen as a battle with an invasive Real through his identification with the object *a*. My proposition is that in other, more clearly melancholic cases, the real presence of object *a* is the source of those features so characteristic of melancholia.

Having set out to understand a certain type of subject that we encounter in our clinical practice, the "melancholic," and having looked for ways to explain their response to analytic treatment, I have argued that we can best understand melancholia as a sub-type of psychosis.

Lacan's structural account of the difference between neurosis and psychosis has been essential to my approach, even though Lacan talks of melancholia very rarely and does not offer much of an account of affective or passional psychoses, despite Clérambault's attention to it. I have sketched out a way of understanding melancholia based on the idea that while the neurotic's access to any libidinal object is via its semblants, in melancholia the veil of semblants falls from the object, leaving the melancholic exposed to the object in the real and at its mercy. This object can be either persecutory, as it is in paranoia, or abject-making, as in melancholia. Thus, Freud's approach, which proceeds by comparing and contrasting mourning and melancholia, is at best misleading. The melancholic suffers not from eternal mourning but from an inescapable proximity to the object in the Real. I have focused on the depressive aspect of melancholia, but there is the expectation that we may now be able to understand other phenomena as well. For instance, it may be possible to regard the presence of anxiety in melancholia as resulting from an encounter with the real of the object. Another line of exploration would pursue further the distinction touched on here between the two different modes of presence of the object: the phallic presentation based on the object and its semblants, on the one hand, and on the other the object in the Real, where the encounter with the real object is at stake in melancholia.

Notes

1 See "Foreclosure" in my (2008) *Lacan, Language and Philosophy* (Albany: SUNY Press), 3–24; Anne Lysy, "What One Calls 'Untriggered Psychoses,'" http://www. ch-freudien-be.org/Papers/Txt/lysy-fc12.pdf; Stijn Vanheule (2011) *The Subject of Psychosis: A Lacanian Perspective* (London: Palgrave Macmillan); and Jonathan Redmond (2014) *Ordinary Psychosis and the Body: A Contemporary Lacanian Perspective* (London: Palgrave Macmillan).
2 See, for instance, Gordon Parker, Julie Roussos, Philip Mitchell, Kay Wilhelm, Marie-Paule Austin, and Dusan Hadzi-Pavlovic (1997) "Distinguishing Psychotic Depression from Melancholia," *Journal of Affective Disorders* 42: 155–67.
3 On the significance of diagnosis in relation to addiction and substance abuse, see the valuable collection Y. G. Baldwin, K. R. Malone, and T. Svolos (eds.) (2011) *Lacan and Addiction: An Anthology*, London: Karnac.
4 On psychotic transference, see J.-L. Gault (2007) "Two Statuses of the Symptom," in V. Voruz and B. Wolf (eds.), *The Later Lacan*, Albany: SUNY Press.
5 See, for one example among many, B. S. Wiese (2011) "Geriatric Depression: The Use of Antidepressants in the Elderly," *British Columbia Medical Journal* 53, 7: 341–7.
6 See in particular G. G. Clérambault (1921–24) "Les psychoses passionelles," in *Oeuvre Psychiatrique*, 1 (323–27), Paris: Presses Universitaires de France; trans. J. Cutting and M. Shepherd (1986) "Psychoses of Passion," in *The Clinical Roots of the Schizophrenia Concept*, Cambridge: Cambridge University Press.
7 *Hamlet*, act 1, scene 2, 180–81.
8 I'm grateful to Stijn Vanheule for bringing these remarks to my attention.
9 Since the focus of my study is melancholia rather than mourning I have limited the discussion of the topic of mourning. I will however make a comment on Jacques Derrida's reflections on mourning expounded, in particular, in P.-A. Brault and M. Naas (eds.) (2001) *The Work of Mourning*, Chicago: University of Chicago Press. Derrida emphasizes the continuity between mourning the loss of a friend and the fact that the knowledge of eventual loss is inscribed in the friendship itself *ab initio*; mourning is prepared for and expected from the start (Brault and Naas 2001: 146). As true as this observation is, it does not describe the specific process of the work of mourning, that is, the process by which the loss is memorialized. A friendship while the friend is alive and a friendship after the friend's death are not the same thing, whatever the continuities, and it is what is specific to the loss that is of interest. Perhaps the loss is already inscribed in the relationship from the start. But then, how inadequately do we turn out to be prepared for the loss when it actually occurs?
10 See also U. May (2012) "Karl Abraham's Revolution of 1916: From Sensual Sucking to the Oral-Aggressive Wish of Destruction," *The Psychoanalytic Quarterly* 81: 83–109.
11 "At the higher stage of the pregenital sadistic-anal organization, the striving for the object appears in the form of an urge for mastery, to which injury or annihilation of the object is a matter of indifference" (Freud 1915:138–9).

12 I would stress this comment, "In the two opposed situations of being most intensely in love and suicide the ego is overwhelmed by the object, though in totally different ways" (Freud 1917a: 252).

13 Freud had already noted the similarities between the sense of guilt in obsessional neurosis and melancholia in Draft N (Sigmund Freud [1897], Draft N, May 31, 1897, *The Complete Letters of Sigmund Freud to Wilhelm Fliess*, 1887–1904, 250–2), as had Karl Abraham in their correspondence (Karl Abraham [1915], Letter from Karl Abraham to Sigmund Freud, March 31, 1915, *The Complete Correspondence of Sigmund Freud and Karl Abraham*, 1907–1925, 303–6). Freud returns to the question again in *The Ego and the Id*.

14 This is very well analyzed by K. Abraham (1994) "A Short Study of the Development of the Libido, Viewed in the Light of Mental Disorders (Abridged)," in Rita V. Frankiel (ed.) *Essential Papers on Object Loss*, New York: New York University Press. See also K. Abraham (1942) "Notes on the Psycho-Analytical Investigation and Treatment of Manic-Depressive Insanity and Allied Conditions," *Selected Papers on Psycho-Analysis*, London: Hogarth.

15 See R. Grigg (2012) "Treating the Wolf Man as a Case of Ordinary Psychosis," *Culture/Clinic* 1: 86–98; on ordinary psychosis, see (2013) "Psychosis Today," *Psychoanalytical Notebooks* 26 and (2009) "Ordinary Psychosis," *Psychoanalytical Notebooks* 19.

16 See J. Lacan (2004) *Le Séminaire, Livre X, L'angoisse*, Paris: Seuil, where Lacan refers to the object *a* as the function that roots the subject in the Symbolic.

17 "Les hommes libres, les vrais, ce sont précisément les fous. Il n'y a pas de demande du petit a, son petit a il le tient, c'est ce qu'il appelle ses voix par exemple. . . . Il ne tient pas au lieu de l'Autre, du grand Autre par l'objet a, le a, il l'a à sa disposition. . . . Lui [le fou] disons qu'il a sa cause dans sa poche, c'est pour ça qu'il est un fou."

18 I am indebted for these comments on Genet to Pierre-Gilles Guéguen (2009) "Ordinary Psychosis: The Extraordinary Case of Jean Genet," *Lacanian Ink* 34: 95–105.

Bibliography

American Psychiatric Association (5th edn. 2013) *Diagnostic and Statistical Manual of Mental Disorders*, Arlington: American Psychiatric Association.

Falzeder, E., Brabant, E. and Giampieri-Deutsch, P. (eds.) (2000) *The Correspondence of Sigmund Freud and Sándor Ferenczi Volume 3: 1920–1933*, Cambridge, MA: Harvard University Press.

Fichtner, G. (ed.) (2003) *The Freud-Binswanger Correspondence: 1908–1938*, London: Open Gate Press.

Freud, S. (1911) "Psycho-Analytic Notes on an Autobiographical Account of a Case of Paranoia (Dementia Paranoides)," *Standard Edition*, 12.

—— (1915) "Instincts and Their Vicissitudes," *Standard Edition*, 14.

—— (1917a) "Mourning and Melancholia," *Standard Edition*, 14: 237–58.

—— (1917b) "Introductory Lectures on Psycho-Analysis," *Standard Edition*, 16.

—— (1923) "The Ego and the Id," *Standard Edition*, 19.

Genet, J. (1968) "Ce qui est resté d'un Rembrandt déchiré en petits carrés bien réguliers, et foutu aux chiottes," *Oeuvres complétes* Paris: Gallimard.

Guéguen, P.-G. (2009) "Ordinary Psychosis: The Extraordinary Case of Jean Genet," *Lacanian Ink*, 34: 95–105.

Kernberg, O. (2010) "Some Observations on the Process of Mourning," *International Journal of Psychoanalysis*, 91: 607.

Kraepelin, E. (8th edn. 1913) *Psychiatrie: ein Lehrbuch*, Leipzig: Barth.

Lacan, J. (1967) "La formation du psychiatre et la psychanalyse," speech delivered at the Cercle d'Études directed by Henry Ey, 10 November 1967. Online. Available http://www.ecole-lacanienne.net/pastoutlacan60.php (accessed 5 August 2013).

—— (1977) "Desire and the Interpretation of Desire in Hamlet," *Yale French Studies*, 55/56; also in (2013) *Le Séminaire, Livre VI, Le désir et son interprétation*, Paris: Martinière.

—— (2006) "On a Question Prior to Any Possible Treatment of Psychosis," in *Écrits*, New York: W. W. Norton & Company.

Sartre, J.-P. (2012) *Saint Genet: Actor and Martyr*, Minneapolis: University of Minnesota Press.

Shakespeare, W. (1877) *Hamlet: A New Varorium Edition*, ed. H. Furness, Philadelphia: Lippincott & Co.

Taylor, M. A. and Fink, M. (2006) *Melancholia: The Diagnosis, Pathophysiology and Treatment of Depressive Illness*, Cambridge: Cambridge University Press.

11

MADNESS, SUBJECTIVITY, AND THE MIRROR STAGE

Lacan and Merleau-Ponty

Jasper Feyaerts and Stijn Vanheule

Introduction

In his 1949 essay on *The Mirror Stage as Formative of the I Function*, Lacan discusses the function of the ego within psychoanalytic experience. Here, he holds that "the subject's capture by his situation gives us the most general formulation of madness—the kind found within the asylum walls as well as the kind that deafens the world with its sound and fury" (Lacan 2006b: 80). In a similar way, in his *Phenomenology of Perception* from 1945, Merleau-Ponty considers pathological subjectivity as "a loss of plasticity" (Merleau-Ponty 2002: 151) in the subject's intention to renew its perceptual field. Moreover, both Lacan and Merleau-Ponty contend that the "capture" or "loss of plasticity," which are distinctive for madness, reveal something of the nature of human subjectivity as such.

In this chapter we discuss the intimate relation between subjectivity and madness as treated in Lacan's early writings[1] and in Merleau-Ponty's seminal work the *Phenomenology of Perception*. In doing so, we outline the difference between Lacan's and Merleau-Ponty's readings of Henry Wallon's psychogenetic model of the mirror stage. Both authors took a special interest in this model because of its potential to clarify their own theoretical positions: whereas for Merleau-Ponty the mirror image is an illusion that needs to be reduced to lived experience, Lacan considers the specular image non-reducible, and as formative for the experience of subjectivity. We reframe this difference in terms of the above stated convergence between the two authors on the status of madness vis-à-vis subjectivity. This brings us to the conclusion that the point of difference separating Lacan's and Merleau-Ponty's viewpoints on the relation between madness and subjectivity is related to the function they ascribe to misrecognition in the formation of subjectivity, as well as to the subsequent possibility (Merleau-Ponty) or impossibility (Lacan) of overcoming this misrecognition.

The metaphysics of madness

Before addressing Lacan's and Merleau-Ponty's appropriations of Wallon's theory of the mirror stage, it will be helpful to turn to Lacan's paper *Presentation on Psychical Causality*, dating from 1947. This text presents a remarkable similarity to the thread followed by Merleau-Ponty in his *Phenomenology of Perception*. In the same vein as Merleau-Ponty's phenomenological critique of science's naturalistic attitude,[2] Lacan takes issue with the "organicist theory of madness" of French psychiatrist Henry Ey, who, according to Lacan, "cannot relate the genesis of mental problems [. . .] to anything but the play of systems constituted in the material substance (*l'étendue*) located within the body's integument" (Lacan 2006a: 124). Such play "always rests in the final analysis on molecular interaction of the *partes-extra-partes*, material-substance type that classical physics is based on" (Lacan 2006a: 124). In making this critique, Lacan confirms the phenomenological refutation of the naturalistic attitude, which assumes that madness, qua natural kind, is a determined object among other objects in the world. He proposes that instead of yet another mechanistic biological model, a theory of psychic causality is required, one that actually transcends the particular issue of madness:

> The problem that madness thus kindles in us owing to its pathos provides a first answer to the question I raised about the human value of the phenomenon of madness. And its metaphysical import is revealed in the fact that it is inseparable from the problem of signification for being in general—that is the problem of language for man.
>
> (Lacan 2006a: 135)

Far from reducing psychical causality to a fortuitous curiosity, Lacan stresses its metaphysical dimension. The existence of madness illuminates the nature of subjectivity as such. More particularly, madness is bound up in signification, and points towards the problem language poses for man. Language enables the human being to fictionalize reality and to live it through as a problem of truth, believed in conditionally. Lacan contends that "[t]he madman believes he is different than he is" (Lacan 2006a: 139), but in a decisive way the same holds for "the king who really thinks he is a king" (Lacan 2006a: 139). This split in subjectivity between "being" and "believing" takes us to the heart of subjectivity itself. Rather than viewing madness as an expression of biological frailty, or as a deplorable adversity that goes against true human subjectivity, Lacan holds that madness is the "permanent virtuality of a gap opened in his essence. And far from being an 'insult' to freedom, madness is freedom's most faithful companion, following its every move like a shadow" (Lacan 2006a: 144). Madness is a permanent possibility for human subjectivity and this is what makes up its metaphysical significance. Instead of being an aberration, subjectivity cannot be genuinely comprehended, and would not be what it is, without madness as the limit of its freedom. We return to this idea later in the text.

In 1947, Lacan relates psychical causality to the concept of the "imago." Subjectivity takes shape as a "more or less typical series of ideal identifications" (Lacan 2006a: 145) start to define "who one is." These successive imaginary identifications, taken as an ever-developing ensemble, constitute the ego. More precisely, the "imago" is the specular image by which the ego of the subject is constituted through identification, without thereby conflating the actual being of the subject with this image. It is the image by which man believes himself a man, and by which the madman believes himself other than what he is. The imago is the image by which man recognizes himself (as an image) while at the same time misrecognizing his being.[3] In other words, at the basis of both madness and human subjectivity the same kind of identification can be found. This is why madness partakes of the metaphysical condition of the subject and should be comprehended in terms of the problematic relation between being and believing as such.

Similarly, Merleau-Ponty (1945) fulminates against reducing madness to the mere outcome of numerous causal factors that would determine its make-up. Rather than placing madness beyond human existence, he believes that madness reflects a state of subjectivity that can be comprehended in its own right:

> There can be no question of simply transferring to the normal person what the deficient one lacks and is trying to recover. Illness [. . .] is a complete form of existence and the procedures which it employs to replace normal functions which have been destroyed are equally pathological phenomena. It is impossible to deduce the normal from the pathological, deficiencies from the substitutive functions, by a mere change of the sign. We must take substitutions as substitutions, as allusions to some fundamental function that they are striving to make good, and the direct image of which they fail to furnish. The genuine inductive method is not a "differential method"; it consists in correctly reading phenomena, in grasping their meaning, that is, in treating them as modalities and variations of *the subject's total being.*
> (Merleau-Ponty 2002: 123–4; emphasis added)

For Merleau-Ponty, madness reflects a "modality or variation" that concerns "the subject's vital area," as an expression of "the subject's total being" (Merleau-Ponty 2002: 123–4), which should be revealed through phenomenological analysis.

Interestingly, Lacan explicitly addresses this phenomenological analysis in his 1947 paper. More specifically, he revisits Merleau-Ponty's point that lived experience needs to be considered prior to any objectification and even prior to any reflexive analysis that interweaves objectification with experience. As Lacan contends:

> For Merleau-Ponty's work decisively demonstrates that any healthy phenomenology, that of perception, for instance, requires us to consider

lived experience prior to any objectification [. . .]. Let me explain what I mean: the slightest visual illusion proves to force itself upon us experientially before detailed, piecemeal observation of the figure corrects it; it is the latter that allows us to objectify the so-called real form. Reflection makes us recognize in this form the a priori category of extension [*l'étendue*], the property of which is precisely to present itself *partes-extra-partes*, but it is still the illusion in itself that gives us the gestalt action that is psychology's true object here.

(Lacan 2006a: 146)

However, Lacan's recourse to Merleau-Ponty's phenomenological maxim is highly ambiguous. After all, Lacan only focuses on the lived experience of the mirror image, and not on the lived experience of perception in its pre-objective dimension, which is what interests Merleau-Ponty. Before turning to our discussion of Lacan's and Merleau-Ponty's respective readings of this mirror stage, we present Merleau-Ponty's analysis of lived experience and his critique of the naturalistic attitude.

Naturalistic attitude and lived experience

As indicated by Lacan, a principle guiding Merleau-Ponty's phenomenological account of perception is that of uncovering the unreflective ground of lived experience, which is both presupposed and forgotten within the naturalistic attitude. For Merleau-Ponty, the first task of a genuine philosophy is the phenomenological critique of this attitude, which tends to ignore the subjective ground on which it operates. The naturalistic attitude obfuscates the constitutive role subjectivity plays in perception and sees the world as an already constituted entity that hence appears as a whole of ready-made objects. Merleau-Ponty thoughtfully summarizes the logic of this naturalistic repression:

Obsessed with being, and forgetful of the perspectivism of my experience, I henceforth treat it is as an object and deduce it from a relationship between objects. I regard my body, which is my point of view upon the world, as one of the objects of that world. My recent awareness of my gaze as a means of knowledge I now repress, and treat my eyes as a bit of matter. They then take their place in the same objective space in which I am trying to situate the external object and I believe that I am producing the perceived perspective by the projection of the objects on my retina. In the same way I treat my own perceptual history as a result of my relationships with the objective world; my present, which is my point of view on time, becomes one moment of time among all others, my duration a reflection or abstract aspect of universal time, as my body is a mode of objective space.

(Merleau-Ponty 2002: 81–2)

As this passage indicates, Merleau-Ponty suggests that the body determines our view of the world, which leads him to elaborate a bodily phenomenology. In this way, Merleau-Ponty attempts to acquire knowledge of how things are genuinely experienced when the veil of the naturalistic forgetfulness of experience is dissolved. This return to the things themselves is "a return to the world which precedes knowledge, of which knowledge always *speaks*, and in relation to which every scientific schematization is an abstract and derivative sign-language—as is geography in relation to the country-side in which we have learnt beforehand what a forest, a prairie or river is" (Merleau-Ponty 2002: x). Such pre-predicative knowledge of lived experience can be gained through the body. The naturalistic attitude, by contrast, represses embodied subjectivity.[4] As a consequence of this repression, the body is hence treated as a desubjectified object among other objects, owing nothing to the experience of the world. Therefore, Merleau-Ponty's phenomenological analysis aims at lifting naturalistic repression, which should enable the pre-objective, lived experience to come to the fore. Pathological subjectivity is an important issue within this phenomenological effort to go beyond fixed representation. It points to the ambiguity of existence, and, like a real-life thought experiment, it elucidates the dimensions operative in normal subjectivity.

Lacan reads Wallon

In order to refine our analysis of this phenomenological rapport that conjoins madness and subjectivity, we now turn to Lacan's and Merleau-Ponty's readings of Wallon's psychogenetic theory of the mirror stage as formulated in *Les Origines du Caractère chez l'Enfant*, and study how these bear on their respective theories of subjectivity.

In the chapter of *Les Origines* entitled "The Body Proper and Its Exteroceptive Image," Wallon introduces a whole menagerie to demonstrate that animals and humans relate differently to the mirror image. For Wallon, the distinctive feature separating the human infant from, for example, the drake consists in the former's ability to grasp the reciprocal relation between the self and its reflection. An animal, by contrast, is unable to identify with its image, as is illustrated by the example of a drake that had acquired the strange habit, since the death of its partner, of staring at a reflecting windowpane. Wallon writes: "Without doubt his own reflection could more or less fill in the void left by the absence of his companion" (Wallon 1949: 219; our translation). The ability of the drake to find consolation in the image results from its inability to identify with the mirror image. In a similar way, Lacan contrasts the behavior of the human infant and the chimp when confronted with their mirror image: the infant engages in triumphant jubilation and playful self-discovery, while the chimp displays sheer indifference. Lacan relates this fundamental difference qua lived experience to the remarkable contrast between the early instrumental self-sufficiency of the animal and the human's prematurity at birth, which he tentatively associates with the perceptual propensity for recognizing the human Gestalt early in life.

A second important idea from Wallon's work that resonates in Lacan's study of the mirror stage is the consideration of the jubilant mirror experience as the mythical beginning of self-differentiation. The mirror stage enables the transition from a passive state of raw immediacy to a situation of imaginary mastery and then to symbolic representation: "The development of the infant demonstrates by what degrees immediate experience, the undifferentiated, dispersed, and transitory impressions of brute sensibility must become dissociated, fixed by images initially concrete and seemingly coextensive with their object, and then give way to symbolic transmutations of pure and stable representation" (Wallon 1949: 183). For Wallon, the mirror experience is thus also the "prelude to symbolic activity," enabling a transition from partial, sensorial perceptions to what he calls the "symbolic function" (Wallon 1949: 230–1). Lacan's early work is often read in the same way: the mirror experience forms the imaginary ground for the symbolic "I" to come to the fore.

Wallon's detailed observations clearly function as a paradigm for Lacan's theory of the mirror image. However, the Lacanian appropriation of the mirror stage is more than the simple juxtaposition presented thus far. In several respects, Lacan's ongoing revision and articulation of the mirror mechanism throughout his teachings represents a complex synthesis of several strands of thought in psychoanalysis, philosophy and experimental psychology. Let us address this issue by means of the following questions:

Why does the yet to be constituted subject look in the mirror?

What does the yet to be constituted subject see in the mirror?

The first question concerns the anterior ontogenetic conditions that drive the infant towards the seductive lure of the mirror image. In the opening chapter of *Civilization and Its Discontents*, Freud already poses the same question a propos the genesis of his psychical topography. In a discussion of the "oceanic feeling"— the lived experience surrounding the ego—Freud argues:

> The idea of men's receiving an intimation of their connection with the world around them through an immediate feeling which is from the outset directed to that purpose sounds so strange and fits in so badly with the fabric of our psychology that one is justified in attempting to discover a psychoanalytic—that is, a genetic—explanation of such a feeling.
> (Freud 1929: 65–6)

Freud thus concludes, "a unity comparable to the ego cannot exist in the individual from the start" (Freud 1914: 77). Lacan endorses this Freudian "genetic explanation" of the ego:

> In effect, if one starts from the notion of original narcissism, perfect as regards libidinal investment, if one conceives of the primordial object

164

as primordially included by the subject in the narcissistic sphere, as a primitive monad of enjoyment (*jouissance*), to which is identified the infant nursling (*nourisson*), one has difficulty seeing what would be able to lead a subjective way out (*sortie subjective*).

(Lacan 2001: 410)

Lacan's concerns about the notion of original narcissism are relatively straightforward here: original narcissism, as the blissful state of a self-sufficient and unified wholeness, is, considered from an ontogenetic perspective, untenable insofar as it curtails the possibility of conceiving of the development of any subjectivity whatsoever. The question as to "why" the Lacanian *sujet-à-venir* looks in the mirror should thus point to the non-all of human nature prior to the acquisition of ego-like subjectivity.

Contra Wallon, Lacan consequently stresses that man is, by definition, a disadapted animal burdened with a disordered Gestalt-like imagination. The mythical tale of the mirror stage is not so much the *nec plus ultra* of human teleological development that Wallon described as it is the expression of a "primordial discord" that characterizes man's relation to nature.[5] More specifically, Freud and Lacan relate this non-all of human nature to the idea that all human beings are born prematurely. As a consequence, human infants are utterly dependent on others for carrying out all basic vital tasks. Adopting Freud's terminology, Lacan defines this prolonged "primordial discord" as a state of helplessness (*Hilflosigkeit*). It is against this ontogenetic background that the peculiarly (de)formative function of the specular image has to be understood: the illusory completeness of the subject's body image as reflected in the mirror provides him with the promise of a unified wholeness that compensates for human helplessness. Yet, the attraction exercised by the seductive lure of the Gestalt-illusion responds to a completely different logic than the one observed in other animals: animals respond instinctively to (Gestalts of) other animals, but they do not alienate themselves in the mirror image. Humans, by contrast, do. This is why Lacan holds that "the mirror stage is a drama whose internal thrust is precipitated from insufficiency to anticipation" (Lacan 2006b: 78): the non-all of human nature is supplemented and warded off by the mirror image.

This brings us to the second question: what does the yet to be constituted subject see in the mirror? Or what does the image in the mirror reflect? For Wallon, the reflected mirror image seen is in a certain way indifferent: the developmental task the infant has to accomplish consists of integrating the real model and the mirror image. For this integration to occur the reciprocal relation between the child's own body and the mirror image is not needed; other bodies can affect the same developmental shift. According to Wallon, the pre-mirror stage child has difficulties with *spatial realism*: it does not yet understand that the bodies located at two points in space—the introceptively felt body and the virtual image in the mirror—constitute only one body. The insight acquired during the mirror phase concerns the recognition of spatial values. The child's behavior suddenly demonstrates a

165

jubilant comprehension of the reciprocity between model and image. The *Aha-Erlebnis* of the mirror stage thus concerns an epistemological breakthrough; spatial realism is replaced by a more accurate conception of the relation between model and image.

For Lacan, by contrast, the account of the mirror image is far less heroic. Lacan stresses that the image seen in the mirror is not indifferent at all. The mirror image concerns the child's own body image and henceforth helps transcend any "human or artificial support" (Lacan 2006b: 76). The triumphant jubilation accompanying the subject's identification demonstrates the sudden experience of mastery over the premature distress, the possibility of being "*maître/m'être à moi-même*" via the reflected totality of the salutary imago. This identification with the imaginary totality of one's own body lays the foundation for the formation of the ego and later for successive secondary identifications. However, identification with the mirror also sets the stage for structural misrecognition: experiences that do not fit the seductive wholeness of the mirror image are subsequently warded off. Indeed, in Lacan's theory, the epistemological status of the subject's identification with the mirror image is far removed from the epistemological breakthrough Wallon accentuates. To put it in the words of Mladen Dolar: "when I recognize myself in the mirror, it is already too late" (Dolar 1996: 138). The fundamental price paid for recognizing oneself in the mirror is that one misrecognizes oneself in the alienating illusion of totality. However, this misrecognition is structural and cannot be simply corrected. The presumed choice between the illusion of the Gestalt and the mythical state of "self-being" is above all a Hegelian one. To reformulate Lacan's favorite example of the forced choice between "Your money or your life" in terms of our discussion: either one chooses the illusion of the mirror image or one loses both. For Lacan, subjectivity itself is engendered by a loss of being; it is, in its essence, the loss of the immediacy of "self-same being." Consequently, the forced choice between "subjectivity" and "being" is no choice at all: choosing the illusory nature of mediated subjectivity is the only option for the yet to be constituted subject.

To conclude: Lacan proposes a reading of Wallon's mirror experiments that differs from Wallon's original interpretations. For Lacan, the specular image by which the ego takes shape is without any doubt an illusion. Nonetheless, it is an illusion that has the structure of a truth. As Lacan puts it in his 1947 essay: there is a "law of our becoming" commanding you to "become such as you are" (Lacan 2006a: 145). This illusion is indeed the human illusion par excellence, by which one obeys this "law of our becoming" through which one pays the price of becoming by separating oneself from one's own being. In this respect, madness is a permanent possibility for the human subject because it is the faithful expression of "this gap opened up in his essence" (Lacan 2006a: 144). The liberation from the slavish adhesion to the immediacy of "being" enables the subject to experience his freedom as detached from what there is. Madness is the *nec plus ultra* of this freedom. In madness, alienation in the illusory image that makes up subjectivity is most extreme. Rather than being a mockery of human subjectivity, madness provides the most faithful expression of the mechanism that commonly makes us think that we are who we are.

Merleau-Ponty reads Lacan and Wallon

Merleau-Ponty's phenomenological reading of Wallon's mirror stage differs from Lacan's and was delivered in a series of lectures in 1950–1, entitled "Les relations avec autrui chez l'enfant." As noted above, Merleau-Ponty takes a special interest in Wallon's theory because of its potential to enhance his own phenomenological project of "returning to the things themselves." Moreover, Wallon's description of the mirror experience explicitly points towards the constitutive relation between visual perception (the Gestalt discerned in the mirror) and any subsequent symbolic activity. As such, it opens up the ambiguity of perception, so cherished by Merleau-Ponty, since it sets the stage for a critique of the naturalistic attitude. Let us recall Merleau-Ponty's description of naturalistic repression, which denies the embodied subjectivity that nonetheless functions as its constitutive ground:

> I detach myself from my experience and pass to the *idea*. Like the object, the idea purports to be the same for everybody, valid in all time and places, and the individuation of an object in an objective point of time and space finally appears as the expression of a universal positing power. I am no longer concerned with my body, nor with time, nor with the world, as I experience them in antepredicative knowledge, in the inner communion that I have with them. I now refer to my body only as an idea, to the universe as idea, to the idea of space and the idea of time. Thus "objective" thought (in Kierkegaard's sense) is formed—being that of common sense and of science—which finally causes us to lose contact with perceptual experience, of which it is nevertheless the outcome and the natural sequel.
>
> (Merleau-Ponty 2002: 82)

For Merleau-Ponty, phenomenology is about returning to the original perceptual experience. In this respect Wallon's description of the mirror stage, and specifically the gradual subordination of the proprioceptive real body to the virtual body as seen in the mirror, is interesting to Merleau-Ponty. Wallon considers the mirror stage as the phase during which the child overcomes its premature epistemological attitude of believing in the independence of the interoceptive "felt body" and the "virtual body" in the mirror. The child overcomes this faulty belief by relating the pre-objective perception of the body to the mirror image. This transition reflects the naturalistic attitude through which the lived body is repressed by the specular illusion. The objectified body in the mirror departs from the original body, which nonetheless "is always near me, always there for me, [. . .] that is never really in front of me, that I cannot array [. . .] before my eyes, that remains marginal to all my perceptions, that is *with* me" (Merleau-Ponty 2002: 104).

In the same vein, Merleau-Ponty addresses Lacan's interpretation of the mirror stage as a drama of alienation in an ideal ego:

> The self-image, at the same time that it enables self-knowledge, enables a kind of alienation: I am no longer what I immediately felt I was, I am this picture of me offered by the mirror. There occurs, in the words of Dr. Lacan, a "captivation" of me by my spatial image. Suddenly, I leave the reality of the lived experience of myself for a constant reference to this ideal self, fictitious or imaginary, of which the mirror image forms the first draft. In this way, I am torn from myself and the mirror image prepares me for another, even more serious alienation, which will be the alienation by the other.
>
> (Merleau-Ponty 1997: 203; our translation)

Merleau-Ponty thus seems to read Lacan in the following (phenomenological) way: the mirror stage represents the dramatic transition from a lived experience of the self to the fictional experience of an ideal imago. This fictional experience sets the stage for seeing the subject as an object in the world. Just like Lacan, Merleau-Ponty stresses that the subject is captivated by the illusory ideal image of its reflection. However, contra Lacan, the formative illusion of the mirror image is henceforth treated as a hindrance to authentic phenomenological subjectivity. For Merleau-Ponty, the illusion seen in the mirror deceives the subject about its own true origin. Instead of treating the body as the way "I am" in and for the world, the subject captured by the mirror image sees the body as something "I have." The body is thus reduced to an image that is nothing more "than an appearance in a visible world which has nothing to do with me" (Merleau-Ponty 1997: 197). Consequently, imaginary recognition is above all a misrecognition vis-à-vis the original bodily experience of the phenomenological subject.

Three conclusions can be drawn from Merleau-Ponty's interpretation of the mirror stage. First, Merleau-Ponty adheres to what we might call a "subjective dualism." On the one hand, he discerns authentic phenomenological subjectivity, which is intrinsically linked to the pre-objective experience of the body. On the other, he recognizes ideal subjectivity, which is concomitant with alienation within an image.

Second, apart from being a neutral ontological analysis, his phenomenological rendition of the mirror stage seems to engender a *normative* analysis of subjectivity, which he explains as follows:

> The task of a radical reflection, the kind that aims at self-comprehension, consists, paradoxically enough, in recovering the unreflective experience of the world, and subsequently reassigning to it the verificatory attitude and reflective operations, and displaying reflection as one possibility of my being. [. . .] Hence reflection does not itself grasp its

full significance unless it refers to the unreflective fund of experience which it presupposes, upon which it draws, and which constitutes for it a kind of original past, a past which has never been present.

(Merleau-Ponty 2002: 280–2)

Although Merleau-Ponty seems to waver with respect to the question of the precise ontological status of the unreflective fund underlying any original experience of the self and the world, he nevertheless sees it as a *conditio sine qua non* for any genuine account of subjectivity.

Third, this ontological/normative scheme permeating Merleau-Ponty's reading of the mirror stage and the greater part of his *Phenomenology of Perception* obviously bears on his phenomenological analysis of pathological subjectivity. Indeed, more than anyone else, it is the madman who, for Merleau-Ponty, represents the subject as completely immersed in the constituted pole of a blocked subjectivity, cut off from the permanent possibility of renewing the sense of his own existence, imprisoned in the static world of former habits and lost prospects: "For these patients the world exists only as one readymade or congealed, whereas for the normal person his projects polarize the world, bringing magically to view a host of signs which guide action, as notices in a museum guide the visitor" (Merleau-Ponty 2002: 129).

In Merleau-Ponty's view, the normal person is capable of overcoming the deceiving illusions and objectifying tendencies that are installed with the mirror stage. For him, the mirror image can be eclipsed whenever he returns to the genuine subject of phenomenological corporeality. The madman, by contrast, is completely absorbed by the constituted pole of his own existence. In his delusions, all contact with the phenomenal ground of every deliberate *Sinngebung* is lost. In this respect, the madman personifies the naturalistic fallacy itself, and provides a counter-example to the definition of true subjectivity.

Subjectivity and madness: Lacan versus Merleau-Ponty

Whereas both Lacan and Merleau-Ponty take madness seriously, and assume that madness teaches us something about the nature of human subjectivity, they actually arrive at contrasting conclusions. From a Lacanian perspective, three fundamental remarks can be made about Merleau-Ponty's analysis of the mirror stage, as spelled out above.

First, whereas Merleau-Ponty believes in the relevance of distinguishing between phenomenal and ideal subjectivity as two concomitant subjective states, Lacan juxtaposes "subjectivity" and "being" as mutually exclusive categories. From a Lacanian point of view, it is not only "too late" when I recognize myself in the mirror, there is also no way to return. Thus considered, the phenomenological project of "returning to the things themselves" is nothing but a reverie that takes shape as an *après-coup* effect of a fundamental loss of being. For Lacan, there is no true subject to return to beyond the alienation: phenomenological reduction as the royal road to a more original self-experience is ultimately a dead end. Lived experience is an effect of the alienation in the image, not something one could return to.

Second, and closely connected to what we called Merleau-Ponty's normative analysis, the very notion of a pre-reflective embodied subjectivity can be thought of as a contradiction in terms. Despite many similarities, Lacanian psychoanalysis and Merleau-Ponty's phenomenology are fundamentally at odds with regard to the (non-) rapport between mediated subjectivity and its corporeal conditions. Merleau-Ponty tends to replace the Cartesian dichotomy between *res cogitans* (thinking substance) and *res extensa* (extended substance) with a more Aristotelian fusion between mind and body as it is expressed in the concept of the lived body. Like Merleau-Ponty, Lacan objects to considering the cogito as a point of certainty or a metaphysical first principle. However, unlike him, Lacan does not reject the Cartesian *cogito*. In his view, the "I" is not a point of certainty, like it is for Descartes, but an instance that comes into being through symbolic-imaginary (mis-)recognition and identification. It is an illusory instance indeed, but at the same time it also makes up the seat of subjectivity. To explain why Lacan continues to refer to the Cartesian cogito, Miller productively resumes Lacan's distinction between "being" and "having" in its relation to the body:

> "Having a body" is significant in its difference from "being a body." We justify the identification of being and body in the animal, but not in man, because no matter how corporeal he is, corporified, he is also made a subject by the signifier, that is to say, he is made lack-in-being. This lack in being as effect of the signifier divides being and body, reducing the body to the status of "having it."
>
> (Miller 2001: 21)

For Lacan the subject is only a subject because of its subjection to symbolic-imaginary mediation. Therefore, it cannot identify itself with its body. This is also the reason why Lacan continues to refer to a cogito-like subjectivity and why his theory is a critique of Merleau-Ponty's phenomenology: for Lacan, the only outcome of the normative call to return to the phenomenological "lived body" is the ultimate effacement of the subject.

Third and finally, given these Lacanian reservations vis-à-vis Merleau-Ponty's phenomenology, it becomes clear how Lacan's reflections on the mirror stage fundamentally differ from the phenomenological version and how they consequently lead to a different view of the relation between subjectivity and madness. As Lacan contends in his paper on the mirror stage:

> This misrecognition [the one that characterizes the ego] can be seen in the revolt through which the madman seeks to impose the law of his heart onto what seems to him to be the havoc of the world. This is an "insane"

enterprise—but not because it suggests a failure to adapt to life, which is the kind of thing people often say in our circles, whereas the slightest reflection on our experience proves the dishonorable inanity of such a viewpoint. It is an insane enterprise, rather, in that the subject does not recognize in this havoc the very manifestation of his actual being, or that what he experiences as the law of his heart is but the inverted and virtual image of that same being. He thus doubly misrecognizes it, precisely so as to split its actuality from its virtuality.

(Lacan 2006a: 140)

In Lacan's view, "the insane enterprise of madness" is a fundamental expression of human subjectivity. Rather than being a failure to adapt to life as it actually is, madness is the proper heir of the subject's lack of being. Madness is the price we all pay for the loss of the immediacy of being. It is the offshoot of the so cherished freedom that is considered to be the distinctive feature separating man from the animal. Although the madman is indeed blocked in a constituted subjectivity, and although he is indeed "the limit of our freedom," the madman is—instead of being the perfect opposite of enlightened subjectivity, or the counter-example of a more original phenomenological subjectivity—our most faithful companion. In short: both madness and freedom are possibilities of a human being due to "the permanent virtuality of a gap opened up in his essence" (Lacan 2006a: 144). To deny this gap in a nostalgic movement towards phenomenological subjectivity is to deny subjectivity itself.

Notes

1 Lacan's discussion of madness and psychosis changed substantially through the course of his career (see Vanheule, 2011). In this chapter we focus only on Lacan's discussion of psychosis and madness prior to his public seminar.

2 "The 'naturalistic attitude' is the stance taken by he who aims 'to grasp the nature of reality' and describe such 'reality' in terms of some objective description which will accurately characterize the 'thing-in-itself' apart from one's experience of it" (Toombs 1993: 40).

3 As such, Lacan's subject as subjected to the image/signifier is closer to a certain "ontological dualism" where "thought is in disharmony with the soul" (Lacan 1990: 6). Moreover, this brings Lacan in closer proximity to Descartes, in that Lacan tends to place the imaginary/symbolic orders that engender subjectivity and the organic body in separate domains. However, this does not imply that Lacan is uncritical of Descartes. Lacan's alleged proclamation for "a return to Descartes" should not be taken as the uncritical return to the *res cogitans* of the Cogito-like subject. As Adrian Johnston observes (2008: 53–4), Lacan's formulations on the relation between subjectivity and the body allow for the rejection of a false dilemma tacitly governing many contemporary discussions. That is, the choice between, on the one hand, a strict mind-body dualism (à la Descartes) and, on the other hand, a reduction of subjectivity to its corporeal substance (whether this substance be the organic body of the natural sciences (e.g. "the brain") or the lived body of modern phenomenology). We will return to this issue in our conclusion.

4   Nevertheless, the question remains: why is the body repressed in the first place? In our opinion, the concept of the body is indeed a step in the right direction for any effort to elucidate the conditions of possibility for subjectivity's genesis. However, to the extent that Merleau-Ponty's recourse to the body results in an unproblematic *embodied subjectivity*, it also represents the unthought remainder that threatens to haunt the temporal logic of naturalistic repression and concomitantly proves to be a serious drawback to his phenomenology. It is precisely at this point that Lacan's conceptualization on the relation between Cartesian subjectivity and the *Real of the body* can provide a welcome alternative.

5   Although Wallon similarly stresses the child's prematurity at birth, he considers it to be a positive condition for the subsequent sociability of the child. The difference with Lacan's reading lies in the fact that Wallon thinks of prematurity as an anterior condition that is replaced by a more adaptive sociability. Lacan, by contrast, emphasizes the fundamental impossibility of abolishing this primordial discord and maladaptation to the natural environment.

Bibliography

Dolar, M. (1996) "At First Sight" in R. Salecl and S. Žižek (eds.) *Gaze and Voice as Love Objects*, Durham, NC: Duke University Press.

Freud, S. (1914) "On Narcissism" in J. Stratchey (ed. & trans.) *The Standard Edition of the Complete Psychological Works of Sigmund Freud*, vol. 14, London: Hogarth Press.

—— (1929) "Civilization and Its Discontents" in J. Stratchey (ed. & trans.) *The Standard Edition of the Complete Psychological Works of Sigmund Freud*, vol. 21, London: Hogarth Press.

Lacan, J. (1947) "Presentation on Psychical Causality" in J. Lacan and J.-A. Miller (eds.) (2006a) *Écrits*, New York and London: W.W. Norton & Company.

—— (1949) "The Mirror Stage as Formative of the I Function," in J. Lacan and J.-A. Miller (eds.) (2006b) *Écrits*, New York and London: W.W. Norton & Company.

—— (1960–1; 2nd edn 2001) *Le Séminaire 1960–1961, Livre VIII: Le transfert*, Paris: Seuil.

—— (1990) "Television" in J. Copjec (ed.) *Television/A Challenge to the Psychoanalytic Establishment*, New York and London: W.W. Norton & Company.

Johnston, A. (2008) *Žižek's Ontology: A Transcendental Materialist Theory of Subjectivity*, Evanston: Northwest University Press.

Merleau-Ponty, M. (1945; 2nd edn 2002) *Phenomenology of Perception*, trans. P. Kegan, London: Routledge.

—— (1997) *Parcours*, Lagrasse: Editions Verdier.

Miller, J.-A. (2001) "The Symptom and the Body Event," *Lacanian Ink*, 19: 4–47.

Wallon, H. (1949) *Les Origines du Caractère chez l'Enfant*, Quadrige: Presses Universitaires de France.

12

NARCISSISTIC NEUROSIS AND NON-SEXUAL TRAUMA

Hector Yankelevich

How to write about narcissistic neurosis from a perspective that acknowledges the transformative influence of Lacan's teachings? Even the term, narcissistic neurosis, seems like a concession to a terminology that Lacan, when he did not oppose it, tried to render more rigorous, all the while noting that this was a Herculean task, comparable to the cleaning of the Augean stables. How to systematize a notion that Freud first employed to describe psychosis (excluding dementia praecox) but later became a subdivision within classical neurosis? Freud developed this notion in lesser-known texts, such as "Introduction to Psycho-Analysis and the War Neuroses" (1919). In this short text, Freud notes that many patients identified as "narcissistic" present a trauma identical to the one found in war neurosis, that is, a trauma that is not sexual in origin. Soldiers during the Great War witnessed traumatic scenes of the mutilation and death of their peers in combat while they remained uninjured. The exposure to danger was experienced as if the reality of death was a second traumatic scene. Their symptoms, which Ferenczi and Abraham strove to treat and name, were not formations of the unconscious, but rather powerful inhibitions that prevented them from returning to combat, leaving them stuck in a never-ending mourning of their dead comrades.

Freud's text is brief but suggestive. Those suffering from so-called narcissistic disorders experience a type of pain that Lacan rendered precisely by using Freud's term: *Liebesversagung*, the "refusal of love," a term that had been lost by analysts and translators. The word *Versagung* in this compound form merits some discussion; it is often mistranslated as "frustration." This word acquired an important place in post-Freudian psychoanalytic theory, developing connotations that had little to do with Freud's ideas. Since neurotics suffer from the unrelenting demands of their drives (*Triebanspruch*),[1] they suffer from "frustration"[2] (*Versagung*). In their cure, the analyst is to recreate the same frustration-inducing conditions that caused frustration in order to offer outcomes other than aggression and regression to that measureless exigency of the drives. Lacan reorients analytic discourse, making a distinction between "object frustration" and "refusal of love." The first is a fact common to every speaking-being; it is a result of language, since the signifier itself deprives us of our first object and not the Other. What is frustrated, more than a demand for an object, is the demand for jouissance. The loss of this primary jouissance gives speech to human beings. The "refusal of love" refers not simply to an absence or to a rejection, but to the falsity implied in the promise of love. What is this falsity about? Since not all promises given are broken, which first promises of the parents were not kept and continue to function psychically?

On the one hand, speech is speech; it promises to give something no subject can ever give. This is a structural fact that would trigger the mourning for that unreachable horizon. But, on the other hand, in the clinic, we often hear the effect of words said without faith, words that are misleading, and we find the impossibility of a parent occupying the place of the Other. The key given by Lacan is the idea that a refusal of love makes the drives even more unwieldy. One might say that this causes us to bite someone else, and then ourselves, exactly on the spot where we failed to be caressed.

One finds in Freud's work two case histories that can be read as instances of narcissistic neurosis; in both, sexual life has been marked by rigidity and poverty. Regarding the first case, in his analysis of the Wolf Man (1917), Freud coined the term "*Narzisstische Versagung*," usually translated as "narcissistic frustration" (Freud 1918: 117). This frustration leads to a breakdown, to narcissistic depression. The Wolf Man's almost complete inhibition and depression without melancholia proved resistant to analysis even when the phobic and obsessive symptoms were resolved. Let us note that Freud places the term *Versagung* in quotation marks, suggesting that he is not employing it in the usual way. This is not the case with the term frustration, which is part and parcel of analytic discourse. Here we follow a semantics from "failure" to "refusal." The first term is a consequence of the second. In terms of the Wolf Man, this means the Other's refusal to recognize the subject as a male, as a phallophore. Its consequence is a failure to separate gonorrhea (admittedly, an annoying illness) from the meaning it acquired for the Wolf Man: the failure of his virility, an inhibition of all sexual activity. This collapsing of meaning implied the disappearance of all that can be signified by the phallus. The seduction by his sister was deeply traumatic. Because the experience was incestuous, it deprived him of the chance to define his phallus and any phallicity. It convinced him that there was such a thing as a "sexual rapport." Furthermore, for the Wolf Man, all "sexual acts" would imply incest. The Wolf Man's delusional episodes, however, were not psychotic. In his commentary, Lacan criticized Freud for cutting the analysis short and, even more, for his *furor theorisandi*: his dogged attempt to demonstrate the reality of the primal scene against Jung's skepticism towards its reality.

The second case is Freud's analysis of the so-called "Young Female Homosexual," which is worth revisiting in terms of narcissistic neurosis. A recent biography, written shortly before the death of the patient, provides interesting new perspectives. The fact that the young woman fell in love with a *demie-mondaine* and later had other liaisons of a similar kind did not actually define her. Nor did her marriages to men, or for that matter, her lack of sexual enjoyment, or even her relationship to her dogs. What defined her was that women, men, and even animals were for her poor substitutes. For this woman, all living beings were sexually poor, and not worthy of love. This shows a problem that she had with her neighbors and others of her kind (*semblables*), an issue that Freud could not theorize because he considered it to derive from the object libido's reversal into narcissistic libido.

The first modality of the subject's existence in his relation to the Other is that of offering himself as the object that covers over the Other's lack. He only offers himself as either lost or dead so as to interrogate the Other's desire. Alienation, in this sense, offers the possibility of formulating a question, which implies a first separation. This movement goes towards a new alienation, since separation consists of an appropriation of a signifier of the Other that is emptied of meaning. This structural level of primary narcissism makes of the world a place where the ego identifies as a lovable object, and the subject can only place meaning where it was meant for him, believing all along that he is the one who gives the world meaning. This is the pinnacle of alienation.

The first structure of alienation-separation only offers two outcomes for the subject trapped in primary narcissism: losing oneself in the Other (that is, a real death or a longing for death), or continually depending on the meaning the Other gives. A non-delusional interpretative modality of thinking will be the only refuge to try to attempt a separation.

For Lacan, there is no passage from primary to secondary narcissism, no passage from narcissism to the identifications that will decide the subject's sexuality. There is no movement from narcissism to the formation of fantasy without a prior

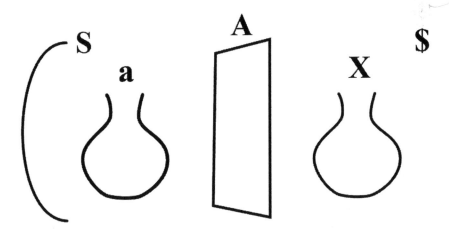

Figure 12.1 Double mirror device. Set-up of a concave mirror and a plane mirror. Plane mirror and disappearance of the object. Drawing by Lacan on January 16, 1963, *Seminar on Anxiety* (personal notes).

Source: Lacan 2004: 162

passage through castration. All this happens very early on in structure formation. The object *a*, as real object, cannot have any representation in the mirror.[3] The specular double is virtual, never completely an other and never totally oneself. An explanation of Lacan's theoretical line of reasoning around his use of the model of the two mirrors will help us discuss this further.

The most extended and durable effect of Lacan's teaching has been, paradoxically, the belief that the mirror stage is an evolutionary stage in the neurobiological development of the speaking-being. The predominant role of the stage that spans from 6 to 18 months of age is the myelination or development of myelin sheaths around nerve fibers of the central nervous system, allowing for the acquisition of both voluntary motor skills and the ability to identify with the neighbor (*semblable*) supported by another person. Initially, for Lacan, the *semblable* will play the role of "master," since it has better control of movements. The subject will launch, in anticipation, into a conquest of the surrounding space, remaining identified with this other and jealous of it. If this were all that were at stake, there would not be much new in regards to the Freudian ego, conceived of as a psychic surface and at the same time as a projection of the body on it. Yet Lacan turns a corner in the 1960s.

After the seminar *On Anxiety* (1962–3), Lacan radically changed his concept of the mirror. While it is true that this phenomenon would not exist without neurobiological maturation, maturation is not the actual cause of an "intrapsychic" mirror, which produces an ideal ego as a point of support and conflict for the ego. Instead, the offer of love coming from the Other is the primary cause. This is why in the double mirror schema consisting of a concave mirror and a plane mirror, the flowers are surrounded by the image of an inverted vase; they symbolize precisely the jouissance that appears in the baby's body as a transformation of this offer of love coming from his mother, or whoever occupies the place.

The first significant novelty illustrated by the schema is the disappearance of the flowers, *a*, in the virtual space behind the plane mirror. This will be a capital innovation in Lacan's thought. Even though Lacan does not make it explicit in the seminar *On Anxiety*, this issue will be developed in the next seminar, *The Four Fundamental Concepts of Psychoanalysis*.

The *a* that disappears is the real jouissance that falls from the body, emptying it, like the mouth empties the nipple and breast that were experienced as belonging to the child's body. This first oral object is thus constituted *après-coup* before disappearing. This loss is what Lacan writes as "x" and the barred subject S next to it indicates that the subject of the unconscious is not just between two signifiers; at stake is the loss of that of the first object of jouissance, not the breast as such, but of the jouissance of the entire body.

Lacan's second schema, shown overleaf, implies two ideas. The first is that the border zone or rim of the mirror comes to be the edge and rim of every neighbor, of every imaginary other in our life. This other as mirror image covers over an abyss of otherness, and the neighbor thus is and is not an image of myself.

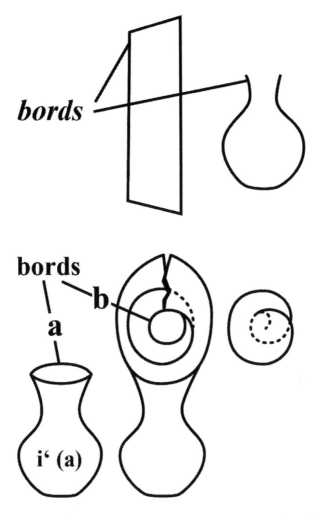

Figure 12.2 Borders of the mirror and borders of the neighbor (*semblable*); the object as border of the hole. Lacan's drawing of January 16, 1963, *Seminar on Anxiety* (personal notes). See also Lacan (2004).

This second proposition is that the real object *a*, which is forever lost, dwells on the rim of the orifice of the imaginary body i'(a). This is because the disappearance of the real jouissance leaves investments in the erogenous zones and in the body's rims. The rest of the object *a* will be left to reappear in the fantasy. Only under these conditions does the *semblable*/neighbor represent the secondary narcissism of everyone.

This operation is not achieved fully in narcissistic neurosis. From this lost jouissance what is left is the phallicization of the body, achieved by the impact of the Other's desire, directed in its name to the subject. If some leftover of this operation remains in the ego, it hurts there.

What would be discursive proof that this loss, in essence, took place? The relation to ourselves is made out of believing and not believing in ourselves. The radical suppression of the second term (not believing) leads to paranoia, and suppression of the first (believing) to melancholy. These two poor outcomes leave open or closed the first identification to primary narcissism.

From here stems the interpretative or depressive coloration of all remainders of primary narcissism in every subject. The clinical problem appears when this affective chromatism taints the entire life of the analysand, appealing before the symptoms as formations of the unconscious, even when no episode would make us think that we are facing a pre-psychotic state.

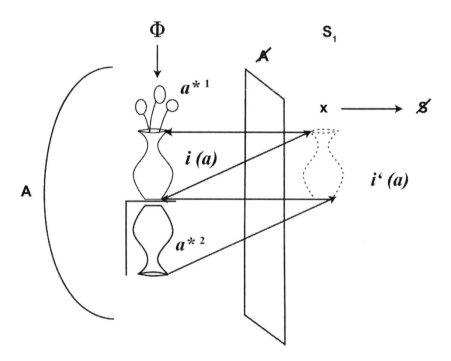

Figure 12.3 Mirror S1. The flat mirror is an effect of S1 over the real jouissance of the object (Lacan's schema modified for this chapter). See also Lacan (1981).

There is first unity of the body i(a), a unity that the neurophysiologic body lacks and that is achieved by the care of the Other. First, the future subject exists as named; the Other addresses him, talks to him, and interprets the chance-movements of the real body as spoken replies. This unity is not sufficient to secure the structure and to protect the body from fragmentation in its confrontation with the Other's desire.

In this third schema, the letter A symbolizes the real Other as such, and the effect produced by the care and offer of love. They make the brain cortex work as an aspheric mirror, giving erogenous unity to the fragmented neurophysiologic body, a*1, making the entire body into an erogenous zone. This is what creates the first ego i(a). The most important aspect of the care is loving speech; it configures the first object of jouissance, a*2, around which the first imaginary body closes up. The letter represents the primordial identification, only possible if the Other desires, giving his lack to the subject as such.

The plane mirror represents the symbolic acquisition produced by the identification to a master signifier, S1, that is separated from the others and functions as an ideal. The plane mirror makes it possible for the object of jouissance in the real space, to the left of the schema, to disappear in the virtual space to the right. What does this mean? The breast as an oral object can never become a scopic object. This is to say that the two-year-old child can look at and envy the newborn at the breast, but can no longer remember the experience of feeling the breast as a part of his body. For the body to acquire its scopic status something new takes place—a loss. The imaginary character of the neighbor (no longer real) i'(a) offers the structural root for the potential to displace it, even if this loss is painful, as Freud proposed. What is painful is that, to access the status of neighbor, the other, any other, has to have for me a remainder of lost jouissance (a).

Let us return to what we call narcissistic neurosis. What does Freud mean by non-sexual trauma when discussing war neurosis? Why did Lacan highlight the Freudian notion of *Liebesversagung* (love refusal) in those terms? Was Lacan referring to someone who as a child had been mistreated, humiliated, neglected and deprived of any protection? Lacan showed that the issue was not a lesser affective quantity but a loss of symbolic reference. It was in this sense that Freud had coined the concept *non-sexual trauma*, bringing it closer to the field of neurosis. Freud writes, " 'narcissistic libido,' that is to say, a mass of sexual energy that attaches itself to the ego and satisfies itself with this as otherwise it does only with an object" ("*«narzisstischen Libido»*, *d.h. eines Masses von sexueller Energie, welches am Ich selbst hängt und sich an diesem ersättigt, wie sonst nur am Objekt*") (Freud 1999: 3, modified). Freud talks here of a modification (*Veränderung*) of the ego, which is not the modification described in *Mourning and Melancholia*, even though both texts were written at about the same time. There is a sexual object in the ego itself, and the ego is treated as an object not by the ideal, but by the libido that finds its satisfaction in it. What would this object in the ego be but the subject itself when invested as an object by an Other from which the subject is not separated, by an Other that continues investing the subject as an object of its own narcissism? At the same time, this object with which the subject identifies stands for the father or the mother, for those who maintained this type of relation with the subject.

The subject's problems with narcissism are the problems of the narcissism of the adult who represents the Other; they establish that the subject will be always both opposed to and completely sustained by that adult. Lacan mentions this inclusion of an object in the ego, thus opening not only a clinical issue of the Real, but also a theoretical problem that goes beyond the resolution of neurosis through the paternal metaphor. This metaphor does not fit with the theorization of what at that time had a double relation to castration. Lacan states:

> Effectively, it is insofar as the castration complex is both crossed, but without being fully realized by the subject that there is an identification with a sort of raw image of the father, an image that carries a reflection of his real particularities in what they have as heavy, even crushing. Here we see once more a renewal of the mechanism of the reappearance in the Real, but this time a Real at the limit of the psychic, within the boundaries of the ego—of a real that imposes itself to the subject, in a quasi hallucinatory way, insofar as this subject, at some point, abandons the symbolic integration of the process of castration.
>
> (Lacan 1994: 415)

This is a singular and rich passage. In this seminar, Lacan comments on the case of Freud's Little Hans, but here, without further ado, he launches into a long explanation about a different subject, who is not exactly Hans. We can hypothesize that he suddenly remembered the Wolf Man. He refers to a hallucination, like that of the cut finger hallucinated by the Wolf Man. Lacan remarks that what is at stake is not a return of something foreclosed in the Real, which rules out any diagnosis of psychosis. Lacan leaves open the issue of an ego, which includes an impassable Real, since the Real imposes itself. In Lacan's thinking in the 1970s, this was schematized as an imaginary cord, or string, failed in the place where it goes above the Real in the Borromean knot. Lacan never spoke of this error in the knot,[4] but I am inviting us to revisit it, especially in the neurotic structures, where a splinter of the Real never leaves the ego in peace. It satisfies itself without allowing us the simpler solution of assuming that this Real is just a remainder of jouissance asking for an encore.

The jouissance at play here is precisely the jouissance with which the subject struggles in narcissistic neurosis. It exercises its effects on the unconscious chain. This type of jouissance interferes with the creation of signifiers via metonymy and metaphor, thus impoverishing the investment of memories. It attacks the formation of dreams and parapraxes, and even symptom formations, because the subject cannot even articulate them as such. It is not what Lacan calls parasitic jouissance, but an opaque jouissance, useless for desire, love, and sublimation. Only a great poet such as Rainer Maria Rilke was able to transform this jouissance into something else, since he managed to testify to it by turning it into poetic work. Rilke made letters with it, used it as a lever and point of support for a possible love life. He consented to it, as a dimension from which, as a man, he had always been excluded, and that he had excluded himself from, because he considered it incompatible both with speech and writing. This is exactly what Lacan called "*savoir y faire*," to be able to manage things.[5]

Freud tells a story in a short, yet famous essay, "*Vergänglichkeit*" ("On Transience"), of taking a walk through a landscape in full summer bloom in the company of a taciturn friend (Lou Andreas) and a young and already well known poet, a transparent allusion to Rilke: "The poet admired the beauty of the scene around us but felt no joy in it. He was disturbed by the thought that all this beauty was fated to extinction, that it would vanish when winter came, like all human beauty and all the beauty and splendor that men have created or may create. All that he would otherwise have loved and admired seemed to him to be shorn of its worth by the transience which was its doom (*Schicksal der Vergänglichkeit*)" (Freud 1982: 305).

Freud responded: "But this demand for immortality (*Ewigkeitsforderung*) is a product of our wishes (*Wunschlebens*) too unmistakable to lay claim to reality: what is painful may none the less be true. [. . .] But I did dispute the pessimistic poet's view that the transience (*Vergänglichkeit*) of what is beautiful involves any loss in its worth. [. . .] *On the contrary, an increase!*" Freud continues:

> What spoilt their enjoyment (*Genuß*) of beauty must have been a revolt in their minds against mourning. The idea that all this beauty was transient was giving these two sensitive minds a foretaste of mourning over its decease; and, since the mind instinctively recoils from anything that is painful, they felt their enjoyment of beauty interfered with by thoughts of its transience. [. . .] I believe that those who think thus, and seem ready to make a permanent renunciation because what was precious has proved not to be lasting, are simply in a state of mourning for what is lost. [. . .] Mourning, as we know, however painful it may be, comes to a spontaneous end. When it has renounced everything that has been lost, then it has consumed [aufgezehrt] itself, and our libido is once more free [. . .]."
>
> (Freud 1982: 306–7)

He was spelling out his canonical theory of mourning: mourning consumes the subject when renouncing the lost object. Logically, Freud, *nolens volens*, allows us to see it, at the same time, as a condition of impossibility: one cannot renounce something lost when what is lost was never possessed. Two years later, under different circumstances, this will designate a particular modality of trauma, whose cause is a (theoretically) novel modality of refusal and failure.

Freud thus attributes to narcissistic libido a character that we can rethink through Lacan. Freud could not define it without renouncing his own attack on Jung, who clearly held that narcissistic libido was desexualized. Lacan introduces the Other's jouissance as not having acceded to the subject the status of signifier or object of the fantasy. Rilke confirms this insight in one of his last poems, "Unfinished Elegy":

Don't allow childhood, that nameless compact
with the heavenly, to be repudiated by destiny;
the prisoner himself broken in the dry prison
still has it to nurse him secretly to the end. Timelessly
it holds his heart. The diseased one too,
when he stares out and comprehends that even the room no more
offers an answer, because it can yet be healed—healable also
his objects lie about among his losses, feverish and diseased,
but still healable—: for him
childhood yet bears fruit. Purely
amid decaying nature it tends its welcoming bed
Not that it is innocent; its prettied up deceptions,
its bed-shams and bolsters, only fleetingly delude us.
Never more certain than we, never more naïve.
Nothing godly can weigh against its weight.
Defenseless just like we are; like animals in winter are, defenseless.
But more so because childhood has no hiding places.
Defenseless as if itself were the threat.
Defenseless like fire, like a giant, like poison, like goings-on
behind locked doors at night in a suspicious house.
For those who fail to see that the hands of the home
Lie, those that protect—are themselves in danger. Who has the
     right then?

(Rilke 1972a)

This poem, written four years after that summer walk with Freud, seems not just to answer but to agree with Freud's interpretation. Rilke clarifies here the nature of mourning that he could not complete earlier. This poem exhibits a tendency we find in many patients, which can be called a wish to be death's neighbor. Here we find not the suspicious collision with death that aims at obtaining secondary gains, but a state of endless mourning. Proximity to death can obtain a surplus jouissance, the extra jouissance with which death has been invested. In Rilke's case, this manifests itself in the attempt to approach death in writing. The erogenous temptation of death appears meaningful in a world that has been annihilated. There is still a hope of separating from the first Other, of tearing oneself from it, a hope comparable to the dangerous belief that the act of killing oneself would make someone be born again.

The work of a great poet sheds some light on the attention we should pay to what gets written in the analysis of each analysand, as an effect of speech, which makes each cure a sort of letter that becomes readable. This is a letter that did not exist before the analytic work, and such a letter comes to find its proper place between the voice and the gaze. The wish to remain, at any cost, in the proximity of death allows us to see something that was not fully accomplished in the first dialectic of alienation and separation. This is what Lacan has described as the "lethal factor" (Lacan 1981: 208, 213), a point of death that marks the jouissance of life. If it is not spoken, at least it is written. "Lethal"[6] is the forgetting of one's previous existence after one has crossed the waters of the Lethe. It is the jug from which the souls of the dead drink when arriving to Averno. It is the forgetting of forgetting, and here it acquires a positive value. Lethal is what is hidden forever from that period of life, or the original repression, *Urverdrängung*.

The narcissistic subjects we treat have not been blessed by that water of oblivion and by its lethal effect that create an incorporeal space[7] for words. It allows a satisfaction in speech without thinking that speech always carries consequences. Those not blessed by Lethe will carry the task of deciding not just to keep on living their lives, but to sustain life with a saying that belongs to them alone. They suffer from an excessive speech that is not free from jouissance, and at the same time from a speech with a jouissance that was scarce. We see this theme in one of the Sonnets to Orpheus, written in 1922 as a funerary monument in the Castle of Muzot:

> Who, with the dead, on poppy dine,
> need nevermore fear:
> the true sweetness in his rhyme
> shall never disappear.
> (Rilke 1974)

Rilke's poetry, like any great art, asks without idealization what sublimation means in an analysis. Sublimation is a work on jouissance but, as defined by Freud, it is *zielgehemmt*, i.e. inhibited as to its sexual goal, which strictly means that it loses it aptitude for reaching orgasm. This does not mean that it would not maintain its nature of jouissance in regards to its sexual aim, with all the inherent difficulties implied by jouissance. It may cause anxiety, inhibitions, and symptomatic formations, as a jouissance not inhibited in terms of its objective would. An object that is also an instrument provides this jouissance, as Real. This is much more attractive for a great artist, at least an artist who engages in a deadly struggle with words, sounds, or colors, who finds that mere reality is greyer and far more secondary than what common mortals think. In general, this requires a share of pain that readers or spectators will want to pay to ignore.

Sublimation does not mean de-sexualization; on the contrary, it is the raising of an object to the dignity of the Thing, thus providing a jouissance thanks to the words used by the poet when writing. These are not strictly words from ordinary language but those that the poet has extracted from it, so as to mold them anew. This task is as dangerous as that of the mountain climber who risks death, reaching summits by way of the steepest paths, like the explorer who defies lands never traversed to leave on them, and in the memory of everyone, the trace of his passing.

An artist is not someone who manages to give shape in writing to his own fantasies, as Freud seems to imply in *The Poet and Daydreaming*. An artist is someone who, because of a failure in fantasy, uses writing to relate to others, which allows him to have a semblance, while at the same time not being himself. A great poet is his work; it is the trace of his existence. Thanks to his work, he maintains himself in the despair of failing to say something that before it was written he did not know.

There is analytic work to be done here which does not primarily concern the formations of the unconscious. When patients feel that they have to be "unique" but, not psychotic, they have not been subjected to foreclosure, such patients strive for a signifier of the One by which they hope to obtain human stature. If not for this desperate attempt, they would be reduced to refuse. Only by fulfilling that improbable task will they return to the "one amongst others" that defines human society. They will be redeemed from moral fault, whether the fault be one really committed or simply attributed to their parents. Once more, Rilke expresses this well:

> Who, if I cried out, would hear me among the Angelic
> Orders? And even if one were to suddenly
> take me to its heart, I would vanish into its
> stronger existence. For beauty is nothing but
> the beginning of terror.
>
> (Rilke 1972b)[8]

What is this terror? Freud's metaphor, referring to narcissistic neurosis as war neurosis, is more profound; he suggests that these analysands live in a state of war, and that such a belief can be a weapon against the precariousness that was the previous norm. If it is true that the death drive is found when drives unravel themselves, then a last quatrain, written in French by Rilke, can show how this unraveling has become a creative instrument:

> *Il faut fermer les yeux et renoncer à la bouche*
> *Rester muet, aveugle, ébloui*
> *L'espace tout ébranlé qui nous touche*
> *Ne veut de notre être que l'ouïe.*
>
> [One has to close one's mouth and eyes
> Stay mute and blinded by light rays,
> Space a trembling around us all touching
> Only wants of us we keep hearing.]
>
> (Rilke 1972a: 42)

In this poem, Rilke confesses his will to lose all senses for the benefit of only one, hearing. The jouissance of an isolated drive is superior to that of entangled drives. Writing is an instrument of re-enmeshing—after having enjoyed the creation of metaphors, the gift of only one drive is accepted in silence because the pen is also a sword filled with an ink replacing blood. Then the poet gathers the invocatory drive with the other senses, making life possible. This is how Rilke finally answers Freud, beyond the death of both. Mistrust in transience, in the perishable beauty accessible to the senses, is justified and true, and indeed it allows the poet to recreate the Other as a poem. In the poem, there are no seasons in which the flowers wither; the written words know nothing of spring, neither do they know of icy winters, since this is the constant temperature of the heart. This is why there is always a fear of abandoning pain, as if pain was more real, for any distancing of pain will immediately produce a feeling of unreality.

But the Other born with the poem disappears once it is written. What does not vanish, however, is the absolutely singular use of the words that say something that nobody else has ever said, and that nobody will say. In this we see the invention of the Real. Writing replaces a speech that never, or almost never, carried a saying. It luminously recreates so much that it is blinding, for here is the other Φ, not the undernourished or perishing desire of the Other. This poetic Real puts order in what is offered as a signifier for life. Maybe a woman, Baladine Klossowska, who was already the mother of the future Balthus and of Pierre, fulfilled for some time the role of what a woman can be for a man: Merline, she was as he named her.

When we listen to some analysands, the impression they leave us is not so much an unfinished mourning as a lack of jouissance in the relation with the other, or of a jouissance that was badly directed. One may imagine that the little bit of jouissance is like the flowers from the first mirror that disappear in the second mirror. Those flowers may have been lacking in sun or in sap, since they are barely sketched, an opaque background of said words, or perhaps even this thought is nothing but a retrospective optical illusion. The question remains: how can we mourn what never was?

The work of Rilke as a poet (*Dichter* in German means creator) teaches us how human speech can find meaning again when the desire of the Other, which only existed intermittently as a contradiction, prevented the language of the mother from giving it beforehand. This entailed a path through writing as recreation of the mother tongue, giving to his words a meaning that they never had because they never were gathered in that way. The "infancy" of which he talks as poet is not even the originary helplessness in early life, but a childhood reinvented so as to receive from language words that did not mean anything. Those meaningless words made it impossible to have a body for oneself and for the others; he returns them written with a signification that makes them forever new, impossible to be worn out. Ultimately, Rilke teaches us that poetic saying passes through a letter that was not yet written.

Translated by Patricia Gherovici and Manya Steinkoler,
and revised by the author

Notes

1 Freud was always devoted careful consideration to the verbal roots of the terms that he used in his teaching. "Exigency" or "vindication" are expressed by the term *Spruch*, which comes from the verb *sprechen*, "to speak," and means judgment directed to something or someone, *An*. In the choice of this word, Freud links the drive to language.

2 We will soon offer another translation for what was not yet clear between the structural frustration of an object, and that of love, a clinical feature that needs to be founded on other bases.

3 Lacan uses a mirror device to illustrate a residual component that does not appear in the mirror reflection; thus, it is radically outside the field of the Other. Lacan calls it the object *a*: "the *a* is what remains irreducible in this total operation of the advent of the subject to the locus of the Other, and it is from there that it is going to take on its function" (Lacan 2004: 189).

4 Pura Cancina proposed this in her book (2012) *El dolor de existir, la melancolía*, Buenos Aires: Letra Viva.

5 Editors' note: This "*savoir y faire*" does not have to do with knowledge in the traditional sense but rather it is a know-how with the real.

6 Lacan plays with one of the roots of the classical Greek verb *lanthano*: "to be hidden"; "to forget."

7 This is the incorporation of the central hole, of the torus of the Other in the subject, as the subject's "soul." Lacan's seminar *L'Insu que sait de l'une-bévue* ..., first three sessions, unpublished.

8 Rilke, "Wer wenn ich schriee, hörte mich denn aus der Engel/Ordnungen? und gesetzt selbst, es nähme/einer mich plötzlich ans Herz: ich verginge von seinem/ stärkeren Dasein. Denn das Schöne ist nichts/ als der Schrecklichen Anfang [. . .]."

Bibliography

Freud, S. (1916) "Bildende Kunst und Literatur," in *Studienausgabe*, reprinted in Band X (1982).

—— (1917) "Er erkrankte also an einer narzisstischen Versagung," in *Studienausgabe*; reprinted in Band VIII (228).

—— (1918). "From the History of an Infantile Neurosis," in *The Standard Edition of the Complete Psychological Works of Sigmund Freud*, vol. XVII, London: Hogarth Press, 1–124.

—— (1919) "Introduction to Psycho-Analysis and the War Neuroses," in *The Standard Edition of the Complete Psychological Works of Sigmund Freud*, vol. XVII, London: Hogarth Press.

—— (1999) "GW, XII," in *Werke aus den Jahren 1917–1920*, Frankfurt: Fischer Verlag, 323–4.

Lacan, J. (1962–3; 2nd edn 2004) *Le Séminaire L'angoisse. Livre X*, Paris: Le Seuil.

—— (1994) "Le Séminaire. Livre IV," in *La relation d'objet*, Paris: Seuil.

—— (1981) *The Four Fundamental Concepts of Psychoanalysis*, trans. A. Sheridan, New York: W. W. Norton.

Rilke, R.M. (1972a) *Œuvres 2, Poésie*, Paris: Seuil.

—— (1972b) "Première Élégie," *Les Élégies de Duino* (édition bilingue), trans. P. Jaccottet, Paris: Seuil.

—— (1974) "Nur wer mit Toten vom Mohn/aß, von dem ihren,/wird nicht den leisesten Ton/wieder verlieren," in *Sonnets à Orphée* (édition bilingue), Paris: Seuil.

13

SHE'S RAVING MAD

The hysteric, the woman, and the psychoanalyst[1]

Claude-Noële Pickmann

It is well-known that the hysteric led Freud to his discovery of the unconscious. In return, she made the psychoanalyst the privileged addressee of her question, and the enigma of femininity immediately took center stage in the development of psychoanalysis.

"What is a woman?"—That is the question for the hysteric. Looking for a response to this intractable enigma, she addresses her question to the father, pushing him unremittingly all the way to his jouissance; or just as well, by identifying herself with a man, she cross-examines man's desire for a woman.

This question that the hysteric emblematically sustains is also the one at the heart of psychoanalytic knowledge. Indeed, the thesis that the unconscious is determined by the phallus, a fact that Freud highlighted in what he gleaned from his patients—and most especially from his hysterical patients' speech—demonstrates that the feminine sex, as such, is excluded from the unconscious. While there are in fact two anatomical sexes, the unconscious does not recognize this biological reality. It neglects it, Freud concludes in his "Three Essays on the Theory of Sexuality" (1905), and recognizes the phallus as the only sexual symbol. Since the difference between the sexes is not inscribed in the unconscious, what is inscribed in its place is a failure in jouissance that Freud designates by the term castration, whose effects are different for boys and for girls.

This is the scandal that Freud has been violently reproached for, namely, that he did not understand the feminine. His error was in wanting to explain the feminine by way of a conceptual tool that cannot be applied to it. Indeed, how can Freud successfully define the specificities of the feminine when he uses the theory of the primacy of the phallus and the logic of castration implied by it?

Jones and the British school criticized Freud already in the 1930s, opposing his phallocentrism, which they considered as theoretically inadequate with regard to women. They posited a "natural" or "primary" femininity that daughters would inherit directly from their mothers and that would orient both their feminine desire and their jouissance. This "natural" femininity was ascribed to anatomical determination, in contradiction with clinical evidence that men and women are both beings of language and that their relation to sex is subverted by this fact.

187

On the other hand, the Freudian thesis makes us aware that unconscious knowledge does not say it all and, notably, it says nothing about the female sex, which, as such, is excluded. Indeed, the unconscious is founded on this rejection. The irreducible phallocentrism of the unconscious is an obstacle to the male-female relation. This failure in jouissance inherent to human sexuality is related to the absence of complementarity or harmony between the sexes. We can thus summarize this major discovery of psychoanalysis: at the fundament of the world, the world that is ordered by phallic semblants, there are not two sexes; there is no primary complementarity,[2] but only a non-rapport. This is the Real of sexuation[3] that both men and women must confront in their encounter with the other sex.

S(A̶): Lacan's love letter[4]

If woman, as such, does not exist in the unconscious, then we cannot find a distinctive feminine trait that would pertain to all women. Therefore, we must renounce the possibility of finding the essence of femininity. Lacan will summarize this fundamental axiom of the Freudian discovery in an aphorism that is at once provocative and concise: "T̶h̶e̶ woman does not exist" (Lacan 1998b: 7). He writes this in barring the definite article, "the." What does not exist is the predicate that would accompany all women, the feminine universal, the identificatory trait that would determine what is a woman. Women, of course, exist! Consequently, each woman will have to invent her own solution to make up for this flaw in sexual identity, her own way of being a woman.

Due to this fact, what a woman encounters when confronted with castration is not only an unbearable inequality between the sexes. We know that women have always been able to make the best of being of the so-called "weaker sex," but it is "the profound *Werwerfung* of the woman, her rejection as a being" (Lacan 1998a: 350) that is at stake. Lacan designates this emptiness of existence (for women)— the one that women face insofar as they are women—with the matheme, S(A̶): the signifier of the barred Other, the "fault, hole, or loss in the Other" (Lacan 1998b: 28). This illustrates the dimension of inconsistency, that the Other qua locus "does not hold up."[5] In this sense, the S(A̶), expresses that the Symbolic is "not-all." Furthermore, it points to an irreducible Real, which is produced as an excess to every symbolization process. This Real cannot be written: the Other is definitively irreducible to the one of the identifiable,[6] i.e., *hétéros*. Lacan's thesis in "Encore": "By S(A̶) I designate nothing other than woman's jouissance" (Lacan 1998b: 64). Feminine jouissance appears as heterogeneous to phallic jouissance; it is not its symmetrical feminine counterpart. Nevertheless, it is situatable in relation to phallic jouissance as an opening to another dimension. This is why Lacan called it supplementary jouissance. As such, feminine jouissance escapes the phallic signifier, producing an Other dimension, which is its own beyond, and which doesn't allow any complementarity of the partner in the sexual relation.

Lacan designated this Other jouissance by the term "*pas tout*" (not-all),[7] showing that the universality of the phallic order is already flawed. The "not-all" is a subjective position that is not limited to women, yet the way women encounter the castration of the Other produces a more immediate relation with the failure in the Other than it does in men. Indeed, a woman, in search of a referent to identify herself with the signifier "woman," finds an absence instead of the signifier she had hoped for.[8] The feminine position is thus revealed as divided with regard to the phallic function: this relation to the phallic function is only partial; it is not generalizable, and as such, it is undecidable. This is why one cannot confuse the feminine position with hysteria; hysteria is the position of the one who has decided not to play in this undecidability and consequently cannot enjoy it.

Following Freud and then Lacan, if an anti-phallic essence of femininity does not exist, that is to say, if the feminine exception does not exist, if there isn't anybody or anything from the woman's side that is able to found the existence of a non-phallic sex,[9] how can a woman enjoy this part of herself where she is radically Other for herself?

Why is there nothing rather than something?[10]

If the phallic law that structures the world fails to make woman an "all" (complete) subject, what happens to the unsubjectifiable part of herself? Is it not this very question that the hysteric addresses to the father when she demonstrates the failure of the phallic order to account for the possible existence of a feminine being? She thus denounces the limits of the Symbolic order by questioning the structure at the very point of its failure. It is in this way that the hysteric has an almost natural vocation to make herself a symptom of the Master's discourse, and to incarnate at each historic moment the symptomatic truth of the social malaise. Her symptom takes various forms in regard to this malaise in order to better point it out.

The hysterical phallic gripe, her general complaint, demonstrates the failure of identification of woman with the phallus, showing that a type of jouissance exists beyond the phallus. The hysteric reminds us that the question of femininity can only be posed where the phallic function meets its limit, opening to an infinite beyond, that of an Other jouissance. The hysteric refuses to acknowledge that the phallus as semblant could serve jouissance. Her mistake consists in trying to demonstrate that because it escapes the phallus, it would not owe anything to it and tries to testify to a magnified and untouched "essence" of femininity. Recall Dora in ecstasy, "rapt in silent admiration" (Freud 1905a: 95) in front of the Dresden Madonna or the hypnotic ravishing of Lol V. Stein when the cause of desire appears in the form of Anne Marie Stretter whom she ideally recognizes as "The woman."[11]

Correlatively, the hysteric has been and remains just as much an example of the fact that a girl, during the Oedipus complex, chooses the father and his desire as a privileged partner in order to pose the question of the woman. Dora and the young homosexual woman both showed Freud, even before he was able to fully understand it, that a girl learns to use the father or his desiring gaze; if these fail, she uses the signifiers of his desire in order to become a woman. This is due to the fact that in the relation to the father, lack becomes possible. This possibility offers her a way out; while she doesn't have the phallus, she can still try to be it . . . for masculine desire. She will thus be able to play—at times with some pleasure—at being the phallus, experiencing the ravaging effects that a woman can obtain from making herself the object cause of desire for a man.

Because the mother was the first big Other of the demand, the negativization of the phallus was excluded, and thus this assumption of lack remains impossible as a metaphor. Consequently, the relationship between a girl and her mother always remains contaminated by the question of the satisfaction of maternal jouissance that the daughter either consecrates herself to, or refuses. It is why the question of "What is a woman?" cannot be posed in the mother-daughter context, where it is saturated by the maternal reference and hence leads to a dead-end.

It is particularly noteworthy that after the recognition of the primacy of the phallus for both genders in 1923, Freud will always maintain that the daughter's access to femininity can only happen when she ceases to be captive to the desire of the mother and to the auto-erotic jouissance of the relation to the mother. Only then can she become interested in the desire of the father, which necessitates a partial renunciation of infantile masturbatory jouissance. This allows a more specifically feminine relation to jouissance to emerge. In "On Femininity" (1933), Freud thus designated two arduous tasks in becoming a woman: a change of object and a change of jouissance.

The feminine Oedipus

In consenting to the Oedipal metaphor, a girl fails to find a signifier that could say what a woman is. Even worse, the apparent universality of phallic significa-tion only returns her to the radical absence of a trait of feminine identification. Left stranded by the faulty phallic signifier, she risks being swallowed up by the jouissance of the Other. There where the father fails to produce a universal law, he exposes the daughter to a return of the phallic mother's jouissance, thus demonstrating that the paternal metaphor can only separate the daughter from the mother's jouissance imperfectly. Since a woman is "not-all," as determined by the father's phallic law, she is "not-all" protected from the temptation of "mad reunions" she might experience with maternal jouissance. This can happen at the end of a love affair, or when confronted with professional failures, as well as when traversing the stages of a woman's important biological life cycles. In these moments, she confronts a point in the structure where phallic signification lacks, leaving her without recourse in a world without bearings in which limits and forms dissolve.

The girl's primary love for the mother as phallic first big Other turns into hate when she discovers that the mother does not have the phallus. A remainder of this first attachment can create an indissoluble and ravaging bond, often taking the color of hate. A second love for the father is also disappointing because the paternal metaphor cannot say it all, leaving the girl with a persistent demand for love.

The feminine Oedipus complex appears as a kind of secondary structure that only partly recovers the originary bond between the daughter and the mother and never succeeds in completely consigning it to oblivion. However, Freud never confuses this remainder of the attachment to the mother or the auto-erotic modes (sometimes very archaic) of jouissance that they entail with what could be the essence of a feminine jouissance. On the contrary, he clearly shows that the remainder of this attachment to the mother acts as a handicap for the femininity of the daughter. He remarks that the fact that the little girl turns away from the mother is a very significant step in her development. Furthermore, the passage to the paternal object is only accomplished by the passive tendencies that have remained after the "catastrophe" of the Oedipus complex (the abandonment of incest and the institution of conscience and morality).

The remainders of the mother-daughter pre-Oedipal bond only constitute an obstacle if they remain omnipotent. The originary love for the mother may remain as a devastated and devastating place, an infernal love, a relation nourished principally by guilt and by incessant reproaches towards this Other, "the prehistoric, unforgettable other person whom no one coming after can equal" (Freud 1954: 239). The feminine clinic, and notably the clinic of hysteric women testifies largely to this terrible alienation that constitutes the love of the phallic mother in which they camp, sometimes without defection, making themselves prey to mortifying effects and to the law of the disaster that this love bears with it.

The ravage of the other: a psychic catastrophe

Freud never used the term ravage to qualify the mother-daughter relation. However, in the course of his elaboration of feminine sexuality, he gave great importance to the high point of this primary relation of rage. This rage is ravaging for the figure of the mother and it is what allows the daughter to leave this devastated place to turn towards the father. For Freud, if there is ravage, it is the ravage of the mother. It concerns the first object of the girl's love and its consequence is to make her exit the maternal space and push her towards the space of the father. This is indeed what we still find today in the treatment of hysteria.

Freud noticed that a remainder of this bond indissolubly subsists throughout the girl's access to femininity. Indeed, if the mother's love initially eroticizes the body of the daughter, the mother's hold over the sexual drives of the daughter always represents a catastrophe for the daughter's femininity. In "On Feminine Sexuality" (1931), Freud sheds light on hysteria in this regard:

> this phase of attachment to the mother is especially intimately related to
> the etiology of hysteria, which is not surprising when we reflect that both
> the phase and the neurosis are characteristically feminine, and further,

that in this dependence on the mother we have the germ of later paranoia in women. For this germ appears to be the surprising, yet regular, fear of being devoured by the mother. It is plausible to assume that this fear corresponds to a hostility which develops in the child towards her mother. . . .

(Freud 1931: 226)

Psychoanalysts often forget this originary bond between daughter and mother when they concern themselves with the love of the father and the fantasy of seduction that underscores it.

The castration of the other and the alterity of the body

What for Freud is the specificity of the feminine experience with the mother that produces hysteric daughters? Freud discovered that while castration weighs menacingly on the sexual life of boys, the girl experiences it as an already accomplished fact. Let us leave aside the debate that ends up throwing out the baby with the bath water. Instead, let us designate more precisely the subjective consequences of this experience of castration as the girl is confronted with it. The irruption of sexual difference leaves the girl with a lack of identity when she is confronted with the lack in the Other, depriving her of an ideally phallic Other worthy of love. Freud speaks here of an impossible completion to show that privation is already inscribed at the very heart of the relation to the first Other of the demand in which subjects alienate their desire. This Other is said by Freud to be unforgettable precisely because the signifiers of the Other's desire enter our body and in so doing eroticize it; that is to say, they cut it up into zones of drive. Lacan described the drive as the "treasure trove of signifiers" ($ \lozenge$ D) before defining it in the 1970s as "an echo of a saying in the body" (Lacan 1975). The first seductress of the child, the mother, eroticizes the body with the signifiers of the Other. Language parasites the body with a transitivist jouissance insofar as it is not attributable to a subject or to the Other. The notion of jouissance of the Other (*la jouissance de l'Autre*) as designated by Lacan takes on its very meaning in the equivocation in the French preposition "de."[12] There is an equivocation between the jouissance that the subject could take from the body of the Other and the jouissance that the Other could take from the body of the subject. The identification with the imaginary phallus of the mother is correlative to this equivalence. The illusion that the girl and the mother could have something in common, bound between them indissolubly by way of their bodies, is found in this equivocation. This is why it is so ravaging for the subjectivity of the girl as well as for the mother.

The kernel of the ravage seems thus to be constituted by a fixation on a remainder of this modality of jouissance as jouissance of the Other. Ravage continues to occur as long as a woman has not yet disinvested the maternal Other from its ideal position, and is continually alienated in her demand.

We thus see why, in the rupture of the semblants, when the illusion that constitutes our sense of reality breaks down, when the names of the father become untied, and when what had been paternal reference points are demolished, nothing bars the ravage any longer. At such times, the jouisssance of the Other returns in the subject as unbarred, submerging the body and threatening to swallow it. This can often give the hysteric a psychotic allure and disturb the analyst, especially when witnessing the irruption of a minor hallucinatory episode (for instance, being poisoned or possessed by the mother). Importantly, this type of event risks being considered a "psychiatric case." The psychoanalyst, however, should remain vigilant, not giving up on a diagnosis of hysteria. The term "borderline" is weak because it does not allow for distinctions to be made between hysteria and psychosis. Nevertheless, such cases are indeed a paranoid version of feminine hysteria.

Just as spectacularly, in those moments where the names of the father unravel, one can witness the irruption of psychosomatic phenomena that sometimes leads the hysteric, having exhausted all the usual medical resources, to ask for an analysis.

The hatred of the castrated mother

Freud did not cease underlining that the remainder of the relation mother-daughter is not love but hate. This is why he thought that the first husband would only inherit this incurable discord, often putting first marriages in danger. Freud emphasizes that this hate comes from the phase preceding Oedipus and is reinforced and exploited in the following phase. Such a hate can be quite striking and can persist throughout one's life. What is the motivation for the little girl's love turning into hate?

In order to respond to this question, Freud patiently addresses the catalogue of motives of complaints—frustrations of all sorts—that a girl could reasonably address to her mother, to finally conclude that these complaints are secondary in constructing the *après-coup* of the Oedipus complex. For Freud, there is no motive for this hate other than maternal castration. With maternal castration, it is the phallus as imaginary phallus that is lost. That the Other is castrated reveals that the phallus is only a lure, a postiche, confronting the girl with the flaw in the Symbolic order and depriving her of any identification in a world where nothing seems unified or real anymore, since the one that would guarantee the stability of the word and the equality of beings has disappeared. This is why there is "betrayal"—to use the term that is spoken most often by our patients—when they discover that the identificatory support that their mother offered them was only a lure. This betrayal of the Other we designate by the German vocable *Versagung*, which Lacan proposed to translate as "perdition" (Lacan 2001a: 353).

Ravage and femininity

Following Freud, Lacan took note of the radical disharmony that is the core of the mother-daughter relationship and in the 1970s he designated it with the term

193

ravage. Lacan used this expression to introduce the formulae of sexuation in "L'étourdit" (1972), formulae written so that the phallic function is common to both sexes, thus defining masculine or feminine positioning. Let us first explore this term "ravage," first used by Lacan as a psychoanalytic concept in 1972. This is a term from daily language that stems from the French verb *ravir* from the Latin *rapere*, which means "to take away by force." In a figurative sense, it means "transported by admiration or joy." The *Littré* dictionary defines it as "damage by violence and rapidity," but also "destruction caused by something that is propelled, like an impetuous flow." In the eleventh century "impetuous flow" and "ravage" were synonymous. One can thus rank different orders of ravage from the various meanings of the verb *ravir*. These range all the way from ravishment to swallowing up, furrowing, rapture and to devastation. It is impossible not to evoke the writing of Marguerite Duras in this context, recalling her texts *The Barrage against the Pacific* and *The Ravishing of Lol V. Stein*, to which Lacan paid written homage in 1965. Duras admitted that these works stemmed from her own ravage and she wrote them in order to make something else of it. She famously asserted during a television interview that writing is the only thing more powerful than the mother.

The term "ravage" not only designates a symptomatic failure of the mother-daughter relation, but is a logical effect of the "not-all," due to the fact that a woman is "not-all" inscribed in the phallic function. The ravage is tied to a doubling between sense and absence that makes woman be "not-all" subjected to castration. As a consequence, her inscription into the phallic order will be contingent and not universal. In this sense, ravage is a logical effect of the "not-all," stemming from a direct rapport to the default in the symbolic order.

To pose the problem in this way has immediate clinical implications: the daughter-mother bond should not be restored. The cure does not aim at repairing the harm caused by a frustrated, castrated, possessive mother, even a destructive one, by making the analyst into a "good mother." We should add here that any analysis that has the aim of restoring this original bond relies on a denial of the structure by trapping the woman in the position of a girl.

The mother-ravage

Lacan criticized Freud for not having noticed that the feminine escapes phallic law and obligates women to pass directly through castration. Since women are not-all, they have the choice to position themselves in the phallic function or not.

While often a shelter, the love of the father is, however, a risky one for the girl. When the imaginary father falls from his place and nothing can hold the world together, an abyss of unsubjectifiable jouissance opens, which necessitates the law of a castrating Other. It is here that Lacan returned to Freud to tell us that a certain number of women seem to expect more support from their mothers than from their fathers. Lacan uses the term "subsistence" here in a double sense. "Subsistence" means to stop, to stay, to endure. The etymology of the word invokes nutrition as well as the ensemble of goods necessary for existence. This relates to care-giving

194

by way of food, implying frustration, and dependency on the mother. This maintains the daughter in the register of demand, which organizes the drive, but not the register of desire.

However, "to subsist" is also a philosophical term that has an ontological seat, a kind of unshakable foundation that could not fail: it is not just a question of living but the question of feminine being that is posed by way of the use of this word. Lacan denounced the very feminine belief that where the signifier failed women—"She is called woman (*on la dit femme*) and we defamed (*dit-fâmed*) her" (Lacan 1998b: 85)—femininity's real substance could be found in the relation to the mother. Here, Lacan evoked the ideas of a feminine essence, of a substantial and solid foundation for femininity that a rapport with the mother's body could give the illusion of, not to mention the vertigo of a body-to-body. In actuality, all this covers up the abyss in which the daughter's relation to the sex is lost.

We should recall that Lacan, who had several militant feminists in analysis, addressed them on several occasions in his seminar *Encore* (1972), saying that there is woman only from the nature of things, which is the nature of words. Furthermore, he maintained that "one should not go into a head-spin with the anti-phallic nature of the woman which has no trace in the unconscious" (Lacan 1980).

It would be even more misguided and specious to look for woman in the pre-Oedipal or even less in a body-to-body experience before language. Lacan denounced, in not a very gallant manner, a number of post-Freudians who theorized the existence of a pre-Oedipal femininity: "Horney, or Deutsch for whom the tendency—when speaking of women—is to prefer 'the voice of the body' to the voice of the unconscious as if it was not precisely from the unconscious that the body finds a voice." He added, "it is curious to see that, right there in analytic discourse, the excess that there is between the authority with which these woman speak gathered with the superficiality of the solutions that this speech produces" (Lacan 2001b: 463).

As we have previously seen, the mother is always the first seductress of the child, be it a girl or a boy, to the extent that care—the touching that she engages in with her child—is a "stimulant" (*Reiz*) for them. Yet, clinical practice amply reveals that what mothers—in good faith and even in the name of love—are capable of making their children endure (in particular their daughters) is absolutely without limit. The child, in effect, occupies a particular function in the economy of feminine desire due to the imaginary equivalency between child and phallus. The baby is the principal object of jouissance for feminine desire. If it weren't for the interdiction imposed by castration, nothing would prevent a mother from using her child for her own satisfaction. This version of the "maternal instinct" opens the way for every sort of excess, for all the abuse that it is necessary to qualify as "sexual," since the child, having been a very real object, can be played with like a play thing, a plug. The child, in trying to respond to this aspiration, is only by way of the erotization, without limits of a body.

Women in analysis relate, sometimes with shame and sometimes with rage, memories of the practices they were subjected to as children and even adolescents under the guise of "bodily hygiene." The rage emerges when the woman on the couch realizes that she has been as a girl an object of her mother's jouissance. The shame arises from their realization of their own participation in the jouissance of this incestuous relation. For these women an indelible and privileged fixation of jouissance remains that, if repressed, can burden their subsequent sexual life.

One discovers that the fantasy of the father's seduction can unfold during the cure, permitting the erotogenic zone concerned with the mother to serve feminine sexual jouissance instead of remaining a handicap, as Freud had put it. The fantasy of paternal seduction has the potential of inscribing the sexuality of the daughter as a subject of desire while limiting maternal jouissance. Femininity is the price of the inscription under the interdiction of the limitless jouissance of the Other. By making use of the father, the girl will subsequently be able to traverse the limit beyond the semblance and "do without the father." Only the denial of castration can give such extraordinary force to the implacable and exclusive alienation that one sometimes encounters between a mother and a daughter.

Feminine jouissance is only encountered beyond the phallus, on the condition that the phallus works as a semblant. At the same time, let us highlight that the more the daughter looks for the answer to the question of woman in the relation with her mother, the more ravaging this is for her subjectivity and jouissance. Between mother and daughter there is denial of castration when the daughter gets stuck with the body of her mother unable to develop femininity. Dora understood: she scorned the jouissance of her mother's "good housekeeping" and preferred to relay the question of femininity to her father. Often single-parent families insulate themselves in the maternal model. Today's hysterics do not always have someone serving in the paternal function to whom they can pose this question. The analyst should be careful about not pushing a woman towards ravage, where she will only find the obscenity of maternal jouissance. There is no "practice of ravage" in the cure.

When a patient comes to us to speak about femininity, it is often to distinguish it from the mother's femininity. Sometimes the traits inherited from the mother are actually an obstacle to femininity. The analyst must grant a space for the analysand to be able to create her own way of being a woman.

The popular idea that femininity is transmitted from mother to daughter under the pretext that they are from the same sex is a favored illusion in our modern Western society, in which patriarchy in the traditional sense no longer exists. Yet there is surely something difficult for today's modern women, which is how to accept a limit. This limit is precisely the limit of the transmission of femininity. A woman can transmit to her daughter no more than to any other woman what it is to be a woman, any more than another woman can. Whenever a mother uses her daughter to give consistency to a "being woman," she will make it even more difficult for the daughter to find her own path to her own femininity. This is why each time the mother is questioned during the cure of a woman, psychoanalytic ethics demand sustaining this disjunction between the mother and the woman, in order not to add to the ravage.

Clinically, for the subject who is its prey, the ravage can take resistant and enigmatic forms in each case. This is illustrated by the following examples: I evoke the waves of ravage that senselessly overtook a young woman, leaving her stupefied and stranded in a deep depression. Her concerned mother assiduously recruited the help of a doctor to prescribe "happiness pills." For another, on the occasion of a pregnancy, the ravage took the form of the sensation of an alien invading her body during sleep, menacing her to the point of disintegration. For this analysand, the repeated irruption of a surge of hatred against her own unborn daughter was an extreme irrational violence that made her fear the worst and left her stranded, feeling like an empty bag. For yet another analysand, an edema of Quincke, a rapid, dramatic, inflammation of skin, menaced her each evening at dinnertime, pushing her inexorably towards anorexia and leaving her swollen and ravished.

Man-ravage

Lacan defines the function of the sinthome as a "supplement" (*suppléance*) to make up for the lack of a rapport (Lacan 2005: 101). The sinthome corrects the knotting precisely where its failure occurred. He adds, "there is a rapport only where there is a sinthome. It is the sinthome that allows the other sex to be tolerated. I take the liberty to say that the sinthome is the sex to which I do not belong, that is to say, a woman. A woman is for every man a sinthome. For what a man is for a woman, we must find another name, since the sinthome is characterized by non-equivalence. A man is for a woman, anything you please, an affliction, worse than a sinthome, even a ravage" (Lacan 2005: 101).

In Lacan's formulations in this late seminar, woman is a sinthome for a man and man is a ravage for a woman. There is a radical distinction between ravage and sinthome. If the sinthome is what allows to make up for what does not stop not being written, it seems that in the sexual relation with a man, insofar as a woman enters into it as not-all (*pas-toute*), her jouissance will be other than phallic jouissance, and therefore she will not find the union that she expects.

The solitude of the jouissance has not left her many opportunities to take on a ravaging aspect, something we have a number of clinical testimonies of. Often after the daughter has experienced ravage with the mother, the woman will experience ravage with the man. Freud noted this ravaging dimension in a woman's sexual relations with a man. However, when confronted with this, Freud makes of the phallic cause something dear to women. According to him, it is the principal motive of their affliction, "a hostile bitterness" (Freud 1918), towards the man who took their virginity. Freud tells us we should never ignore the impact of this bitterness in the relation between the sexes.

According to Freud, it is not so much the narcissistic wound (Freud 1918: 205) felt during the first sexual encounter but the raging phallic plaint present in the stormy mother-daughter relation that contaminates a woman's first amorous relationship with a man. Defloration "unleashes an archaic reaction of hostility" (Freud 1918: 208). Thus, the first husband will simply inherit the bad mother-daughter relationship. Freud asserts that, as a rule, "second marriages so often turn out better than first" (Freud 1918: 207). Freud writes, "I think it must strike the observer in how uncommonly large a number of cases the woman remains frigid and feels unhappy in a first marriage, whereas after it has been dissolved she becomes a tender wife, able to make her second husband happy. The archaic reaction has, so to speak, exhausted itself on the first object" (Freud 1918: 203).

This clinical remark Freud made in 1918 illuminates the entire field of the psychology of the amorous life of the woman. This field is often neglected by psychoanalysts, who prefer to relegate it to the hysteric woman's neurotic dissatisfaction. Is it the kernel of maternal ravage that is reactivated in a woman's amorous passion, or is there something else at stake in the ravage with the man she loves, the man who provides her with sexual jouissance? Freud notes that under the auspices of marriage, the expectation and the act do not match up in coitus. He adds that the woman finds tenderness only in an illicit liaison that must remain secret; the only one where she can act on her own influence and not by the influence of others (Freud 1918: 203). Freud recognizes a disjunction in women's difficulty in choosing between the man who gives her his name, i.e., the husband, and the man who gives her sexual jouissance, i.e., the lover. If this painful demand exists in women, namely that only one man should give them both, isn't it simply because these demands are within themselves antinomic?[13] When a woman chooses a man for his name, identity, and social status, this phallic realization will take place at the expense of feminine jouissance. Many women show day to day satisfaction in being the wife of a man and the mother of his children; this works as long as the fantasmatic or real seducer does not appear to disturb the conjugal peace and open the space of ravage. As we see in some hysterical patients, as soon as a husband is suspected of taking a mistress he suddenly becomes an object of fantasy, a sexual seducer. Here the effects of ravage cannot be simply reduced to the reality of the infidelity or the presence of the other woman. The conjugal betrayal is inflected by an earlier maternal disappointment.

Why does the relation to the beloved man, the one she experiences jouissance from, evince ravaging effects beyond the ones that she gets from being the object of his desire? Why does man become woman's ravage? We might find the answer in considering the complex and rich question of feminine jouissance. Woman has the Other as her partner, and in Lacan's formulation, a very particular Other, that in his development of the formulae of sexuation he calls the "*l'hommoinsun*" (Lacan 1973: 35), one who will not exist, much like Lacan will also say of "The woman."[14] At the same time, it is possible to say that the *hommoinsun* exists by pure contingency, a contingency that one finds specifically in love, that is, by being the one who supports feminine jouissance. Also spelled *au-moins-un* ("at-least-one" who is not castrated), as the partner of feminine jouissance, he is identified with the figure of exception. This is why, in love, whereas the man believes he creates the woman, actually, he puts her to work supplementing the failure of complementarity so that the "at-least-one," this partner for feminine jouissance, will ex-sist. Lacan writes ex-sist with a dash to underline the *au-moins-un*'s enigmatic exterior, peripheral existence, since the *au-moins-un* exists most often by being denounced as "not it."

The *au-moins-un* is the figure that subtends feminine jouissance. Valuable insofar as he is denounced, he is at the same time all the more enjoyed since there will never be a man qualified to be the exception she is looking for. She can thus nourish the precious dissatisfaction she enjoys—recognizing in her man the one from whom she wants to get an enjoyment beyond his castration. It is in this regard that the hysteric refuses to give the value of the universal to the particular. She would rather go on strike than compromise in allowing jouissance to condescend to desire.

If, as a consequence, the hysteric's quest for the exception is ravaging, it is because she unceasingly repeats, verifying again and again the impossibility of finding the "one" who would finally match up with her jouissance. She thus bears the entire weight of the *hétéros* and this is ravaging for her. The man's desire, on the other hand, when he makes a woman the object of his jouissance, uses a phallic yardstick for measuring that can be all the more obliterating when his desire inscribes and reduces her to a simple phallic exchange value. Here we often see that at the heart of the relation to the beloved man who gives her sexual jouissance we find the replication of the feeling of "being nothing for him" or of being rejected by her mother.

One hypothesis we could propose on the basis of the insistence of this scenario in clinical work with women would be that by way of man-ravage the hysteric protects herself from a more devastating ravage, where she would experience a subjectless pain impossible to name or identify.[15] She thus allows herself to be divided by the jouissance that a man takes by way of her, making a partner of the solitude she encounters, while the real union will never materialize (Lacan 1973: 23).

In so doing, she experiences the painful realization that the sexes will not meet, and that the two modes of jouissance will never coincide; Achilles will never join with the tortoise, finally making a "whole" where she could belong once and for all. In fact, woman will never join up with the One, since, insofar as she supports the Other sex, she will just be able to differentiate herself from the other sex in producing the *One au moins* (at-least-One/subtracted One), ad infinitum.

Insofar as she is "not-all" phallic, a woman can encounter the limit where all supplementation fails. This limit reveals that there is no order to existence, and no partner who could respond to restore order. There is no rapport between man and woman where what never ceases to not be written would finally be written or where subjectivization would finally hold. This is the structural reason why women are more affected by ravage than men.

Translated by Manya Steinkoler and Patricia Gherovici

Notes

1 This text was abridged by the editors. The original version was published in French: Pickmann, C.-N. (2001) "L'hystérique et le ravage," in A. Michels (ed.) *Actualité de l'hystérie*, Paris: Erès.

2 The thesis of a primary complementarity (*mixité originelle*) has served as a support for creating a citizenship with parity as its principle. See A. Fouque (1995) *Il y a deux sexes*, Paris: Gallimard; or S. Agacinski (1998) *Politique des sexes*, Paris: Du Seuil.

3 Sexuation is the Lacanian term to explain how, when confronting the enigma of sexual difference, we position ourselves as men or women, a positioning that is not based on anatomical differences but on modalities of jouissance.

4 During lesson VII, this letter, a logical scripture of the Other that is not marked by the signifier, can illuminate the abyssal mystery of Freud's dark continent of femininity. Indeed, this writing shows that the feminine sex, insofar as it is the Other sex, escapes the signifier only in reference to it, and is one of its most radical effects. The feminine demand for love stems from the failure in a direct relation to the fault in the symbolic order, as *not-all*. We must distinguish between love, as love of the same, and love in love letters or lovers' declarations, which aim at the *semblant* of the Other. Consequently, they are outside sex, *beyondsex* (*horsexe*). Love letters aim at the *hétéros* and thus give place to the Other. J. Lacan (1998) *The Seminar of Jacques Lacan: Book XX. On the limits of love and knowledge, 1972–1973*, ed. J. A. Miller, trans. B. Fink, New York: W. W. Norton & Company.

5 Ibid.

6 "How then can we situate the function of the Other? How—if, up to a certain point, what remains of any language when it is written is based simply on knots of the One—are we to posit a difference? For it is clear that the Other cannot be added to the One. The Other can only be differentiated from it. If there is something by which it participates in the One, it is not by being added. For the Other . . . is the One-missing (*l is the One-*)" (Lacan 1998b: 129).

7 With the notion of "not-all," Lacan, in the early 1970s, succeeded in theorizing something new about feminine sexuality, notably in taking up what Freud had expressly left by the wayside (Lacan 1998b: 57, 80). See also J. Lacan (2011) *Le Séminaire. Livre XIX Ou Pire*, Paris: Seuil.

8 Instead of unifying herself and finding unification and identity, she doubles herself between phi and S(-A).

9 As is verified everywhere, every image of woman placed imaginarily in the place of the exception, from the mother to the star, anywhere from the virgin to the drag queen, falls into the "all-phallic."

10 B. Toboul (1997–8) "The Question 'ex,'" unpublished.

11 "Lol, stricken with immobility, had seen, as he did [Richardson] the relinquished bowing grace of a dead bird. She was thin. She must have always been this way. She dressed this thinness in a low cut black double sheath dress in an equally black tulle. She wanted to make and dress herself this way and she was as she wished, irrevocably. One could glean the admirable bone structure of her body and of her face as she appeared, she would die with her desired body." M. Duras (1964) *Le ravissement de Lol V. Stein*, Gallimard: Folio, 15–16.

12 In French, de means both of and from, objective and genitive.

13 It is Gerard Pommier's thesis that "[a] man thus supports two extreme and irreconcilable functions for the woman who loves him. His existence offers a hold on this discord; he holds the middle and is the figure of the hole that exists between sex and name." And a little further, he adds: "The ravage from then on carries the name of a man; it supports him. The presence silently unites what is disjointed, what any action or word

200

disjoints, an errancy, incommensurability, of death or life." G. Pommier (1989) *L'Ordre sexuel*, 44–7, Aubiers.

14 The "*aumoins un*" is homophonic with the "*homme moins un*" or the masculine category of exception, the "uncastrated man" whose exclusion from the set of men allows for general masculine identification. The "*au moins un*" is the figure of exception and fantasmatically related to feminine jouissance as "inheriting" the Imaginary phallus of the primal mother.

15 The lack in being is a modality of existence possible for the subject in that it allows the Other of love to exist.

Bibliography

Freud, S. (1901; 2nd edn 1905a) "Fragment of an Analysis of a Case of Hysteria," in *The Standard Edition of the Complete Psychological Works of Sigmund Freud, Volume VII (1901–1905): A Case of Hysteria, Three Essays on Sexuality and Other Works*, London: Hogarth.

—— (1905b) "Three Essays on the Theory of Sexuality," in *The Standard Edition of the Complete Psychological Works of Sigmund Freud, Volume VII (1901–1905): A Case of Hysteria, Three Essays on Sexuality and Other Works*, London: Hogarth.

—— (1918) "The Taboo of Virginity" (Contributions to the Psychology of Love III), in *The Standard Edition of the Complete Psychological Works of Sigmund Freud, Volume XI (1910): Five Lectures on Psycho-Analysis, Leonardo da Vinci and Other Works*, London: Hogarth.

—— (1931) "Female Sexuality," in *The Standard Edition of the Complete Psychological Works of Sigmund Freud, Volume XXI (1927–1931): The Future of an Illusion, Civilization and its Discontents, and Other Works*, London: Hogarth.

—— (1933) "On Femininity," in *The Standard Edition of the Complete Psychological Works of Sigmund Freud, Volume XXII (1932–1936): New Introductory Lectures on Psycho-Analysis and Other Works*, London: Hogarth.

—— (1954) *The Origins of Psychoanalysis*, ed. M. Bonaparte, A. Freud and E. Kris, New York: Basic Books.

Lacan, J. (1973) "L'étourdit," in *Scilicet* 4, Paris: Seuil.

—— (1975) "Le Séminaire Livre XXIII, Le sinthome, session of 18 November 1975," in *Ornicar?* 6.

—— (1980) "Seminar of 15 January 1980," reprinted in *Le Monde*, January 26, 1980.

—— (1998a) *Seminar V, Les formations de l'inconscient*, Paris: Seuil.

—— (1998b) *The Seminar of Jacques Lacan: Book XX. On the limits of love and knowledge, 1972–1973*, ed. J. A. Miller, trans. B. Fink, New York: W. W. Norton & Company.

—— (2001a) *Seminar VIII, Le transfert, 1960–1961*, Paris: Seuil.

—— (2001b) "L'étourdit," in *Autres Ecrits*, Paris: Seuil.

—— (2005) *Le Séminaire Livre XXIII, Le sinthome*, Paris: Seuil.

Toboul, B. (1997–8) "The Question 'ex,'" unpublished seminar.

Part III

MADNESS AND CREATION
Environs of the hole

14

THE *OPEN* EGO

Woolf, Joyce and the "mad" subject

Juliet Flower MacCannell

Virginia Woolf and James Joyce: two "mad" authors of the early twentieth century. One a woman, one a man; one English, one Irish. Each equally revolutionary for their "stream of consciousness" literary techniques; each equally refusing the premises of psychoanalysis. Woolf declined analysis, fearing harm to her creativity; Joyce rejected it for his schizophrenic daughter Lucia: she was merely "telepathic," he said.[1] Each regarded *writing* as freeing them from the conditions that ordinarily shape the child, its cast of mind, its ego. Which elements configuring their egos—family, language, gender, or the political discourse that encircled them—explain why Woolf's rebellious ego ends with despair and "madness" (and her suicide), while Joyce's opens jubilant possibilities for art and thought?

The Lacanian psychoanalysis developed in Freud's wake confirmed his thesis that the unconscious is linked to language—to what is said and what cannot be said. The ego makes every effort to repress the unconscious, barring by means of its power of formalization, from entering linguistic expression. Woolf and Joyce both broke radically with such ego-centered policing of language, to be sure, but how did their particular writing egos permit this? And what was the effect of this rupture on their own psyches?

Woolf and Joyce both wrote *against* their families of origin, but their antagonism cannot be termed simply Oedipal. Rather, their work attests to how the family by their time had *already* become effectively post-Oedipal. Whether for its subjects or its masters, British imperial order destroyed something vital in the family, in society, and in literature. Woolf knew this all too well, as its victim and its (literal) daughter: the government official who organized the British Empire on the model of a patriarchal family was her very own grandfather, and her father's Milton-inspired misogyny curtailed his daughter's reading and writing on the theory that they harmed her mental health.

James Joyce's revolution in language was also aimed at his own family, according to Lacan, particularly at his hapless alcoholic father, who railed impotently against British rule. But Joyce had another objective in his sights: he could see that his father's malaise was rooted in the contemporary sociopolitical order of Ireland, disfigured as it was by an empire that had colonized its language its culture, its men and women.

Virginia Woolf began her revolt by rewriting the feminine story in opposition to the authorized male ego empowered by empire, and she became the theorist of a *feminine ego* that could challenge the unrestricted dominion the male ego exercised over culture. Her work has resonated throughout the years with women and feminists of all kinds. But Joyce more radically aimed to overturn, at its linguistic root, what was impeding his people, men and women both, from saying what very much needed to be *said* and *written*. He would moreover ultimately address a greater stumbling block than colonial (and male) rule. Only if the ego itself were reconfigured would it ever really be able to *speak*. Joyce reinvented the ego as what I call "the *writing* ego" and he did so for the sake of man and woman, family and nation.

One may object that Joyce has a thoroughly masculine voice and that, apart from Molly Bloom's infamous soliloquy in *Ulysses*, he is seldom called a feminist. I do not intend to call him one here. However, while he comes at writing from the opposite side from Woolf, like hers his writing seeks to un-house and de-throne the insufferable male ego at the center of a destructive political order, an order that had mythified and reified that ego. And he was perhaps the more effective of the two.

The family and the ego—under imperialism

The *primary family* shapes how an individual child comes to terms with its drives, destructive to itself and to the society into which it is born. Families prepare children for social coexistence: getting children to manage their drives is the precondition for all socialization, the most important task for any family formation—matriarchal, patriarchal, clan, et al. Contending with our drives' lethal power forces us into cultural creation: aesthetic enjoyments, especially, would literally be unthinkable were civilization's strictures, sacrifices and limitations not imposed.[2]

Even repressed, however, drives linger in the unconscious, where unavowable fantasies of their *satisfaction*, impossible in society, nourish conscious desires. Although they always seem oppressive to the child whose enjoyments they check, *Oedipal families* by and large succeed in preparing their children for social coexistence. (Women often complain that the Oedipal family schema places them too sternly under paternal authority.)[3]

However, in the *post-Oedipal* family (as experienced by Joyce and Woolf) the subject is no longer required to *inhibit* its lethal drives, but to *give in* to them. And this is the crux of the matter. Woolf's family exemplifies this. Her grandfather James Stephen, Permanent Under Secretary for the Colonies, was the architect of British "benevolent imperialism." He is known for popularizing the phrase "the mother country" for Britain, promoting the Empire as a parent and benign protector of its children.[4] The British Empire, colonizing much of the world by professing to offer it a better and more powerful mother, in reality visited upon its children the *destruction of the family*, for the Empire's model family this "mother" brooded over required absolute male supremacy, according to Stephen, with women and those deemed culturally inferior (like the Irish) tightly controlled or suppressed.[5]

For Joyce, the decimation was not just of his immediate family, but of Ireland itself. It was absent a whole, fully formed Irish society for its families to contribute their children to—whether as simple "citizens" or creative "artists." Under English rule, Irish subjects were born to a condition that permitted them to form only small, politically impotent social circles (like that of the maiden aunties Morkan in Joyce's "The Dead"). Irish paternal authority was debilitated since its Irish children could see there was *no society* their fathers could prepare them for. The over-inflation of patriarchal power in the empire's own core seemed to extract its sustenance from the far-flung fathers it colonized.

Woolf's own family, of course, was very much in charge, on top. Yet it, too, suffered from the very patriarchal tyranny it helped to create. It granted its male members far too much unchecked power for their own mental good. Woolf's grandfather would overwork himself, often on purpose, to induce a nervous collapse. He would then take time off to recover from the breakdown, after which he would start right in again, working himself once more into madness, and "curing" it once again with rest.[6]

A longstanding human essential—the *paternal* family—had become, under imperial sway, a brittle, rigid *patriarchy*, formed around a puritanical ideal of misogyny that was especially detrimental to its daughter Virginia, whose texts illustrate its awful effects on all women. But Woolf did not fully realize how destructive it was also for the men themselves who administered it. Because they could discount half of humanity, the Stephen men became in essence less than men.

Woolf tried valiantly to free herself from the blighting effects of the masculine ego her family inflicted on her, by meeting its overwhelming power with a strong, resistant female ego. But her efforts were stymied by her implicit acceptance of its definition of masculinity. She was unable to see the feminine as anything other than a wavering subjectivity in unhappy communication with the disorders of Nature and the vagaries of the body and its emotions—the very things the severely formal masculine ego casts out of its purview. Any opening or weak spot in the feminine was to her a potentially incurable wound.

In her novel *The Waves*,[7] sometimes called her "portrait of the artist," Woolf meticulously enters into the consciousness, individual and collective, of a set of male and female children to explore the correlation between their egos and their language use. She divides the male children (whose aim, she says, is the fixation of a sturdy self, a tree that goes to "the root of the world") from female ones, who are always in imminent danger of losing themselves—their bodies, their faces, their separate identities, the unity of their bodies and their heads. All the children in the novel at one time or another hold to an ideal of merging indistinctly into all the others, but none, not even the girls, can let go of the opposing ideal of possessing a firm, clear, distinct ego. For all the subjectivity revealed by the stream of consciousness style Woolf perfected in her rendering here, none of the children, not even the girls, has the ability, the empathy, to grasp the small *o* other as a subject. And none attempts to reclaim the enjoyments taken from them by the political, symbolic, educational, military and religious orders in which they are placed.

Woolf attacked the male ego by conjuring a feminine one, but she never quite managed to question the very structure of the ego itself—which is why centering on the ego may have been the real trap for her. Despite her direct attacks on male rule, in the end she feels the ego *must* be closed; it *must* defend itself against the dissolution that always threatens it. Her comment on the courtesan Harriette Wilson's memoirs illustrates this:

> Across the broad continent of a woman's life falls the shadow of a sword. On one side all is correct, definite, orderly: the paths are strait, the trees regular, the sun shaded, escorted by gentlemen, protected by policemen, wedded and buried by clergymen, she has only to walk demurely from cradle to grave and no one will touch a hair on her head. But on the other side, all is confusion. Nothing follows a regular course. [. . .] The trees roar and rock and fall in ruin.[8]

This is a striking description. On one side, "phallic" order (I use this term technically) positions her as a defined object in a patriarchal culture of militarily organized formal arrangements that constrain both Nature-in-General and her specific Nature-as-Woman. She is confined to walking straight paths, just as the trees are constrained to grow in rows. Policemen regulate her public behavior while husbands and clergymen manage her private love life. On the other, Woolf sets up a wild Nature free of all restriction, all order. This alternative site potentially locates woman outside the shelter of phallic order, along with the pleasures of the sublime—terrifying excess.

Woolf's description is hardly reassuring. Her point seems to be that in either case, woman is reduced to impotence, to being overwhelmed—it makes little difference whether by male dominated society or by lethal Nature. But to assume Woolf imagines that woman's only options are these two versions of powerlessness would be a mistake. There was something else, indefinable (to or by her), that she desperately wanted. To see better what that is, let me turn to Lacan and his conception of how language and sexuality are linked.

Language and sexual difference

> [Man] thinks as a consequence of the fact that a structure, that of language—the word implies it—carves up his body, a structure which has nothing to do with anatomy.[9]

Lacan explains how masculine and feminine subjects differ. Each speaking being adopts a certain logical position in its unconscious, and this, Lacan says, is either masculine or feminine. It is not correlated with one's biological or anatomical gender. The "carving" of the body is universal—it works this way for all humans, who become bodies-without-organs under the regime of language. Such bodies are neither constrained nor governed by their physical organs: sexual difference has nothing to do with anatomy. Rather, the basic unit of language, the signifier, has a phallic function, φx (the phallic signifier, φ, structures the subject). It "castrates" masculine and feminine subjects differentially.

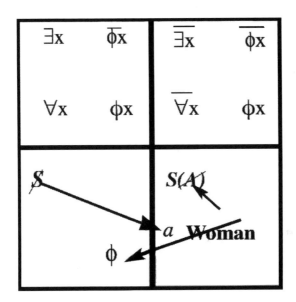

Figure 14.1 Jacques Lacan's diagram of sexuation in Seminar XX: Encore, Lacan (1998), p. 78.

Lacan provides a diagram of the two logics.[10] On the left (masculine) side, all *people* are seen to be organized by the phallic signifier—and unconsciously by the object *a* (the little residue of enjoyment—half real, half imaginary—of the signifier's cutting process). In masculine logic, castration by language is universal: all are under the phallic function, all but one. Just one escapes castration: the unbarred Other, the all-enjoying totemic father; the exception that proves the rule.

The logic of femininity, on the right, offers no such absolute clarity. Its rule is equally universal—everyone is submitted to castration. But the structure of negation for the feminine universal is of a different order from the masculine exception. There is no one exempt from castration—except for some. Not all are submitted to the phallic function: not all people, and not all of my particular body either.

Feminine logic makes the phallus her subjective focus (see the arrow pointed at his φ). The masculine subject's focus is her object *a*. So far, a traditional view of sexuality: she envies his phallus (and cultural power); he desires her *a* objects (her breasts, et al.).

Masculine logic fits the feminine object into the phallic order, policed and arranged like the trees in Woolf's description. Masculine unconscious logic demands she be his object if he is to submit to castration.

But feminine logic, unlike the masculine, has a dual focus. Castration organizes only one of her facets, her objective side (the part that is object for and objective of the masculine). The other face of her logic, her subjective side, is not all under the phallic function. Instead, it is organized by something that compensates her for being used as an object in the phallic regime: the S, the sign, the word, of the ~~Other~~ (A). Her second arrow points, let us note, away from the phallus, toward this barred ~~Other~~.

Lacan is indicating that the feminine requires a sign from the ~~Other~~ that supports the non-phallic side of her being—the part to which phallic eyes are blind. Only a word (of love) from the ~~Other~~ permits her to go beyond her phallic definition as an object, and grants her existence other than as Victorian "angel in the house," or servant of the phallic order.[11]

What did Woolf really want, then? She needed affirmation of this "other" side of her being. She declared repeatedly in her letters to her husband, Leonard (Freud's English language publisher) that she depended on his love to support her existence. In the end, even Leonard's words of love were not enough; still signifiers, they seemed unable to support her against her own death drive. Why? She was never convinced that any man worthy of the name must be prepared to face down the death drive—his and hers. In this she was, at the last, her father's daughter. To her, the feminine ego was incurable and undesirable: trapped by her idealization of a decisive masculine ego, the feminine ego she proposed was insufficient to ward off the damage caused by a patriarchal family that kept Woolf (like all women) forever at a disadvantage.

Joyce found what Woolf missed in her battle with the signifier, something that might have offered her deliverance. I hinted at the matter of openness to the other above: that the subject struggles not only against the death drive (lethal jouissance), but also for an enjoyment lost to Oedipus (and more so to the pseudo patriarchy)— lost, first of all, by means of our language practices.

Each of the ever-proliferating signifiers that make up language is meaningless in itself. Signifiers can only point to other signifiers, promising possible (future) meaning. But meaning as such is never finally delivered: living languages require a "next" signifier to produce the semblance of meaning. Full meaning=dead language.

Signifiers are also the bearers of our desires, of the promise that someday they will deliver the very enjoyment they have carved away. The structure of deferred satisfactions is the same as what holds for language's promise of finally meaning— satisfactions are necessarily deferred until death. These are, it seems, the rules for speaking beings.

But Joyce changed the rules. He found his way to an enjoyment carried by the signifier, not repressed by it. Which is why his joy-filled writing does not take language (or the phallic signifier) entirely seriously.

Joyce's "The Dead"

My approach to Joyce, language and the ego differs from Jean-Michel Rabaté's in *The Politics of Egoism*,[12] mainly because I look for Joyce's writing ego less in his major stylistically innovative novels than in one short story, written in plain style, from *Dubliners*.[13] In "The Dead," Joyce frames a new masculine ego and a new feminine one with, I believe, revolutionary effect. In it he paints a devastating portrait of the fatuous male ego produced by the deadened language of patriarchal/imperial order. The story's hero, Gabriel Conroy, is a "writer": he pens book reviews for *The Daily Express*. (Miss Ivors, an Irish political agitator for Home Rule, chides him for writing for such a paper, saying he is becoming a West Briton (188).) He also composes speeches for his aunts' annual Christmas dance.

As he and his wife Gretta arrive for the party, Gabriel contemplates the evening ahead. He takes in the party so he can fine-tune his speech, going over the headings used to organize it, rather a sad catalogue of clichés from hospitality in Ireland, the Three Graces, Paris, sad memories, Browning (192). He worries it will not come up to the standard of last year's speech, and wonders if the partygoers will applaud as much as they usually do.

His aunts fawn over his writing talents and his deftness at steering the party's guests away from anti-social behavior—guests must not become intoxicated or enter into political and religious quarrels. (Only differing opinions on classical music are allowed at the holiday table.) Aunt Kate is relieved to have Gabriel there, and Gabriel succeeds at weaving the gathering together in a kind of impartial order, an achievement topped off by his carving the Christmas goose perfectly and serving it around in equitable portions.

His speech is well received, the more so—he believes—as he has taken pains to adjust it to his audience's lower grade of culture by removing some arcane poetic allusions. Yet Gabriel is at a loss for words (as is everyone else in the company) when the inebriated Freddy Malins disrupts the discussion of an opera at the Theatre Royal by praising a singer at the low-brow Gaiety pantomime, describing a Negro chieftain who had one of the finest tenor voices he has ever heard (198). When the partygoers silently smirk at his opinion, Freddy demands to know why the chieftain cannot also have a voice, wondering if it is because he's only a black. Apparently, these cultivated Irish subjects of the British Empire have unwittingly adopted its views of racial superiority—the same views used against them by the British to smother their own "inferior" Irish voices.

Toward the end of the evening, Gabriel accidentally catches a faraway look in Gretta's eyes as she listens to an unseen pianist playing an old ballad. He sees grace and mystery in her pose—she seems to him to be a symbol of something (210). He would name a painting of her "Distant Music."

Gabriel imagines her dreaminess echoes his desires for the passionate evening her romantic mood would only enhance. He eagerly anticipates their arrival later at the hotel room (for once, without the children) and vows to use this night to erase their years of dull existence; to recall their ecstatic moments. He feels sure that despite their dull marriage, children, his writing and her household duties their souls' "tender fire" has not died out (214).

Gretta is his "angel in the house," her feminine life cramped by maternity and housewifery. But not by these alone: for, as Gabriel admits, she has also been stifled by his writing.

What follows is one of the most horrifying affronts to a self-centered male ego—and to the bad writer Gabriel unmistakably is—ever depicted. Alone together in the hotel, Gabriel is stung to discover that he has been quite mistaken about his wife's reverie. She tells him the song she overheard at the party, *The Lass of Aughrim*, made her sad (218–19). When he asks why, she says it recalled to her the memory of a boy, Michael Furey, who loved her and who had sung that song for her. The boy had died. He had stolen out of his sick bed to stand in the cold rain under her window one night to say farewell to her before she went away to convent school in Dublin. Already so ill, the exposure to the damp chill hastened his end; he did not last a week after she left.

Gabriel, upset at having his designs thwarted by the memory of his wife's lost love, and more than a little jealous, asks snidely what he had died of so young, venturing the ever-romantic "consumption" as his guess. Gretta answers that she thinks he died for her (220), in response to which Gabriel is seized by a vague "terror," just when he had hoped to triumph.

Why "terror"? Because although he was only a boy, Michael Furey was more of a man than Gabriel could ever be, and Gabriel knows it. Furey's dying for her voids the claim of Gabriel—who smugly thinks one night will make up for the years of their dull existence together, and who has surely never sung to her—to be his wife's true lover. At seventeen, Furey was already constituted a man, defined by his willingness to face death for his love.

Gabriel was "the man of the hour" at the party, the center of attention of the close-knit society around him that has willingly given him the dominant role. He was even a hero: he "saved" the party from the poor drunk Freddy Malins; he was gracious and treated everyone respectfully, although he stumbled a bit with the serving girl, Lily. Yet, alone before the other, his Gretta, the small *o* other, he is dispossessed of the verbal and social powers granted him by his adoring little circle. Facing her, he sees himself as a fatuous, inconsequential little creature, humiliated by this dead figure. He sees himself for what he is: ludicrous, a "pennyboy" for his aunts, writing for the vulgar.

His sheer unawareness of Gretta's unfathomable subjectivity—that she has an interior life ungoverned by his stale narratives—exposes his ego's superficial narrowness and obtuseness, as well as what a bad writer he is. From an artistic point of view, his every thought is conventional and hackneyed (including his imagined portrait of his wife as a symbol of "something").

Joyce lets us know that Gabriel's person and his writing are products not of a lack of talent, but of an ugly and oppressive political order. Gabriel's entire existence is under the thumb of the English and of an English language that restricts him to writing innocuous reviews and making pointless little speeches to his small circle of family friends. And if Gabriel is a model patriarch, secure at the center of a family circle sustained by the work of women, the tragedy is that he is merely a pale imitation of the real imperial patriarchy that rules him.

He has literally, that is, been confined to his small circle. He exercises no power in the wider world, nor can he. Even when Miss Ivors challenges him to put his writing in the service of Home Rule, he knows deeply that he can have no real say in an Ireland ruled from afar by the Empire. And because Irish society does not depend on his contributions, his manliness is diminished. He is reduced to being an unexceptional man—but an exceptionally good servant of the tyrannical order that has robbed him of the kind of masculinity that might have allowed him, as a man, to see Gretta as a subject. He cannot afford to realize even himself as a subject.[14]

A postgraduate student of mine objected to my interpretation. He admitted that Joyce does see Gabriel this way, but claimed that egocentrism is the very essence of masculinity: the very definition of a "man" is that he is a self-centered, insensitive creature, domineering over his women and children. Besides, he added, haven't feminism and popular culture taught us that men are simply egotistical brutes that can never change? When I countered that Joyce was suggesting Gabriel was rather less than a man because he was not prepared to give his life for others, the student bristled: we can't possibly hold men to that standard in this day and age.

The judgment the serving girl Lily in "The Dead" passes on men—that nowadays they are all talk, and what they can get out of a girl (178)—constitutes her bitter reproach to men who have used her, a proto-feminist sentiment. And it is perfectly applicable to Gabriel himself who, despite his moderation and tact, is nothing but his "palaver" (talk) and what he can "get out of" Gretta later in the hotel room. This is why Michael Furey's gesture, more than his words, moved Gretta: it was the subjective support she needed, this sign of love from a barred O̶t̶h̶e̶r̶.

What then is the shape of the writing ego Joyce attempted to set in the place of the destructive ego (and bad writing) engendered—and gendered—by the politics of the day? Why did Joyce need to assail language to make it accomplish, or be the accomplice of, a liberation from personal and political oppression? For clearly Joyce did change something essential in the operations of language itself.

One enjoys fully, we thought we knew, only in the unconscious. Unconscious enjoyment was, for Freud, lodged in the symptom whose unspeakable jouissance is brought to light only in slips, and it can be dispelled only by analytic treatment. Joyce, however, found his own way to untangle enjoyment from the symptom that impounds it under a phallic regime that has stolen it from us unawares. He altered the very way the signifier works, inventing something Lacan named the sinthome—a signifier that, rather than sequestering jouissance, frees and opens it to conscious experience.

Language and the ego

Lacan tells his students: "The symptom in Joyce doesn't concern you at all,"[15] and he is both astonished and excited to discover that Joyce is "not hooked up to the unconscious" (*JSI*: 5). Extrapolating from Joyce's proper name ('*Joy*-ce'/ jouissance) and his family psychiatric history, Lacan find that Joyce does not exhibit the psychosis that would be expected by his rejection of the Name-of-the-Father. Rather, something unparalleled emerges from the Irish author's singular (though not uncommon) relation to language*s* ("*l'élangues*"). Joyce is situated, Lacan says, by the *English* he speaks and writes, but also by the *Irish* tongue the British Empire so forcefully cut out of his native Ireland. Imperial English is a language Joyce "plays upon" because "his own was wiped off the map, that is, Gaelic [. . .] not his own, therefore, but that of the invaders, the oppressors" (10). The manner in which Joyce responded to this double linguistic/political imposition/privation culminated in a revolution in language—and something more.

In his late work, Lacan recognized that the crucial task of mediating the Real and the Imaginary is no longer shouldered by language / the Symbolic / the paternal metaphor. Language not only fails to be a shelter against the Real any longer; it has become a threat, a danger in itself. Nearly dead, language has ceased to shape our bodies. It seems to proffer unlimited jouissance to (some of) its (male) subjects—and none to others. It pretends to free us from Oedipus, claiming we have no need of symbolic language to render us human. Yet the dead language this leaves us with lacks poetic, metaphoric resonance—and it is a straitjacket far worse than any Oedipal constraint.

Lacan says that the menace of and to language arises where the signifier has become tone-deaf, if it has no echo, no resonance in or for the body any longer. "There must be something in the signifier which *resonates*. [. . .] [P]hilosophers imagine that there are drives and so on [. . .] for they don't know what a drive is: the echo in the body of the fact that there is speech. For speech to resonate, [. . .] the body must be sensitive to it" (*Sem. 23:* 4). Such was the tone-deaf Anglo-Irish tongue that found itself very much in need of a Joyce to recalibrate its relation to the subject, to civilization. But Joyce also had to overcome the specific deadness of the languages at his disposal. He had to reintroduce language to the body it would affect with its resonance, its poetry. First Joycean revolution, then: "Joyce wrote in English in such a way that [as] . . . Philippe Sollers has remarked in *Tel Quel* . . . the English language no longer exists."[16]

He did this by inventing the *sinthome*: a unique adequation to a fundamental discursive shift in the relation of subject to culture, of ego to other—and of men to women.[17] It also provided a fresh way to confront the challenge posed by the rancid politics of his time—and ours.[18] Joyce did more, that is, than shake off the fetters of colonial English. He created a *lalangue,* a babble that conveyed without repressing the specific jouissance of its author:

> Read some pages from *Finnegans Wake* without trying to understand anything. It reads, but as someone of my circle remarked to me, that's because we can feel present in it the *jouissance* of the one who wrote it. [...]
> This joy, this *jouissance* is the only thing that we're able to get a hold of in his text. [...] Joyce gives it all the power of language without, for all that, any of it being analyzable, which is what strikes the reader and leaves one literally dumbfounded [...].
>
> (*JSI:* 5; 8)

Thus the second Joyceian revolution: he had to alter the very form of the ego, which could no longer be modeled on the phallic signifier. To refashion the subject's relation to language and oppressive discourse,[19] Joyce had to play with language(s), a play that was deadly serious in its urge to reinvent the ego itself. Not the indefinite ego of Woolf's feminine; not the imperial male one, closed, armored; not even an Orlando-like androgynous one: but instead, an open ego.

Recall that Joyce's very definition of Hell was that it was an unbreakable circle, the walled in Hell of the *Portrait*'s sermons. Joyce broke this circle, broke this Hell of an ego, smashing it apart, along with the colonial English that was strangling him.

The open ego

Toward the end of *Seminar 23*, Lacan describes an ego not bounded by the form of a circle: an ego that has opened itself to the Real through the Imaginary. The armature of symbolic language is gone: it is a set of open 'brackets' (Figure 14.2). He discovers it in Joyce's *Portrait of the Artist as a Young Man*. Stephen Dedalus, beaten mercilessly by his peers, responds as if there has been no assault on his body, no wound to his ego. One cannot therefore imagine his ego as a closed circle, a walled in fortress that if breached wreaks havoc. Stephen, Joyce writes, is simply "emptied out," without rancor toward his tormentors. This puts Stephen, Lacan says, beyond the ideal of the ego as an intact body—and vice versa (*Sem. 23*: 59).

If a body-image is not engaged in Joyce, Lacan says, it can only be a sign that the ego has a quite particular new function—that of opening up, rupturing and freeing the imaginary from supporting the consistency of body, of mind and body. Joyce "set the imaginary relation free" from control by the signifier: "One thinks against a signifier [...] one leans against a signifier in order to think" (*Sem. 23*: 63).

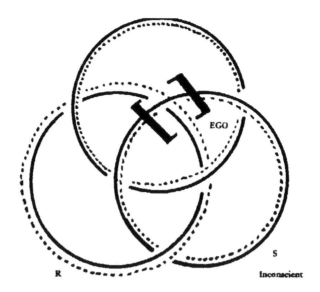

Figure 14.2 Diagram of the "open ego"

To free the Imaginary from its sterile relation to the ego-as-circle is to put it in touch with another kind of ego—one capable, like Baudelaire's, of taking a "bath of multitude." An ego open to, not walled off from other egos. Experience and enjoyment flow through the open ego—out of the fortress of the closed ego.

Notes

1 Jacques Lacan, *Seminar 23*: 43. "Le Sinthome," 1976, in *Ornicar?* 6–11, 1976, ed. J.-A. Miller, trans. L. Thurston. I used this translation, with occasional references to the manuscript of the French seminar because I did not have access to the published edition. I refer to "Joyce the Symptom I," the address Lacan delivered at the invitation of Jacques Aubert for the opening of the fifth International Joyce Symposium, 26 June 1975, as *JSI*.

2 "[Drive] is [. . .] a measure of the demand made upon the mind for work." Sigmund Freud (1895) *Project for a Scientific Psychology, SE I,* p. 317.

3 Woman's inability to place herself entirely under the Oedipal phallic signifier is, for Lacan a valuable cultural resource Freud overlooked. See my discussion of Lacan's sexuation formulae regarding the way the feminine responds to castration.

4 See Jane Marcus (1987) *Virginia Woolf and the Languages of Patriarchy*, Bloomington: Indiana University Press, p. 83. "The mother country" is, psychoanalytically, a triumph of political perversion: according to Lacan, the sadist's fundamental fantasy is that the Mother possesses uncastrated power. See my *The Regime of the Brother: After the Patriarchy*, London and New York: Routledge, 1991, on the sadistic superego displacing the paternal with the patriarchal.

5 The era's proponents of male superiority (e.g., the secret society at Cambridge, The Apostles, to which Woolf's brothers belonged) based their claims on the ideology of colonialism. Marcus writes, "[. . .] Virginia Woolf's grandfather was more than a petty patriarchal tyrant over his own family. He was actually the architect of an ideology of oppression that used the model of patriarchal domestic tyranny as a basis for colonial imperialism" (Marcus 1987: 83).

6 Marcus (1987), p. 99.

7 Woolf (1923) *Jacob's Room & The Waves,* New York: Harcourt Brace and World, Inc.

8 (1947) *The Moment, and Other Essays,* New York: Harcourt Brace, p. 179.

9 J. Lacan, *Télévision,* Paris: Éditions du Seuil, 1974, p. 16 [English, p. 6]. « L'homme [. . .] pense de qu'une structure, celle du langage—le mot le comporte—de qu'une structure découpe son corps, et qui n'a rien à faire avec l'anatomie. »

10 See Joan Copjec's unsurpassed exposition of the diagram: "Sex and the Euthanasia of Reason," in her (1994) *Read My Desire,* Cambridge, MA and London: The MIT Press.

11 Feminist efforts to return the male gaze try to turn his symbolic phallus into an object *a,* if not a purely physical organ. This puts them on the "masculine side," an undesirable outcome for most.

12 Cambridge: Cambridge University Press, 2001.

13 (1960[1916]) "The Dead," in *Dubliners,* New York: The Viking Press, 1960, pp. 175–224.

14 Most people do not, of course, read Joyce's story this way. The last film by the great John Huston was *The Dead.* Despite his feel for literature, Huston treats Gabriel as a decent, sensitive husband. But the story is written otherwise; it is Joyce's stinging critique of the brittle, controlled male *ego*—a brittleness that voids Gabriel of any originality, sensitivity or passion, controlled by prevailing colonial powers.

15 Encountering Joyce altered Lacan's own psychoanalytic theory.

16 *Seminar* 23, 18 November 1975. The French manuscript reads a bit differently.

17 From "master's" discourse to "university discourse," correlated with the ethics of capitalism: (1976) Seminar 23, in *Ornicar?* 6–11, 1976.

18 "Joyce's personal *malaise* in his own (Irish) civilization was that of a double encirclement by the hell of an English language that had been forcibly imposed over his culture and that had remained fixed at the moment of its imposition. It had no freedom to change or evolve. [. . .] It brooked none of the playful, metaphoric outlets for the *jouissance* that language represses—outlets open to any 'native' speaking-being. English stagnated in its Irish iteration. [. . ..] Joyce was oppressed not simply by *language.* His oppression was aggravated specifically by its being the language, deeply foreign to his culture, of his imperial oppressor." Juliet Flower MacCannell (2008) "Nowhere, Else: On Utopia," *Umbra.*

19 In the introduction, *Joyce the Symptom I,* "University and Analysis," Lacan writes that Joyce means the turning from this dominant: "Joyce himself knew it would happen to him posthumously, the university in charge. It's almost exclusively academics who busy themselves with Joyce [....]. And he hoped for nothing less than to keep them busy until the extinction of the university. We're headed in that direction" (*JSI:* 3) 9.

Bibliography

Freud, S. (1895, 1966) *Project for a Scientific Psychology, SE I,* London: Hogarth.

Joyce, J. (1960) "The Dead," in *Dubliners,* New York: Viking Press.

Lacan, J. (1974) *Télévision,* Paris: Seuil

—— (1976) "Le Séminaire Livre XXIII, Le sinthome, session of 18 November 1975," in J-A Miller (ed.), L. Thurston (trans.), *Ornicar?*

—— (1975) Joyce the Symptom I; in Xerox copy, personal communication.

—— (1998) *The Seminar of Jacques Lacan, Book XX, Encore: On Feminine Sexuality, The Limits of Love and Knowledge 1972–1972,* trans. B. Fink, New York: W.W. Norton.

Marcus, J. (1987) *Virginia Woolf and the Languages of Patriarchy*, Bloomington: Indiana University Press.

Woolf, V. (1931) *Jacob's Room & The Waves*, London: Hogarth.

—— (1947) *The Moment, and Other Essays*, London: Hogarth.

15

PAOLA MIELI

Normality and segregation in Primo Levi's *Sleeping Beauty in the Fridge*

> To sink is the easiest of matters; it is enough to carry out all the orders one receives.
>
> Primo Levi, *Se questo è un uomo*

Nazi extermination camps were places where a vast number of new scientific applications were first tried out. The complicity of both the industrial complex and the medical and university establishments enabled Hitler's regime to set up a machine of alienation and annihilation based on an aberrant ideology of production: human beings were handled as an expendable commodity.

In his testimony as a survivor, Primo Levi has conveyed the devastating effects of this desubjectivizing experience and has given an extraordinarily human voice to the unspeakable. *Se questo è un uomo* [*If This is a Man*], *La tregua* [*The Truce*], and *I sommersi e i salvati* [*The Drowned and the Saved*] are the fruit of the moral necessity to speak, of making known, that "forced" Levi to write.[1] When Levi mentions, in November 1967, the possible reasons that allowed his survival in the camps, he lists luck, his mountaineering training, and the fact of being a chemist, which allowed him some privileges in the final months of his imprisonment. He also notes his interest in human psychology and the will to live "with the precise aim of relating the things that we witnessed and that we endured" (Levi 1985: 260). This is a crucial need that squarely confronts the Nazi desire to eliminate, in every possible way, all traces of the extermination as well as all testimony regarding it. *I sommersi e salvati*, the last book to emerge from this need, is one of the most important reflections on the human condition written in the twentieth century.

As is well known, Levi also wrote several stories of a special character that do not fit into pre-established categories. Generally defined as science fiction, they nonetheless bear the trademark of his writing: the reflection on the causes and consequences of the "immense biological and social experience" of the concentration camps (Levi 1980: 117). With subtlety and irony, Levi the storyteller ponders the issue of segregation in our own time, and the heritage that the camps have bequeathed to the present. In so doing, he establishes a disconcerting continuity between past aberrations and present normality, showing how "normality" could be understood as a shared form of madness. In some of his most dazzling fiction, Levi the storyteller indicates with great acumen and perspicacity the close relationship between science, new technologies, and subjective alienation, as well as the ways in which normality or the tranquility of a prosperous life are in fact the product of a biopolitical normativity embraced with careless complicity.

The watershed between normality and madness is problematic. Not by chance does the word "alienation" refer both to the human degradation caused by predetermined systems of production and to the so called "madness." As Foucault has amply shown, the concept of madness itself is the outcome of specific biopolitical types of normativity.

As a reminder of our present situation and of the lessons learned in the experience of the camps, Levi writes: "Monsters exist but are too few in number to be truly dangerous. More dangerous are the common men, the functionaries always ready to believe and act without asking questions" (Levi 1980: 257).[2] By accepting the status quo, by embracing currents of thought, or "superior" orders, as if they were his own, the ordinary man reveals the alienation that characterizes him: his unwillingness to act in a critically responsible manner. In his uncritical assent, he becomes a willing perpetrator in what Arendt famously named "the banality of evil."

Sleeping Beauty

La bella addormentata nel frigo [Sleeping Beauty in the Fridge] is a short play with eight characters, collected with other fictional writings in Storie naturali, written between 1964 and 1967 and published in 1967 under the pseudonym of Damiano Malabaila.

The play is set in Berlin in the year 2115. The milieu is middle-class, the atmosphere cozy and repetitive—the everyday humdrum. The occasion is a gathering of friends ("la solita festicciola"), one of those parties that one feels obliged to throw a few times a year. Lotte, the mistress of the house and narrator, lets us know immediately that she could easily do without it. Bored and slightly irritated, she leads us through the play with a jaundiced eye. Conversely, her husband, Peter Thorl, seems excited by the unfolding of the event.

The special occasion is Patricia's birthday, December 19. Patricia is above all some sort of heirloom—that is, she has been passed down from father to son across several generations within the Thorl family. She is, in fact, a centenarian. We learn in the play that in 1975 she was selected to be frozen by a scientific committee whose illustrious president was the famous Ugo Thorl, discoverer of the fourth principle of thermodynamics and ancestor of the head of the house.

Between 1975 and 2115, Patricia had been reawakened from her frozen sleep for a total of around 300 days.

In the Berlin of 2115, the Thorls are proud owners of their precious object of social attraction. Lotte explains that some people own a Renoir, a Picasso, or a Caravaggio, others "a conditioned hurricane" ("*un uragano condizionato*") or even a live dog or cat, but the Thorls have Patricia, the beauty preserved for ages through refrigeration.

We are instantly made aware of Peter's weakness for Patricia. If, as Lotte explains, Peter has for some years been a changed man—less hospitable, more serious—we're soon let in on the reasons for this change: his secret passion for Patricia, who is lovely as ice cream, even if a little soft ("*faisandée*"). In the course of the play, we learn about Peter's secret defrosting and sexual assaults of Patricia—this latter also part of a family tradition passed from father to son.

The guests who arrive first for the birthday celebration are Robert and Maria Lutzer, representing middle-class comfort and the virtues of money, which, as Peter puts it, "one inherits along with blood" (Levi 1990: 92). Then, with their customary tardiness, the "perfect" couple arrives, the fiancés Baldur and Ilse, the former a PhD candidate and the latter a mindless bimbo, both of them head-over-heels in love at the start of the evening, but by midnight irreparably separated, thanks to the unceasingly seductive force that Patricia exerts over Baldur's erotic and scientific curiosity.

The key to the evening is the defrosting of Patricia. Once reawakened, the immaculate and courageous Patricia, who devoted herself to scientific experimentation and eternal youth, and has had ample time to ponder on her situation, appears to be essentially bored but cunning and calculating.

The play takes place over the duration of one night and an early morning. By the end of the evening, Patricia plots with Baldur to flee the house of her confinement and leave with him for good, while Baldur has managed to break his engagement. But when finally freed, Patricia confesses that she has no interest in Baldur: her only motivation for turning to him was to extricate herself from her slavery. Finally, Lotte informs us that Patricia plans to leave the country. Indeed, she will go on to a colleague of hers, another frozen human being who had also devoted his life to science and youth—in America.

Continuity

This is the plot. With it comes a fabric of observations and sharp, chilling cross-references that turn the representation of a banal future reality into the mirror of our present-day normality. The play's tone is subtle and ironic. The viewpoint is the seemingly uncritical one of someone who limits himself to establishing a series of facts and taking note of the simple twists of an ordinary social transaction. But the statement of facts is an acute diagnosis of the human heart, its meanings, its contradictions, and its compromises. And it is this viewpoint that is characteristic both of Levi's humor—a humor with a bitter aftertaste—and his talent as a careful observer and analyst. The experience of the camps ensured that Levi, a chemist by profession, would apply his passion for scientific observation to human reality.

The play is so rich in implicit references to Levi's other writings, and in implications of an anthropological, political, and social order, that a long and detailed textual analysis would be necessary to fully bring out its complex and particular nature. I will limit myself here to a few observations concerning the way in which this play, although set in a register radically different than that of political analysis and testimony, may reveal its roots in the experience of the camps. Like other stories by Levi, it retrieves from contemporary reality the symptoms of a social and subjective attitude that nurtured Nazi "reason"—seeing in the present the development of a past fabric. The way of the future allows us to study the effects of the past. This is a lesson that brings Levi's position extremely close to that of Freud.

In this perspective, Levi's choice for the title of the collection in which *La bella addormentata* appears, *Storie naturali* [*Natural Histories*] must be emphasized for all it represents. The word "natural," in contrast to the stories' bizarre and science-fictive content, highlights the intrinsic naturalness and obviousness of the facts mentioned, as well as the indifference that surrounds them. In oxymoronic fashion, this shifts attention to the manner in which the social integration of scientific and technological discoveries may become second nature and settle into the normal, daily rut. It shows how much the idea of "natural" merges with that of habit.

We know that the theme of science is central to Levi in a way that is deeply personal. His training as a chemist and his passion for chemistry constitute an essential characteristic of his relationship to the world, to life, as well as to his work. Levi thought that his survival from the camps was due, to a large extent, to his profession as a chemist. To his understanding of chemistry he was indebted for what is most characteristic of his writing, his personal style. In the camps, his passion for science and for intelligent and productive rationality was confronted brutally by the other face of science: its use for destructive ends. Chemistry was the key tool of annihilation and of the final solution. This confrontation will never cease to influence Levi in his covert, critical, and disenchanted look at the implications of scientific technologies.

On the jacket flap of *Natural Histories*, Levi is quoted as saying that he wrote these stories in an attempt to give narrative form to a very specific insight:

> I wrote about twenty stories and I do not know if I will write more of them. For the most part I wrote them in one sweep, trying to give narrative form to a pointed insight, trying to relate in other terms (if they are symbolic, they are unconsciously so) an insight that today is not rare: the perception of a flaw in the world in which we live, of a large or small crack, of a "formal defect" that thwarts one or another aspect of our civilization or our moral universe. . . . In the act of writing them I feel a vague sense of guilt, like someone who is consciously committing a small transgression. . . .
>
> I entered (unexpectedly) the world of writing with two books on the concentration camps. It is not up to me to judge their worth, but they

222

were undoubtedly serious, dedicated to a serious audience. To propose to this audience a volume of joke-stories or moral traps that are perhaps entertaining but detached and cold: is this not a commercial fraud, like someone selling wine in oil bottles? These are questions I asked myself while writing and publishing these "natural histories." Well, I would not publish them if I had not noticed (not immediately, to tell the truth), that there existed a continuity, a bridge between the camp and these creations. The camp, for me, was the largest of the "defects," of the distortions of which I spoke earlier, the most threatening of the monsters generated by reason.

Levi establishes a logical continuity between the segregationist project of which he himself was an object and aspects of present-day alienation. People adapt to biopolitical normativity with heedless complicity. Concurrently, a sense of abysmal solitude accompanies the arrival and triumph of the era of technology in the service of productivity.

Alienation

La bella addormentata is set in Berlin, which contextualizes the scene exactly. We could observe that each character in the play is symbolically representative of a form of alienation, each one more or less satisfactorily set into his/her own middle-class role, each one part of the workings of a system that s/he supports, but of which s/he is, simultaneously, its effect and its object. The rich schemer, his consumerist and absent-minded wife, the woman of the house who is a betrayed accomplice, her pathetic husband, the young doctoral student crushed by the bureaucracy that he feeds, and his silly fool of a companion, similar to all the other foolish girls who can be seen on the streets of Berlin and New York.

The play opens with a sardonic and horrifying image, a silver Martian fur coat that Maria wears, a coat that is immediately admired and envied by Lotte. This article of clothing, the latest word in fashion, instantly brings to the stage all the violence of consumerism and the market that supports it. It instantly portrays the relationship between exploitation, colonialism, and racism, and the individual and collective indifference that surrounds it.[3]

But what species is a Martian? Neither human nor animal, she/he/it is a figure of what is radically "other"—that which evokes all the consequences of the racist gaze toward the "different." But who the Martian is, here, is a secondary consideration. What matters most is what it is. Above all, "it" is something that can be exploited and transformed into an object of consumption—and no longer even a rarity, since the Russians have imported a large quantity of them and they can be found on the black market. It is difficult not to recall the systematic exploitation of the corpses in the camps, bodies "treated like any other raw material,"[4] to use Levi's words, the most extreme example of the use of the body as an object, of its commodification. But objectification and commodification, in forms that are obviously different but logically not so distant, pervade the current reality, often protected by the scientific and medical discourse; just think of the numerous cases of exploitative pharmacology or the markets for vital organs.

The position of object of consumption is also the one that Patricia occupies in the play. She too belongs to the category of that which is radically "other"; but Patricia is a special monster: a fruit of the most sophisticated science. Her *coté freak*, her century-long and intermittent memory, her eternal beauty, and her ancient and immaculate youth render her an object of attraction. As Baldur, seduced by this dazzling encounter expresses it, "before her, I feel the way I do before the pyramids" (Levi 1990: 103), in awe, before an immemorial monument. Unlike the Martian turned into a fur coat, Patricia occupies her role as object of science by her own choice. And yet degradation and reification unite them in a subtle way.

With thinly veiled sarcasm, Levi describes the characteristics required by the hibernation competition, announced in Berlin in 1975, in which Patricia ranked first: "She had all the prerequisites: a heart, lungs, kidneys, etc., in perfect working order; the nervous system of an astronaut; a determined, unflappable character; limited emotional ability; and lastly, a decent [level of] culture and intelligence."[5]

Levi puts his finger on a key tool of the logic of power and control: that of assessment and evaluation. This is a tool that spreads like an oil stain in contemporary society, in all sectors of the working world, school, training, and culture.[6] As Jean-Claude Milner observes, "Thanks to evaluation, control achieves its pure form; it is nothing but the free circulation of obedience. Michel Foucault called it a knowing-power [*un savoir-pouvoir*]. The expression must be taken in its full force; by virtue of the hyphen, Foucault was seizing on the mutual domestication of knowledge by power and power by knowledge. All of us being subordinated to the same degree, such is the new form of liberty and equality" (Milner 2005: 59–60).

Evaluation is the first step toward selection. In the play, the word "selection" does not appear, even if it is intrinsically present in the choice of the candidates in question. The withheld word has, in the universe of Primo Levi, an immense resonance. It is the key word for the horror of the camps, that which expresses their most ruthless logic, the logic of deportation, assignment to labor in the camps, and the choice of humans for scientific experiments, up to the final step toward the gas chambers. Withheld, the word casts on the notion of evaluation all the weight of history and all the consequences of its isolating effects.

As a heroine of science, Patricia has a special assignment: that of being the spokeswoman for essential events of history. The program of which she is part calls for her reawakening for a few hours every year, her birthday, and "other occasional reawakening in circumstances of particular interest such as important planetary expeditions, famous crimes and trials, marriages of rulers or screen stars, international baseball matches, telluric cataclysms and the like. In other words, all that which merits being seen and passed down to the distant future" (Levi 1990: 97). One cannot help but pause over the bitter irony brought out by Levi, who surely knows something about oblivion in history, its instrumental political quality, and its subjective and collective consequences.

The gray zone

To Baldur's naïve, relentless curiosity about the experiment of which she is the protagonist—what can she say about it; what goes on; how is "our world seen through your eyes?"—Patricia replies: "There is nothing extraordinary about it. You know, you get used to it immediately."

These words strike us as familiar. With clarity and a sense of vertigo, they bring to mind another statement in Levi's writings, from *I sommersi e i salvati* and its famous chapter entitled "The Gray Zone." Addressing the difficult question of the *Sonderkommando* (the special squads of prisoners—for the most part Jews—who were entrusted with running the crematoria, putting the prisoners to death, and sorting the corpses), Levi quotes the statement of one of the few survivors of those tasks: "Doing this work, you either go crazy the first day, or you get used to it" (Levi 1987: 689).

Despite the temerity of the approach, its literalness reveals the network of implications underpinning Levi's writing and the association he establishes between different contexts, between different forms of exception and norm and between the various "monsters" generated by reason, whether they are the fruit of Nazism or of the biopolitical discourse in a democratic regime.

The special squads of the *Sonderkommando* are an "extreme case" (Levi 1987: 686) of the "gray zone," that famous hybrid zone of prisoner-functionaries, masterfully analyzed by Levi, which constituted the very framework of the camps' totalitarian system. This is a zone that exists universally in regimes organized by power, hierarchy, and privilege, and it is consubstantial with them. "It is a gray zone," as Levi says, "of ill-defined boundaries that at once separates and combines the two camps of masters and servants" (Levi 1987: 679). It is the zone of compromise and collaboration, the bridge connecting the oppressed and the oppressor. It is the zone of being the products of a system in which one finds oneself performing the role of hinges.

The analysis of the gray zone, the detailed study of its facets, is surely one of Levi's greatest psychological, political, and "ethnological" (to use Lévi Strauss's definition of Primo Levi's writings) contributions. It is an essential tool for thinking about the consequences of the relationship between power and alienation in all its forms and in all kinds of regimes, totalitarian or not.

Should Patricia not be viewed as an example, in time of peace, of such a gray zone? And if so, is it not precisely because, with its form changed but not its essence, the *raison d'être* of this zone persists in the current biopolitical system? Is this not an invitation addressed to readers/spectators to reflect on the defect of form of which they themselves are participants?

"There is nothing extraordinary ... you get used to it immediately" is a statement that condenses, simply and dryly, the settling of a disenchanted position in which the extraordinary or the unheard-of are emptied of all surprise. Does not acceptance begin where surprise, curiosity, uncanny feelings and scandal end? Thus, habit shows its political implications: it is the scheme of not thinking, of adapting oneself, of letting things run—something that is ever closer to alienation. It dwells in the ethics of tacit collaboration. At the same time, this "getting used to" that occupies the opposite pole of madness reveals the latter's ethical value: madness as the only possible ethical response to the loss of all human dignity.

Levi provides Patricia with a way out: flight. This does not, however, make this story of alienation a story with a happy ending. But it introduces a direction, a hope, and it makes Patricia's act a radical one: the interruption of a predetermined destiny, a first step toward an exit from the gray zone. The play comes to an end; the scene falls apart.

Taking one's destiny into one's own hands is a political message. In order to do so, the task must be, above all, ethical and based on wanting to know, on reasoning in order to not give up, on confronting one's own role in the discourse of which one is a product.

In 1976, Levi wrote about the camps and about Nazi hatred: "Perhaps what happened cannot be understood, actually, *it must not be* understood, because understanding is almost the same as justifying. . . . We cannot understand it; but we can and we must understand where it comes from, and be watchful. If understanding is impossible, knowing is necessary, because what happened can return; consciences can be newly seduced and darkened: even our own" (Levi 1980: 256). Wanting to understand, never ceasing to try to understand even where understanding ends, is a historical and political necessity. As Domenico Scarpa rightly observes, what pushes Levi to write is the will to change the world, and understanding the world is what allows the transmutation of its values (Levi 1991: 242).

The perfectly integrated figure

Among the figures in *Se questo è un uomo*, Elias is the one most perfectly integrated. Unlike Patricia, he is completely suited to the task that he is carrying out. He is a dwarf, with the build of a Hercules and beast-like strength, of an indeterminate age between 20 and 40, a bewildering worker to whom nothing seems impossible. Even the Germans stop to admire his work and seek his services. Elias sings and declaims incessantly in Polish and Yiddish, with the violent gestures of someone suffering from dissociation, amid the applause and laughter of his circle of listeners. He systematically and innocently steals without ever getting caught *in flagrante*. "He is a good worker and organizer, and for this twofold reason he is sheltered from the danger of selections, and respected by bosses and companions" (Levi 1980: 131).

In the camp, Elias "prospers and triumphs," and he is probably "a happy individual." The question that moves Levi—*is this a man?*—is raised in respect of Elias:

We can now ask who is this man Elias. If he is a madman, incomprehensible and para-human, who ended in the Lager by chance. If he is an atavism, different from our modern world, and better adapted to the primordial conditions of camp life. Or if he is perhaps a product of the camp itself, what we will all become if we do not die in the camp, and if the camp does not end first.

There is some truth in all three suppositions. Elias has survived the destruction from outside, because he is physically indestructible; he has resisted the annihilation from within because he is insane. So, in the first place, he is a survivor: he is the most adaptable, the human type most suited to this way of living.

If Elias regains his liberty he will be confined to the fringes of human society, in a prison, or in a lunatic asylum. But here in the Lager there are criminals and no madmen; no criminals because there is no moral law to contravene, no madmen because we are wholly devoid of free will, as our every action is, in time and place, the only conceivable one.

(Levi 1985: 96)

Elias is the perfect product of the logic of the camp, the outcome (adaptation and satisfaction) founded on totalitarianism, violence, and desubjectivization. In this equation, interpretive categories of the free world do not apply: since action here finds itself completely determined by the circumstances that produce it, it is the only action possible. But this laboratory of alienation says a lot about alienation in general. Levi's personal reflection continues:

That said, one might perhaps be tempted to draw conclusions, and perhaps even rules for our daily life. Are there not all around us some Eliases, more or less in embryo? Do we not see individuals living without purpose, lacking all forms of self-control and conscience, who live not *in spite of* these defects, but like Elias precisely because of them?
The question is serious.

(Levi 1985: 98)

This serious question formulated at Auschwitz remains after Auschwitz, affecting Levi's writing and view of the so called free world. Despite all their differences, Elias and Patricia belong to the same zone. And if it is true that Patricia enters it by choice, we must ask ourselves to what extent her choice was not determined by the system in which she found herself perfectly integrated—a choice not so distant from that of many young men and women who enthusiastically embrace an ideal, ready-made identity, assuring themselves of their own roles as little monster consumers and collaborators. The fact that Patricia escapes it through boredom does not diminish the disruptive effect of her act, since her action reinserts—into a mechanized, repetitive, and determined world—the very possibility of free will. In Levi's mind, this possibility seems unthinkable in the case of Elias.

Entering the camp entailed immediate dispossession: stripping, cutting of hair, branding, removal of one's own name and one's own language. It involved the systematic destruction of the narcissistic and libidinal envelope that sustains the subject of language and his/her right to shield himself/herself behind an image cut to fit, where modesty meets human dignity. Furthermore, those who entered were immediately struck, insulted, humiliated, and disoriented. Levi very clearly showed how this voluntary work of eradication and stripping had a primary and specific goal: that of breaking the capacity for resistance among the camp's new arrivals—who were always and above all considered adversaries—and in this way dissipating every possible idea of rebellion. Its implicit goal was, of course, the final exploitation of all the human resources and their extermination.

The expansion of such an operation, the application of industrial technologies to achieve it, the determination to eliminate an entire race, and the number of people exterminated make the Nazi camps a reality without equal in history, an epochal watershed that sets out a radical Before and After. This "After" involves us all, and the systematic desubjectivization carried out in the camps remains part of our horizon. It never ceases to make its effects felt in the present, in the traces transmitted from one generation to another, on the part of survivors and victims and on that of executioners and accomplices.

It is not by chance that after the silence of the immediate postwar era surrounding *Se questo è un uomo* and the lukewarm reception on its publication by Einaudi in 1955, it was the psychiatrist Franco Basaglia—founder of the anti-psychiatric movement in Italy—who highlighted the crucial importance of Primo Levi's observation, enabling him, as Bucciantini puts it, to emerge from his "shell as witness and guardian of memory" (Bucciantini 2011: 69) and to achieve with his discourse a deep social resonance.

In Levi's analysis of objectification and exclusion, Basaglia immediately recognizes implications similar to those with which he has direct experience in psychiatric confinement. If it is true that, in referring to Levi in a partially instrumental manner, Basaglia tends to homogenize aspects of experiences that are not compatible—the camps and the psychiatric institution—it is also true that he finds in Levi's text crucial elements of the process of "dehumanization" typical of all segregationist environments. He identifies their common space and coordinates:

> The fact that the outcast of the Nazi camps might have the same aspect as a mental patient does not mean that—through deprivation, hardship and torture—the prisoner has gone mad. Rather that, interned in a place where mortifications, humiliations and arbitrary events are the norm, a person—whatever his mental state—gradually becomes objectified within the rules of internment and identifies with them. His construction of a

crust of apathy, lack of interest, insensitivity is probably then just his extreme act of defense against a world which first excludes him and then annihilates him: the last personal resource that the patient, as internee, sets up in opposition in order to protect himself against the unbearable experience of living consciously as an outcast.

(Basaglia 1966: 137–8)

Understandably, Levi reacted with reticence and annoyance to the exportation of his thoughts on the experience of the Nazi camps into other forms of confinement. The difference of the camps remains inescapable and fundamental, since the first and last goal of subjugation was not confinement, but death. However, it is Primo Levi himself who outlines the continuity between the logic of desubjectivization and the logic of alienation in contemporary society. "Imagine now a man who is deprived of everyone he loves, and at the same time of his house, his habits, his clothes, in short, of everything he possesses: he will be a hollow man, reduced to suffering and needs forgetful of dignity and restraint, for he who loses all often easily loses himself" (Levi 1985: 33).[7] Basaglia adopted this line of thinking when he denounced the system of psychiatric confinement, recognizing in it the de-humanizing process the so called mental patient was forced to undergo: very soon one can't tell whether the mental discomfort is the outcome of an actual illness or the effect of confinement itself.

It is Basaglia's great merit to have denounced the scandal of the human degradation perpetrated by psychiatry—which, 50 years after his denunciation and the dismantling of various departments of psychiatry, remains a problem as serious as it ever was. If certain forms of confinement are mitigated, special treatments and pharmacology often remain a means of segregation and aggressions upon respect, modesty, and subjective dignity—sadly commonly accepted as "normal" by professionals, relatives, and institutions. The fact that science and norm are called on to justify the silencing of a human being—rather than addressing the social and psychological causes of its discomfort—shows that there is no breach in the continuity of past and present rationalizations. A subtle biopolitical thread links alienation, control, and profit.

The sounds of thawing

Primo Levi radically demonstrates how the human cannot be reduced to an organic and/or purely genetic materiality. The human being is *the subject of language*, the product of the collective relation from which it emerges, in perpetual transferential relation with the Other. And it is within the logic of this relation that human beings can express—or not—their own free will and their own style, that which has a radical impact on their physiological and corporal reality. As Levi puts it: "part of our existence has its seat in the souls of those who come near to us: this is why the experience of those who lived through the days when a man was a thing in

229

the eyes of another man is not human" (Levi 1985: 225). But if this applies to the reality of the camps and to the exploitation and degradation of men in general, it also applies to the logic of a certain scientific discourse so in vogue in contemporary society, thoughtlessly embraced by many (intellectuals, scientists, media, consumers, and so on). Largely supported by the medical and pharmacological industry, this discourse reduces the human to a purely chemical or material formula, to determined neuro-chemical behaviors and reactions, foreclosing the subject of language and its transferential relation to the world.

It is not by chance that Levi associates the most heartbreaking aspect of dehumanization in the camps with the removal of language, the impossibility of communicating, of understanding and making oneself understood, an incapacity that led directly to death. Speech, this *"necessary and sufficient mechanism that makes man a man"* (Levi 1987: 723; italics mine), was prohibited, crushed, and eliminated. To the word zeroed out in the throats of the victims, there came, as *pendant*, the fierce yell of orders shouted, incomprehensible, and incoherent, the "non words" of a language "extant unto itself," *"orts- und zeitgebunden*, tied to place and time" (Levi 1987: 728), a corrupted variant of the *Lingua Tertii Imperii*, where the voice's sound is reduced to that which is ever more essential and enigmatic in speaking: the pure imperative, the undecodable. Incomprehensible and ineffective at it was, this imperative was followed by punches, beatings, and so on, to the point of death. As in dealing with animals, no substantial difference is seen between gesture and word.

"All human races speak; no non human species knows how to speak" (Levi 1987: 721). This is what defines the universal to which man belongs, and it is precisely this universal that was attacked and challenged in the camps, with the intent to undo it, to demonstrate its insignificance—a project that never ceases to haunt contemporary society.

In *Sleeping Beauty in the Fridge*, there is an eighth character, Margareta, the daughter of Lotte and Peter Thorl. She does not appear on the stage; her voice comes from offstage. She speaks just once to ask her mother from the next room if Aunt Patricia woke up and what she brought her this year. To the list of the figures of middle-class alienation gathered in the play, this curious detail adds a young representative of infantile consumerism. But her offstage voice summons the voice of future generations, of all those who, born innocently in a particular environment, are forced to deal with a world that has determined their existence and within which they will have to articulate their own word, their own free will.

There is yet another presence in the play that is particularly relevant, since it accompanies its rhythm and its parsing; it is the noise of science and technology. This is the noise of the machinery that accompanies the operation of thawing Patricia, the beating of the metronome, the creaking of the hatch, the sound of the scissors, and so on. Following it is a series of chemical and mechanical details related to the process of thawing that Peter and his guests exchange with interest.

Science and technology are protagonists of the play, both ironically and seriously. Set in Berlin, this implicitly raises a crucial question: to what degree are the advent of Nazism, and its creed of aesthetics and hygienics, part and effect of an aberration of the discourse of science, in the dominance of the technological age? To what degree are we all participants and collaborators in such a discourse?

Patricia's running away to reach a frozen colleague in America underlines the German/American axis of scientific experimentation—and brings to mind how the American research on eugenics in the early years of the twentieth century was efficiently exploited by German internment centers. Any close study of the classification process of immigrant labor arriving in the US in centers such as Ellis Island amply demonstrates the segregational efficacy of collusion between the production and medical systems.

Levi's is an ethical interrogation of modernity. In 1981, he participates as a man of science in the debate over the responsibility of scientists in contemporary society. Here he addresses the scientist, admonishing him/her:

> Whether you are a believer or not, whether you are a "patriot" or not, if you are allowed a choice, do not let yourself be seduced by material or intellectual interests, but choose within the field that can render the route less painful and less dangerous for those of your cohort and your descendants. Do not hide behind the hypocrisy of "scientific neutrality." You are gifted enough to know how to evaluate whether the egg you are hatching will release a dove or a cobra, a chimera or perhaps nothing.
>
> (Levi 1986: 977)[8]

Speaking in vain

Levi relates that, while in Auschwitz, he as well as many other prisoners had the same recurring dream, one in which, suddenly, they saw themselves at home, and able, at long last, to tell their story: the horror, the hunger, the beatings, the death, and all the unheard-of and unimaginable experiences to which they had been subjected. But the dream would inevitably become a nightmare: relatives and friends paid no attention, they remained indifferent, talked about other things and eventually left. The anguish caused the inmates to wake up: a woeful pain assailed them, "sorrow in its pure state" (Levi 1980: 83). The real of human deafness reawakened them to the Real of life in the camps.[9]

It is to be hoped that, instigated by Levi's ethical fight to show the continuity between past aberrations and current logic, his contemporary readers will not behave like his friends in the nightmare, not to ignore, that is, his uncomfortable questioning and seek refuge in the normalcy of the everyday.

Notes

1 "It was the experience of the Camp . . . that forced me to write" (Levi 1985: 396).

2 "I mostri esistono ma sono troppo pochi per essere pericolosi; sono più pericolosi gli uomini comuni, i funzionari pronti a credere e obbedire senza discutere . . ." (Levi 1985: 394).

3 In *The Sixth Day and Other Tales* (1990), Rosenthal translates marziano as "silver marten." Rosenthal has Robert say: "It's a silver marten: it seems the Russians have imported a large quantity of them." A significant mistake:—was this an oversight? But what does this oversight say about the difficulty of accepting the radicalness of Levi's thought?

4 "L'empio sfruttamento dei cadaveri, trattati come una qualsiasi anonima materia prima, da cui si ricavavano l'oro dei denti, i capelli come materiale tessile, le ceneri come fertilizzanti agricoli; gli uomini e le donne degradati a cavie, su cui sperimentare medicinali per poi sopprimerli [The cruel exploitation of the corpses, treated like some ordinary raw material, from which they extracted the gold of their teeth, the hair as textile material, the ashes as agricultural fertilizer; the men and women reduced to guinea pigs on which to experiment with medications, then do away with them]" (Levi 1980: 254).

5 "Possedeva tutti i requisiti, cuore, polmoni, reni ecc. in perfetto ordine; un sistema nervoso da pilota spaziale; un carattere imperturbabile e risoluto, una emotività limitata, ed infine una buona cultura ed intelligenza."

6 Paraded as regulatory and precautionary methods, assessment and evaluation are agents of normativity whose operations are rooted first in selection and then in segregation. Just think of the IQ tests on which the destiny of so many schoolchildren depends nowadays: What classes will they be permitted to attend, what type of school etc.? This is based on some contrived parameters, which, at best, reflect the pseudo-scientific preconception of the people who have formulated them or are charged with their application. Prerequisites corrupt even those activities in which the presence of a vocation should be determined a posteriori, and are based on a subjective experience. Ironically, the series of prerequisites required by the Berlin competition calls into mind those requested by the Consortium for candidates applying to psychoanalytic training. The criteria of admissibility ("the applicant's personal qualities that are considered as necessary to undertake the psychoanalytic education") listed by the Consortium include: "evidence of integrity of character, maturity of personality, reasonable indication of capacity and motivation for self-reflection ... appropriate intellectual ability" ("Standards of Psychoanalytic Education, Accreditation Council For Psychoanalytic Education, The Psychoanalytic Consortium," Accreditation Council for Psychoanalytic Education, www.ACPEinc.org).

7 The term "organizer" (*organizzatore*), refers to the term "organized," which in this context has the meaning "obtained illegally," as Levi explains in a note. "Il vocabolo [organizzato] assunse questo curioso significato durante la seconda guerra mondiale, non solo nei Lager ma anche in molti paesi d'Europa, forse con allusione ironica alla nota "organizzazione" tedesca che spesso si risolveva in puro furto o truffa ai danni dei paesi occupati [The word [organized] took on this curious meaning during the Second World War, not only in the camps but also in many countries of Europe, perhaps as an ironic allusion to the well-known German "organization" that often turned to pure theft or swindling of the damages of occupied countries]" (Levi 1980: 106).

8 "Si immagini ora un uomo a cui, insieme con le persone amate, vengano tolti la sua casa, le sue abitudini, i suoi abiti , tutto infine, letteralmente tutto quanto possiede: sarà un uomo vuoto, ridotto a sofferenza e bisogno, dimentico di dignità e discernimento, poiché accade facilmente a chi ha perso tutto, di perdere se stesso" (Levi 1980: 20–1).

9 This recalls the ambiguity of the function of reawakening, and within it, the role played by the Real. "Le réel, c'est au-delà du rêve que nous avons à le rechercher—dans ce que le rêve a enrobé, a enveloppé, nous a caché, derrière le manque de la représentation dont il n'y a là qu'un tenant lieu [The real has to be sought beyond the dream—in what the dream has wrapped, enveloped, hidden from us, behind the lack of representation of which there is only a substitute]" (Lacan 1973: 59).

Bibliography

Basaglia, F. (1966) "Un problema di psichiatria istituzionale. L'esclusione come categoria socio-psichiatrica," in *Rivista Sperimentale di Freniatria*, no. 6; Re-published in Massimo Bucciantini (2011), *Esperimento Auschwitz*, Torino: Einaudi, pp. 136–9.

Bucciantini, M. (2011) *Esperimento Auschwitz*, Turin: G. Einaudi.

Lacan, J. (1973) *Les quatre concepts fondamentaux de la psychanalyse, Le Séminaire Livre XI*, Paris: Seuil.

Levi, P. (1958; 2nd edn 1980) *Se questo è un uomo*, Turin: G. Einaudi.

—— (1985) *Survival in Auschwitz (Se questo è un uomo)*, trans. S. Woolf, New York: Summit Books.

—— (1986) "Covare il cobra," *La Stampa*. Rebublished in *Opere*, Vol. III, Torino: Einaudi, 1990, pp. 974–7.

—— (1987) *I sommersi e il salvati, Opere*, Vol. I, Turin: G. Einaudi.

—— (1990) *Storie naturali, Opere*, Vol. III, Torino: Einaudi, pp. 5–183.

—— (1990) *The Sixth Day and Other Tales (Storie naturali and Vizio di forma)*, trans. R. Rosenthal, New York: Summit Books.

—— (1991) "Chiaro/Oscuro," in M. Belpoliti (ed.), *Primo Levi*, Milan: Marcos y Marcos edizioni.

Milner, J. C. (2005) *La politique des choses*, Paris: Navarin.

16

SPELL IT WRONG
TO READ IT RIGHT

Crashaw, psychosis, and Baroque poetics

Stephen W. Whitworth

In his early and later work, Lacan claimed that once the Symbolic has been robbed of its ec-centric center, its anchoring point, the Name-of-the-Father, the Symbolic Other falls away and is replaced by the cruel, sadistic, jealous, castrating Real Father of jouissance, the murderous father of the primal horde Freud discussed in *Totem and Taboo*. When this occurs, all signifiers slide about without any limitations of a specific range of signifieds. Then, the productions of the psyche, both in their destructive, phantasmagoric, jouissant imaginings and in their delusional metaphor, may eventually preserve something where the subject once was, if they acquire a creative, artistic, or even literary quality. In Lacan's words, when this happens, "the discursive products characteristic of the register of paranoia usually blossom into literary productions" (Lacan 1975: 77). The delusional metaphor impels the psychotic to "write" himself over and over again with language experienced as objects, as letters (the material substratum of the symbolic signifier); through creativity, the psychotic is consequently enabled to hold himself together psychically and be relatively functional, staving off the persecutory, haunting, and ever-returning primordially foreclosed Real Father of jouissance—with creative, literary endeavor.

Long before Lacan poetically interpreted the remarkably lucid delusional system of President Schreber and described the psychotic structure sinthomatically through the works of James Joyce, seventeenth century English poet Crashaw's career maps out a similar trajectory, from the optimistic yet somewhat traumatic "break" in "To the Name above Every Name." This "break" inadvertently instantiates a Real, not a salutary symbolic castration through the suffering ecstasy of his devotional poems, including the final relative "calm" of his last, great Theresa hymn, "The Flaming Heart," where delusional creative systems functioning as ersatz Symbolic orders provide a last, preservative, and literary refuge for the remains of a subject.

The son of a virulently anti-Catholic Anglican pastor Reverend William Crashaw, Richard Crashaw was converted to Catholicism. This was already a "break," a break that eventually leads him to exile, penury and, probably, death by poisoning at the hands of some of the very Catholics he has spent his life defending. Crashaw's break, however, begins long before the excesses of his hypertrophied, mystical visions get him expelled in 1644 from even Peterhouse College at Cambridge, with its strongly Catholic sympathies, and he is forced to take refuge on the Continent when the Puritans gain the upper hand in the ensuing English Civil War. From early childhood, in fact, Crashaw's break is the suggestion of an underlying psychic structure, a structure predicated on the absolute exclusion of the father and a subsequent (or probably precedent) clinging to the mother and maternal figures. William Crashaw seems to play no role whatsoever in his son's "formation" (in the French sense of both "education" and "the development of character"). Crashaw's psychic structure is determined by a fixation at a position prior even to that of alienation: for him, the mother is not a prototype for the Other, not a (m)Other, but the All, the cosmic pleroma, the One of/as everything.

And so, long before Crashaw's official conversion from Anglicanism to Catholicism, in a literary pietà entitled "Sancta Maria Dolorum: Stabat Mater Dolorosa" ("Holy Mary, Mother of Sorrows"), the inspiration for Crashaw's ecstatic visions is a voyeuristic picture of an all-too-fleshy, all-too-immanent, close and touching (in the literal sense) "miracle": the vision of Mother Mary and her son Christ exchanging wounds during the Passion. The proximity and visionary nature of what Crashaw describes is emphasized by the poem's emblem of the pietà; it is as though he were witness—as Crashaw insists in the poem itself—to the pathos-filled scenes unfolding.

"In shade of death's sad Tree," he tells us, "Stood dolefull Shee" (Crashaw 1927: 284, lines 1–2). Though Mary is separated from her son on the cross by physical space, they are one; his wounds are mouths that speak to/with her own:

> O costly intercourse
> Of deaths, and worse,
> Divided loves. While son and mother
> Discourse alternate wounds to one another;
> Quick Deaths that grow
> And gather, as they come and goe;
> His nailes write swords in her, which soon her heart
> Payes back, with more than their own smart;
> Her Swords, still growing with his pain,
> Turn Spears, and straight come home againe.
> (Crashaw 1927: 285, lines 21–30)

And Crashaw, witness to this "discursive intercourse" of mother and son, yearns to play his part, his participation mystique in their holy, painful communion. "O Mother turtle-dove!" he cries,

That these dry lidds might borrow
Something from thy full seas of Sorrow . . .
O teach those wounds to bleed
In mee . . .

(Crashaw 1927: 285,
lines 51, 53–4, 61–2)

He begs to be "soft subject for the siege of love" (Crashaw 1927: 285, line 59), so that, like a "yonger brother" (Crashaw 1974: 286, line 88), he may, with Mary and Christ, watch his "life dy" (Crashaw 1974: 285, line 48).

This drive to participate in the subjectively shattering union of mother and child, or, more specifically, in the phallicized Mother who precedes sexuation (what Julia Kristeva calls the "semiotic chora" and Michèle Montrelay first calls the "floating field") finally leads Crashaw to write one of his most shocking and profoundly misunderstood poems: a text in which he seems to imagine a mother performing fellatio on her son. The poem is an epigram, purportedly a translation of Luke 11:27, but the Biblical passage is doubtlessly metamorphosed as it passes through Crashaw's psychotic psychic structure. "Suppose He had been Tabled at thy Teates," the poet begins, addressing Mother Mary,

"Thy hunger feels not what he eates":

Hee'l have his Teat e're long (a bloody one)
The Mother then must suck the Son.
(Crashaw, 1927: 94, lines 1–4)

This poem, perhaps more than any other, is what for many generations caused literary critics to consider Crashaw's poetry "impious," "lewd" and even "obscene" in the excesses of its spiritual "enthusiasm." It is what caused Crashaw's fascinating poetry, sadly, to be excluded from the canon of English literature for so long, before Lacan and other psychoanalytic theorists of his age insisted that the so-called "litter" of literature can teach literature students about the mind, and even psychoanalysis itself how to renew its conceptual categories. Here, the poem obviously invokes the Catholic conceit that the wound in Christ's side and the blood that flows from it are the "breast" whose "milk" is the eternal life-giving salvation of the congregation of the faithful, as Carolyn Walker Bynum has demonstrated in *Jesus as Mother* (1982) and *Holy Feast and Holy Fast* (1988). And here, certainly, the poem invokes the traditional counter-reformation iconography—detailed by Leo Steinberg in his *Sexuality of Christ in Renaissance Art and in Modern Oblivion* (1996)—of the blood from Christ's side flowing down to his genitals to emphasize his "humanation" or incarnation. Yet the final line—entirely Crashaw's invention—is, without a doubt, surprising, to say the least. It is understandable that the already sexuated, normativizing, compulsory, and compulsive obsessionally heterosexual neurotic egos of early nineteenth and early twentieth century Renaissance literary critics and historians would think that Crashaw is representing something sexually untoward and incestuous between the sacred mother and the child in this epigram.

Crashaw's epigram has been read through the lens of neurosis, whose eternal, post-sexuated search in culturally valorized work for the lost object has been affected by the rock of symbolic castration and the assumption of the Name-of-the-Father by the subject, who has passed through both stages of castration: alienation and separation. The psychotic psychic structure of Crashaw's texts has not passed through alienation or separation; it has not faced the rock of symbolic castration (only the anxious trauma of an all-too-real castrative threat). Furthermore, it does not realize that the Other, as such, does not exist and therefore does not need to be foreclosed, and has not assumed the hole at the heart of the transcendental Name-of-the-Father. Moreover, it has not been sexuated and, consequently, has no lost object. According to Lacan, the psychotic never passes through the two castrations that produce the "normative" neurotic subject engaged in culturally valorized "work" that defers gratification and recognizes the Other as the treasury of signifiers "presumed to know" the "answer" to the subject's definitive life question, the question of his desire. The psychotic, unlike the neurotic, never even begins to experience the first castration of "alienation." He does not begin to realize that the Mother is sometimes called away from the child by social obligation, work, the pursuit of her own desire—what in Lacanian theory is a structural (not biological) phenomenon known as the Symbolic Father. This Father is refused access to any form of symbolization whatsoever by the psychotic: he is foreclosed and relegated to the deepest depths of the unconscious. Unlike the neurotic, therefore, the psychotic does not begin to experience the Mother as a (m)Other, a synecdochic anticipation of the world of others with desires distinct from the needs of the child himself. Nor, consequently, does the psychotic experience the second castration that the normative neurotic subject experiences: separation. He does not extend the initial synecdochic anticipation within the (m)Other that there may be much more out there in the world than just a Mother who occasionally disappears to a full-scale recognition of the Other as absolutely distinct. Nor does he, like the neurotic, ever realize that finding one's place in the familial, social, and linguistic world of symbolic others involves psychically assuming the "first signifier" of the Father's name, the name that situates him culturally. On the contrary, for the psychotic, there is never even an anticipation of this socially situating "first signifier." It is foreclosed and castration can only ever be experienced phantasmagorically as a terrifying *Real*, as a possibility for the Real Father of jouissance, who, like every object of Symbolic foreclosure, returns persecutorily in the Real.

What are we to make, then, of Crashaw's insistence that "The Mother, then, must suck the Son," if we read it through the lens native to it, the lens of psychosis? Firstly, we must read the poem as a whole, as an *All*: Christ—in Crashaw's eyes, the eternal child held in his mother's arms, as the emblem to "Sancta Maria Dolorum" indicates—feeds from her breast, and she, in turn, sucks from the life-giving blood. She feeds from his death, and then returns that life to him as he feeds from her breast, in an ouroboric, oral-stage circuit reminiscent of the origins of life, the intrauterine state and birth, long before the separation of subject and Other, long before the penis has become the Phallus and the breasts objects for anything but appetitive satisfaction. The so-called "obscenity" and "incestuous fellatio" of Crashaw's divine epigram, then, are the products of our own critical, psychically anachronistic perception, not of any salacious "impiety" in the Thing itself.

In his hymn "To the Name above Every Name," this sensitive English mystic, transported by his Baroque visionary ecstasy, announces, "I Sing the Name which None can say/But touch't with an interiour Ray" (Crashaw, 1927: 239, lines 1–2). And like every good counter-reformation Catholic driven to speak, to sing by overwhelming affective piety, he thereby pays homage to the transcendental unrepresentability, the unsayability, of the name of God, of the sacred tetra-grammaton. Yet Crashaw, anticipating Senatspräsident Daniel Paul Schreber two hundred fifty years later, also—somewhat paradoxically—makes a special claim for himself in these lines: like Schreber, enraptured by the "nerves" and "rays" of the "hinder God" to produce the "bellowing miracle" heralding his imminent salvational "unmanning," Crashaw separates himself from the common lot of humanity. He, unlike others, has been "touch't by an interiour Ray," and can say the unsayable; for him, the transcendental signifier, the Proper Name, the Name-of-the-Father or paternal metaphor—in short, the *Vorstellungrepräsentanz*—that, unlike other signifiers, unites being and meaning, is not transcendental, not a significative anchoring point for the Symbolic order. On the contrary, he, "in the wealthy Brest/Of this unbounded Name," will "build [his] warm Nest" (Crashaw 1927: 239, lines 11–12).

Clearly, this spiritual, jouissant, and poetic "warm Nest" has been built not, as its title might initially suggest, on disavowal—the unconscious maintenance of two mutually exclusive propositions within the psyche—but on the foreclosure—the absolute exclusion from symbolization, even in the form of the lack at the heart of symptoms—of the transcendence of a primordial or first signifier. And as we learn from Lacan in Seminar 3, "the object of a *Verwerfung* [foreclosure] reappear[s] in the Real" (Lacan 1997: 190). And this return does not lead to the paradise Crashaw initially foresees; it leads to psychosis. It is haunting, often persecutory, linked, as Lacan indicates, to paranoiac hallucinations, producing creativity and poetry. This is because, as the introduction to the seminar on "The Names/Prohibitions of the Father" tells us, "the supposition of the pure erotic bliss of the father viewed as primordial" (Lacan 1990: 89) must be mediated by a Symbolic Father, a Symbolic Other. As real Thing, which Crashaw suggests he can touch, which he insists he, unlike all others, can put in his mouth and sing, the Father is unbearable. "God," we are told by psychoanalysis, must be "something one encounters in the Real, inaccessible. It is indicated by what doesn't deceive: anxiety"; yet here, unlike the case with the neurotic, it is an anxiety so strong it makes subjectivity an impossibility (Lacan 1990: 90).

But what, some will ask, of the "effeminacy" so often attributed to Crashaw, of his passive wish to be the "soft subject for the siege of love," of his repudiation of identification with the position of the father, of his lifelong unmarried state, of his only truly intimate bonds being platonic and with much older maternal "great ladies," such as the Countess of Denbigh and the exiled Queen Henrietta Maria? Don't these facts indicate, as Freud concluded in his analysis of Schreber's infamous *Memoirs of My Nervous Illness*, that Crashaw's psychosis was the result of an "outburst of homosexual libido" that had been long repressed (Freud 1963: 142)? Not at all. Crashaw's psychic structure is much more archaic than any lifting of a secondary repression (*Verdrängung*) or unsatisfactory situating on the chart for which the formulae of sexuation can account. It involves a profound difficulty with the fundamental phenomenon of signification, not of sexuation; it is what some would call a "signifying illness."

Crashaw, as we have seen, has no signifying "anchor" and his consequent paranoid persecutory anxiety is, as Lacan eventually decides, "not without an object" (Lacan 1990: 82); its object is the small object *a*, the lost object, which, for the neurotic, functions as "cause and support of desire" in fantasy when it "falls away in anxiety" and is expressed in the (usually) socially productive "act." But Crashaw's small object *a* has not been lost, has never been renounced (*Versägt*); he has not received the small fragment of nonsense left by the lost object, but is, rather, the victim of so much sense that it all becomes nonsense, all becomes the nonsensical "material medium that concrete discourse borrows from language" (Lacan 1996: 413). He is not a subject of desire. His anxiety emanates from elsewhere, from the Real Father of jouissance, his foreclosure of the Symbolic Other released. And so Crashaw takes refuge in the object he never renounced, the Mother, and his poetry becomes a flight from the persecutory Father he fears, leaving within it no empty space for a Proper Name that could prevent the treasury of signifiers usually held in the Other from sliding in an endless, nearly meaningless, metamorphic nightmare. This metamorphic, phantasmagoric infinite sliding of the signifier over a universe of signifieds is demonstrated nowhere more evidently than in "The Weeper."

In this hymn, Mary Magdalene, whose eyes are hailed as "sister springs/. . . Ever bubbling things/Still spending, never spent!" (Crashaw 1927: 308, lines 1, 3, 5), is seen (once again literally, in an introductory emblem designed by Crashaw's own hand, an emblem that represents both Mary's eyes and her ripped-open heart streaming tears) as crying endlessly over the broken body of her savior and in penitence for her own past sins. At first, her tears are "Heavens of ever-falling stars" (Crashaw 1927: 308, line 8) that, as seeds, are "sown" to make the Earth shine as Heaven does. Yet they quickly become a stream flowing upward to Heaven as the Milky Way, the "creame" of which "Heaven the cristall ocean is" (Crashaw 1927: 309, lines 25, 27). Soon they are the "breakefast" of cherubs (Crashaw 1927: 309, line 30), but also the "pearles bedecking Sorrow" (Crashaw 1927: 309, lines 34, 42) as she bewails the going down of the golden Sun/son. Quickly they begin to metamorphose into a host of things: they become the morning dew; medicinable balsam; a "richer wine"; a "golden stream" more golden than Midas's Tagus; the month of April; a sweet spring fountain; "flouds"; fires; "love's sweet powres"; the site where the lamb "dipt his white foot"; "walking baths"; the crown of all kings; and, finally, "*all* places, Times, and objects" (Crashaw 1927: 313, line 131, emphasis mine).

Some have found this continual metamorphosis grotesque. Others have quite simply found it bizarre and poetically ineffective and inartistic. And still others have—somewhat absurdly—pointed out that the progression of the poem's stanzas is "illogical." Regardless of how critics have responded, Crashaw himself seems eventually to become afraid of this endless sliding of the single signifier "tear" over a host of signifieds that could possibly go on forever in the maternal "floating field" or "semiotic chora" of his psyche, and he abruptly puts an end—after twenty-six stanzas—to the phantasmagoric chain with the only signifier at his disposal that can do the trick: death. Suddenly interrupting the transformational chain, he declares:

> Not so long ago she lived,
> Shall thy tomb report of thee;
> But so long she grieved,
> Thus must we date thy memory.
> Others by monuments, months, and yeares
> Measure their ages; thou, by TEARES.
> (Crashaw 1927: 313, lines 211–16,
> caps in original).

No longer the divine "starres" of a touchable and immanent heaven, the tears of the Magdalene—a female figure, with whom, once again, Crashaw clearly feels an affinity—are now an epitaph, the writing on a tombstone. They are the marks of death—the "tears" in the punning sense of "rips"—that Crashaw senses are beginning to destroy his mind.

Fortunately, Crashaw discovers the biography of the Spanish mystic Saint Theresa of Avila, and the beautifully bound commingling of pleasure and pain, of ecstasy and jouissance he finds there inspires him poetically and creatively, and enables him to at least provisionally and repeatedly repair the tears in his psyche memorialized in "The Weeper." This enables him, in short, to go on living. In "A Hymn to the Name and Honor of the Admirable Saint Theresa, Foundresse of the Discalced Carmelites, both Men and Women; A Woman of Angelicall Heighth of Speculation, for Masculine Courage of Performance, More then a Woman, Who, Yet a Child, out Ran Maturity, and Durst Plott a Martyrdome," a poem whose exceptionally long and associational title at first displays some of the metamorphic and sliding signifying qualities of "The Weeper." In this poem Crashaw begins to construct the delusional system that will be his psychic "salvation."

In this poem, Crashaw immediately announces to God that, in this praise of holiness, "Wee'l appeal to none of All/those thy old souldiers, Great and Tall/That

240

could reach down/with strong armes . . ./[and] speak lowd into the face of Death/Their Great Lord's glorious name" (Crashaw 1927: 317, lines 3–9). Instead, he will be concerned with what he calls God's true abode, the place where God is forever "Making his mansion in the mild/And milky soul of a soft child" (Crashaw 1927: 317, lines 13–14), the breast of St. Theresa as a young girl. No more will Crashaw "sing the name which none can say" in a failed identification with strong, adult, masculine figures; he will find/see himself in the psyche of one closer to the primordial bond prior to the entry of the "strong armes" of the Father, one still living in the infant state. Crashaw proceeds to detail the childhood of St. Theresa, and to tell us that from the start, the little girl was more than half in love with death. "Scarse," he says, "has she learn'd to lisp the name/of Martyr, yet she thinks it shame/Life should so long play with that breath/Which spent can buy so brave a death/. . ./Though she cannot tell you why/She can love, and she can dy" (Crashaw 1974: 317, lines 15–18, 24–25). This is a sentiment not so very different from that expressed at the end of "The Weeper."

He proceeds to narrate her childhood, how she slowly but surely learns how much stronger love is than death; how age—either chronological or psychic, it seems—does not make the Martyr; and how, finally, this urge for death grows stronger even than her close bond with her mother: "Her weake brest," he tells us, "heaves with strong desire/Of what she maye with fruitlesse wishes/Seek for amongst her Mother's kisses" (Crashaw 1927: p. 318, lines 40–2). Crashaw's identification with the young saint tells us that life, even in the constantly satisfied need of union with the mother, eventually becomes unbearable when tortured relentlessly by the phantasmagoric signifying sliding of a Symbolic devoid of the paternal metaphor. This leads one to yearn for the end death offers, which, after all, is just another ceaselessly sliding signifier that Crashaw thinks he needs, "though (s)he cannot tell you why" (Crashaw 1927: 317, line 24).

At last, the young St. Theresa makes the decision to leave the shelter of her "Mother's kisses" and "Since 'tis not to be had at home/She'll travail to a Martyrdome" (Crashaw 1927: 318, lines 43–4) among the Moors. "Farewell, then, all the world! Adieu!/Teresa is no more for you!" Crashaw, speaking in the young saint's voice, says to us enthusiastically: "She's for the Moores and Martyrdome" (Crashaw 1927: p. 318, line 64). Yet here Crashaw falters, and calls the young saint back. "Sweet! Not so fast! Lo thy faire Spouse/Whom thou seekst with so swift vowes,/Calls thee back, and biddes thee come/T'embrace a milder martyrdom" (Crashaw 1927: 318, lines 65–8). He proceeds to explain that in life she may embrace a thousand martyrdoms, a thousand "deaths," each time God's seraphim come to practice their "archeries" on her tender heart with their golden arrows. Martyrdom, he insists, is not a once-and-for-all "act" at the hands of an all-too-brutal Saracen embodying the cruel, jealous, persecutory, Real Father of jouissance; it is a series of physical and intrapsychic experiences, whose infinitely and simultaneously painful and joyous pleasures will keep unbearable life at bay. When these seraphim—less awful representations of the terrible Father—visit, he concludes, speaking to the young saint, "O how oft shalt thou complain/Of a sweet and subtle Pain./Of Intolerable Joyes;/Of a death, in which who dyes/Loves his death and dyes again/And would forever so be slain./And lives, and dyes; and knowes not/why/To live, But that he thus may never/leave to Dy!" (Crashaw 1927: 319, lines 97–104).

And so Crashaw, perilously close to ending his life at the nightmarish conclusion of "The Weeper" because of his entrapment in a Symbolic order gone mad in the absence of its anchoring Proper Name, begins to build, to create, to dwell poetically in a delusion that tenuously, provisionally approximates the foreclosed Name-of-the-Father. And this is not so surprising, for as Lacan says quite specifically in his *De la psychose paranoïaque dans ses rapports avec la personnalité*, "If reality is perverted in psychosis, it retains an order, retained . . . in thought, in action, and in will" (Lacan 1975: 55; my translation). The psychotic can remain functional by constructing a system that makes "sense" of experience and building poetically a provisional substitute for the absent Symbolic Name-of-the-Father. Yet this "substitute," as Crashaw already intuits in this first of his Theresa hymns, requires constant work, a thousand "deaths," "forever being so slain," in which "death" is the necessarily repeated confrontation with and staving off of the terrible, primordial Real Father of jouissance, who forever haunts the psychotic's creations.

This *sinthome* of the psychotic, or as Lacan calls it earlier in "On a Question Prior to Any Possible Treatment of Psychosis," this "delusional metaphor" that holds the psychotic together and allows him to create, live, and pass as a reasonably "functional" citizen (Lacan 1996: 481) finds its "completion" (in the sense of "completed birth," not in the sense of "finishing touch") in Crashaw's second Theresa hymn, "The Flaming Heart." In this piece, Crashaw uncharacteristically opens by addressing his readers (of whom he usually remains blissfully ignorant) directly, and tells us that, in our interpretations of the now anonymous Baroque visual artwork that inspired this poem, we are the subjects of a serious misreading. "Well-meaning readers!" he begins, "you that come as friends/. . . Make not too much hast t'admire/That fair-cheek'd fallacy of fire./That is a SERAPHIM, they say/And this the great TERESIA" (Crashaw 1927: 324, lines 1–5, caps in original). But the painting dupes us, he says: "Painter, what didst thou understand/To put her dart into his hand?/See, even the yeares and size of him/Showes this [Theresa] the mother seraphim!/This is the *mistresse* flame. . ." (Crashaw 1927: 324, lines 13–17, emphasis mine). The arrow, he complains to the painter, belongs not to the angel but to Theresa, the "mother seraphim," who is much larger than he who has been sent to serve, or perhaps "service," her. We, in reading the painting, therefore, must "give him the vaile, give her the dart" (Crashaw 1927: 325, line 36), for we "could'st not so unkindly err" to "mocke[] with female frost love's manly flame" and see her as "some weake, inferiour woman saint" (Crashaw 1927: 324–5, lines 21, 24, 26). She is "the *mistresse* flame" who possesses not only the piercing penile "dart," but, in Crashaw's still somewhat archaic, infantile representation of the sexual act, the "pierc'd flaming *heart*" as well.

Thus, he says finally to the painter and the (implicitly male) reader, "Give her the Dart for it is she/. . . shootes both *thy* shaft and Thee" (Crashaw 1927: 325, lines 47–8). And because her "weapon" is more "potent" than the "dart," she apparently keeps all the ensuing pleasurably painful, incomprehensibly orgasmic pain for herself as well: "In love's field was never found/A nobler weapon than a Wound./Love's passives are his activ'st part/The wounded is the wounding heart" (Crashaw 1927: 326, lines 71–4), and in having her heart or "wound" pierced by the flaming golden arrow, she will "love and dy and kill:/And bleed and wound: and yield and conquer still" (Crashaw 1927: 326, lines 79–80). Our task in reading this painting, it is implied, as well as the entirety of Crashaw's art for which this painting is both the epitome and emblem, is, consequently, to "transpose the picture quite/And spell it wrong to read it right/Read him for her, and her for him/And call the Saint the Seraphim" (Crashaw 1927: 324, lines 9–12).

In Crashaw's art, he is finally able to say: yes, s/he defies the complex categories of even Lacanian sexuation, and, yes, the Name-of-the-Father and the Other on whom we neurotics so depend and in whom—despite our "enlightening" theory— we nonetheless believe have been banished to the abyss, the shadowland, the darkness of the Real. Yet if we are willing to "spell it wrong to read it right" and use some of our most idiosyncratic interpretive powers—to reduce and stabilize rather than multiply significations—we can see that even the psychotic can at times write that Name, even if it be in scrambled, garbled letters, and we can appreciate the poetry of even an unintentionally "lewd," "impious" enthusiast such as Crashaw.

In the end, Crashaw challenges us to practice these techniques of "psycho-analysis in reverse" in a quite simple, epigrammatic/epitaphic poem. "HE WAS CAR," it simply reads: C-R-A-S-H-A-W-E—letters—reordered as a grammatical subject and predicate, in the preterite, or possibly the imperfect. Perhaps because of the creative delusional metaphor he built and rebuilt for himself, Crashaw could imagine inscribing the Name-of-the-Father and tenuously assuming the status of a subject, so long as that Name and assumption were disguised, hidden and safely projected backward into the past, to the "warm nest" of a poetical anagram, not of signifiers, but of concrete, real letters, seductive if only in the nonsense of their music, if only in their poetically, musically reminding us of the "litter" always at the heart of "literature."

Bibliography

Bynum, C. W. (1982) *Jesus as Mother: Studies in the Spirituality of the High Middle Ages*, Berkeley: University of California Press.

—— (1988) *Holy Feast and Holy Fast: The Religious Significance of Food to Medieval Women*, Berkeley: University of California Press.

Crashaw, R. (1927) *Crashaw's Poetical Works*, ed. L. C. Martin, Oxford: The Clarendon Press.

—— (1974) *Complete Poetry of Richard Crashaw*, ed. G. W. Williams, New York: W. W. Norton & Company.

Freud, S. (1963) *Three Case Histories*, New York: Collier Books.

Lacan, J. (1975) *De la psychose paranoïaque dans ses rapports avec la personnalité*, Paris: Seuil.

—— (1990) *Television: A Challenge to the Psychoanalytic Establishment*, New York: W. W. Norton & Company.

—— (1996) *Ecrits*, trans. Bruce Fink, New York: W. W. Norton & Company.

—— (1997) *The Seminar of Jacques Lacan*, ed. J.-A. Miller, trans. R. Grigg, New York: W. W. Norton & Company.

Montrelay, M. (1977) *L'ombre et le nom: sur la féminité*, Paris: Minuit.

Steinberg, L. (1996) *The Sexuality of Christ in Renaissance Art and in Modern Oblivion*, Chicago: University of Chicago Press.

17

MADNESS OR MIMESIS

Narrative impasse in the novels
of Samuel Beckett

Olga Cox Cameron

"The mad have cast upon their tongues words from the unseen and they tell them," wrote the fourteenth-century Muslim historian Ibu Kaldun (Welsford 1935: 78), and a longstanding tradition links these words to the truths that lurk beneath the illusions of sanity. But under what circumstances can these words accede to the status of art? It is not at all the same thing for Shakespeare to use madness as a poetic ploy as for a mad writer to create a work of art. Over time a number of different types of relation have been posited between these domains. Are they mutually exclusive? Is madness the condition for the opening of certain creative depths in, say, the work of Hölderlin? Was Rousseau's writing great not because of but despite his madness? For me the boldest theorist on this topic is Maurice Blanchot, referred to occasionally by Lacan, and who throughout his very varied essays voices the suspicion that there is in the fabric of madness something akin to the literary act itself. To cede the initiative to words, as Mallarmé so famously put it, is the task of the artist, an aspiration that for the psychotic all too easily becomes a tyrannizing imperative.

There is no reason to believe that Beckett, any more than Joyce, was mad, but in problematizing the very possibility of subjectivity as well as meaning and even language itself he appears to shunt the literary artifact into what he himself calls "the spacious annexe of mental alienation" (Beckett 1965: 32) and to entirely undo the particular knotting of Real, Imaginary and Symbolic that earlier and even authentically mad writing such as that of Rousseau supported and strengthened. In replicating the conditions under which the subject ordinarily founders into psychosis, Beckett's work offers a privileged access to a space that is perhaps neither mad nor sane, but impossibly and precariously refuses such differentiation.

It is curious to think of Beckett and Lacan, born on the same date six years apart, living and working alongside each other in mid-twentieth century Paris, both of them, and in not dissimilar ways, interrogating the possibilities and impasses of representation. In his 1975 Yale seminar, Lacan sees the points of convergence between psychoanalysis and literature as quite restricted, but one point of convergence is certainly the topic of representation, central to both. Freud's master of philosophy was Franz Brentano, who viewed the psyche as being in itself representation, and wide swathes of Lacan's work, using various metaphoric underlays, echo the largely Freudian position that the mechanisms known as repression and foreclosure refer to two separate processes: one that permits, perhaps even constitutes, representation; the other that installs a blockage, an impasse, the menace of arrest that threatens the entire weave of psychic life.[1] This distinction was very clearly expressed by Beckett himself in 1949 when he opined: "There is more than a difference of degree between being short, short of the world, short of self, and being without these esteemed commodities. The one is a predicament, the other not" (Beckett 1965: 122).

By the time Lacan was teaching the seminar *RSI* (1974–5) his question about the possibilities of representation had become: What knots the subject? In *Les psychoses* (1955–6) the answer to this question seemed clear; "the ambiguity and the gap in the imaginary relation require something that maintains a relation, a function, a distance. This is the very meaning of the Oedipus complex" (Lacan 1993: 96). Traversing the Oedipus complex is then the process by which we are delivered a world and a self, and Lacan puts it powerfully when he asserts that this network "is necessary so that everything doesn't suddenly reduce to nothing, so that the entire veil of the imaginary does not suddenly draw back and disappear into yawning blackness" (Lacan 1993: 99). In *RSI* his question is still the same, but complicated by reservations as to Freud's solution. Freud, who was not a Lacanian, Lacan says, invented something he called psychical reality, and repeating what he had said twenty years earlier, Lacan elaborates: "What he calls psychical reality has perfectly well a name, it is what he calls the Oedipus complex. Without the Oedipus complex nothing holds together." Thirteen years previously, in the seminar on identification, Lacan had asked the same question, suggesting that it was in fact a very difficult question to answer, and that without the existence of the symbolic order it would be impossible (Lacan 1961–2: 14/3). Here he goes further. There is, he says, something elided in Freud's formulation. What is elided is a particular conjunction of the Real, the Imaginary and the Symbolic, a knotting that he calls a triplicity linked to meaning, but which is predicated on a fundamental circularity. Lacan's very convoluted syntax at this point makes it difficult to ascertain if he is also critiquing the oedipal triangular structure here: "I believe that what Freud stated not, not I am saying about the Oedipus complex is to be rejected" (Lacan 1964–5: 14/1). The problem he is grappling with appears to be that what he calls "the world as representation" depends on the conjunction of the three consistencies named Symbolic, Imaginary and Real, but he suspects, "there subsist in the indefinite order, dimensions supposable as being more than three with which there is constituted our world, namely our representation" (Lacan 1974–5: 21/1). Freud then would have needed not three, but four consistencies. One year later Lacan is talking about the sinthome,[2] which has become literally our only substance, as Žižek puts it, "the only possible support of our being, the only point that gives consistency to the subject" (Žižek 1989: 75). In the seminar on desire, this function had been assigned to the fundamental fantasy in the absence of which, he claims, the subject is exposed to the darkness of trauma. We hence move from Oedipus complex to fundamental fantasy to symptom. Of the symptom, the last avatar in this series, Žižek writes, "symptom is the way we the subjects 'avoid madness,' the way we choose something (the symptom formation) instead of nothing (radical psychotic autism)" (ibid. 75).

The concept of the nothing, psychoanalytic, philosophic or literary, is of course much vaster than Žižek's formulation, which, for purposes of focus, I would like to adopt in this paper, thereby risking over-simplification.

What Žižek presents as a binary opposition—either a self and a world that can subsist, or the catastrophe of madness—may not leave room for the interstitial solutions Lacan was seeking in his year-long seminar *Le sinthome* (1975–6), whereas a year earlier in *RSI* he is trying to effect a shift from Freud's psychical reality to what he, Lacan, calls operational reality. In earlier seminars, Lacan had also explored the possibilities and impasses of representation from a number of other angles, notably perspectivist painting and mathematical numeration. Whatever else they aim to establish, each of these directions would seem to suggest that every representation is as he says of the Borromean knot, an artifice of representation. This is true even of number, with on one occasion Jacques-Alain Miller taking the floor to explain the factitiousness, the grammatical sleight of hand necessitated by Frege's predication of zero as the origin of numeration, which Miller names as an astonishing conjuring trick, since improbably it effects the creation of something from nothing, the emergence from zero of the one that permits all subsequent numeration.

Several of Lacan's middle seminars wrestle with the manner in which the functions of repetition and representation are intricated, and lean heavily, often with impenetrable results, on Frege's writings; a celebrated example being the insight with which he baffled his American audience at the Structuralist Conference at Johns Hopkins in 1966, when he announced that:

> the question of the two is for us the question of the subject, and here we reach a fact of psychoanalytical experience in as much as the two does not complete the one to make two, but must repeat the one to exist. This first is the only one necessary to explain the genesis of number, and only one repetition is necessary to constitute the status of the subject.
>
> (Lacan 1972: 191)

By the seventies, however, the factitiousness of this process is too obvious not to require further commentary. In the seminar *RSI*, interrogating the role of number in terms of that which holds, he refers to science as something that counts. It manages to make some things sure where there is number. We have the greatest difficulty, Lacan suggests, in not taking the sequence of numbers as constitutive of the Real. But number seems. In more than one place in this seminar, number is described as a semblance, the extraordinary thing being that this semblance, created from nothing, from zero, is a highly effective mathematical entity. "It can happen," Lacan says, "that there is no root, that no root exists, and when it does not exist that does not upset us, we make it exist, namely, we invent the category of the imaginary root and what is more, that gives results" (Lacan 1974–5: 11/2). In *On the Way to Language*, Heidegger defines the word as that which brings each thing into being and holds it there. In *RSI* Lacan ascribes this function to the platonic eidos, which he translates as the Imaginary. Without the eidos, the Imaginary, there is no chance that names will stick to things, as he says in the lesson of March 11 (ibid.). Furthermore, consistency, which is of the Imaginary order, is not only that which permits numeration to function, it is what underwrites the world as representation. "Consistency for the speaking being is what is fabricated and what is invented" (ibid.: 11/2), as Lacan says, giving to this statement the widest possible import, including in its ambit all of human history, and specifically the history of religion. He refers to the Book of Genesis as "the first phase of this human imagination that is God" (ibid.: 11/3).

It is not difficult to see that Lacan's lengthy expounding on the genesis of number in *Crucial Problems in Psychoanalysis* picked up on here is applicable to all human genesis and as such to the Book of Genesis itself. This statement has been expanded on by an American scholar, Elaine Scarry, currently Professor of French at Harvard, who describes the Bible as a monumental artifact that is also a monumental description of the nature of artifice, a tireless laying bare of the workings of the imagination, which has managed to substantiate itself so convincingly that it has been able to function as one of the major supports of Western civilization (Scarry 1985: 180). This is a point worth pausing over, since this impetus is exactly opposite to that which fuels Beckett's fiction. A narrative that presumably begins with a telling dependent on a narrator goes on to free itself from this dependency to become not only freestanding but to install the thing brought into being, the created object, God as creator. In other words, the original terms of this activity are now inverted in such a way that the created object, God, is infused with a reality, more densely substantiated than that of the originary narrative gesture. This fictionalized inversion, as Lacan says in *RSI*, marks all of human history.

It is this inversion, this sleight of hand that Beckett refuses, this operational reality that he excoriates. To attempt representation at all is, he says, a fraught project since "the object of representation resists representation either because of its accidents or because of its substance" (Beckett 1983: 135), and in light of such refractoriness what remains for the artist to represent are the conditions of this resistance, this impossibility, resulting, Beckett says, in "a literature of the unword" (ibid.: 54), a place of impenetrable proximities where language becoming opaque and empty opens onto the bleak reaches where there is no more world, a minatory absence, ordinarily screened by the veils of the everyday.

If Žižek describes the sinthome as an answer to the question why is there something instead of nothing, one would have to describe Beckett's work as a sustained attack on both question and answer.

The American critic Hugh Kenner links Beckett's work to a recognizably Irish nihilistic tradition traceable through Sterne, Swift, Joyce and Flann O'Brien, suggesting that, situated as Ireland is on the very edge of Europe, the humanist project that makes of nothingness, pain and death way-stations towards recuperation never really took hold and was always more likely to be reversed than endorsed (Kenner 1962: 37). In the hands of Irish writers, this reversal frequently functions as a comic device, as for example in Flann O'Brien's *The Third Policeman* when Policeman MacCruiskeen shows the narrator the small decorative boxes that he fabricates in his spare time at the barracks, the smallest of all being nearly half a size smaller than ordinary invisibility. "There now," said MacCruiskeen,

> Six years ago they began to get invisible. Nobody has ever seen the last five I made because no glass is strong enough to make them big enough to be regarded truly as the smallest things ever made. The one I am making is nearly as small as nothing. Number One would hold a million of them at the same time and there would be room left for a pair of woman's horse britches if they were rolled up. The dear knows where it will stop and terminate.
>
> (O'Brien 1967: 74).

Here syntax and structure retain a forward momentum while the narrative itself recounts the fabrication of nothingness; in other words, an oxymoron at the level of narrative rather than at the level of rhetoric.

Throughout Beckett's work, oxymoron can be said to function as a signature rhetorical ploy, most typically recognizable as a speech that negates itself in the instant of utterance: "I seem to speak, it is not I, about me, it is not about me," as he writes in the opening phrases of *The Unnamable* (Beckett 1959: 293). Each time the veil of the Imaginary is rolled out, it is rolled up. Nothing is allowed to consist, to subsist. This is a narrative voice that insists only on the expression that "there is nothing to express, nothing with which to express, no power to express, no desire to express, together with the obligation to express" (Beckett 1965: 103); but a narrative voice that in Blanchot's view is the most critical voice, which can, unheard, make itself heard. Whence our tendency when hearing it, he adds, to take it for the oblique voice of madness (Blanchot 1982: 221).

This oxymoron (classically, a statement that negates itself), a something that becomes nothing, carries very varying emotional weight throughout Beckett's writing. In the early work *Watt*, it operates with a balletic formal grace edged with some discomfort but not yet freighted with the anguish it will later bear. Watt living in the house of Mr. Knott finds that happenings that initially appear to be fairly solid, such as the arrival of a father and son, the Galls, to tune the piano, gradually become leached of all semantic import and so reduced in density that they become merely the geometrical games that time plays with space. As the narrator puts it: "What distressed Watt in this incident of the Galls father and son, and in subsequent incidents, was not so much that he did not know what had happened, for he did not care what had happened, as that nothing had happened, with the utmost formal distinctness and that it continued to happen, . . . that nothing had happened with all the clarity and solidity of something" (Beckett 1963: 73).

Even in the first part of the trilogy, *Molloy*, this signature reversal can function as simple irony:

> I wrapped myself in swathes of newspaper, and did not shed them until the earth awoke for good in April. The Times Literary Supplement was admirably adapted to this purpose, of a never failing toughness and impermeability. Even farts made no impression on it. I can't help it, gas escapes from my fundament on the least pretext, it's hard not to mention it now and then, however great my distaste. One day I counted them. Three hundred and fifteen farts in nineteen hours, or an average of over sixteen farts an hour. After all it's not excessive. Four farts every fifteen minutes. It's nothing. Not even one fart every four minutes. It's unbelievable. Damn it I hardly fart at all, I should never have mentioned it. Extraordinary how mathematics helps you to know yourself.
>
> (Beckett 1959: 30)

But these comic overtones become submerged over time, and the negatory ferocity of oxymoron, visible heretofore at the level of rhetoric or narrative, begins to bite into the fabric of language itself. The linguist Roman Jakobson isolates two aspects of language, material and relational, lexical and grammatical. For *The Unnamable*, with respect to the first of these, the factitious demarcations by which language structures the universe have long been laid waste. "Call that morning," he scoffs, or of his own progress, "call that on" as the unraveling of the bond between names and things maroons him among nameless images and imageless names (Beckett 1959: 411). Of the relational aspects, Benveniste, with whom Lacan worked closely for a while, has written lucidly of the tiny but essential grammatical ties by which man constitutes himself as subject.[3] In Beckett's late work, a disaggregation, an unknotting of the relation of the subject to language at the level of these mostly overlooked ties, becomes pervasive.

The most obvious of these ploys is the pronoun "I." "It is the fault of the pronouns," says the Unnamable. "I will not say I again, it is too red a herring" (Beckett 1959: 408), but personal pronouns are only the first instances of subjective mooring. Other pronouns that share the same status are the indicators of deixis, this, that, here, now, and all their correlatives, yesterday, last year etc. which of necessity are defined only in relation to this speaking "I," as are also verbal tenses. "Linguistic time is self referential," as Benveniste writes, "determined for each speaker by the instances of discourse related to it" (Benveniste 1966: 227). These small grammatical ties that knot the speaker to his utterance have all come undone in Beckett's late prose. "How long have I been here, what a question, I've often wondered. And often I could answer. An hour, a month, a year, a century, depending on what I meant by here and me, and being, and there" (Beckett 1974: 8). In the last of his works Beckett called a "novel," *How It Is*, there are three untitled sections written in short recurring prose stanzas that are completely without punctuation. No sentence begins, no sentence ends. The opening stanza does not really begin anything since it is also a constantly occurring refrain:

> How it is I quote before Pim with Pim after Pim how it is
> three parts I say it as I hear it.
>
> (Beckett 1964: 7)

Beckett's previous novel *The Unnamable* had opened with the questions: "Where now? Who now? When now?" interrogating the basic categories of space, time and subjectivity. Here, these have all dissolved. The voice speaks of "great tracts of time" with markers of identity such as memory, images or wishes all reduced to attributes assigned or not to the speaker by some outside force. So, for example: "the wish for something else no that doesn't seem have been given to me this time the image of other things with me there in the mud the dark the sack within reach no that doesn't have been put in my life this time" (Beckett 1964: 12). Furthermore, the voice does not own what it utters. "I say it as I hear it," is a recurring refrain. Words are cited, quoted, repeated, reducing the speaking "I" to the status of echo or automaton.

In the seminar *Le sinthome* Lacan marvels at how seldom we so called normals notice that our relation to language is for the most part precisely this parasitic dependency, this being spoken. In the seminar *Les psychoses* he noted how rare and significant are the moments when the subject really speaks, speaks in his own name. Only the psychotic, who is rigorous in a way the rest of us are not, fully experiences the consequences of this parasitic relation, the fact that in the absence or refusal of the grammatical ploys that permit the subject to lay hold of language, language in a menacing reversal can lay hold of the subject. Not to occupy the nominative position is to be shunted towards the accusative, as is poignantly recognized in *Texts for Nothing*. "Who would I be if I could be? What would I say if I had a voice, who says this, saying it's me? Answer simply, someone answer simply. It's the same old stranger as ever, for whom alone accusative I exist" (Beckett 1974: 22).

In concluding, I turn again to Blanchot who suggests that to write is to become the echo of what cannot stop talking, to endow this endless chatter with the authority of one's own silence. Literature stills the ragged clamor that subtends human existence, the gigantic murmur of uninhabited language that lies in wait for all of us but that besets the psychotic.[4] It is Beckett's formidable achievement to have made accessible this menacing murmurous absence. The most celebrated book in Irish literature, the ninth century Book of Kells, in a reprise of Horace, speaks inspiringly across the centuries of its task as that of "turning darkness into light," but because madness exists there are darknesses that remain dark. Beckett makes it clear that it is one of the signatures of our humanity to acknowledge these darknesses, along with the helplessness to which they can consign us.

Notes

1 "The theory of repression is the cornerstone on which the whole structure of psychoanalysis rests" (*S.E. XIV*, 16). Like almost all Freudian concepts it is vast and wide-ranging. For purposes of definition and clarity here it may be described as a process bearing on potentially overwhelming representations—thoughts, images, memories—that the subject repels from awareness, thus constituting an unconscious knowing separated from the rest of the psyche. In contrast to this process, foreclosure is a primordial expulsion resulting in the absence of unconscious representation, a vortical nothing in the psychic space where repression effects the trace of a minatory something.

2 Predicated on the Borromean knot, this late formulation in Lacan's work focuses on a fourth element in the subject as that which holds the Symbolic, the Imaginary and the Real together, something that functions in a manner analogous to the Oedipus complex of earlier theorizations, but that could be of a quite different order, e.g. the activity of writing. This fourth element in knotting the Symbolic, Imaginary and Real together is the something that prevents the subject from foundering into psychosis.

3 In his seminal work *Problems of General Linguistics*, Benveniste repeatedly insists on the deceptive ease with which habit obscures the profound difference between language as a system of signs and language assumed into use by the individual. When the individual appropriates it, many elements of language are transformed into what he calls "instances of discourse, characterized by a system of internal references of which 'I' is the key" (220) and that include a series of "indicators" "which from their form and their systematic capacity, belong to different classes, some being pronouns, other adverbs, and still others, adverbial locutions" (218).

4 All through *The Psychoses* Lacan makes the point that we are all on the receiving end of an internal commentary all the time but, unlike the psychotic, do not take it seriously (74, 110, 138).

Bibliography

Beckett, Samuel. *Molloy; Malone Dies; The Unnamable*. London: Calder and Boyars 1959.
—— *Proust and Three Dialogues with George Duthuit*. London: Calder 1965.
—— *Watt*. London: Calder and Boyars 1970.
—— *Texts for Nothing*. London: Calder and Boyars 1974.
—— *How It Is*. London: Calder 1964.
—— *Disjecta*. London: Calder 1983.
Benveniste, Emile. *Problems in General Linguistics*. Miami: University of Miami Press 1974.
Blanchot, Maurice. *The Siren's Song*. Trans. Sacha Rabinovich. Brighton: Harvester 1982.
Lacan, Jacques. *The Psychoses*. Trans. Russell Grigg. London: Routledge 1993.
—— "Identification" 1961–2, private trans. Cormac Gallagher, St. Vincent's University Hospital, Dublin.
—— *Crucial Problems in Psychoanalysis* 1964–5, private trans. Cormac Gallagher, St. Vincent's University Hospital, Dublin.

—— *Le sinthome* 1975–6, Publication hors commerce, Association freudienne, Paris.

—— *RSI* 1974–5, private trans. Cormac Gallagher, St. Vincent's University Hospital, Dublin.

—— "Of Structure as an Inmixing of an Otherness Prerequisite to Any Subject Whatsoever," in *The Structuralist Controversy*, ed. R. Macksie and E. Donato, Baltimore and London: The Johns Hopkins Press 1970, pp. 186–200.

Kenner, Hugh. *Beckett, A Critical Study*. London: Calder 1962.

O'Brien, Flann. *The Third Policeman*. London: Hart-Davis McGibbon 1967.

Scarry, Elaine. *The Body in Pain*. Oxford. Oxford University Press 1985.

Welsford, Edith. *The Fool*. London: Faber & Faber 1935.

Žižek, Slavoj. *The Sublime Object of Ideology*. London: Verso 1989.

18

READING MAYHEM

Schizophrenic writing and the engine of madness

Manya Steinkoler

There is a medieval saying that "madness is more a device or engine, an *ingenium,* than a destiny." In the Latin for engine, *ingenium,* we find the root of genius, as well as the connotation of a natural disposition as we read the root, *gen,* appearing in "engendering" and "congenital." Destiny connotes a narrative quest, a drama with a definable "end," and concerns the long-term link between psychoanalysis and tragedy, with the unconscious becoming conscious, Oedipus, awakening to his horror, and tearing out his eyes. *Ingenium* is a creative ability to escape from destiny, like Ulysses and Diomedes' ingenious Trojan horse: it is an invention that both is and allows for the unexpected. The horse was a construction, a work of masterful engineering, related to another definition of *ingenium,* "to engineer." An ingenious invention, we can think of a building, a birth, or in the case I will discuss today, a writing.

A gifted schizophrenic—an actor, a writer, and a homeopathic doctor—would visit the hospital where I worked like a great prince taking the spa waters for a brief respite from his royal duties. It is by recourse to a specific text of his that I will discuss how showing the "engine" at work can be a kind of "genius," one that differs from the work of sublimation in neurosis. This essay contemplates Lacan's notion of the infinite line, not as "repressed" or unconscious, but as Real. In this regard, the delusion (*délire*) is itself a production, an invention, literally off (*de*) the tracks (lira), that exceeds the furrows of the Real. Basking in the Real completely, delusion can often seem utterly unreadable, opaque, impenetrable. Running off the tracks, or inventing new ones, this "madness," a delusional construction, is nevertheless a work, and, at times even—and such a debate is far beyond the scope of this essay—a work of art. Madness is an art, we could hypothesize, that gives form to this "engine." In this case, it reveals our "natural disposition" as highly unnatural, twisted, rambling, careening, circling, and thus more human. This artful madness exposes a fundamental senselessness of the human engendered by language itself.

What form can be given to this engine? Lacan tells us: a circle. He writes in *Le Sinthome*, "But the Freudian unconscious . . . it is just what I said, to know the rapport, the rapport that there is between a body that is a stranger to us and something that makes a circle, an infinite line, that in any event is the one (the D.I. infinite line), one (the circle) equivalent to the other (the D.I.) and something that is the unconscious" (Lacan 1976; my translation).[1]

"Le Jeu mémoire du dieu-serpent Mehen" ("The Game of Memory of the God-Serpent Mehen") is a text that attempts to render the infinite line or circle as the hole of the Real; the writer knows about it. He is inside.[2] This text is the synopsis of a screenplay that has not been written. The author—I will call him Ixidor, the Basque version of Isidor, which means "gift of Isis"—is a supremely functional, widely read, brilliant schizophrenic. He took a screenwriting course and was delighted to "finally understand" how screenplays are constructed. "Screenplays have a pie shape and events happen in a certain order and at a certain time," he explained to me, pleased with the new understanding the screenwriting class had afforded him. Ixidor would insist on the importance of this discovery. "Form" is an imaginary container, an ego, lacking in psychosis and in schizophrenia in particular. The "pie shape" where events "took place in time," was a "find" for Ixidor. We note that the pie (*tarte* in French) shape is round, like the Mehen "board game" from ancient Egypt he will choose for his subject matter. He is literally matching the round form. Ixidor would write nearly 300 pages, "obsessively," he told me. Then, carefully cutting his work down to fit the pie model he had learned in class, he would "now know where to put things that happened, by following the formula." He was thus able to reduce the nearly 300 pages down to eleven dense, almost unreadable single-spaced pages. Those eleven pages are the subject of this essay.

Ixidor's text is virtually unreadable. My exercise of reducing his synopsis is an attempt to focus on what I consider to be crucial to understanding what is at stake in its construction in the first place: *an attempt to restore the Imaginary register.* This is the sense that can nevertheless be salvaged in that blinding, teeming torrent of narration of a constantly traumatic Real, full of accidents, murders and deaths— the mayhem Ixidor inhabits.

Synopsis

Marc Delatour reads to Leila (no last name), *a young woman the same age as he who is in a coma, rescued from a traffic accident* (*accident de circulation*), *in a hospital room. Marc volunteers in the service of Dr. Leroux to read aloud to comatose patients* (*roux* means red in French and is homophonic with "round." We note the theme of turning, of encircling). *Dr. Leroux is a man Marc knew when he himself was hospitalized as a child for burns in a terrible car accident* (another *accident de circulation*) *where he witnessed his father's death.* (Marc and Leila both suffered a "circulation accident": Leila is Marc's double in the mirror.) This is notably where the story begins.

We hear a voice on Marc's car CD player that Marc does not hear, "Marc, help me!" At the same time, Marc sees a text message from his uncle Sethim telling him to pick up a package for his next appointment. His uncle Sethim was responsible years before for the car accident that killed Marc's father and sent Marc to the hospital as a child. *Marc's father had betrayed Marc's mother, Sethim's sister, Isabelle* (let us note the semantic relation to the Egyptian goddess: Isabelle/Isis), *so the vengeful Sethim adjusted the brakes of the car to kill his sister's husband, never imagining that his nephew Marc would be in the car and would suffer terrible burns to his back while watching his father bleed to death.* (Seth is the god of darkness and chaos in the Egyptian pantheon; Seth killed Osiris, his own brother, making Isis, Osiris' consort, lack. We can read a prior story in the Egyptian myth where Isis is rendered incomplete, a tragedy of Seth's doing. The myth explains the primal mother's lack and finds a cause for it, a way that the schizophrenic is posing the question of an originary fault.) *Before visiting his uncle Sethim, Marc finds a holster with four needles, two gold and two silver. They are acupuncture needles that should only be used once. Marc thinks they might be valuable and puts them in his pocket, pricking his index finger accidentally.* (Once again a recurrence of the "*accident de circulation*" occurs in his blood, literally, his "circulation." I will come back to this point of the blood since it concerns the Real of the body as well as the tragic particularity of Ixidor's family history.) *His uncle opens the apartment door sucking his index finger and has a package for Marc in the other hand. Marc takes the package and leaves in traffic which "roule"* (roule means turns, rolls, goes. Like the drive itself, Mehen is the story of the "engine" of the drive. The drive is the fundamental deformation by language that Ixidor's text tries to explain by way of the "game" of the Egyptian god).

We note the doubling of Marc with his uncle; they both have a pricked finger. The doubling is less an issue of "repetition" or coincidence, on the side of the Freudian uncanny, than an insistence of the transitivism of the mirror stage. Transitivism is the mechanism at work through the entire text, making for a series of doublings by way of which Marc, Ixidor's double, tries to understand the logic of being played by Mehen. The snaking, spiraling "plot" doubles on itself as it turns, allowing for a dizzying mirroring that makes meaning impossible and at the same time gives us fascinated pause as we try to make sense in a madhouse hall of mirrors. The text is jam-packed with doublings of brothers and sisters modeled on those of the Egyptian pantheon, with metonymies of blood, circulation and movement utterly impossible to summarize, since they are less about "plot" or any narrative "destiny" than about the construction of these metonymies themselves in a whirling spiral, like the snake Mehen itself as Marc "progresses" inside the serpent's body.

Going to the appointment set for him by his uncle Sethim, Marc rings the bell of Isis Consulting at the same time as his phone beeps, asking him to meet Dr. Leroux at the hospital later that night. Hanging up the phone, now at the appointment to which his uncle sent him, he finds a "sensual and beautiful" woman at the door. "Marc Delatour?" she asks. "Himself," he answers to himself in his head.

The fact that Marc answers the woman "in his head," and she acknowledges his silent answer, should already make us wonder about her "real presence." The reader of this synopsis has heard *both* the voice of the CD that Marc has not heard at the beginning, and the "himself" spoken in Marc's head. While these could be managed by "voice over" in a film, this technique is not mentioned in Ixidor's synopsis. The writing thus implies *a reader* of this text—not a film audience. A reader is necessary to Ixidor's synopsis. The reader is a part of the synopsis, allowing the synopsis to be written, implying the intention for it to be read. In this regard, I am reminded of Gaetano Benedetti's idea of the "transitional subject." The "transitional subject" brings up the question of Ixidor himself as an author who "borrows" the reader he is lacking; the writing is in part made possible as an inclusion of this reader. This concerns the direction of the cure in psychosis as it marks the beginnings of the possibility of reading, the creation of space and of legibility. The text is "about" what it does; it shows how reading becomes possible. When I mentioned to Ixidor that he had made an ingenious series with turning, circulation, movement and spiraling, he was surprised. The choices were not conscious choices of an author expressing an intention. He was thrilled to hear what I had to say about his text and asked me to talk to him about it. I talked about the high level of metonymy that he had put into play. He slapped his knee in sheer delight. He had looked forward to hearing what I had to say. Ixidor was able to look forward to something. I was the reader of this text; he was the writer of his mayhem.

Ixidor was eager to tell me that the ancient Egyptian board game, "the game of Mehen," has rules that no one understands and that historians have not been able to unearth. He spent time at the library and at the Louvre studying the game. His screenplay synopsis is an attempt to give logical sense to this "being played" by the god in whose body we live, the body of language.

"Follow me, young man." Facing him, she states: "I am, myself, all alone, Isis Consulting, CEO, director, secretary, I am everything, including the bank." "You are what I need." She gives him a board on which is a snake rolled seven times on itself; it is the game of Mehen. (In Ixidor's version of the game, crevices find corresponding pieces that *fit* into the serpent's body; the fitting allows for movement to proceed along the inside of the snake into the next inner coil.) The woman tells him: *"The aim, to win: the stakes: memory. The seven circles are also a labyrinth, a clock and a spiral. There are four pairs of gods (Marc walks up the stairs four by four) Osiris and Isis, Seth and Nethys, Anubis and Maat—* and *"Mehen, the encircler."* (We note here that there are four pairs, but Mehen, the serpent himself, is conspicuously not in a pair.) *The woman explains to Marc that the God-Serpent is the master of the Game.* (We further note that there exists a master of the game who is not Isis; Isis is incomplete.) *The buckle on the cross*

of Ankh is the sign of reincarnation, a symbol and a key of locked memory. (It is not truth that is locked, as in neurosis, but the logic of the Real.) I quote: *"A life in another body? One life? Many? Who is the other? And who are you? Him? Half and half? How does memory come? Like a bullet, an arrow or a boomerang?"* (Mehen 2011, unpublished text). It is noteworthy that memory is depicted as something that pierces, like the acupuncture needles earlier and also as something that circulates in terms of the nervous system: it is Real. The "trauma" of being subjected to language is imaginarized in these phallic terms, as a piercing, a making of a hole. The "game of Mehen" is the inscription of trauma that makes meaning possible at the origin of legibility itself. Jean-Jacques Moscovitz has noted that the psychotic is working to inscribe a trauma that has not taken place (Moscovitz 2005: 161).

Marc signs the contract given him by Isis and accidentally pricks his index finger. Blood falls onto the board game. (We note that the "signed contract" is not simply signed—it is "real" and involves the body. This is similarly seen in the early "blood pact" made in childhood with Julie, his childhood sweetheart, whom he met while convalescing in the hospital after his accident; Marc and Julie exchange blood, their pricked fingers touching, and Julie is magically cured.) *A pendulum is heard as the blood falls and clock ticks. In the hospital, Dr. Leroux tells Marc that Julie, his childhood friend, the very one he met in the same hospital some thirty years earlier is back in France and has been hospitalized for a blood disease that cannot be understood* (like the game of Mehen) *and is rapidly dying.* (Importantly, Julie is dying of this blood disease at the very moment Marc signed the contract with Isis; she had been brought back to life as a child by the blood pact made with Marc. Like Leila, Julie is a double of Marc. As such, Julie is also a childhood double for Leila, the woman Marc was reading to in the hospital when the story commenced. The terrifying encounter with Isis is an encounter with the lack of the M(Other). The pricked finger is a real stand in for symbolic castration that does not exist; a hole substitutes for a cut. Not separated from the Thing, castration and death are the same.)

Marc will have sex with Isis "as though drugged" (like Julie is drugged). *We will learn at the same time that Julie's coma was a consequence of a toxin she was forced to consume by her adopted mother. Marc is "drugged" by sex—like the toxin that is killing Julie.* (Blood acts as a Derridean pharmakon throughout the text, curing and killing at once.) *Julie's evil poisoning mother invented a toxin that would magically rekindle its force, giving Julie leukemia if Julie ever left her. Julie wants to go back to Paris, the home of her birth father and her childhood love, Marc. Julie's birth mother had been a criminal and a traitor to her father and to France, her father's country, resulting in her father committing suicide, just as Marc's father had betrayed his mother and his mother subsequently died.* (The reader notes the dizzying mirrors.) *Years later, Julie is back in the hospital, in a coma, her blood poisoned by her adoptive mother.* Julie is poisoned by her mother's toxin; Marc is drugged by Isis' seduction, an encounter he was sent to by his uncle Sethim (the double of Julie's evil mother). What is important is that

Marc and Julie are drugged at the same time. The woman is not metaphorized in schizophrenia; she *is* the mother.) *At the end of the screenplay—after many Hoffmann-esque mad happenings—Julie will die, and her spirit, initially intending to pass into Dr. Leroux's unborn baby, won't be able to since Leroux's girlfriend will abort it. Thus, Julie's spirit will find herself alive again in the no-longer-comatose Leila's as Leila awakes from the coma, and is now, in part, Julie reincarnated.*

Before interpreting this overladen text in more detail, I interject to relate the biography of the author. Ixidor was born on the same day that his four-year-old sister died of gangrene, *of a blood infection* from an accidental shrapnel wound she contracted crossing the street when a bomb detonated. Prior to his birth, his mother had two stillborn babies, both boys, and had named them—despite being stillborn—the very same name as Ixidor. Ixidor's mother was bedridden during the last weeks of her pregnancy with Ixidor and was not able to tend to her daughter, who died as a result. Unable to bear her grief and guilt, she gave Ixidor to his older sister to raise and care for during the first six years of his life. Ixidor's mother was present in the home but absent for him during his early life, often ill and severely depressed; his sister became his primary caretaker. (We note the fraternal couplings of the Egyptian pantheon so important in Ixidor's text.) He was returned to his mother when the sister married and he was six years old. His father was an educated architect, absent most of the time, and his mother, a peasant. There was an older brother who died in young adulthood as well. I point out that we are not speaking of "psycho-biography" in this instance since there is not yet something we could call the psyche or anything by which we could understand the word "biography," or life narrative. Ixidor is the child of all this—of what he was for the father, the mother, the older sister, and even the sister who died at his birth. The "cure" and love-death with Julie is also a solution to the "killing" of his sister by his birth and the loss and subsequent re-finding of his mother. Ixidor is the crypt of what he was for all of these people: an effigy to the dead brothers who died before him and whose name he carries, bearing their death with him as a constant memorial in his psychosis.

The story is Marc's delirium, which comes to explain the animation of Leila, the comatose patient in the hospital. Although taking place at the end of the story, in my reading, it is actually the "animation" of Leila that triggers the delirium—one which we could name Mehen—another name of the subject (Marc) himself since "*je*" (I) is homophonic with "*jeu*" (game) of the *dieu-serpent, Mehen* (the God-Serpent, Mehen). This homophony illustrates that in psychosis, the subject is not separated from the Thing, here the serpent, or what Lacan calls in his later work the circle, a "material Real," the infinite line. The Other and Marc are the same; Marc is the serpent, and is played by the serpent since there is no "I" except the "game of the Other" to which the schizophrenic is subjected unceasingly. We note here Lacan's idea that the Other *is* the body.

The delusion is a subjective creation, naming the subject as not separated from the Other. Moreover, in the form of a serpent, Marc guards the status of the signifier as phallic. We see this identification in his name: "Marc Delatour" means "Marc of the turning," "Marc of the game" or "Marc of the tower (the phallic signifier/snake)" as well as Marc of the *jeu/game* of "Mark-ing Mehen" and "Marc of the turn." "Marc of the turn," identified with the game itself, *shows how the engine works.*

What "encircles" is Mehen, or, in Lacanian terms, the Other, language. The proto-subject is "inside" the body of the serpent. The schizophrenic tries to show a logic to his "being in the hole," a hole whose existence in neurosis is covered up by the metaphor of the Name-of-the-Father, the fantasy, and the symptom. Mehen shows that we are subjected to language without a "cause"; that we are played and mastered, in Ixidor's case, by an unbarred Other, a god whose rules we cannot fathom; playing the game, we are always played. While Ixidor tells a truth that neurosis masks, it is not the "truth of neurosis." This "being played" has nothing to do with truth or revelation. To inhabit the world of Ixidor's text is to be completely subjected to the Real; nothing is missing except the logic of this subjection that Ixidor will try to fathom via his protagonist Marc.

Is the "genius" of a writing that reveals the working of the engine a sinthome? Like the coiling of the serpent Mehen, Joyce's fourth circle as sinthome traces the initial fault-line, making him escape the death of the soul, of the spirit, of the "*ingenio.*" The sinthome is an artifice, a creative prosthesis. Lacan says that there is a reduction to a structure of "LOM," an acronym homophonic with the French word for man, *l'homme.* Written this way, the "is the big Other of Language itself" (Lacan 1976: 1). Further, in the Lacanian neologism "LOM," we hear the eternal "Om" as well as "Eloïm." Like Joyce's, Ixidor's is a writing that shows the engine, revealing the body of the speaking being as the very body as the Other, of language itself as Mehen, inseparable from the body of Marc.

In my reading, Marc experiences mortifying anxiety at the fact that Leila comes to life while he is reading to her, as though her animation is a result of his reading. Is it the spirit of Ju*lie* that reanimates *Lei*la or is it Marc's reading to her (*il lit*) by her bedside (*à côté du lit*) at the beginning of the screenplay synopsis? We can think of the voice object coupled with the stream of words calling to someone in a coma—dead and alive—as a mirror image of the psychotic subject. Life –the psychotic tells us—is made from, and is a result of, language; like Marc, Ixidor is trying to read (*lit/Julie/Leila*). Yet for the psychotic, the cancelling function of language cannot work and a "reading" of the stream of words and of his place in it cannot take place. We have more an insistent echolalia of "*lit*" than anything properly at the level of meaning or metaphor. The fact that the word means: read, bed, dregs, deposit, the third person singular of the verb "to tie" and *il* (he) spelled backwards does not help us at all. He tells us quite clearly at the beginning: his words are the Other's words. He reads to Julie from the books in her knapsack. He reads (*il lit*) to her in her bed (*lit*); what matters in the echolalia is the echo, the mirror.

The delirium serves to explain Leila's re-animation and answer the question: where does subjectivity come from? *How are we alive?* Its answer is Mehen: the cause of re-animation *is* reincarnation, a transfer of spirit passing from one body to another making the word, quite literally, "incarnate." (The fact that Ixidor was named after his two stillborn brothers cannot be ignored here.) We read, *Lei-la*—lit-là—words are there—là, in the Other. Here and there, they are also in the reader, in Marc himself, thus further establishing a mirror between Marc and Leila, his comatose "listener." Mehen is an attempt to give sense to what makes no sense: the "game of the God-Serpent" tries to establish a causal relation between language and the life of a body, to the sense of what it means to be alive. Mehen answers the question, "What causes/makes a speaking being?"

Lacan tells us, following de Clérambault, that the delusion is an elementary phenomenon. Like the Egyptian cartouches, this element *is* the very structure itself, undialectizable and irreducible to something other than itself, "a truth that isn't hidden" (Lacan 1981: 28). Analogical with the function of language itself as metonymy, as stream, as coiling snake, Mehen plays unbeknownst to us—making us "not ourselves." Leila comes to life while Marc reads to her and he does not know why. Subjectivity, here literalized as wakefulness, remains enigmatic and threatening without the Name-of-the-Father, especially for the psychotic for whom the unconscious remains external, a fact this text illustrates so beautifully. It does not make sense that we speak, only that we are spoken. Since without lack, not separated from the Thing, why one speaks and why the other speaks *is a real question*. What do they want, all these speaking beings? To be birthed in language is to be born into senselessness; it is language that is the real monster, the "engine" that Mehen "ingeniously" signifies and tries to make readable.

Marc takes a volunteer job reading to a woman in a coma. He reads books he finds in her bag; the words are always words of the other, words that don't belong to him, aimed at a dead/alive woman's body, whose gaze is a dead one's. We see the contact between words and flesh here in a non-subjective manner. There is no love, no knowledge of "who Julie is" (a subject for another signifier) and no lack. We can only imagine Ixidor's deeply depressed mother, having lost three children, consumed with guilt, dead to her infant. More vividly still, we know she is a mother who names them all, dead and alive, with the same name, Ixidor. We could posit that Marc takes such a volunteer position to protect himself from the void of the feminine *as well as* to establish a mirror that sustains him as the one reading, in the position of the Other of Language, i.e., of the Mother. It is a solution to be on the active side, rather than on the other side of the *in-fans* (literally, without speech), the comatose one, without words. But these positions are nevertheless interchangeable at the mirror stage where the object and the ego have not yet been constituted. In this regard, to deal with the failure of identification that precludes the establishment of a fundamental fantasy, the psychotic subject finds a solution in identification with the mother, and can assume this identification as a kind of proto-subject position. Marc Delatour reading to the comatose patient is in a phallic maternal position. He is "active," with the one caveat: that the words are not his. As the M(Other), he speaks the Other.

In Ixidor's synopsis we will read later on that Marc has a "horror" of the void. The void will emerge with Leila or Julie coming alive—not with their remaining in a coma. Comatose, alive and dead at the same time, an initial distance with the mother allows an establishment of the Imaginary register, the first lack of alienation, and the erection of a phallic veil. Volunteering in the hospital in this manner, Marc can remain unaware of wanting the woman dead; he is in a "curing position" after all, and, at the same time, he alleviates the anxiety of the invasive void signified by the feminine. It is also a way that he "eternally" recalls his childhood love with Julie when the two were face-to-face recovering together in the hospital, in a similar "mirror" cure.

That a comatose woman could be resuscitated is a wish, but when she is actually resuscitated, her very life as a desiring subject provokes real existential anxiety for Marc. The void threatens to overwhelm since there is no way to deal with sexual difference. The woman waking from the coma confronts Marc with the emergence of the void wherein he risks losing this initial proto-lack, his imaginary phallic being. Alive, as a desiring subject, she is mortally threatening, having exited from the Imaginary axis, which served as a kind of protective eternal stasis. The foreclosed element, woman, makes a reappearance in the Real. According to Lacan, woman is one of the names of God. In Ixidor's text, she is Isis herself. Marc is the only thing Isis was missing: the phallus. She "uses" Marc as part of a plan that he cannot understand, where he is forced to play, and he finds himself at the complete mercy of the Other's jouissance. The sexual relation is a kind of death since, unable to experience or engage lack, Marc's very being is at stake. "He is" what she wants, she tells him: all of him. Moreover, given the difficulty of interpreting the desire of the other, Marc is left dangerously close to the possibility of complete annihilation. A "death" becomes necessary to restore and moor the phallic *semblant*, and fix the Imaginary register where Marc is safe. He sacrifices Julie for this, so as to make Leila's life include a death, thereby restoring himself as phallic, in the position of the Other once again.

Unlike the threatening and seductive Isis, Julie is a childhood love. This sexless fraternal love between two sick, orphaned children will function on the Imaginary axis as a way to cure one another, where the *"hainamoration"* (hate-love-enamoration or "jealous-siance") is easily denied and Marc can play the restorative role as the miracle worker. The logic of the text must install a death in Leila that will make Marc's life bearable and sustainable. This is the aim of the game of Mehen. We might point out that Julie/Leila is Marc/Mehen's "partner." She is a sister, one with whom he can make a real pact: she is neither a wife, nor is she a consort; Mehen will never have a consort. We are told there are four pairs of gods, and yet we noted that Mehen was not in a pair: the encircler is only mentioned alone. So who—or what—is the consort of Mehen? There can be no consort since the Other in the mirror who stabilizes the psychotic subject is not yet an Other subject, a point elegantly elaborated in Jean Allouch's contribution to this volume. Mehen makes sure the Imaginary is re-established at the end of the story by re-establishing a live-dead other. This other is not a person: a person is alive *or* dead. Alive *and* dead, this Other is *a reflection*. The "solution" is that Leila is "alive," but as Julie (who is dead). She is bearable "alive" precisely because she is *also* dead and her subjectivity (and the reason she speaks) is subsequently less menacing. We can now hear the various equivocations in the title of the synopsis: *Le Jeu memoire du dieu-serpent Mehen: Je même moi, Je m'aime moi, Je mémoire, Jeu même, jeu m'aime* and in *Mehen, mes haines*. In the words of the title we read very literally the *hainamoration* at stake in the mirror stage.

The aim of the game is to pass to the other side; the image on the other side of the playing board, Ixidor tells us in a footnote, changes. On the other side of the board game, the serpent's seven coilings become nine coilings. The first difference is made in the Imaginary, on the other side of the mirror. The aim of the game is the establishment of difference (without the Symbolic). Julie's death then serves as a necessary *suppléance*; it is a way of constructing an imaginary possibility for Marc, providing a sexless childhood love, an imaginary phallic position and a distance from Isis. Julie's death guarantees Leila's possibility of restoring Marc's reflection, guaranteeing Marc's position as phallic, and "masculine" at least on an imaginary plane.

This imaginary preservation/restoration is seen in the text in a number of ways. First, we see it in the importance of "waking up" or "wakefulness" as distinct from sleep or stupor. The synopsis starts with coffee drinking in the morning and ends with waking up. Mehen is a screenplay about wakefulness. Note that it is called "*le jeu-mémoire*": the game of memory is not the fantasy or the dream. Neurotics need dreams to deal with the Real, but psychotics? In the delusion, the Real is present; it is not repressed: it is in the world. While for neurotics, dreams make no sense, for Marc, it is reality that makes no sense. It is what the psychotic experiences as the mayhem of life itself.

The engine that is Mehen ingeniously shows that what is foreclosed in the Symbolic *re-turns*. The engine is a storyline that never goes anywhere since its "destiny" is itself, always present. The end is the same as the beginning. Despite the "circulation," we witness an Imaginary stasis worthy of the ancient Egyptians whose barren timelessness the *jeu* and the *je* of Mehen preserves.

When the signifier of the Name-of-the-Father fails, something has to hold the mirror in place. Death becomes preserved in the Imaginary (as reincarnation) since it is necessary in order for the proto-subject to exist, stabilized in the mirror stage, infinitely. While lethal, as imaginarized, death is not a total "end." "Winning" the game is going toward the mouth-hole of the snake to the other side (the Egyptian afterlife, a loss that is at the same time a preservation). Here death becomes only a passage; it becomes a way to think language while remaining in the Imaginary register. Since to be played by Mehen is to be always already in the hole, to always already have suffered death—without ever having been alive.

Why then must death be held on to? What allows an image to hold is a remainder. For the neurotic, this remainder is the object *a*. In Mehen, the "remainder" cannot be the object since it has not been separated from the psychotic subject. What holds the mirror is death.

An engine, Mehen is a story of transference in the dynamic sense. Movement is necessary; stasis is death since it invokes the possibility of the emergence of the hole of the Symbolic, a senselessness made manifest in the other's subjectivity, by way of the other's desire. This is clear thematically in the story: Marc's father's accident happened by sabotaging the *brakes*, leukemia is a disease that impedes circulation. The necessity of movement is analogous to the movement of language itself and functions as a *suppléance* for the failure of metaphor. At the same time, paradoxically, this incessant movement only serves to illustrate a much larger Imaginary stasis since Mehen shows that time, past and future, inside and outside, here and there, amounts to an eternal present. *A-letheia*—non-forgetting—is the name of as an omnipresent, eternal, literal re-turn, a constant turning of the engine.

With neurotics we could speak of a *souvenir d'enfance*, a childhood memory; the circle, however, is not the form of a childhood memory. In the circle, everything is simultaneously present on the same plane. Without the possibility of the "*souvenir*," i.e., something that "comes back" as a memory and, without time and without repression, without forgetting that would allow memory, narration, and even fiction itself, the author, present in his protagonist, experiences memory as Real. Memory is what cannot be remembered, since everything is eternally present, repeating uncannily, metonymically, senselessly. Ixidor's eleven page synopsis is an attempt to invent a logic for that eternal present, for the eternal present he inhabits and will allow the marking of returns—not as memories, but as Real events that are simultaneously remembered events. Leila is Julie. What happens to her, happens to him. These densely packed "events," saturated with meaning, make furrowing possible, a crevice-making in the body of the coiling serpent, Mehen, the Egyptian snake god, "the encircler." These markings or "fittings," in a game that Ixidor told me is a "puzzle," allow progression toward the serpent's mouth and emergence on the other side where we find death and reincarnation. The "fittings" are when Marc "moves" forward, gaining knowledge when an event has many meanings at once. The mirroring, the myriad of meaning is a kind of "fit" that allows for a movement from one coil of the snake to the other. This was Ixidor's "invention" of the rules of the game. When something makes sense—for example, Leila wakes up as Julie reincarnated—Marc moves forward in the game. By way of the moves in the Game of Memory of the God-Serpent Mehen, Ixidor has invented a movement, a way of "Marc-ing" the infinite.

In this regard, Francoise Davoine and Jean-Max Gaudillière write in *History beyond Trauma* regarding psychosis that "the impact of disaster has immobilized time; death is no longer possible" (Davoine and Gaudillière 2004: preface 30). Mehen is a way of showing this timeless Real that in psychosis "does not stop being written." In this regard, we cannot say like Hamlet that madness is "out of joint," since Mehen shows, worse, that in madness there is no joint. Thus Marc Delatour's name touches on the existential question for the schizophrenic whose name *is* his task, i.e., to "marc" the infinite line, the infinite turning. The *creux*/spaces in the snake are his attempt to create joints, kinds of proto-holes, that have the function of a hollowing out and creating movement and pauses between spaces and circles allowing something to be at least "marked," if not read. For movement to take place and have meaning, there have to be some marks (*de la tour*) of the interior of the snake. Movement takes place by way of hollows, of "marks"; we can call them proto-holes. "Marc Delatour" is the name of Ixidor's protagonist, and the name of the work that Ixidor's entire life is engaged in. In Mehen, we could say that the hollows in the body of the snake and the pieces that fit into them are both a movement and a pause created via the *semblable*. Paradoxically, it is a fit, i.e., a pause that makes a move possible in the game. These hollows into which the pieces fit show "complementarity" on an imaginary level, demonstrating that in psychosis, *the sexual relation exists*; something really fits into something else. A lack is filled. This is why these "fits" move toward death, since they are a making of two out of the one on the Imaginary axis. The "ah-ha" moments are not moments of understanding as they are in neurosis; "making meaning" is thus equivalent to the "existing sexual relation" and is thus just as lethal as it is relieving: a pause and a movement are thus the same thing. It is at such a point that the text will terminate, at the beginning and ending the story. Eternity is the stopping point of the Imaginary; by making the two, it is an initial separation in the mirror stage.

The Imaginary thus comes as a *suppléance* to handle the Real. The pact between the children is made in blood and replaces a symbolic pact. Needles prick the finger and allow another space for the blood to circulate; the blood is yet another metonymy of the self, of the body, of the snake. The constant pricking and bleeding allows a circulation otherwise than one limited to the body and emanates from the hole in the *index finger*. The word *indice*/index must be read literally; *the Real as Body takes the place of the unconscious; it is the Real unconscious.* Thus the index, the pointer, is the index of meaning pointing to circulation elsewhere, blood/language outside the body. In such a world, pointing to the Real is the same as the Real itself.

I pause here, at the bleeding, to wonder about the transitivism with regard to the physical pain in the story. Marc needs the mirror not to feel, because we never see him feel, but in order to *register* pain. One needs the other to register that one has a body. One needs a body-ego in order to *feel* pain. One's pain had to be felt at least once by an Other in order for it to be registered as such and for a body-ego to be constructed in the first place. "Getting better together" allows an imaginary possibility for the pain to be felt somewhere in the first place; it allows for it to be registered in the mirror. Julie and Leila suffer in a coma, not Marc. Here, one is tempted by Ixidor's emphasis on the Egyptian pantheon to say that whereas in Sade and Klossowski's work, we see quite clearly that "*la jouissance est la sœur de la verité*" (jouissance is the sister of truth), here we could say simply that "*la jouissance est la soeur*" (jouissance is the sister).

Guy Dana has pointed out in his work that the psychotic subject refuses to be "excluded from his own origins." In this sense we could say that Marc witnesses

Leila-Julie's birth as his own; her dead-alive is his own, allowing him to exist. This is why Leroux's new baby is aborted and is not the place for Julie's reincarnation; Ixidor is not concerned with *real birth*. Mehen is not about "real life and death" but the birth of subjectivity: what takes place on the journey by way of the hollowed out parts in the snake. What is at stake in Nietzsche's "midday" in the desert's burning sun, between the eagle and . . . the serpent, as he writes in Zarathustra; "Then it spoke to me without voice: 'What do you matter, Zarathustra? Speak your word and break!' And I answered: 'Alas, it is my word? Who am I?'" (Nietzsche 2005: Bk IV). Is this not what the schizophrenic subject is trying to tell us?

In closing, it is interesting to reflect on the difference between tragedy (a kind of destiny) and this text as engine. It struck me that in this "story" knowledge functions inversely to the way it functions in tragedy. Here, the *peripeteia*, or turning point is not one point, but a constant, endless series of points. There is no turning point, but rather constant turning. Moreover, in the Mehen text, the "increase" in *savoir* (knowledge) marks an increase in the proximity to death. Like Bion's "nameless dread" the increase approaches the totality that can only be separated from by way of the Imaginary. Tragedy, so important to the history and invention of psychoanalysis, to *cathexis*, of the "*Wo Es War*," to the very structure of neurosis as constructing a "destiny," of the revelation of an "unknown known," of a fantasy, an axiom structuring an entire life, is of no use here at all. Mehen shows that the Name-of-the-Father, indeed, that monotheism, which allows for nomination and transmission and history, is a useless imposture. The Egyptians had no need for tragedy, after all; what was important to them was the construction of an image so that their place in history and in the afterlife was guaranteed.

Unlike the unknown known subtending tragedy, the unthought known in psychosis cannot be thought, since unlike neurosis, there is no fault in knowledge that would allow it to be. The aim then is to find a "how to" with what cannot be thought. The text shows that the Real cannot be "treated by" the Symbolic. France of the "father" does not save Julie, although she dies to get there. Papers are lost and stolen, symbolic pacts are useless, parents try to kill children, mothers kill, abort, and abandon their children, etc. "Thought" is not a solution for this knowledge. Solutions concern destinies, not engines, after all. At least the text makes that much clear; there is no solution, but there is the infinity of the Real made more bearable by another kind of infinity, by love, specifically by the love of children, even if it is always as full of hate as it is of love, affects that Lacan calls "careers without limits" (Lacan 1974: 277). For Marc, this is to be taken literally. At best, it allows him moments where he can sit and read to himself-sister, where he can lack-have his live-dead reflection, allowing the circle to end and begin at the same place. For Ixidor, it allows him to be inscribed as Isis's gift that he is named, the phallus, and for this writer to engender something else from her encounter with him and with his writing: this text.

Notes

1 "Mais l'inconscient de Freud . . . c'est justement ce que j'ai dit, à savoir le rapport, le rapport qu'il y a entre un corps qui nous est étranger et quelque chose qui fait cercle, voire droite infinie, qui de toute façon sont l'une (la D.I., droite infinie), l'un (le cercle) à l'autre équivalente (la D.I.), et quelque chose qui est l'inconscient" (Lacan 1976: April 13).

2 A circle is one form of an infinite line. While for the neurotic, it cannot be thought, it is the very Real that the text of Mehen tries to make explicit. Jean-Michel Vappereau writes, "The infinite line (D.I.) writes the real hole that is not thinkable, since we are inside of it. It is primary repression, *Urverdrängung*, the trou-matism of Freud, constitutive of the unconscious. . . . It introduces us to readability as such, to the singular trait (*Einziger Zug*) readable before the letter. Before any writing can constitute itself; it is the possibility of reading itself" (Vappereau 2006: 1).

Bibliography

Benedetti, G. (1977) *Psychotherapy of Schizophrenia*, New York: Jason Aronson.

Bion, W. R. (1962) *Learning from Experience*, London: Karnac.

Dana, G. (2011) *Quel Politique pour la folie?* Paris: Stock.

Davoine, F. and Gaudillière, J. M. (2004) *History beyond Trauma*, New York: The Other Press.

Ixidor (2011) "Le Jeu-Mémoire du dieu-serpent Mehen," unpublished screenplay synopsis, author's private collection.

Lacan, J. (1974) *Seminar I: Freud's Papers on Technique 1953–54*, trans. John Forrester, New York: W. W. Norton & Company.

Lacan, J. (1976) Le Sinthome, Session of April 13, lesson of May 11, private notes.

—— (1981) *Les Psychoses. Le Séminaire III*, Paris: Seuil.

—— (1993) *Seminar III, The Psychoses*, trans. R. Grigg, New York: W. W. Norton & Company.

—— (2005) *Le Séminaire. Livre XXIII. Le sinthome 1975–1976*, Paris: Seuil.

Moscovitz, J.-J. (2005) "L'écoute diagnostique. Sur les entretiens préliminaires avec un analysant et 'sa psychose,'" in *Psychologie Clinique*, 20: 157–67.

Nietzsche, F. (2005) *Thus Spoke Zarathustra*, trans. G. Parkes, New York: Oxford World Classics.

Vappereau, J.-M. (2006) "La droite infinie," Online. Available www.litturaterre.org (accessed October 27, 2013).

INDEX

Abilify 4, 5
Abraham, K. 13, 129, 132, 149, 173
accidie 128, 132
acting out 7, 62, 69, 70
actual neurosis 11, 70–77
addictions 69, 70, 73, 97, 109
agalma 155
Agamben, G. 57
Aha-Erlebnis 166
Aimée 8, 11, 12, 106, 112, 120–125
alienation 29, 118, 166, 168, 170, 175,
    183, 195,196, 223, 225–227, 229, 230,
    235, 237, 245, 262
Allouch, J. 6, 8, 11, 12, 112
analyst's wise ignorance 5
analytic know-how 49
anger 7, 23–25, 132
antipsychiatry 2, 87, 103
antipsychotic medications 4
anxiety 5, 15, 23, 31, 34, 38, 51, 58, 68,
    71–80, 100, 156, 176, 183, 238, 239,
    260–262
Anzieu, M. (*see* Aimée)
aprés-coup 176, 169, 193
Arataeus of Cappadocia 128
Arendt, H. 57
aripiprazole 4
Aristotle 7
Artaud, A. 47, 48, 52
Asad, T. 58
Asher, R. 101
Asperger's syndrome 101
Auden, W. H. 144, 145
Auschwitz 227, 231
au-moins-un 198, 199, 201
autism 5, 89, 101, 247
autoerotism 114
automutilation 106

Baillarger, J. 128
Balthus 185
Basaglia, F. 229
Baudelaire 216
Beauvoir, S. 155
Beckett, S. 9, 14, 245, 246, 248–251
belle indifférence 68
Behrman, A. 131, 135
Benedetti, G. 48, 257
Benjamin, H. 101
Benveniste, E. 250, 252
Bernard, J. 101
Beutel, M.E. 70
Binswanger, L. 130, 131, 147
bipolar disorder 5, 128
Blanchot, M. 245, 249, 251, 252
Bleuler, E. 129
Boothby, R. 2, 10
borderline 11, 13, 69, 77, 86, 110, 140,193
Borromean knot 8, 88, 90, 95, 246, 252
Boyai, J. 102
Braunstein, N. 2, 4, 11
Brawman-Mintzer 70
Breggin, P. 4
Brentano, F. 246
Breuer, J. 3
Briole, G. 105
Bristol-Myers Squibb 4
Broca, R. 107
Brosig, B. 70
Brunswick, R.M. 152
Bush, G. 63

case presentation 107, 109
Casenave, L. 107
castration 30, 33, 41–43, 51, 86, 94, 95,
    153, 176, 180, 187–189, 192–196, 199,
    209, 210, 234, 237, 258

Cavell, S. 59
Cervantes, M. 4
Cheney, T. 131, 135
choice 86, 87
choice of neurosis 85
Chouraqui-Sepel, C. 106
Clérambault, G. de 100, 101, 124, 155, 261
Cocteau, J. 155
cogito 116, 117, 170, 171
Cohen, M.B. 130, 135
Comte, A. 102
Cooper, D. 103
countertransference 70, 71
Courbon, P. 129
Cox Cameron, O. 9, 14
Crashaw, R. 9, 14, 235, 236, 238–243
Cremniter, D. 106
Cusanus, N. 5
cutting 10, 51

Dana, G. 10
Dante 132
Davoine, F. 264
de Beauvoir, S. 155
De Masi, F. 48
death drive 59, 108, 109, 184, 210
delusion (délire) 3, 99, 102, 114, 115, 117, 139, 153, 253, 254, 259, 260; attempt at a cure, 3, 106
death drive 184
dementia praecox 129
depression 5, 12, 53, 99–101, 127, 128, 131, 132, 134, 139, 140, 151, 174, 197
depressive position, 6
Descartes, R. 116, 117
desire 88, 91, 180, 185, 189, 190, 192, 195, 196, 198, 199, 210, 219, 237, 239, 241, 247, 262, 264; of the mother, 29, 88, 95; of the Other, 62, 88, 133, 185, 262
destructive monomania 108
Deutsch, H. 195
diagnosis 5, 71
Diagnostic and Statistical Manual of the American Psychiatric Association (DSM) 2, 11, 71, 99, 107–109, 142
Dickinson, E. 4
Dido 1
discourse 85, 91, 92
divided subject 6
docta ignorantia 5

Dolar, M. 166
Dolto, F. 89, 103
Don Quixote 4
Dora 189
double-bind 5
dreams 3; and insanity, 3; and neurosis, 4
Dresden Madonna 189
drive 71–75, 206; object, 109; formula, 192
Duke, P. 131, 134
Duras, M. 13, 194
Durkheim, E. 2

ego 12, 13, 50, 74, 76, 77, 88, 90, 94, 133, 146–152, 159, 161–166, 169, 170, 176, 180, 205–216, 255, 261, 265
emergence of the unconscious and surprise 6
enactments 76
end of analysis 51
enuresis 23, 24, 28, 31
erastes 120
eromenos 120
erotomania 104, 105, 108, 117, 119, 123, 154
Etchegoyen, H. 102
events of the body 40, 44
Ey, H. 87, 134, 135, 160

Falret, J.P. 100, 128, 131
fantasy 56, 63, 64; formula of, 91, 96
Federn, P. 105
femininity 13, 14, 35–37, 154, 187–196, 209
Ferenczi, S. 147, 173
Ferjol's syndrome 101
Feyaerts, J. 8, 12
Fink, M. 142
Fliess, W. 120
Flor, R. 9
Fonagy, P. 76, 77
foreclosure 7, 8, 37, 40, 89, 91, 93, 102, 103, 105, 125, 127, 152, 153, 248
formal envelope of the symptom 102
Foucault, M. 4, 10, 11, 49, 224
four discourses 86, 91
free-association 68, 70, 106, 121
Frege, G. 247
Freud, S. 3, 7, 8, 13, 52, 53, 60, 62, 68–77, 85, 87, 90, 101–103, 105, 106, 112–115, 117–120, 122–124, 127–130, 133, 140–152, 155, 164,

165, 173–176, 179–182, 184, 185, 187–194, 196–198, 205, 210, 213, 222, 234, 239, 246, 247
Freud, Sophie 147
Fromm-Reichmann, F. 130, 135–136
frustration 173, 174

Gaudilliére, J. M. 264
Gaupp, R. 129
Genet, J. 155
Gestalt 165, 166
Gliederung 52
Goethe, J.V. von 147
graphorrhea 54
Green, A. 69
Greisinger, W. 131, 135
Grigg, R. 2, 12
Gross, O. 130
Guéguen, P.-G. 155, 157

hainamoration 262
hallucination 93, 100, 103, 130, 132
   (see also delusion)
Hamlet 1, 145
Hartacollis P. 69, 73
Hegel, G.W.F. 57
Heidegger, M. 59, 97, 248
helplessness (Hilflosigkeit) 165
heterotopia 49
Hoch, P. 129
Hochman, G. 131, 134
Hólderlin, F. 245
Holocaust 13, 14
holophrase 92, 96, 103
homo sacer 58, 67
Horace 251
Horney, K. 195
hypomania 129
hysteria 40, 128, 191, 193, 196

identity 7
Imaginary, the body's 40, 70, 94, 95, 166, 177, 179; child, 45; conscience, 123; container, 255; elaboration, 75; equivalence, 195; father, 44; fundamental, 103; identification, 38, 39, 41, 44, 45, 161, 170; in psychosis, 54; jouissance, 153; mastery, 164; mediation, 170; other, 176; phallic being, 262; phallus, 94, 192–194; recognition, 168; register, 8, 13, 30, 36, 45, 50, 70, 88, 89, 95, 154, 214–216,

245, 246, 248, 255, 262, 263, 265, 266; threatened, 69; stasis, 264; veil, 249
incest 34, 39, 41
ingenium 254, 260
inverted totalitarianism 66
infans 50, 55
infinite line 267

Jakobson, R. 118
Jones, E. 129, 130, 137, 187
jouissance 30, 31, 49, 50, 88, 90, 93, 100, 103, 108, 165, 174, 176, 184, 188, 191, 192, 195, 215, 265; as compass, 53; body, 176; de-regulation, 51, 104; direct experience, 29; erasure, 52; failure, 188; feminine, 199, 201; interdiction, 6; invasion, 91–93, 104, 105; lethal factor, 183; limit, 22, 89, 108; on the Real of the body, 77; opaque, 180–182; Other's, 95, 104–106, 262, 196, 192; phallic, 108, 197; psychotic, 11, 93, 94, 104; regulation, 54, 93; renunciation, 86, 87; separation, 88; subject of, 92, 93; surplus, 91; unconscious, 213; unregulated, 95, 103, 104
Joyce, J. 8, 9, 13, 45, 95, 205–207, 210, 213, 215, 217, 234, 245
Jung, K. 174

Kafka, F. 96
Kaldun, I. 245
Kanner, L. 101
Kant, I. 3
Kaufmant, Y. 106
Kenner, H. 249
Kernberg, O. 147
Kierkegaard, S. 167
Klein, M. 6, 89, 129, 130, 132–134
Klossowski, B. 185
Klossoski, P. 185
knowledge, 3, 5, 9, 11, 51, 53, 60, 85, 94, 99, 105, 107, 112, 115–117, 121–125, 162, 163, 168, 187, 188, 224, 264, 266
Kraepelin, E. 100, 118, 128–130
Kristeva, J. 86
Kubler-Ross, E. 146

Lacan, J. 3, 5–8, 10–12, 33, 45, 49, 52, 62, 63, 68, 71, 75, 76, 78, 85–87, 89–93, 95, 96, 101–104, 106, 109, 110, 112, 113–125, 127, 130, 132, 133, 137, 139, 144, 152–154, 159–166, 168–171,

173–181, 183, 188, 189, 192–195, 197–199, 205, 208–210, 214–216, 233, 234, 236–239, 242, 245–248, 250, 251, 254, 255, 259–262, 266
lack 52, 63, 64, 73, 77, 92, 93, 95, 175, 178, 179, 185, 190, 192, 197, 238, 256, 258, 261, 262, 265, 266; in-being, 170, 171, 201; of love, 122
Laing, R.D. 2
lalangue 52, 53, 89, 215
Lane, C. 5
Laurent, D. 106
Laurent, E. 106
law, failure of the 5; of the Mother, 33
Leader, D. 2, 5, 8, 12, 133
Lear 1
Le Pen 35
Levi, P. 9, 13, 14, 119, 219–222, 224, 225, 227, 228, 231
Lewin, B. 130
Lewin, K. 54
libido, free-floating 113, 181; and the Other, 133; withdrawal, 148
Liepmann, H. 131
Little Hans 180
Loose, R. 73
love 28, 34, 42, 75, 85, 105, 112, 120–122, 135, 141, 145–147, 150–152, 180, 188, 190–195, 198, 200, 201, 210, 212, 213, 221, 229, 235, 236, 239–242, 259, 261, 262, 266; refusal (*Liebesversagung*), 173–175, 179
Lydiard, R.B. 70

MacCannell, J. 9, 13
MacCurdy, J. 130
Madness 2, 4, 5, 8, 69, 96, 101, 166, 160, 171; antipsychiatric view, 2; boundaries of, 2; chemical imbalance, 2; clinical practice, 5; dreams, 3; definition of 1; diagnosis, 5; freedom, 3, 4, 7, 11, 60–62, 85–87, 89, 90, 96, 130, 131, 154, 160, 166, 177; innovations, 2; organicist theory, 160; pathos of, 1; and rationality, 119; structural disposition, 6; subjectivity, 169–171; and violence, 7; and "wiring" of the brain, 2
Malabalia, D. 220
Maleval, J.C. 2, 11, 106
Mallarmé, S. 245
mania 127, 128, 130, 131; and the Other, 134–137

manic-depressive insanity 129
manic-depressive psychosis 125, 127, 128, 130, 131, 133, 135
Manonni, M. 89, 96, 103
Marx, K. 4
Master's discourse (*see also* discourse), 91, 92
Meadow, R. 101,
melancholia 2, 10, 12, 127–129, 133, 139–144, 148–156, 174, 179
Ménard, A. 106
mental automatism 41, 104
Merleau-Ponty, M. 159–163, 167–172
Merline 185
Michaux, G. 103
Mieli, P. 9, 13
Miller, J.A. 15, 32, 67, 101, 102, 110, 111, 170, 247
Milner, J.C. 224
Milton, J. 205
Minkowski, E. 100
mirror-stage 12, 74, 75, 159, 163–169, 176, 256, 262, 263
mirroring 76
misrecognition 159,
Mitrani, J. 73, 76, 78, 79
money 63
Morel, G. 9
multi-venue treatment 49
Munchausen's syndrome 101

Name-of-the-Father 6, 8, 14, 45, 87–90, 92, 93, 95, 96, 100–103, 153, 214, 237, 238, 242, 243, 260, 261, 263, 266
narcissism 113
narcissistic neurosis 173–185
negative existence 48
negative therapeutic reaction 140, 141
Neurosenwahl (choice of neurosis) 87
neurosis 3, 5–7, 11, 33, 42, 49, 50, 68, 71–79, 85, 87, 89, 95, 102, 103, 105, 113, 114, 120, 129, 140, 148–152, 155, 173, 191, 237, 254, 258, 260, 265, 266
Nobus, D. 5

object 6, 156, 162–164, 174, 186, 210, 261; object *a*, 30, 55, 63, 91, 93, 95, 114, 120, 153–155, 157, 176, 177, 209, 217, 239, 263; change of, 190; loss, 87, 145, 147, 149, 237; of the mother's desire, 6; in psychosis, 103, 120; and mania, 130–132; of segregation, 223

O'Brien, F. 9, 249
Oedipus Complex 113, 193, 246; pre-Oedipal, 191, 195; Oedipus, 8; Oedipal identification, 75
opaque compactness 48
Other 5, 50, 62, 71, 74–78, 87–89, 93, 101, 109, 117, 134, 136, 153, 174–176, 178, 179, 182, 188, 192–194, 239, 243, 259–261; and body, 50, 51; discourse, 103; imposed discordance with reality, 115; jouissance, 93; language phenomena, 130
Oury, J. 49, 103

pain 74
Pankow, G. 49
panic disorder 73, 75
Pape, R. 62
paranoia 8, 56, 86, 127, 234; paranoiac self-punishment, 8; paranoid symptoms, 8, 117
pas-tout 197
passage à l'acte 116, 122–124, 140
paternal metaphor 6; failure of, 50
Penisneid 41
perversion 5, 28, 87, 89, 109, 216
phallus, 10, 30, 33, 40–42, 45, 93, 94, 187, 189, 190, 192, 195, 196, 209, 210, 238, 262, 266
Pickmann, C.N. 6, 13
Plato 63
Porter, R. 1
pousse à la femme (push towards Woman) 93, 107
Proteus 15
psychiatric drugs 4, 87, 99
psychoanalyst's task 110
psychoanalytic theory as resistance 6
psychoneurosis 71–74, 76
psychosis 3, 5, 83, 90–93, 102, 120, 136; depressive, 139; and failure of the law, 5; imposed discordance with reality, 115; jouissance, 93; language phenomena, 41, 49, 117, 130–132, 135, 214, 260, 261, 265; manic-depressive, 125, 127, 128, 130, 131, 133, 135; ordinary, 32, 45, 107, 156, 157; passionate, 8, 59, 144; quiet, 8, 9; testimony, 3, 61, 105, 106, 118, 121, 253, 265
psychotic invention 52
psychotic solitude 47
psychotic transference (see transference)

quiet psychosis (see psychosis)
Quinn, M. 5

Rachlin, H.L. 129
Rasting, M. 70
ravage 13, 194–199
Reagan, R. 65
Real 4, 8, 14, 25, 30, 32, 37, 42, 45, 52–54, 70, 75, 77, 86, 88, 89, 91, 92, 95, 156, 180, 185, 188, 231, 233, 237, 248, 256, 258, 259; piece of the Real, 154; the real of the thing, 88; vréel, 86
reality 4, 86, 90, 93, 96, 100, 106
Rembrandt 155
Renaissance perspective 54
regression 151
repression 40, 252
res cogitans 170
res extensa 170
resistance 71
Rilke, R.M. 13, 180–186
Ritti, A. 128
Rose, J. 59
Rosenbaum, J.F. 70
Rosenfeld, H. 49, 105
Ross, E.K. 146
Roudinesco, E. 123
Rousseau, J.J. 102, 245
Russell, B. 115

Saint Anne Hospital 8
Saint Augustine 63
Saint Teresa of Avila 240, 241
Saint Thomas 132
Salomé, L.A. 52, 181
Sartre, J. P. 155
savoir 266
Scary, F. 248
Scheidung – separation 52, 175
schizophrenia 4, 12, 14, 49, 87, 103, 127, 129, 130, 133, 136, 254, 259, 264
schizo-paranoid position 6
Schreber, D. 3, 8, 50, 93, 95, 102, 104, 117–119, 148, 153, 154, 234, 238, 239
Schmerz – pain 74
science 109, 120
secretary to the insane 6, 11, 118, 120
segregation 131, 219–232
semblable (neighbor) 176, 177
semblance 55, 86
semblant 55, 94, 109, 153, 175, 176, 262; and object, 109; fall, 153, 155, 193;

phallic, 188, 189, 196, 262; specular relation and sacrifice, 106; rupture, 193; transformation in mourning, 153
separation 29, 52, 53, 75, 96, 154, 175, 183, 237, 238, 265; in mania, 133, 136; between self and Other, 133
separation anxiety 77, 78
sexual difference 33, 43, 208–210
sexual discourse 33
sexuation 33, 188, 194, 198, 200, 216, 236, 239, 243
Shopenhauer, A. 3
Shultz, G. 62
Silvestre, M. 104
Sinngebung 169
sinthome 8, 9, 33, 44, 45, 98, 197, 201, 214, 216, 217, 242, 246, 247, 249, 251 255, 260, 267
social anxiety 5
social link 85
Solano, L. 106
Soler, C. 106, 132
Sollers, P. 214
somatic symptom 34
somatization 75
soul murder 50
Soulié de Morand 48, 52
Spaltung 90
Spinoza, B. 132
stabitat 49
Steinberg, L. 236
Steinkoler, M. 3, 8, 9, 14
Stephen, J. 206
stone of madness 1
subject amplification 78
subject-supposed-to-know 6, 68, 70, 112, 115–117, 121
subjective division 92, 93
sublimation 183
sujet-supposé-savoir (*see* subject-supposed-to-know)
suicide 2, 9, 10, 25, 56–66, 87, 106, 133, 134, 140, 142, 151, 157, 205, 258
superego 6, 75, 95
suppléance 11, 51, 52, 54, 96, 102, 106, 107, 110n, 197–199, 263–265
Symbolic, activity 167; acquisition 179; castration, 42, 234, 237, 258; deficit, 194; elaboration, 75; father, 45, 234, 237, 238, 258; flaw, 102; function, 164; hole, 264; language, 214, 215; memorialization, 145, 153; Other,

238–239; order, 8, 12, 30, 40, 79, 88, 89, 95, 123, 148, 153, 154, 189, 193, 214, 234, 238, 245, 246; pact, 265, 266; phallus, 217; place, 40; in psychosis, 54; representation of the body, 94; return in the Real, 8, 133, 154, 237, 242, 263; signifier, 234
Symbolic, Imaginary, Real 30, 45, 88, 89, 95, 234, 245, 246, 263
symbolization 52, 53
symptom 3, 60, 68, 69
synthonia 50
Swift, J. 249
Szasz, T. 2, 115

Taylor, M. 142
Thing (*das Ding*) 6, 88, 90, 94, 95, 183, 238, 258, 259, 261
transference 31, 48, 53, 68, 70, 85, 101, 105, 107, 112; matheme, 115, 117; erotomaniacal, 105; in psychosis, 48, 49,102, 112–125
transference-psychosis 105
transsexualism 101
trauma 74
trepanations 1
truth, 86, 91

Über-Ich, see superego
unconscious 3, 116, 187; discovery, 187; enactment, 116; enigma of the desire of the Other, 62, 88; emergence, 6; fantasies, 76; formations, 90, 173, 178, 184; guilt, 141, 151; discourse of the Other, 115–116; knowledge, 3, 94, 188; and language, 205; Real, 265; rejection of, 104, 132; repressed metaphors, 40; sexual difference, 33, 188, 195, 209; subject of the, 109, 176
unsoundable decision 87–89

Vanheule, S. 8, 12, 77
Verhaeghe, P. 2, 6, 8, 10, 11, 73–75, 77, 78
Versagung 88, 173, 174
Verwerfung 152, 153
violence 7, 57
Voltaire, F.M. 66
von Mayer, J. 102
Vorstellungreprasentänz 238

Wallon, H. 159, 160, 163–167, 172
Whitworth, S. 9

Wilson, H. 208
Winnicott, D. 10, 49, 50, 55
Wolf Man, case of 149, 152, 157, 174, 180
Wolin, S. 66
Woolf, V. 9, 13, 206–208, 210, 217
word-representation 92

Yankelevich, H. 8, 12
"Young Homosexual Woman" 174, 175, 189

Žižek, S. 67, 247, 249, 253

Made in the USA
Middletown, DE
05 June 2023